metamo KISS

Sora Omote **Volume 1**

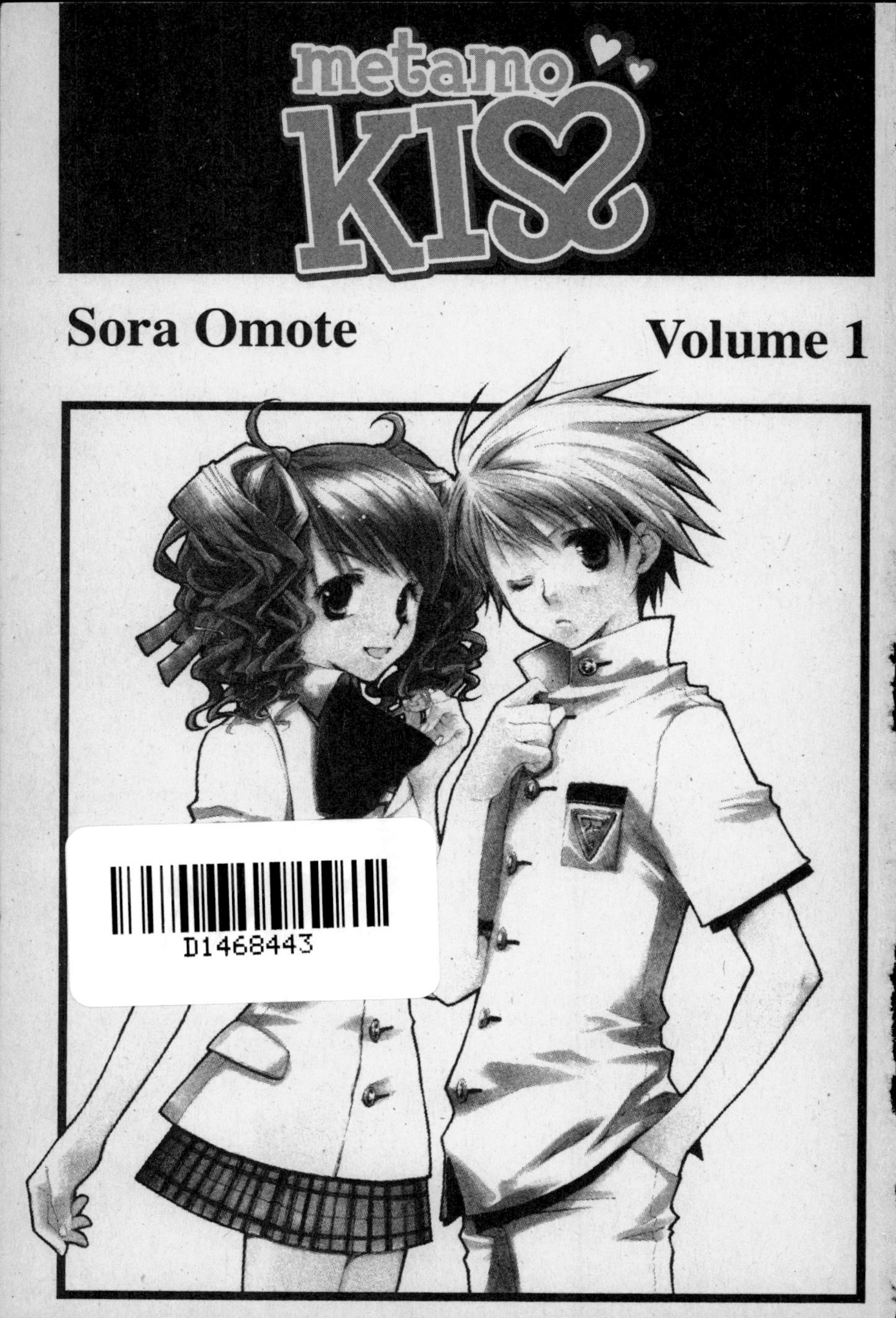

Metamo Kiss Volume 1
Created by Sora Omote

Translation - Alexis Kirsch
English Adaptation - Luis Reyes
Retouch and Lettering - Star Print Brokers
Production Artist - Kimie Kim
Graphic Designer - Fawn Lau

Editor - Carol Fox
Digital Imaging Manager - Chris Buford
Pre-Production Supervisor - Erika Terriquez
Art Director - Anne Marie Horne
Production Manager - Elisabeth Brizzi
Managing Editor - Vy Nguyen
VP of Production - Ron Klamert
Editor-in-Chief - Rob Tokar
Publisher - Mike Kiley
President and C.O.O. - John Parker
C.E.O. and Chief Creative Officer - Stuart Levy

A 🔴TOKYOPOP Manga

TOKYOPOP and 🔴 are trademarks or registered trademarks of TOKYOPOP Inc.

TOKYOPOP Inc.
5900 Wilshire Blvd. Suite 2000
Los Angeles, CA 90036

E-mail: info@TOKYOPOP.com
Come visit us online at www.TOKYOPOP.com

METAMO KISS Volume 1 © SORA OMOTE 2004
First published in Japan in 2004 by KADOKAWA SHOTEN
PUBLISHING CO., LTD., Tokyo. English translation rights
arranged with KADOKAWA SHOTEN PUBLISHING CO., LTD.,
Tokyo through TUTTLE–MORI AGENCY, INC., Tokyo.
English text copyright © 2007 TOKYOPOP Inc.

ISBN: 978-1-59816-827-3

First TOKYOPOP printing: March 2007
10 9 8 7 6 5 4 3 2 1
Printed in the USA

metamo KISS

Volume 1

by
Sora Omote

TOKYOPOP®

HAMBURG // LONDON // LOS ANGELES // TOKYO

CONTENTS

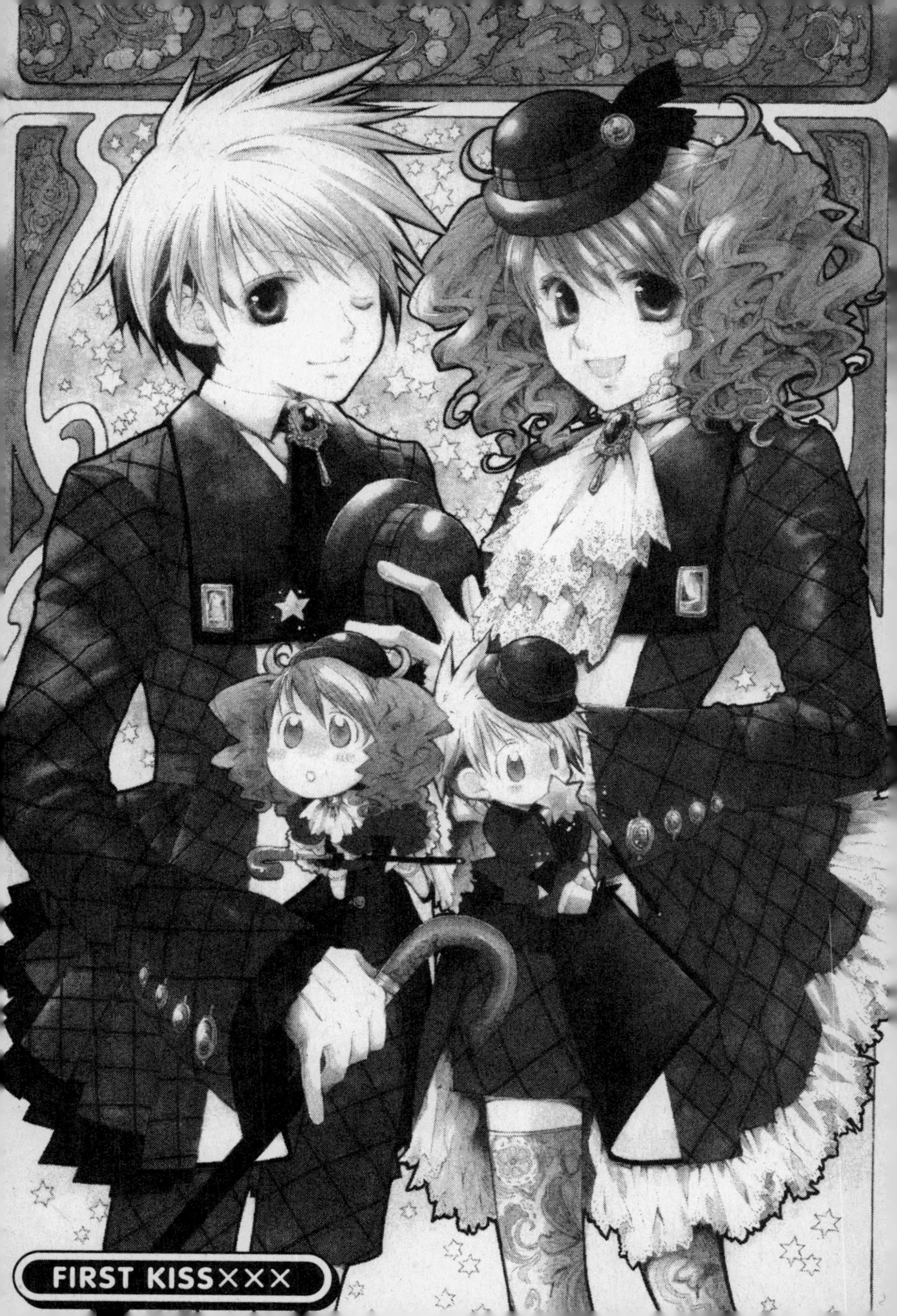

FIRST KISS×××

metamo KISS

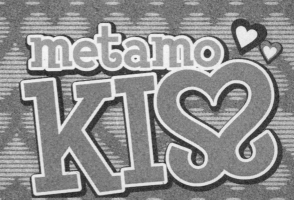

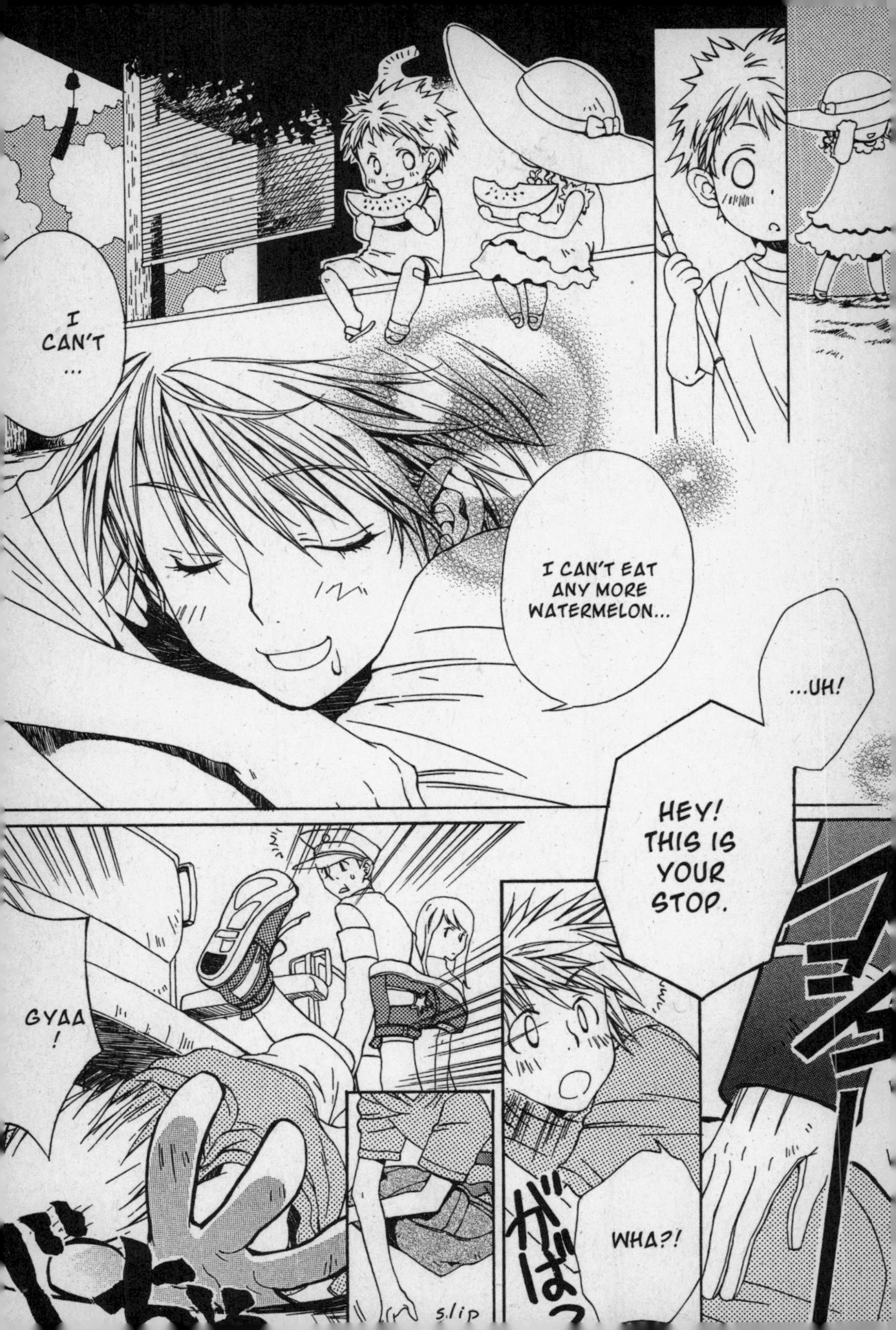
I CAN'T ...
I CAN'T EAT ANY MORE WATERMELON...
...UH!
HEY! THIS IS YOUR STOP.
WHA?!
がばっ
slip
GYAA!

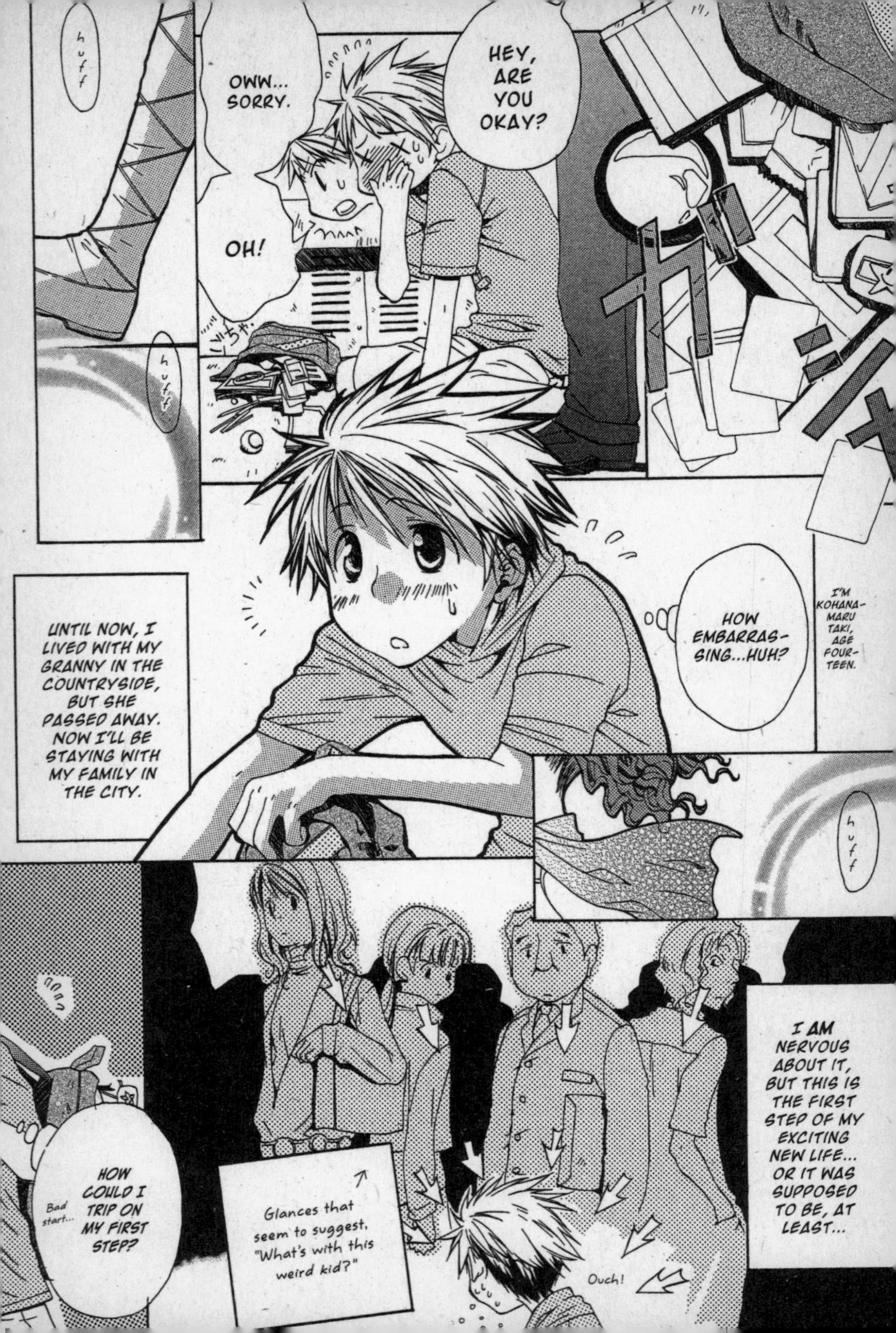
HEY, ARE YOU OKAY?
OWW... SORRY.
OH!
huff
huff
I'M KOHANAMARU TAKI, AGE FOURTEEN.
HOW EMBARRASSING...HUH?
UNTIL NOW, I LIVED WITH MY GRANNY IN THE COUNTRYSIDE, BUT SHE PASSED AWAY. NOW I'LL BE STAYING WITH MY FAMILY IN THE CITY.
huff
I AM NERVOUS ABOUT IT, BUT THIS IS THE FIRST STEP OF MY EXCITING NEW LIFE... OR IT WAS SUPPOSED TO BE, AT LEAST...
Ouch!
Glances that seem to suggest, "What's with this weird kid?"
HOW COULD I TRIP ON MY FIRST STEP?
Bad start...

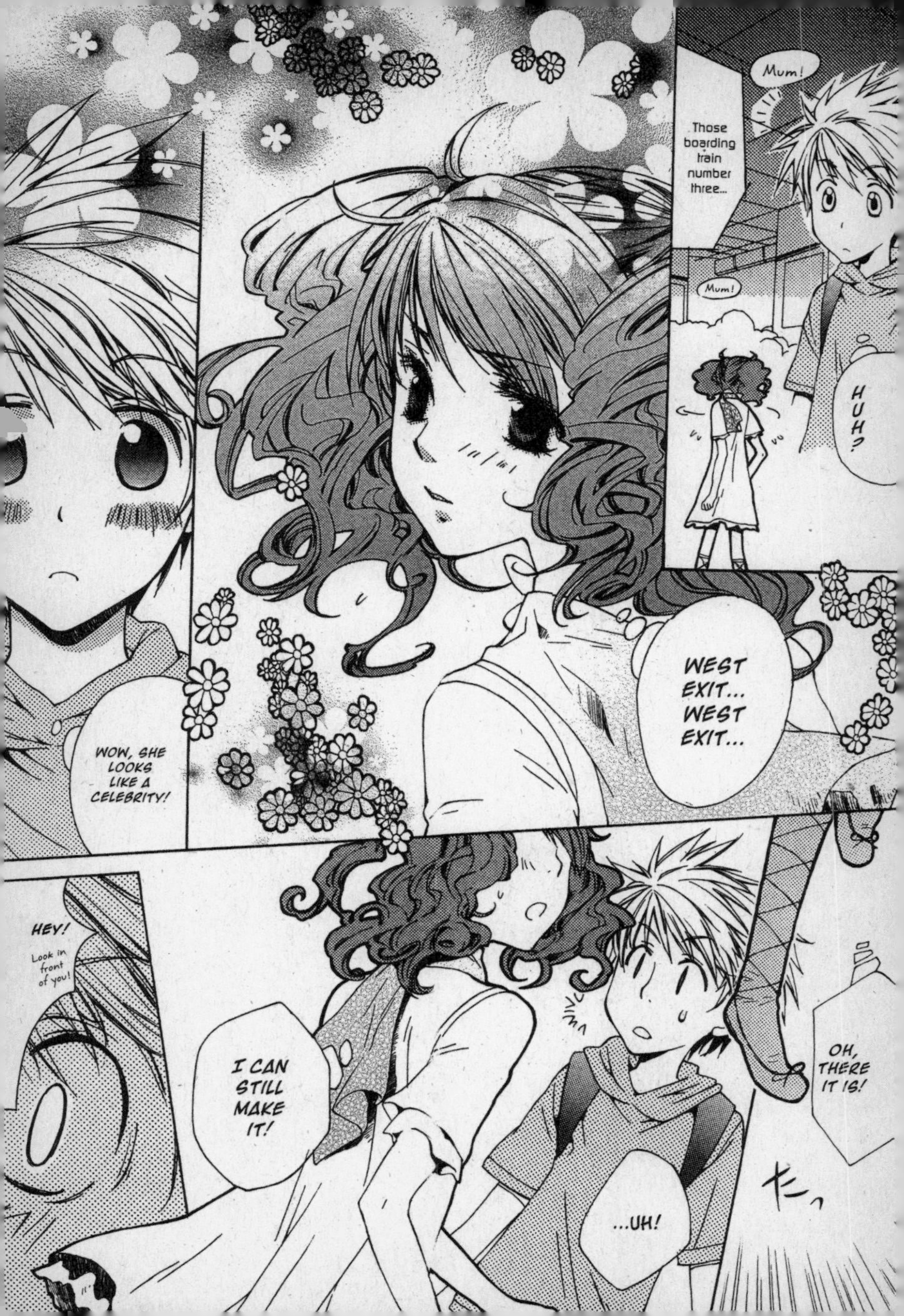
Mum!
Those boarding train number three...
Mum!
HUH?
WEST EXIT... WEST EXIT...
WOW, SHE LOOKS LIKE A CELEBRITY!
OH, THERE IT IS!
...UH!
I CAN STILL MAKE IT!
HEY!
Look in front of you!

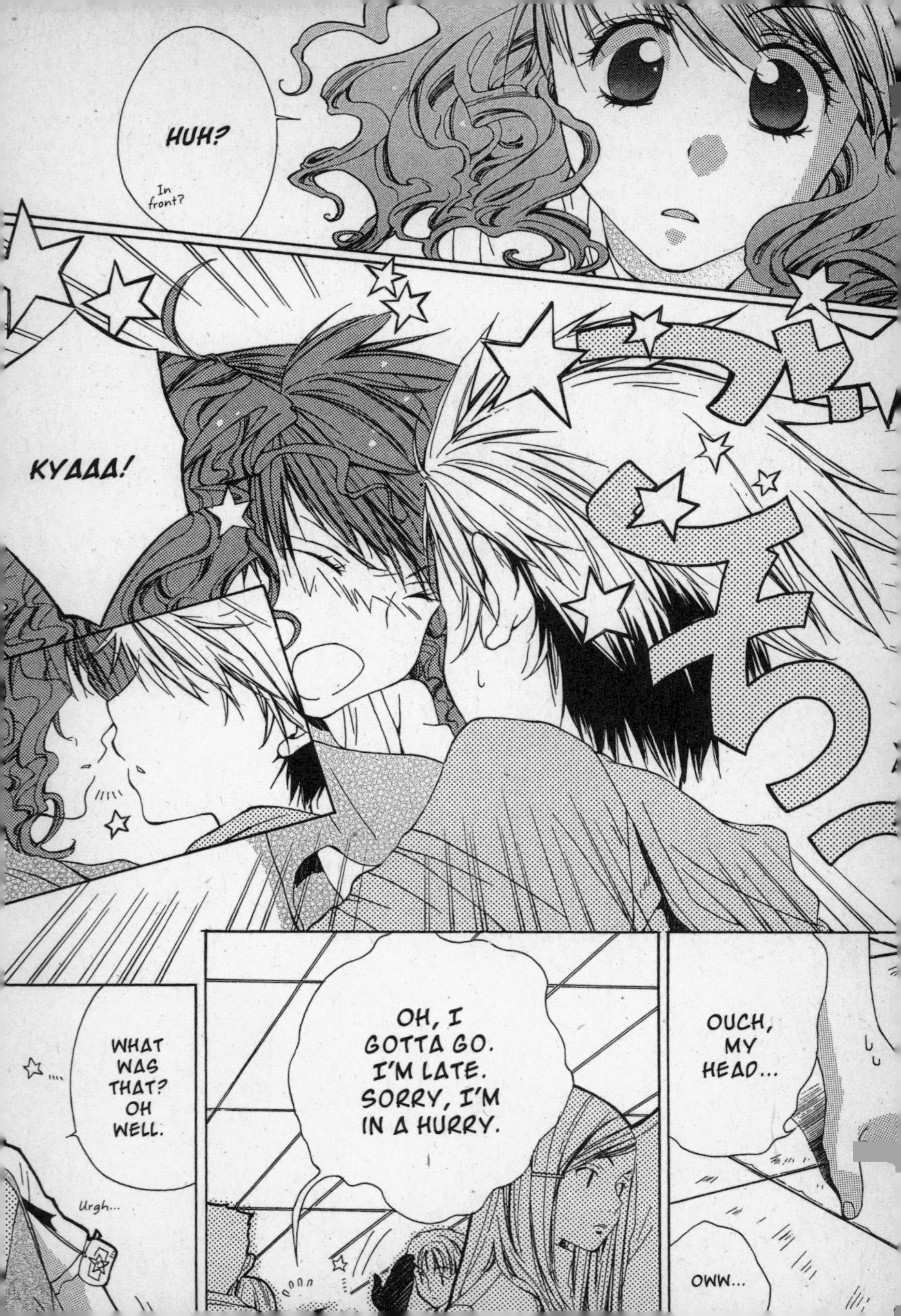
HUH?
In front?
KYAAA!
OUCH, MY HEAD...
OWW...
OH, I GOTTA GO. I'M LATE. SORRY, I'M IN A HURRY.
WHAT WAS THAT? OH WELL.
Urgh...

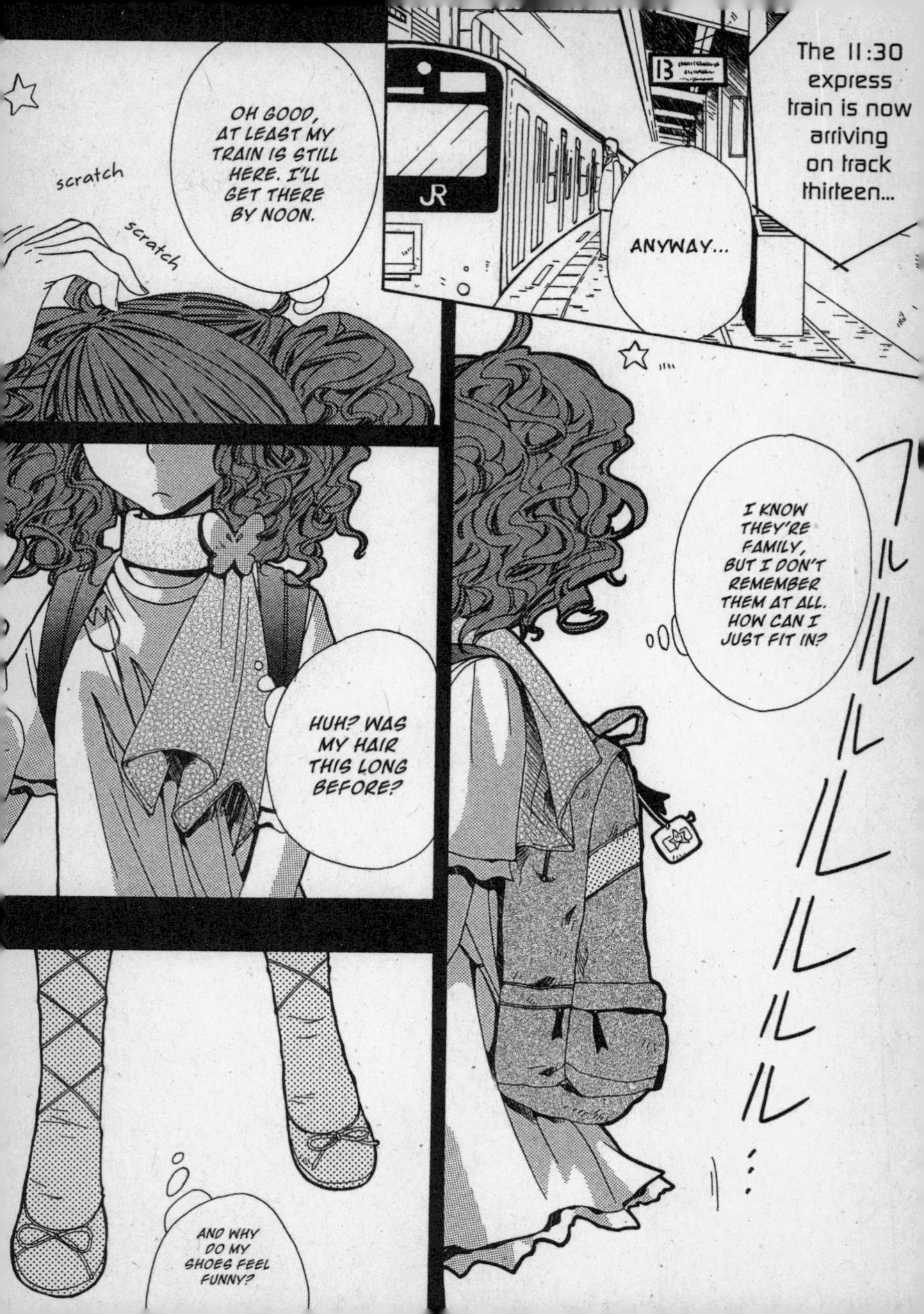
The 11:30 express train is now arriving on track thirteen...
ANYWAY...
OH GOOD, AT LEAST MY TRAIN IS STILL HERE. I'LL GET THERE BY NOON.
scratch
scratch
I KNOW THEY'RE FAMILY, BUT I DON'T REMEMBER THEM AT ALL. HOW CAN I JUST FIT IN?
HUH? WAS MY HAIR THIS LONG BEFORE?
AND WHY DO MY SHOES FEEL FUNNY?

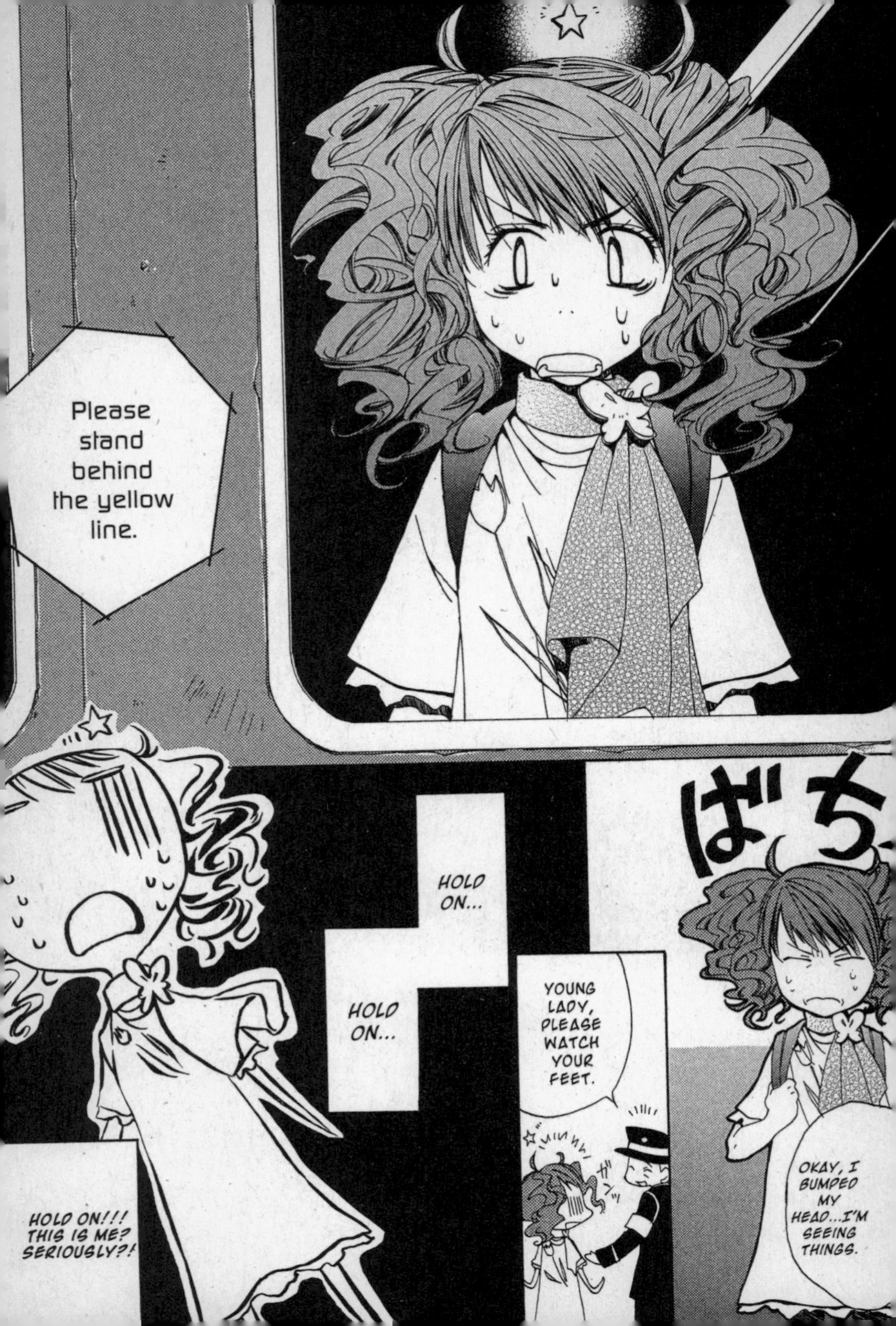

Please stand behind the yellow line.
ぱち
OKAY, I BUMPED MY HEAD...I'M SEEING THINGS.
HOLD ON...
YOUNG LADY, PLEASE WATCH YOUR FEET.
HOLD ON...
HOLD ON!!! THIS IS ME? SERIOUSLY?!

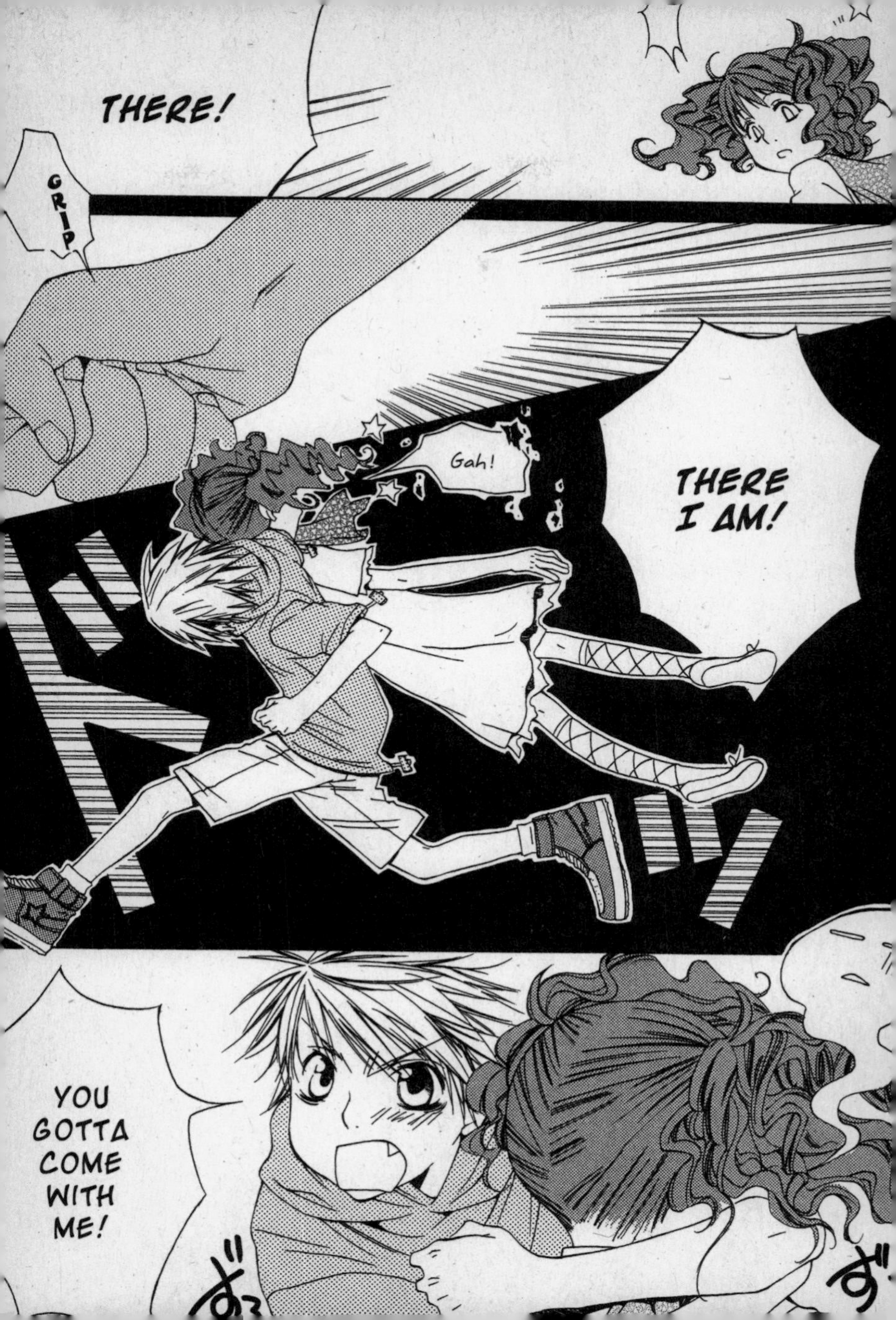
THERE!
GRIP
THERE I AM!
Gah!
YOU GOTTA COME WITH ME!

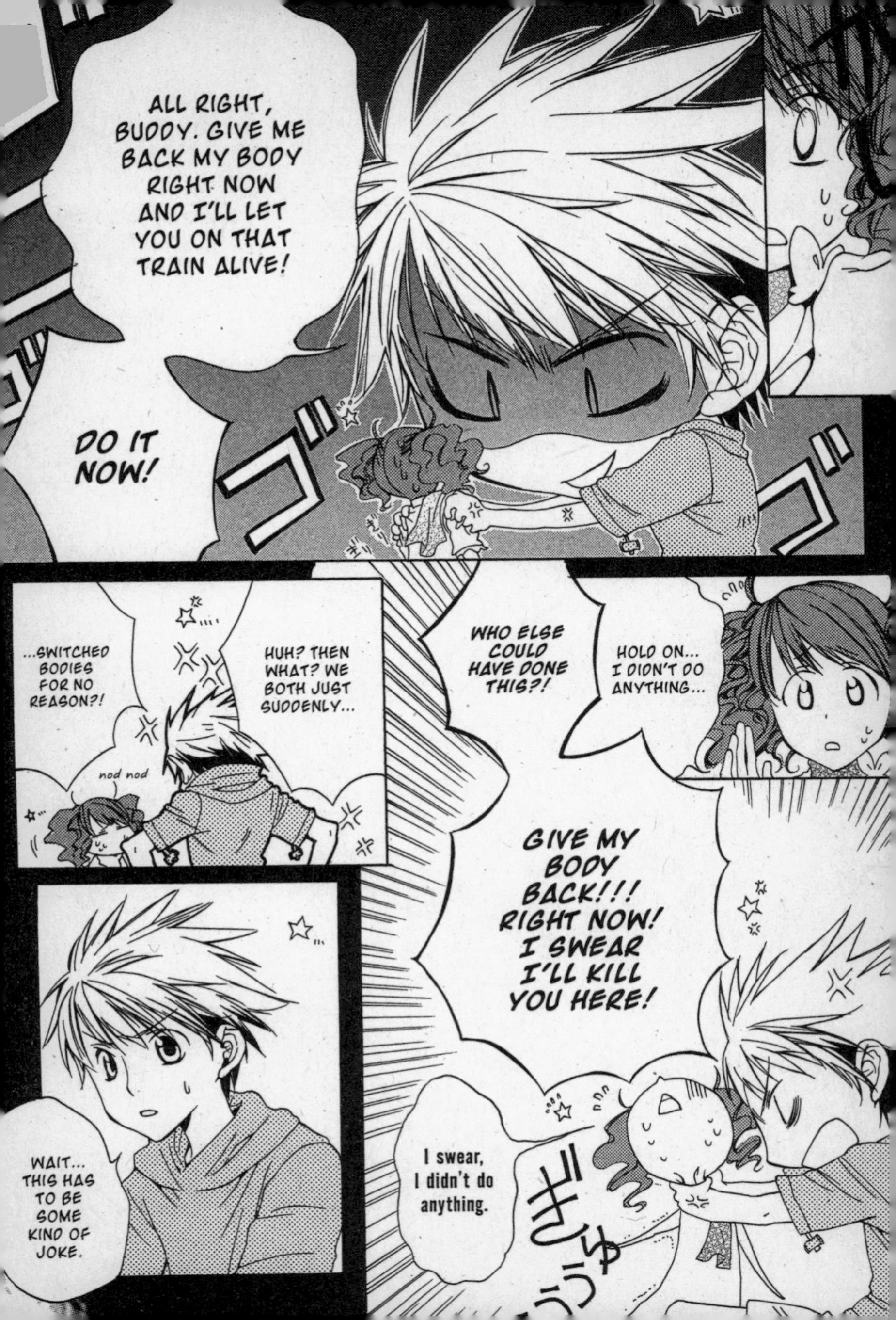
ALL RIGHT, BUDDY. GIVE ME BACK MY BODY RIGHT NOW AND I'LL LET YOU ON THAT TRAIN ALIVE!
DO IT NOW!
HOLD ON... I DIDN'T DO ANYTHING...
WHO ELSE COULD HAVE DONE THIS?!
HUH? THEN WHAT? WE BOTH JUST SUDDENLY...
...SWITCHED BODIES FOR NO REASON?!
nod nod
GIVE MY BODY BACK!!! RIGHT NOW! I SWEAR I'LL KILL YOU HERE!
I swear, I didn't do anything.
WAIT... THIS HAS TO BE SOME KIND OF JOKE.

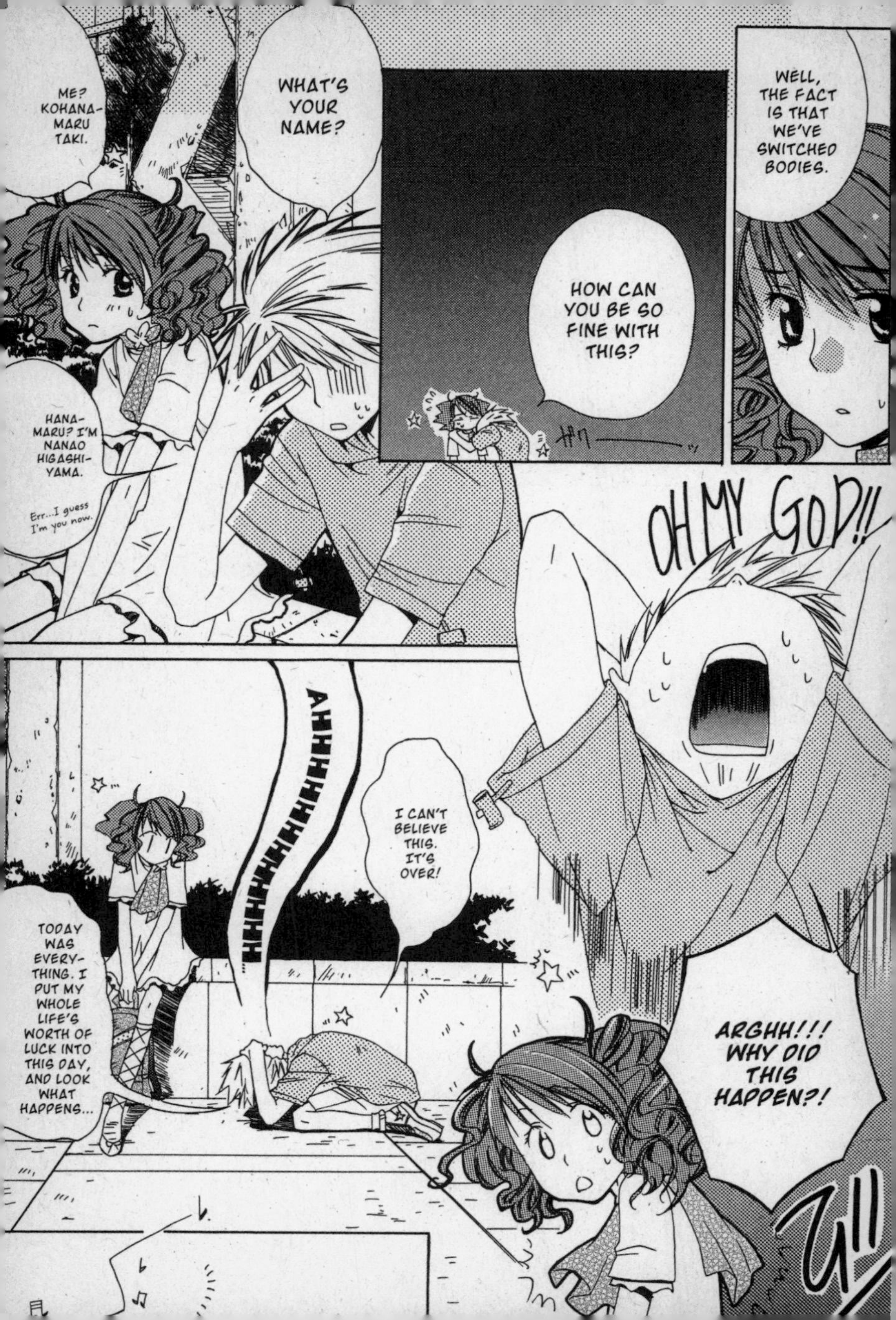

WELL, THE FACT IS THAT WE'VE SWITCHED BODIES.
HOW CAN YOU BE SO FINE WITH THIS?
WHAT'S YOUR NAME?
ME? KOHANAMARU TAKI.
HANAMARU? I'M NANAO HIGASHIYAMA.
Err...I guess I'm you now.
OH MY GOD!!
ARGHH!!! WHY DID THIS HAPPEN?!
I CAN'T BELIEVE THIS. IT'S OVER!
TODAY WAS EVERYTHING. I PUT MY WHOLE LIFE'S WORTH OF LUCK INTO THIS DAY, AND LOOK WHAT HAPPENS...

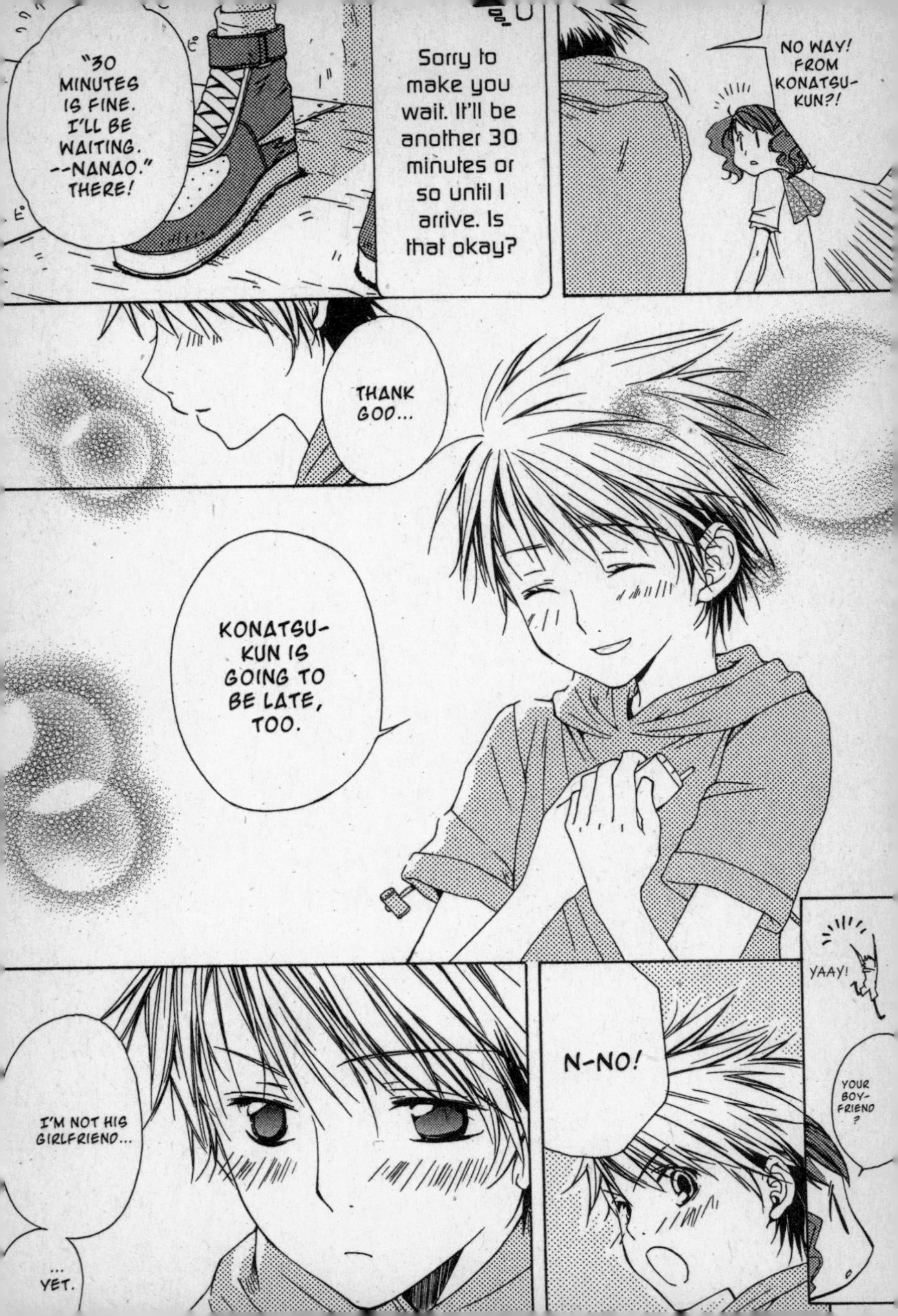
NO WAY! FROM KONATSU-KUN?!
Sorry to make you wait. It'll be another 30 minutes or so until I arrive. Is that okay?
"30 MINUTES IS FINE. I'LL BE WAITING. --NANAO." THERE!
KONATSU-KUN IS GOING TO BE LATE, TOO.
THANK GOD...
YAAY!
YOUR BOY-FRIEND?
N-NO!
I'M NOT HIS GIRLFRIEND...
...YET.

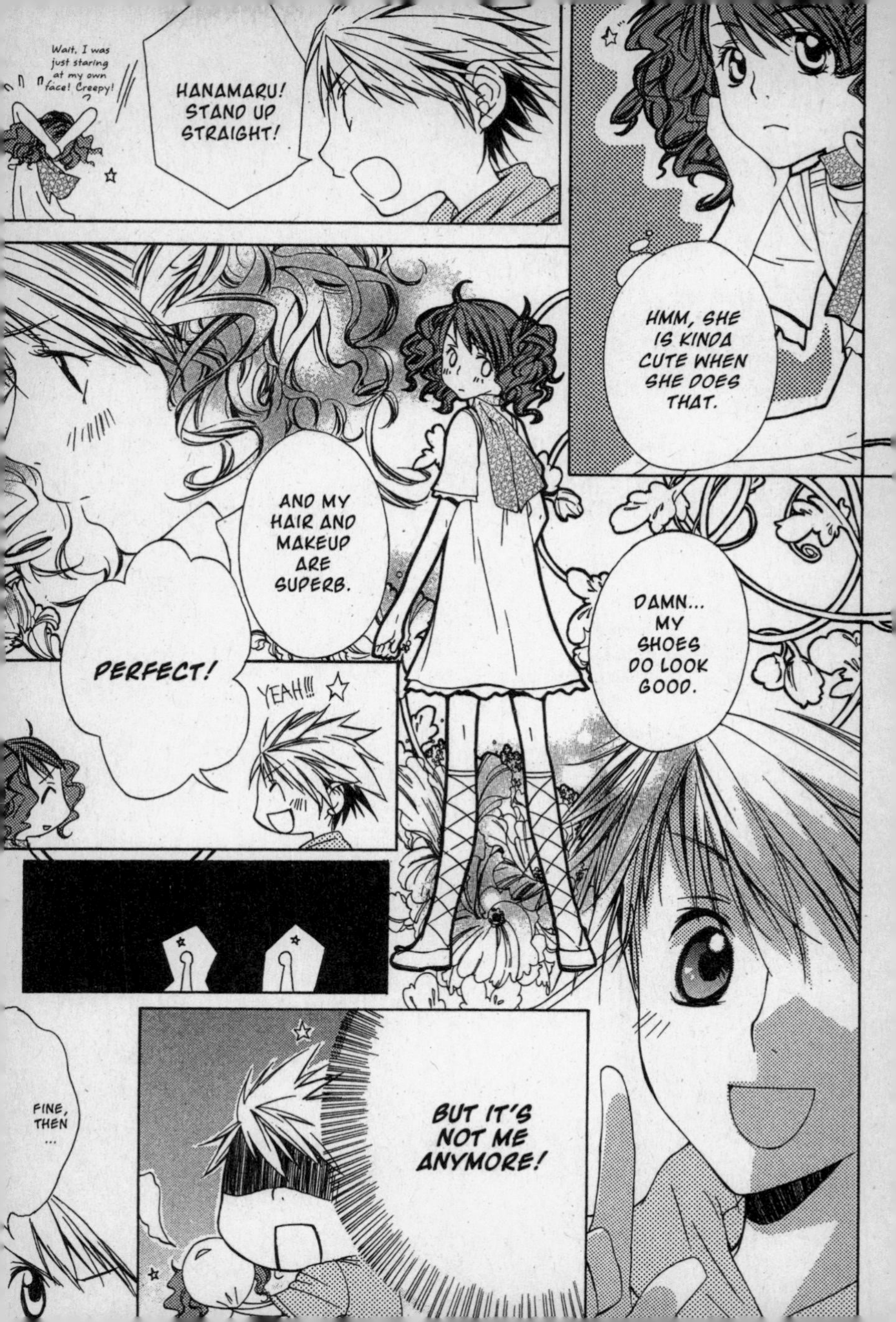
HMM, SHE IS KINDA CUTE WHEN SHE DOES THAT.
HANAMARU! STAND UP STRAIGHT!
Wait, I was just staring at my own face! Creepy!
AND MY HAIR AND MAKEUP ARE SUPERB.
DAMN... MY SHOES DO LOOK GOOD.
PERFECT!
YEAH!!!
BUT IT'S NOT ME ANYMORE!
FINE, THEN ...

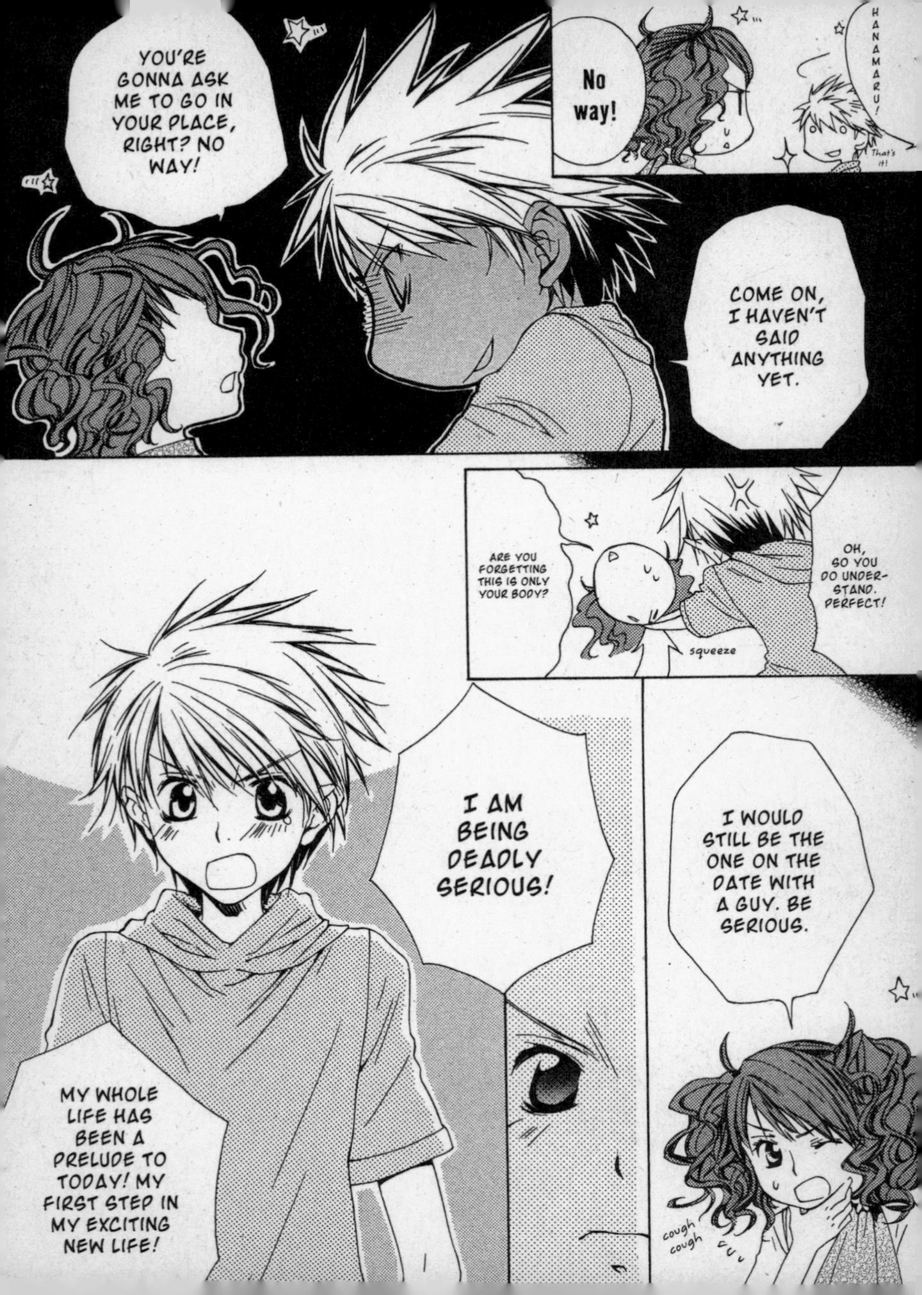
No way!
HANAMARU!
That's it!
YOU'RE GONNA ASK ME TO GO IN YOUR PLACE, RIGHT? NO WAY!
COME ON, I HAVEN'T SAID ANYTHING YET.
OH, SO YOU DO UNDERSTAND. PERFECT!
squeeze
ARE YOU FORGETTING THIS IS ONLY YOUR BODY?
I WOULD STILL BE THE ONE ON THE DATE WITH A GUY. BE SERIOUS.
cough cough
I AM BEING DEADLY SERIOUS!
MY WHOLE LIFE HAS BEEN A PRELUDE TO TODAY! MY FIRST STEP IN MY EXCITING NEW LIFE!

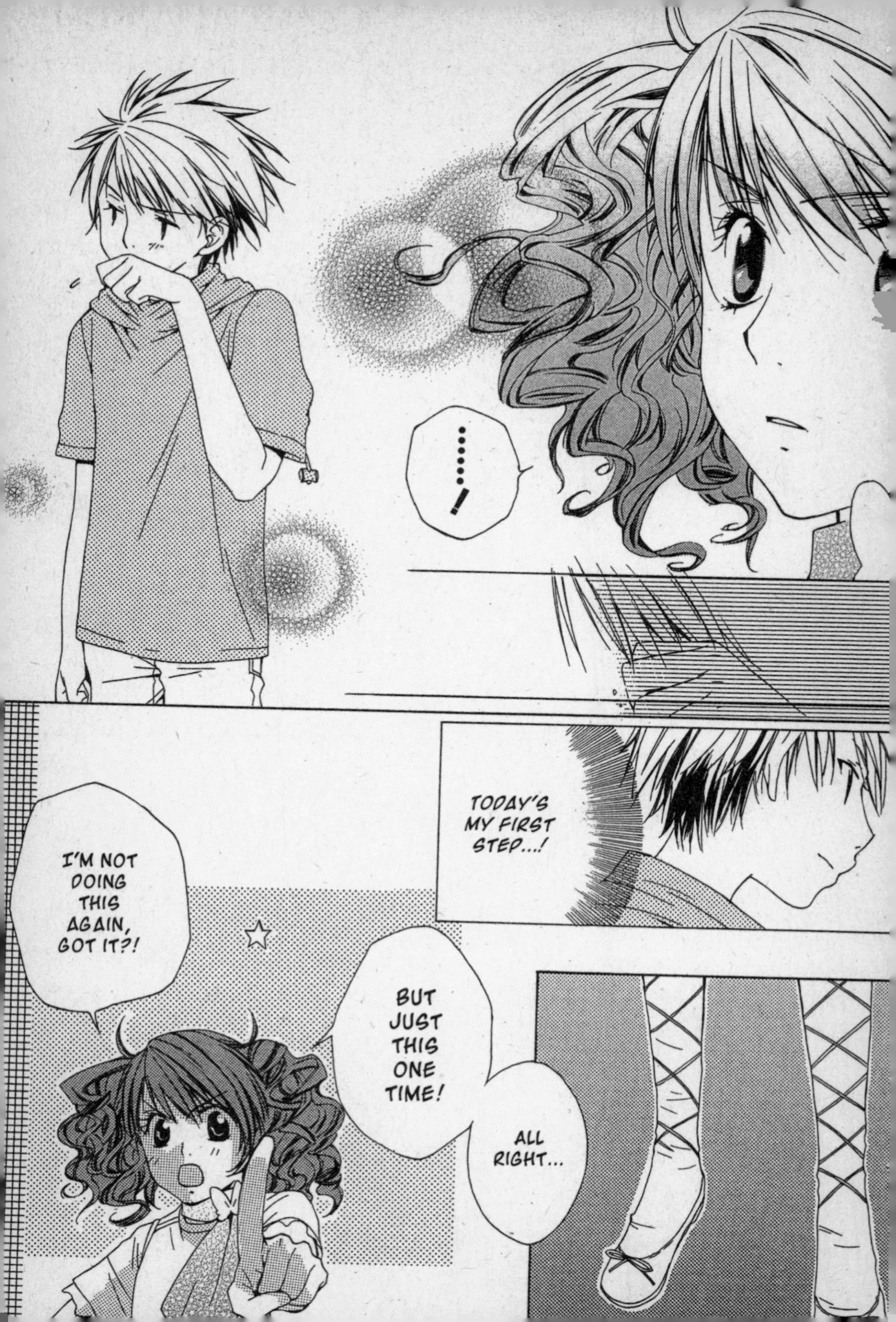
......!
TODAY'S MY FIRST STEP...!
I'M NOT DOING THIS AGAIN, GOT IT?!
BUT JUST THIS ONE TIME!
ALL RIGHT...

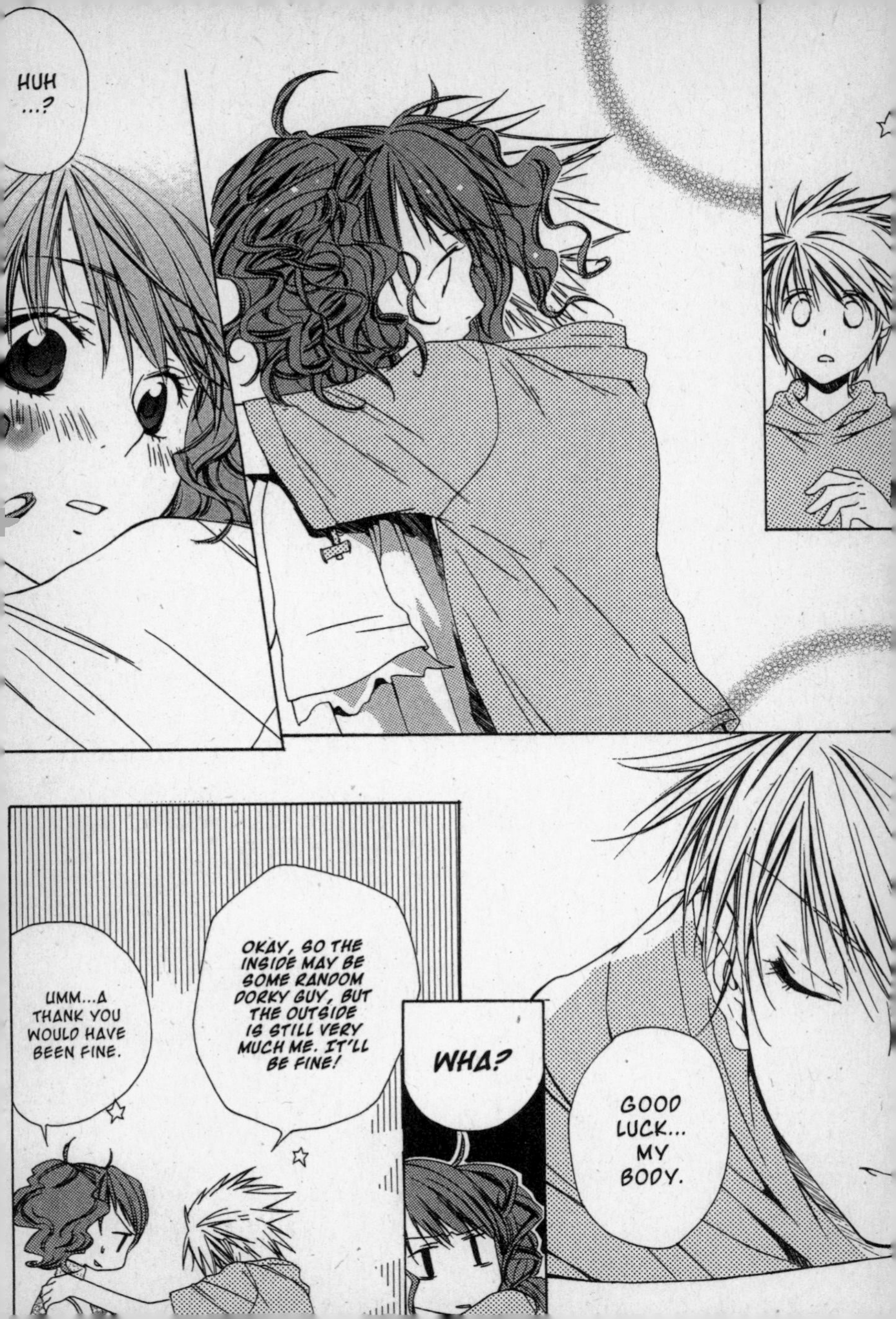
HUH ...?
GOOD LUCK... MY BODY.
WHA?
OKAY, SO THE INSIDE MAY BE SOME RANDOM DORKY GUY, BUT THE OUTSIDE IS STILL VERY MUCH ME. IT'LL BE FINE!
UMM...A THANK YOU WOULD HAVE BEEN FINE.

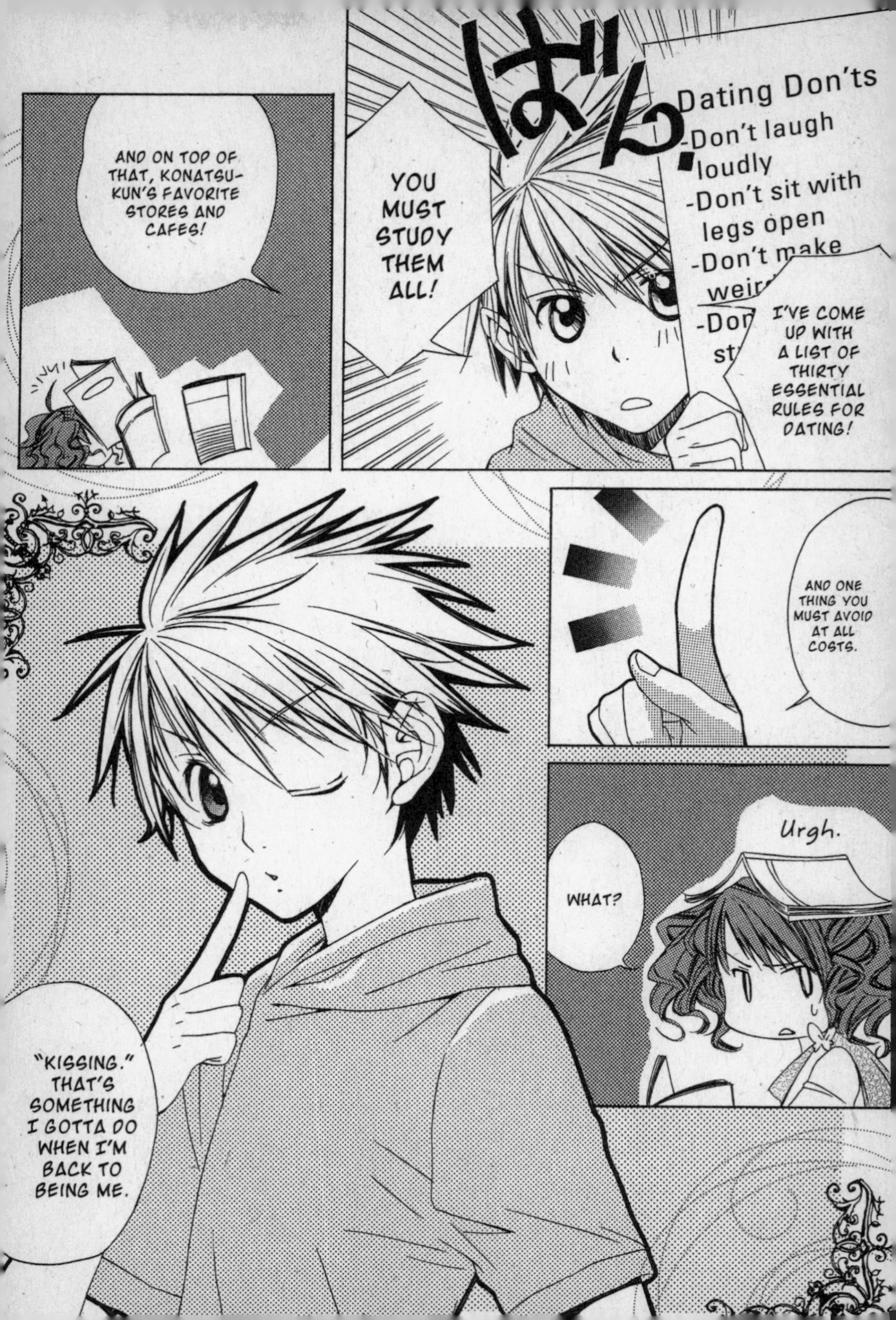
ぱん
Dating Don'ts
-Don't laugh loudly
-Don't sit with legs open
-Don't make
I'VE COME UP WITH A LIST OF THIRTY ESSENTIAL RULES FOR DATING!
YOU MUST STUDY THEM ALL!
AND ON TOP OF THAT, KONATSU-KUN'S FAVORITE STORES AND CAFES!
AND ONE THING YOU MUST AVOID AT ALL COSTS.
Urgh.
WHAT?
"KISSING." THAT'S SOMETHING I GOTTA DO WHEN I'M BACK TO BEING ME.

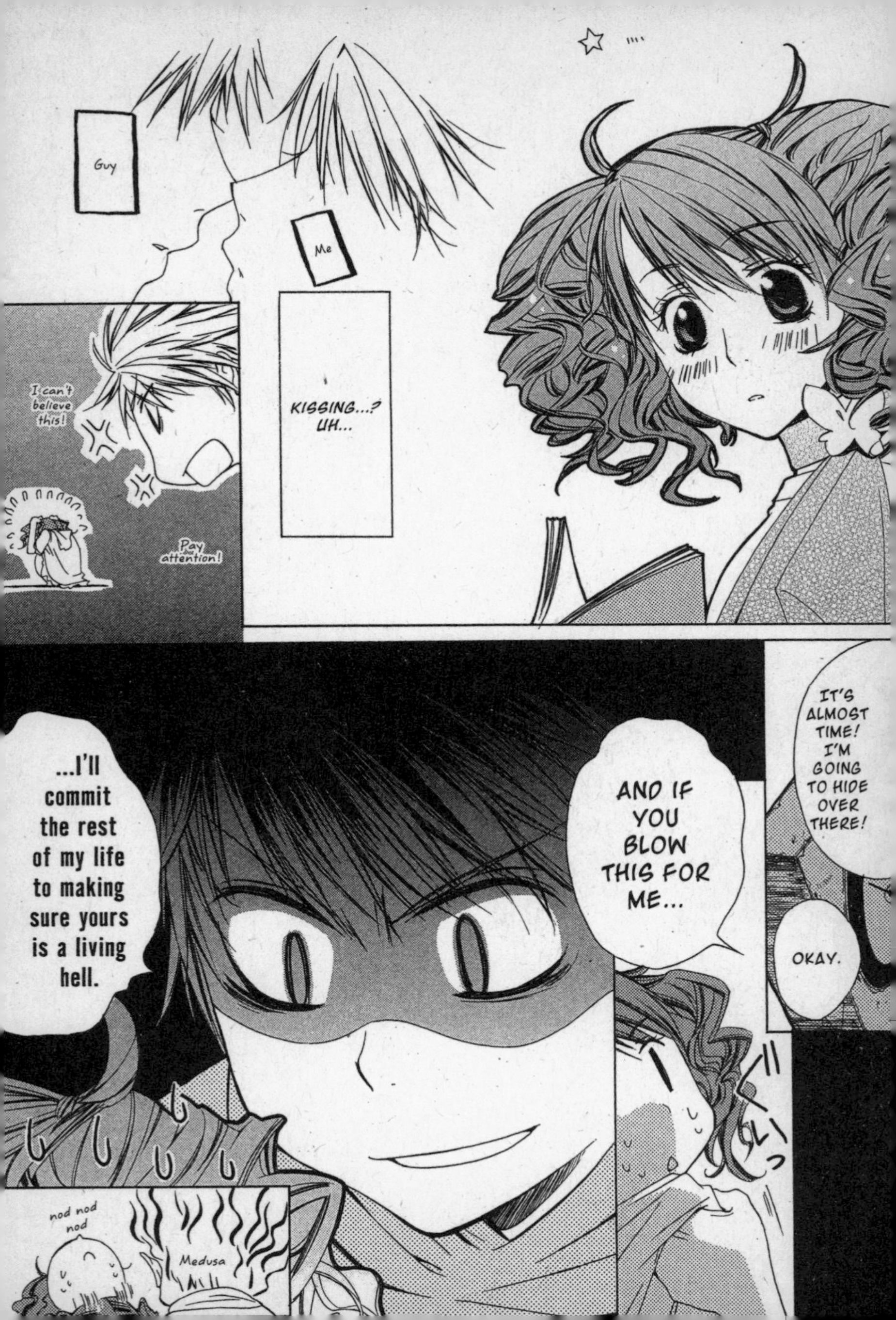
Guy
Me
KISSING...? UH...
I can't believe this!
Pay attention!
IT'S ALMOST TIME! I'M GOING TO HIDE OVER THERE!
OKAY.
AND IF YOU BLOW THIS FOR ME...
...I'll commit the rest of my life to making sure yours is a living hell.
nod nod nod
Medusa

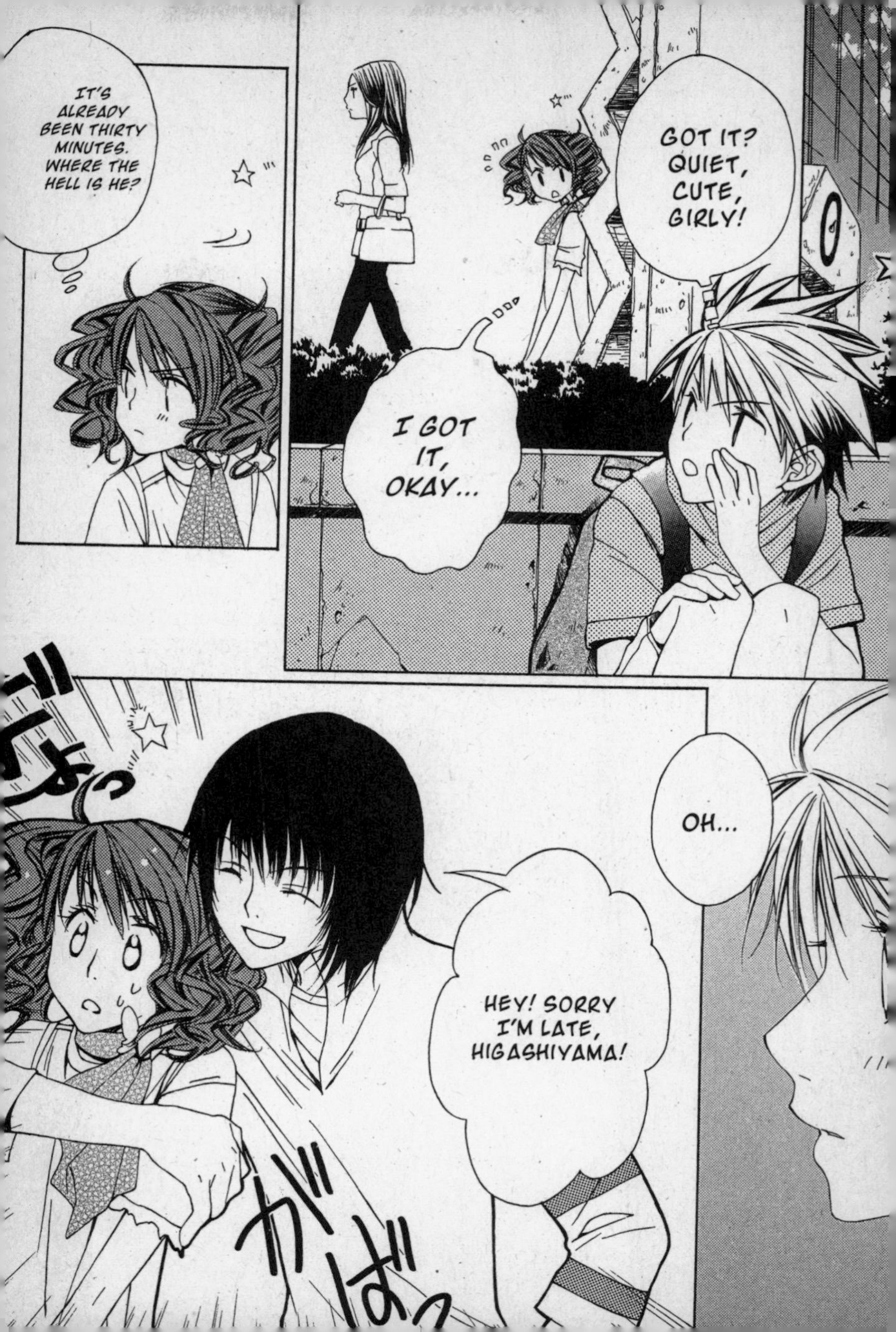
GOT IT? QUIET, CUTE, GIRLY!
I GOT IT, OKAY...
IT'S ALREADY BEEN THIRTY MINUTES. WHERE THE HELL IS HE?
OH...
HEY! SORRY I'M LATE, HIGASHIYAMA!
がばっ

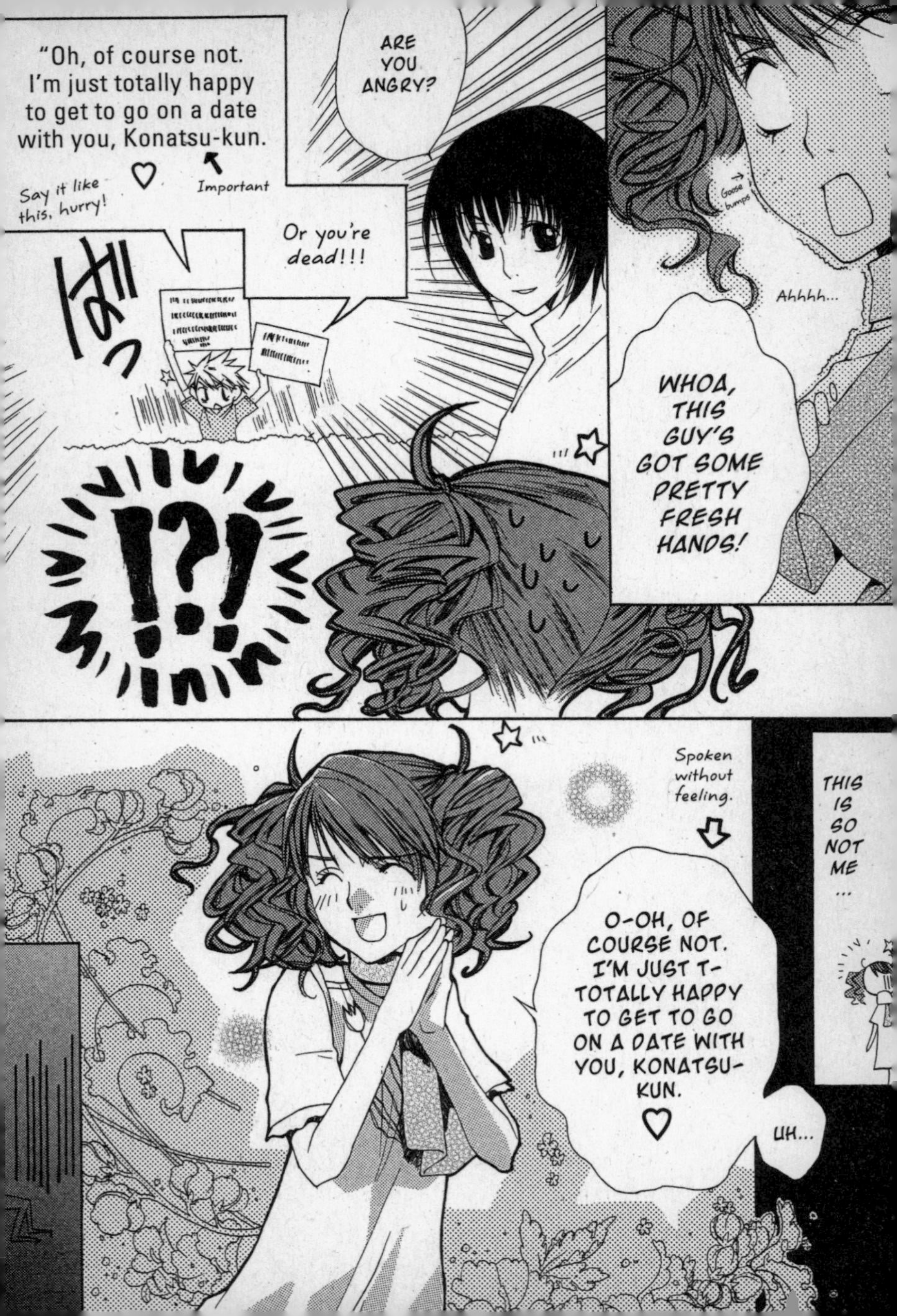

Goose bumps
Ahhhh...
WHOA, THIS GUY'S GOT SOME PRETTY FRESH HANDS!
ARE YOU ANGRY?
"Oh, of course not. I'm just totally happy to get to go on a date with you, Konatsu-kun.
♡
Important
Say it like this, hurry!
Or you're dead!!!
はっ
!?!
THIS IS SO NOT ME ...
UH...
Spoken without feeling.
O-OH, OF COURSE NOT. I'M JUST T-TOTALLY HAPPY TO GET TO GO ON A DATE WITH YOU, KONATSU-KUN.
♡

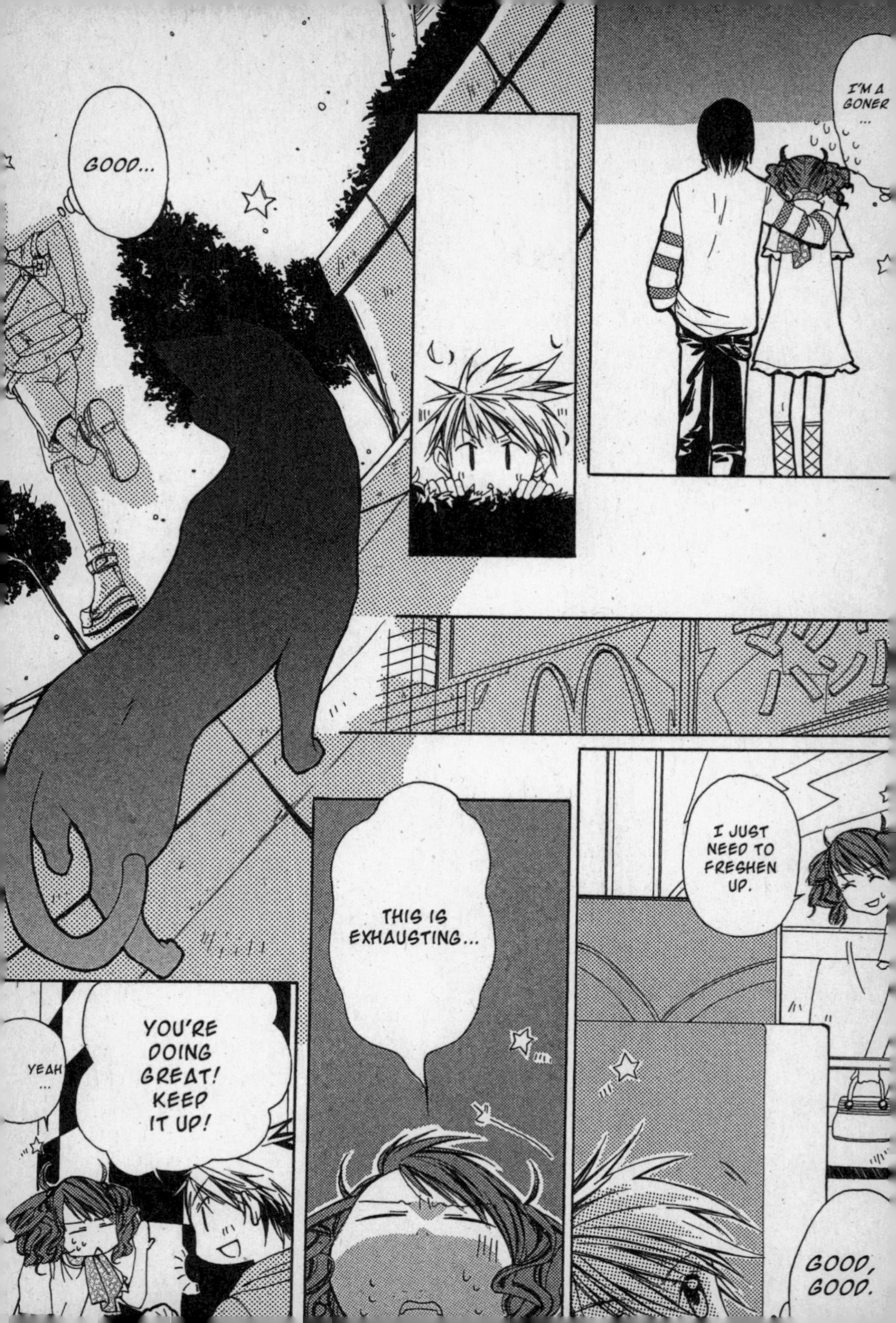
I'M A GONER...
GOOD...
I JUST NEED TO FRESHEN UP.
GOOD, GOOD.
THIS IS EXHAUSTING...
YOU'RE DOING GREAT! KEEP IT UP!
YEAH...

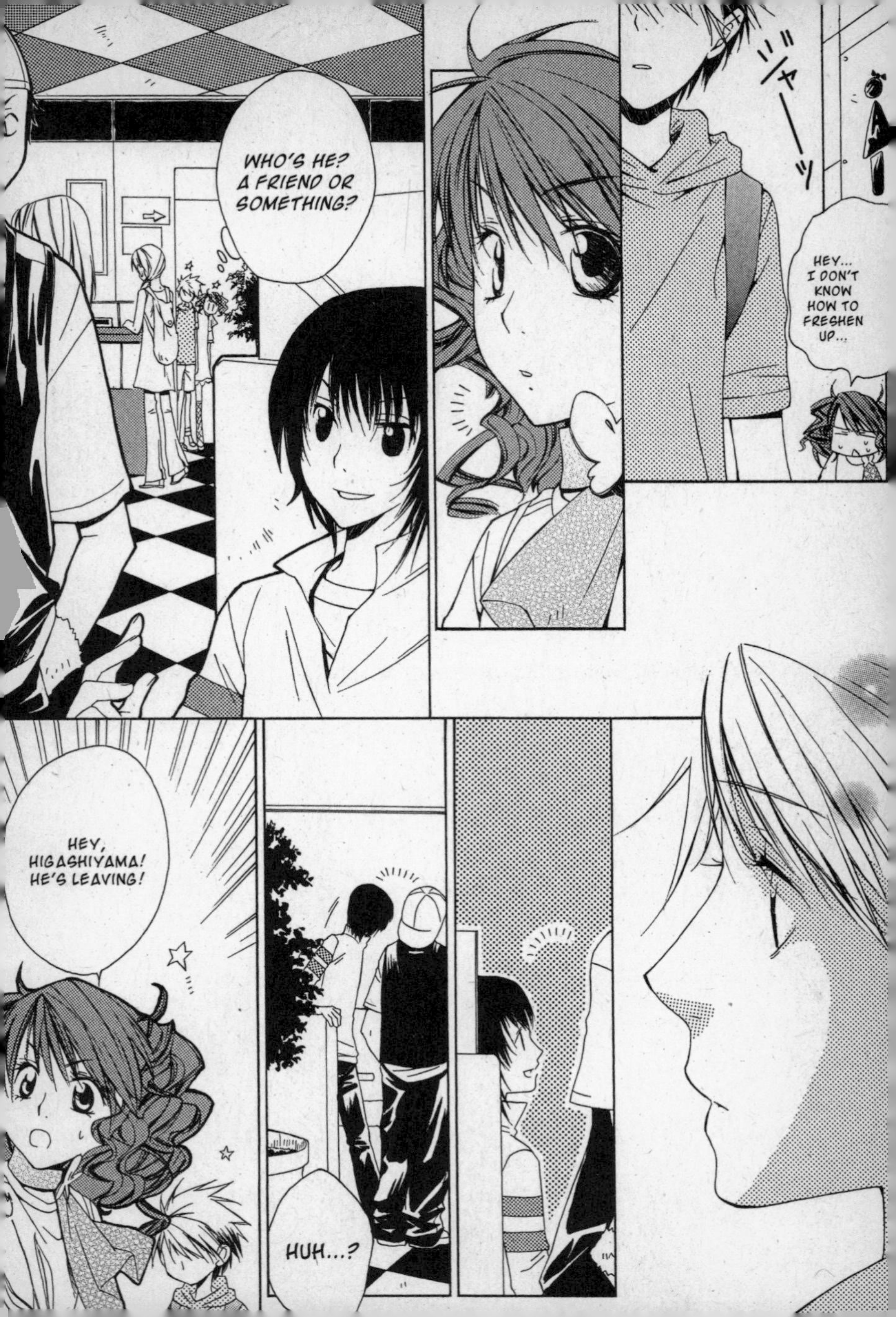
ジャーッ
HEY... I DON'T KNOW HOW TO FRESHEN UP...
WHO'S HE? A FRIEND OR SOMETHING?
HUH...?
HEY, HIGASHIYAMA! HE'S LEAVING!

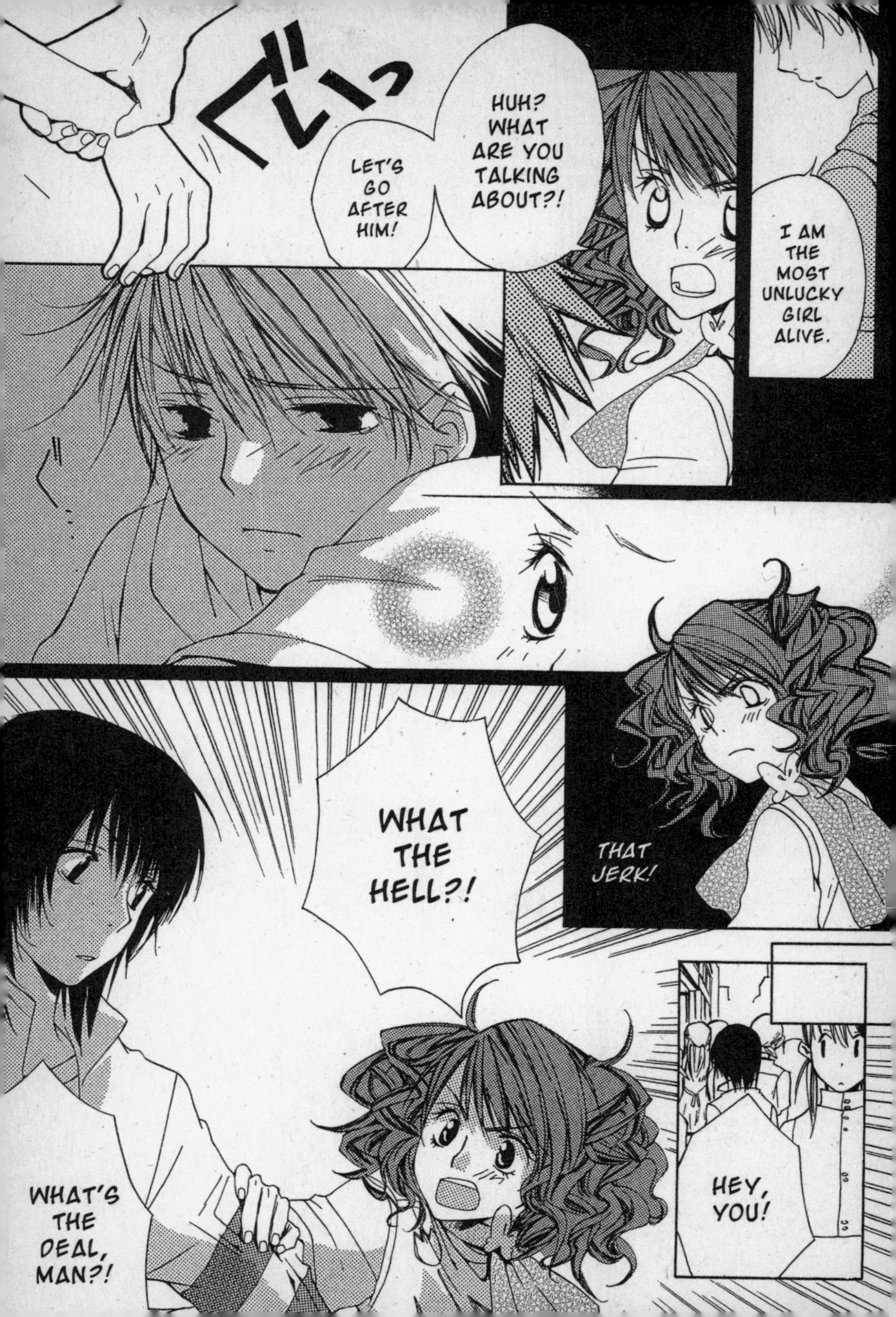
I AM THE MOST UNLUCKY GIRL ALIVE.
HUH? WHAT ARE YOU TALKING ABOUT?!
LET'S GO AFTER HIM!
ぐいっ
THAT JERK!
HEY, YOU!
WHAT THE HELL?!
WHAT'S THE DEAL, MAN?!

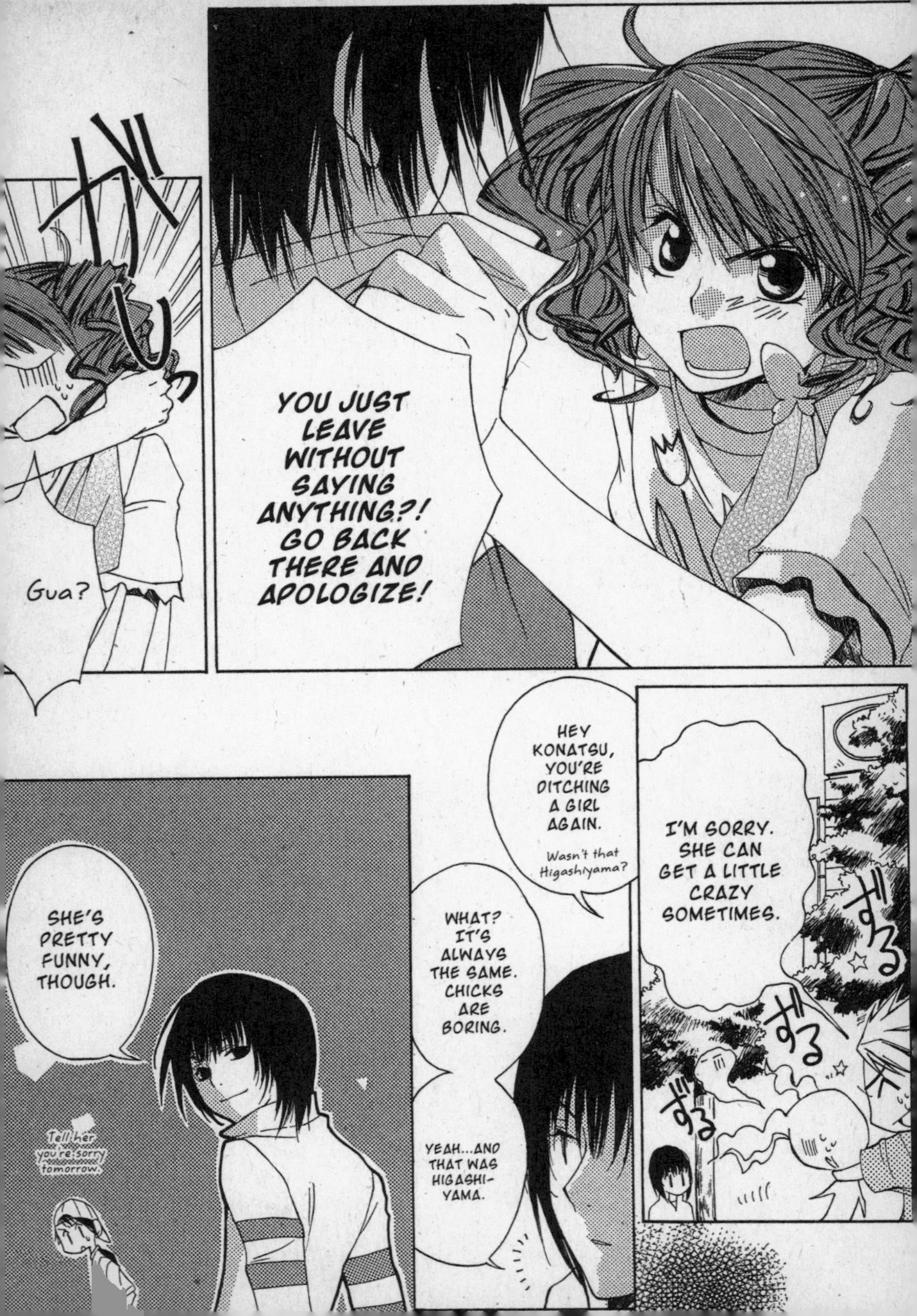
YOU JUST LEAVE WITHOUT SAYING ANYTHING?! GO BACK THERE AND APOLOGIZE!
Gua?
I'M SORRY. SHE CAN GET A LITTLE CRAZY SOMETIMES.
ずる
ずる
ずる
HEY KONATSU, YOU'RE DITCHING A GIRL AGAIN.
Wasn't that Higashiyama?
WHAT? IT'S ALWAYS THE SAME. CHICKS ARE BORING.
YEAH...AND THAT WAS HIGASHI-YAMA.
SHE'S PRETTY FUNNY, THOUGH.
Tell her you're sorry tomorrow.

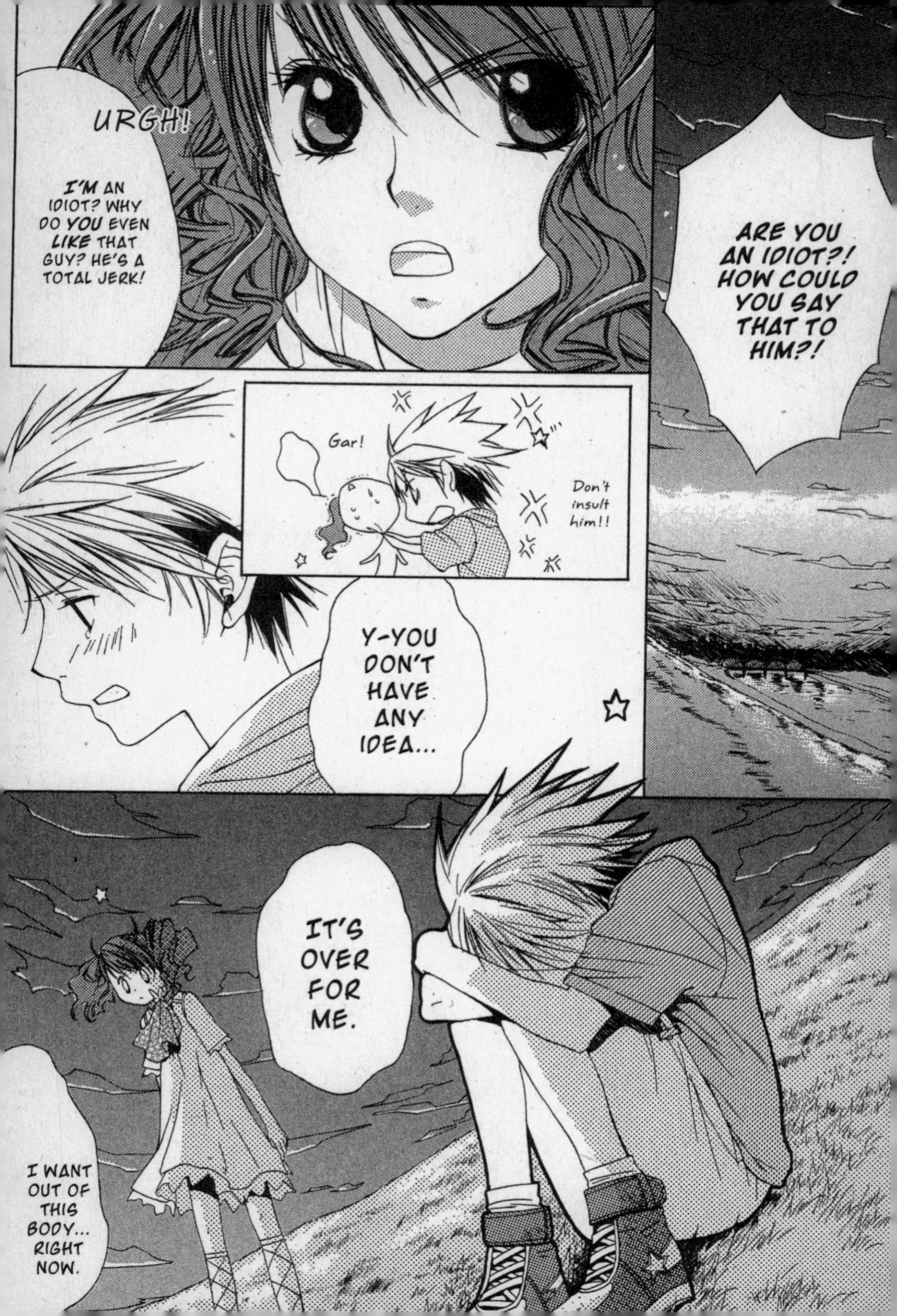
ARE YOU AN IDIOT?! HOW COULD YOU SAY THAT TO HIM?!
URGH!
I'M AN IDIOT? WHY DO YOU EVEN LIKE THAT GUY? HE'S A TOTAL JERK!
Don't insult him!!
Gar!
Y-YOU DON'T HAVE ANY IDEA...
IT'S OVER FOR ME.
I WANT OUT OF THIS BODY... RIGHT NOW.

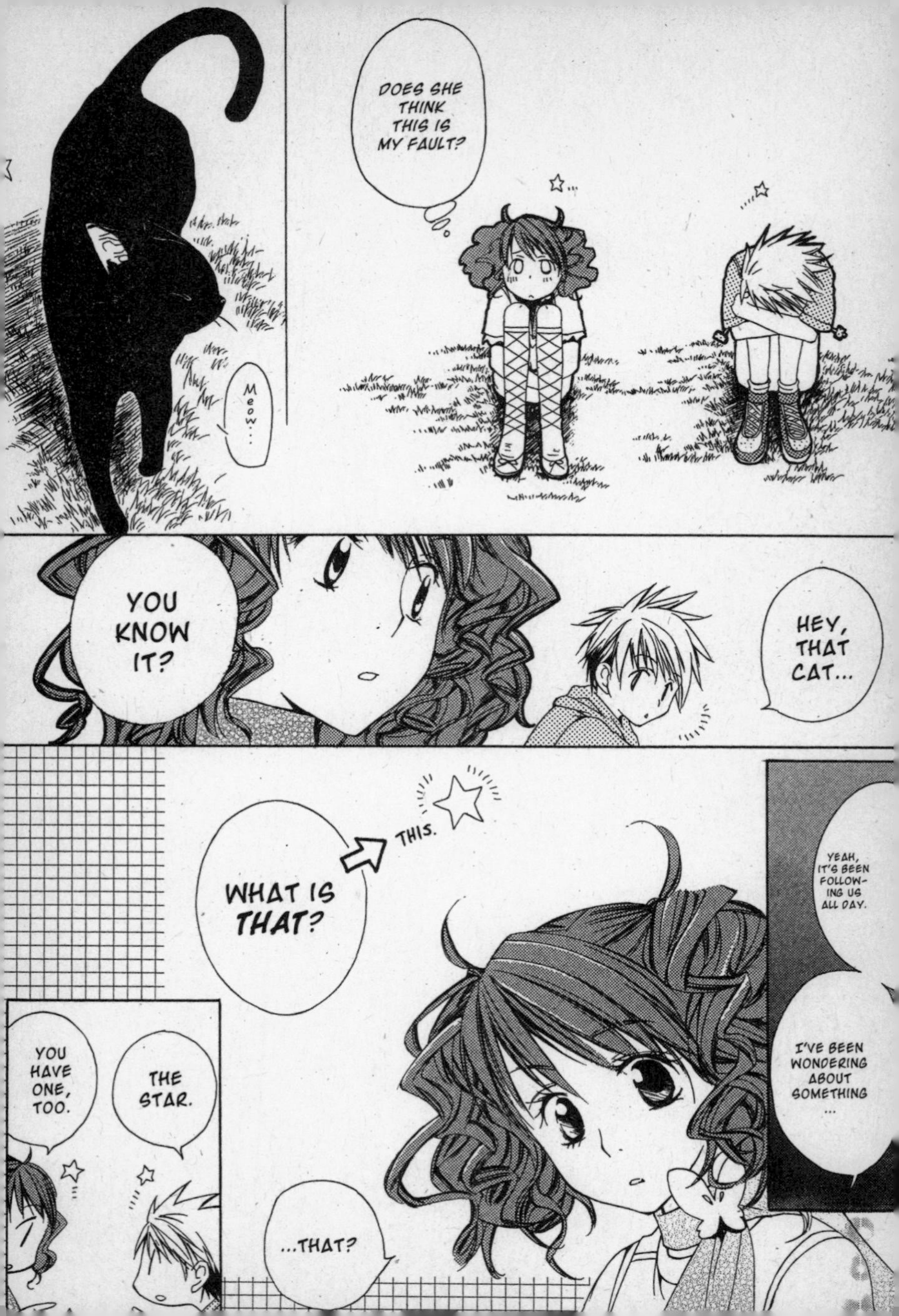
DOES SHE THINK THIS IS MY FAULT?
Meow...
HEY, THAT CAT...
YOU KNOW IT?
YEAH, IT'S BEEN FOLLOW-ING US ALL DAY.
I'VE BEEN WONDERING ABOUT SOMETHING...
WHAT IS THAT?
THIS.
...THAT?
THE STAR.
YOU HAVE ONE, TOO.

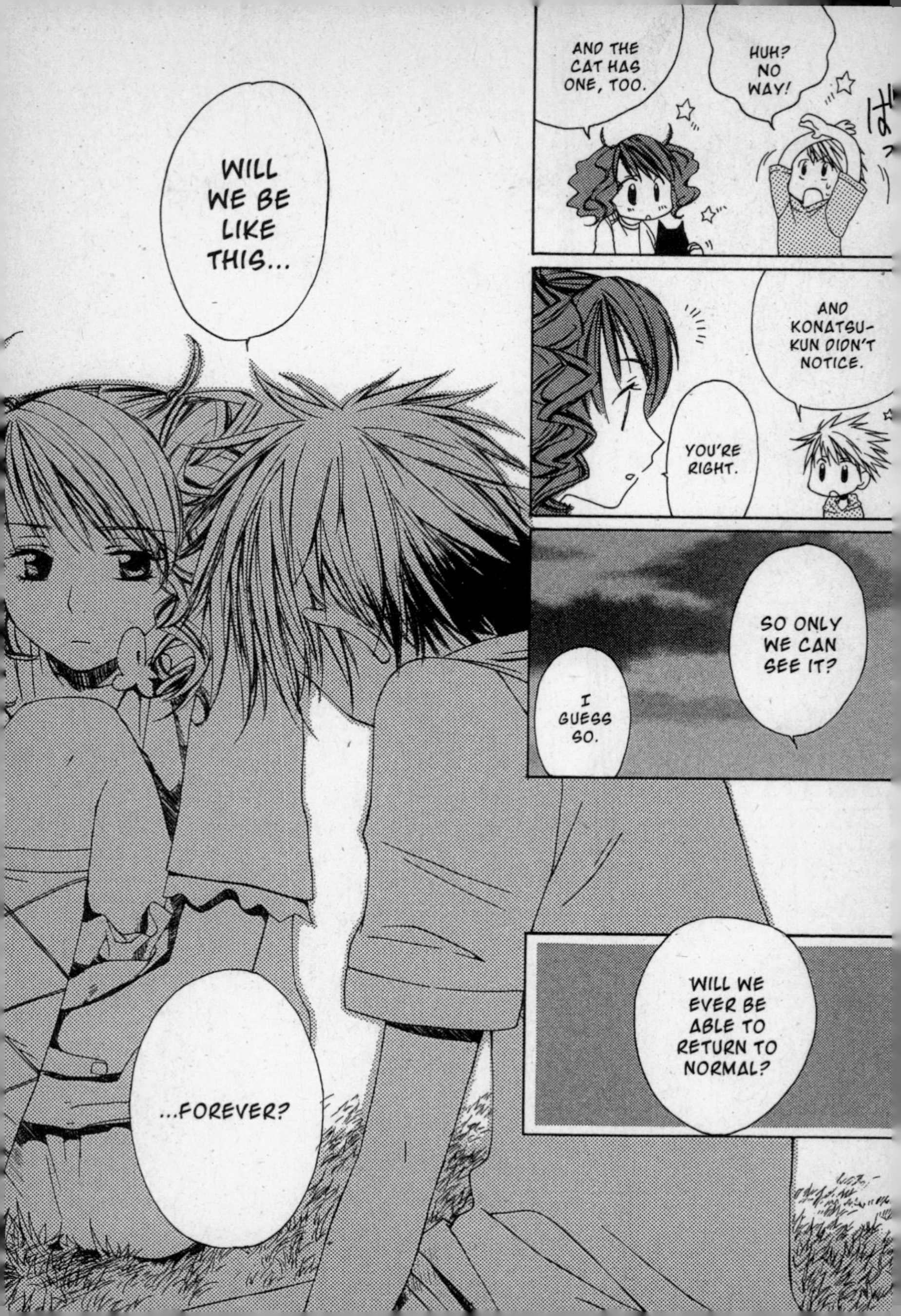
HUH? NO WAY!
AND THE CAT HAS ONE, TOO.
AND KONATSU-KUN DIDN'T NOTICE.
YOU'RE RIGHT.
SO ONLY WE CAN SEE IT?
I GUESS SO.
WILL WE EVER BE ABLE TO RETURN TO NORMAL?
WILL WE BE LIKE THIS...
...FOREVER?

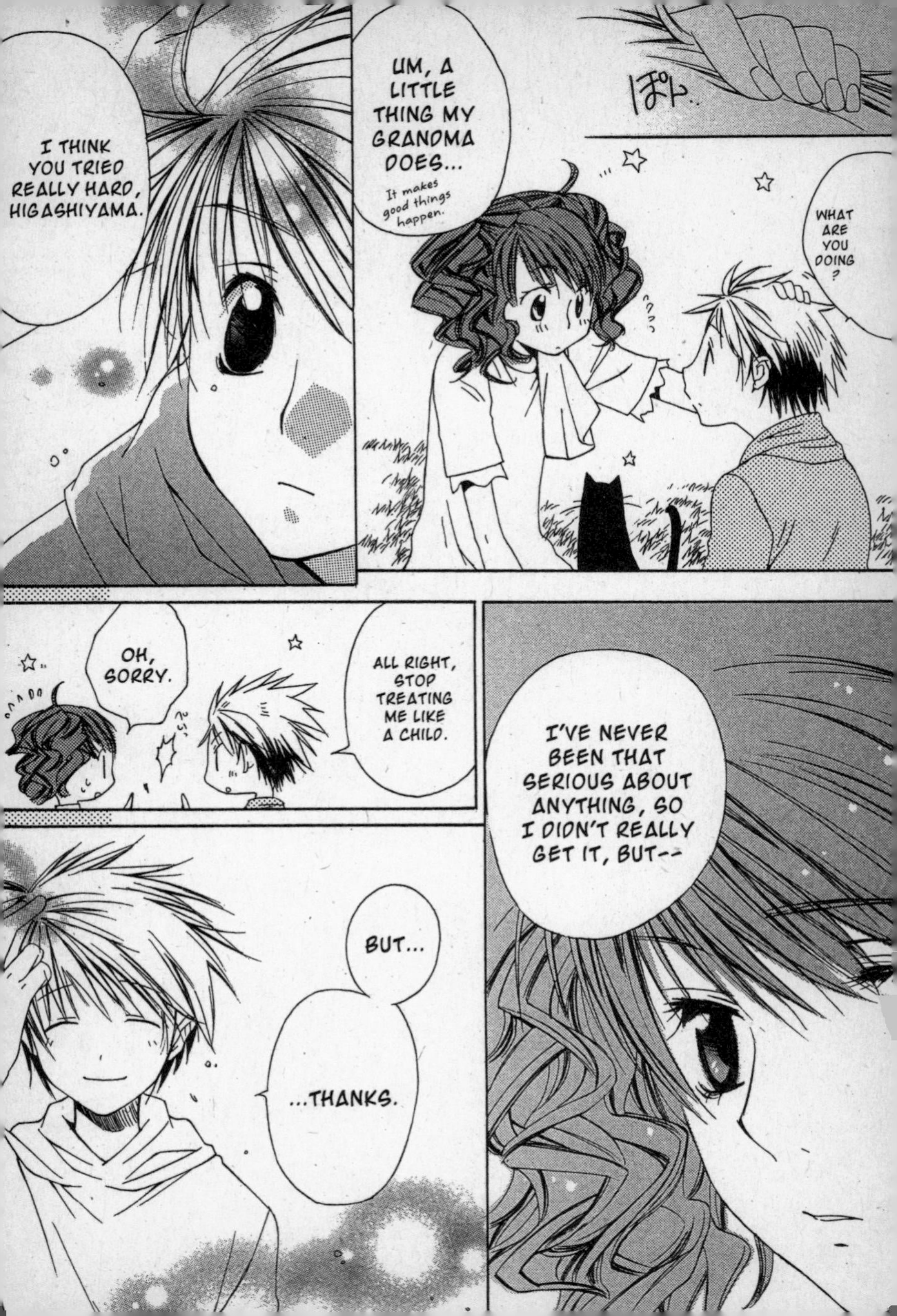

ぽト..
WHAT ARE YOU DOING?
UM, A LITTLE THING MY GRANDMA DOES...
It makes good things happen.
I THINK YOU TRIED REALLY HARD, HIGASHIYAMA.
I'VE NEVER BEEN THAT SERIOUS ABOUT ANYTHING, SO I DIDN'T REALLY GET IT, BUT--
ALL RIGHT, STOP TREATING ME LIKE A CHILD.
OH, SORRY.
BUT...
...THANKS.

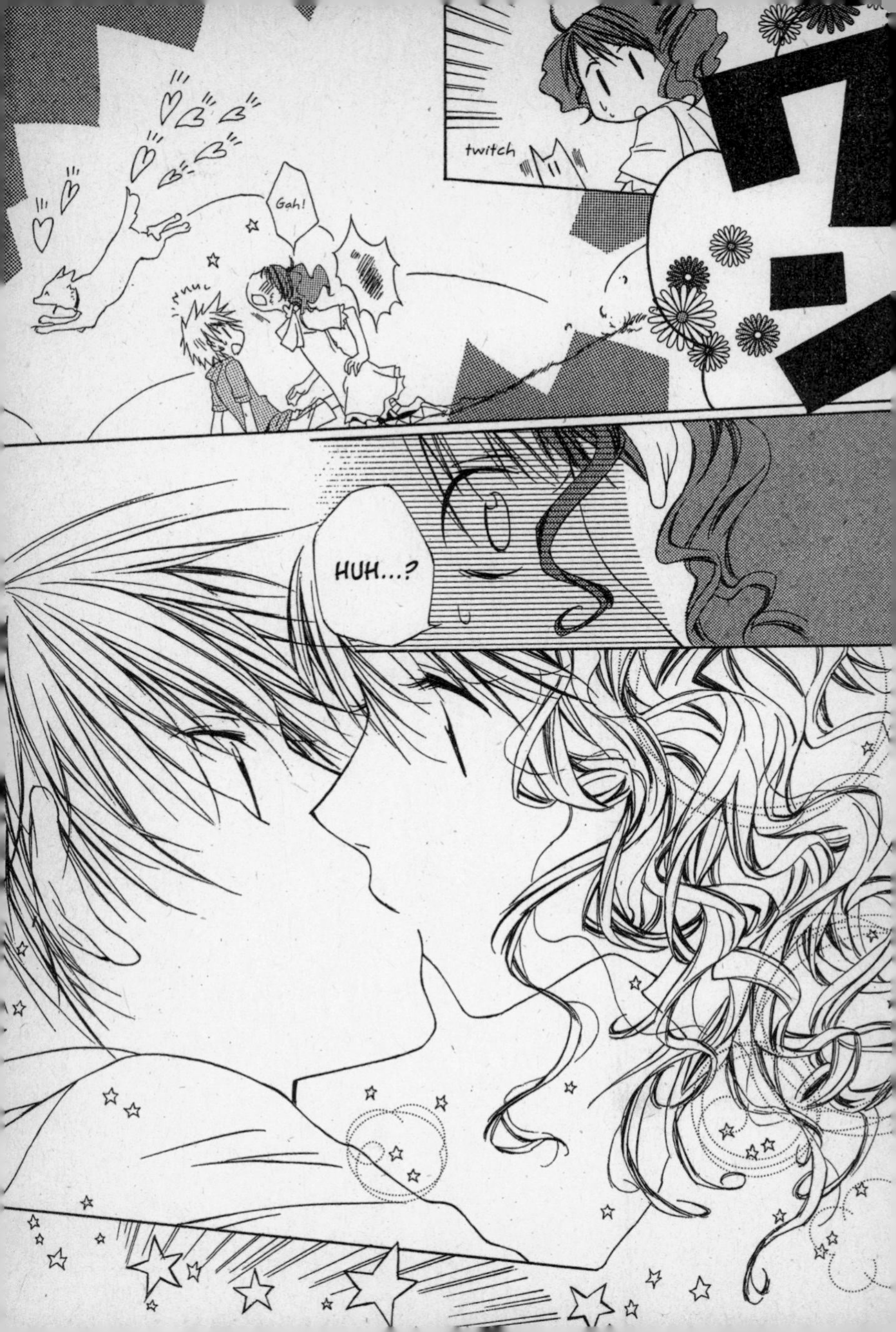
twitch
Gah!
HUH...?

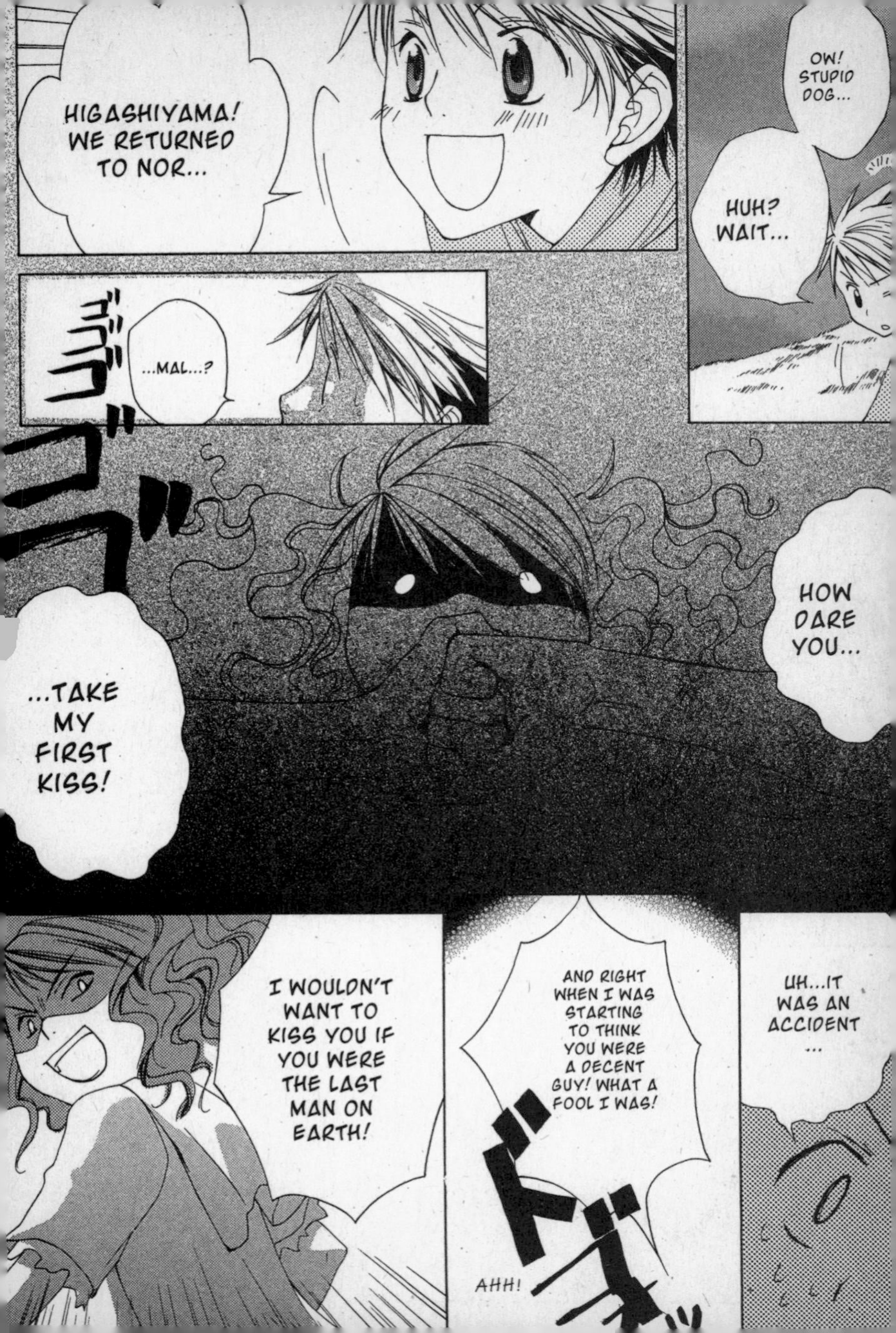
OW! STUPID DOG...
HUH? WAIT...
HIGASHIYAMA! WE RETURNED TO NOR...
...MAL...?
ゴゴゴゴ
HOW DARE YOU...
...TAKE MY FIRST KISS!
UH...IT WAS AN ACCIDENT ...
AND RIGHT WHEN I WAS STARTING TO THINK YOU WERE A DECENT GUY! WHAT A FOOL I WAS!
ドド
AHH!
I WOULDN'T WANT TO KISS YOU IF YOU WERE THE LAST MAN ON EARTH!

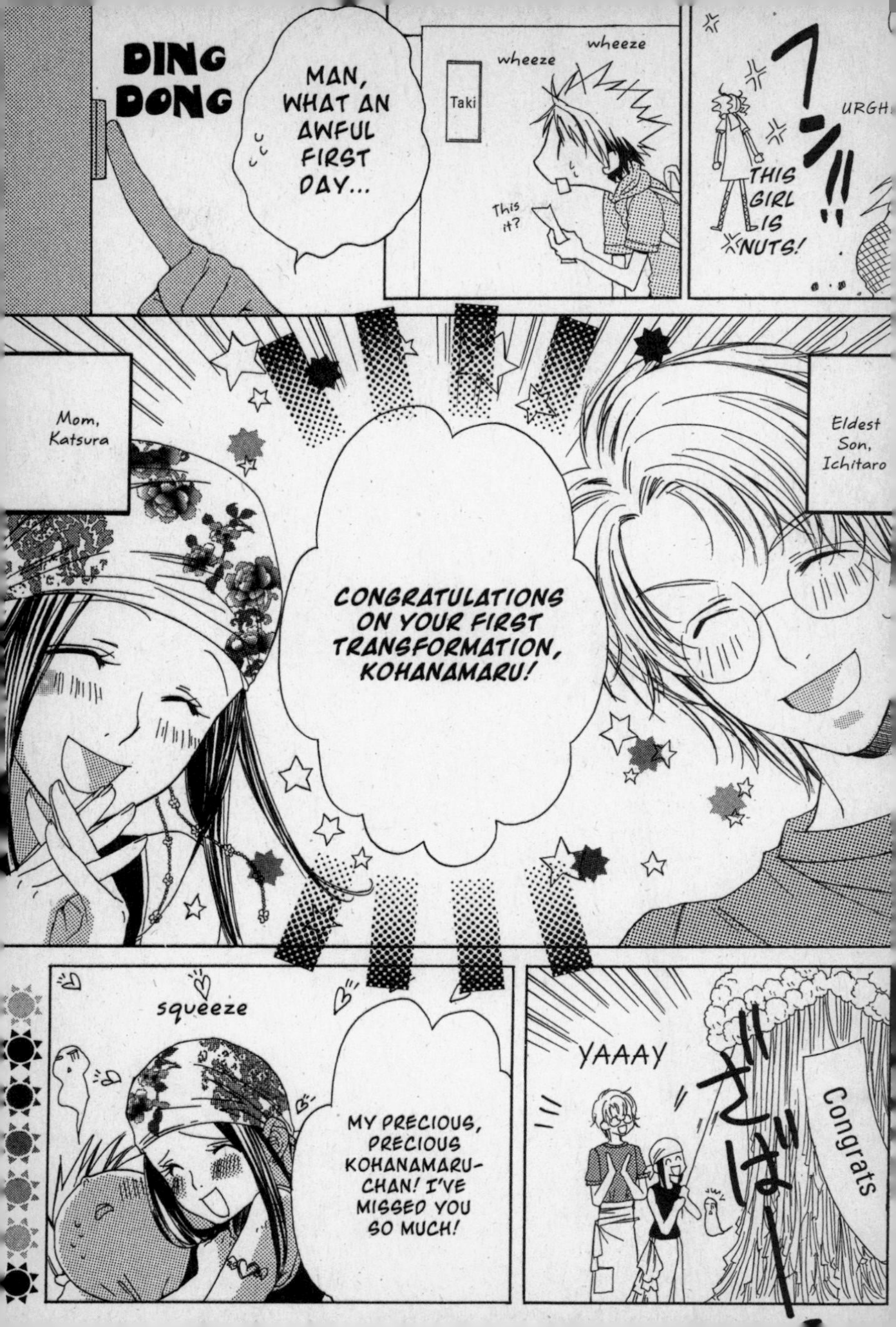
URGH
THIS GIRL IS NUTS!
wheeze
wheeze
Taki
This it?
DING DONG
MAN, WHAT AN AWFUL FIRST DAY...
Eldest Son, Ichitaro
Mom, Katsura
CONGRATULATIONS ON YOUR FIRST TRANSFORMATION, KOHANAMARU!
Congrats
YAAAY
squeeze
MY PRECIOUS, PRECIOUS KOHANAMARU-CHAN! I'VE MISSED YOU SO MUCH!

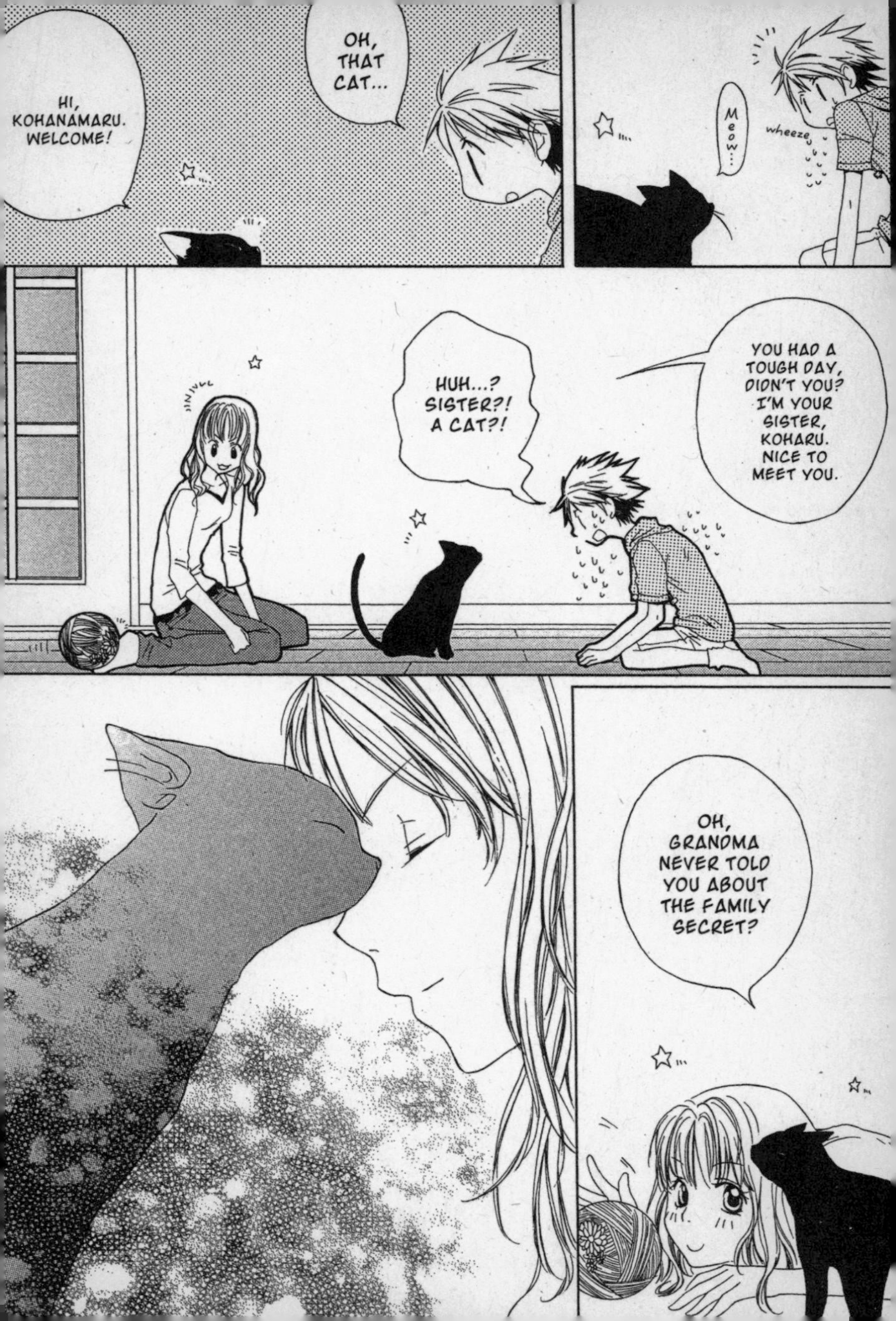
Meow...
wheeze
OH, THAT CAT...
HI, KOHANAMARU. WELCOME!
YOU HAD A TOUGH DAY, DIDN'T YOU? I'M YOUR SISTER, KOHARU. NICE TO MEET YOU.
HUH...? SISTER?! A CAT?!
OH, GRANDMA NEVER TOLD YOU ABOUT THE FAMILY SECRET?

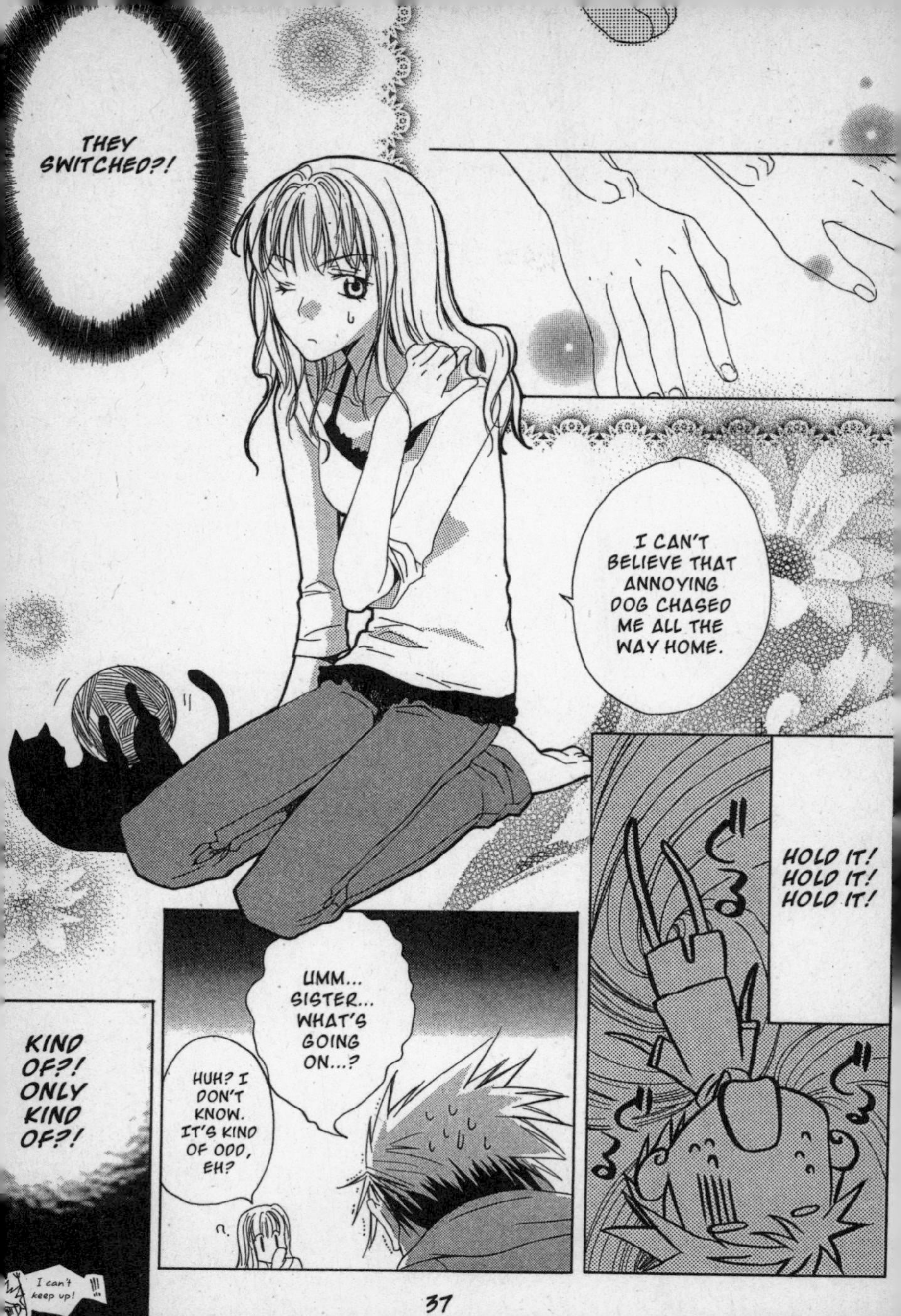
THEY SWITCHED?!
I CAN'T BELIEVE THAT ANNOYING DOG CHASED ME ALL THE WAY HOME.
HOLD IT! HOLD IT! HOLD IT!
UMM... SISTER... WHAT'S GOING ON...?
HUH? I DON'T KNOW. IT'S KIND OF ODD, EH?
KIND OF?! ONLY KIND OF?!
I can't keep up! !!!

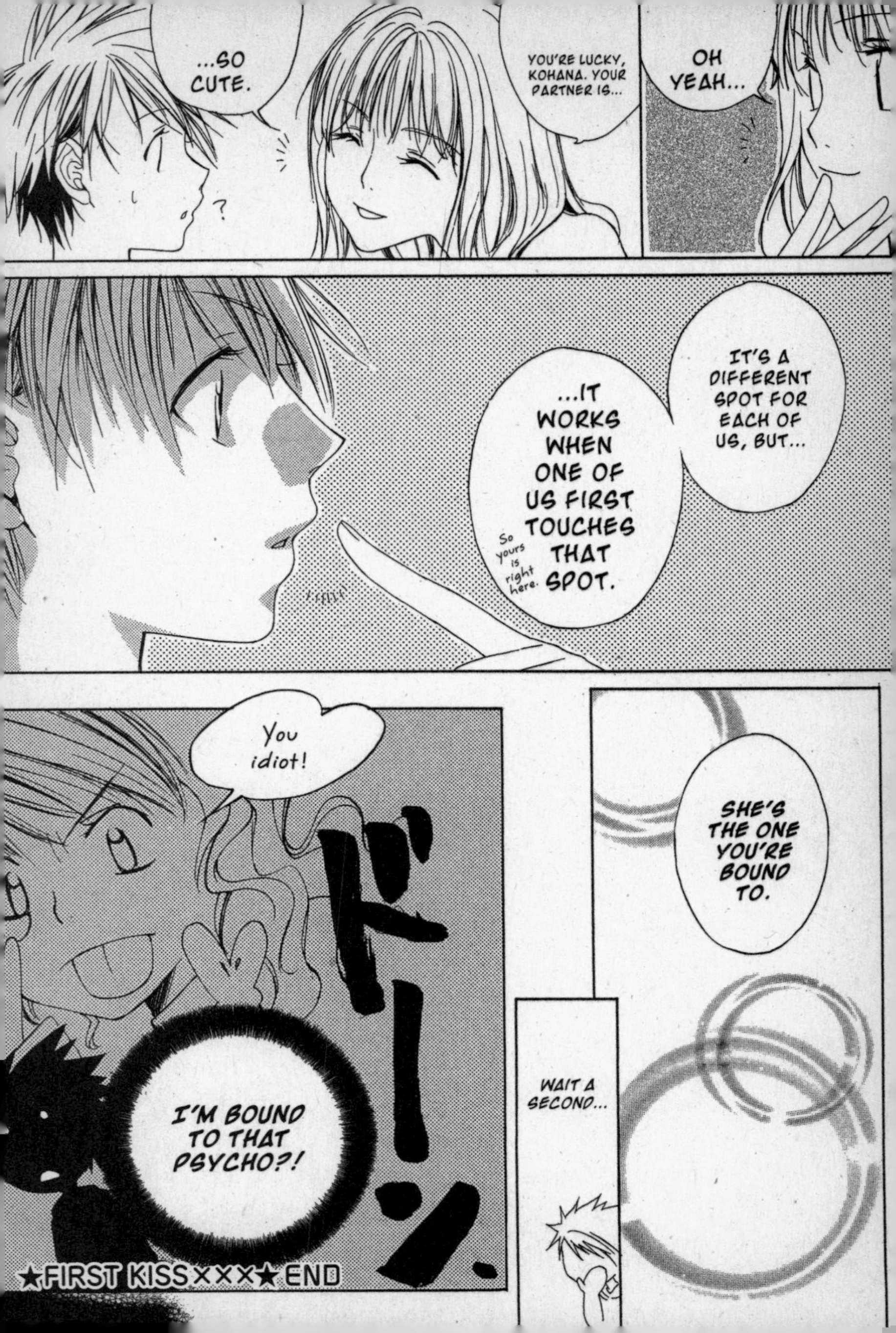
OH YEAH...
YOU'RE LUCKY, KOHANA. YOUR PARTNER IS...
...SO CUTE.
?
IT'S A DIFFERENT SPOT FOR EACH OF US, BUT...
...IT WORKS WHEN ONE OF US FIRST TOUCHES THAT SPOT.
So yours is right here.
SHE'S THE ONE YOU'RE BOUND TO.
WAIT A SECOND...
You idiot!
ドーン
I'M BOUND TO THAT PSYCHO?!
★FIRST KISS×××★ END

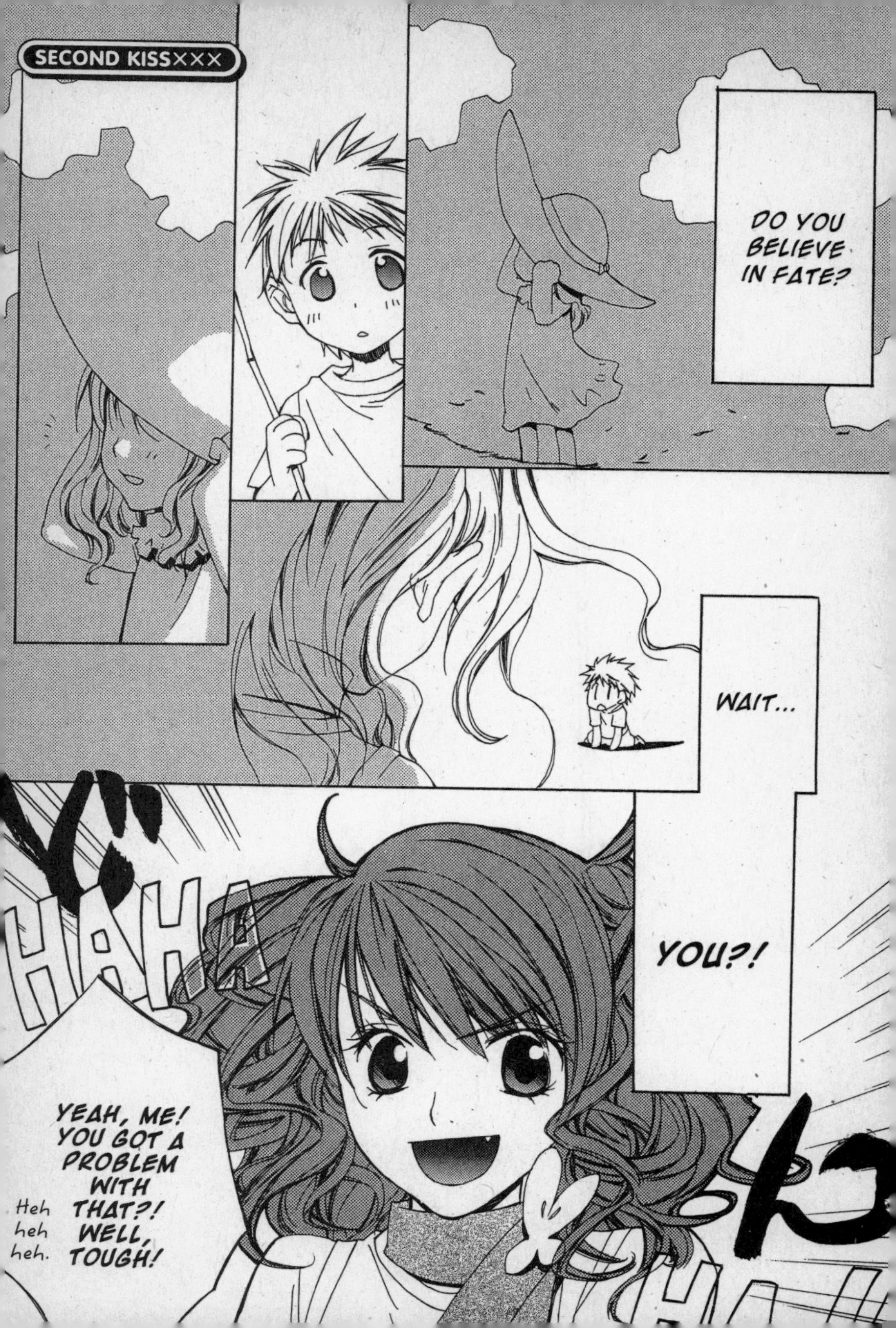
DO YOU BELIEVE IN FATE?
WAIT...
YOU?!
YA HAHAHA
YEAH, ME! YOU GOT A PROBLEM WITH THAT?! WELL, TOUGH!
Heh heh heh.

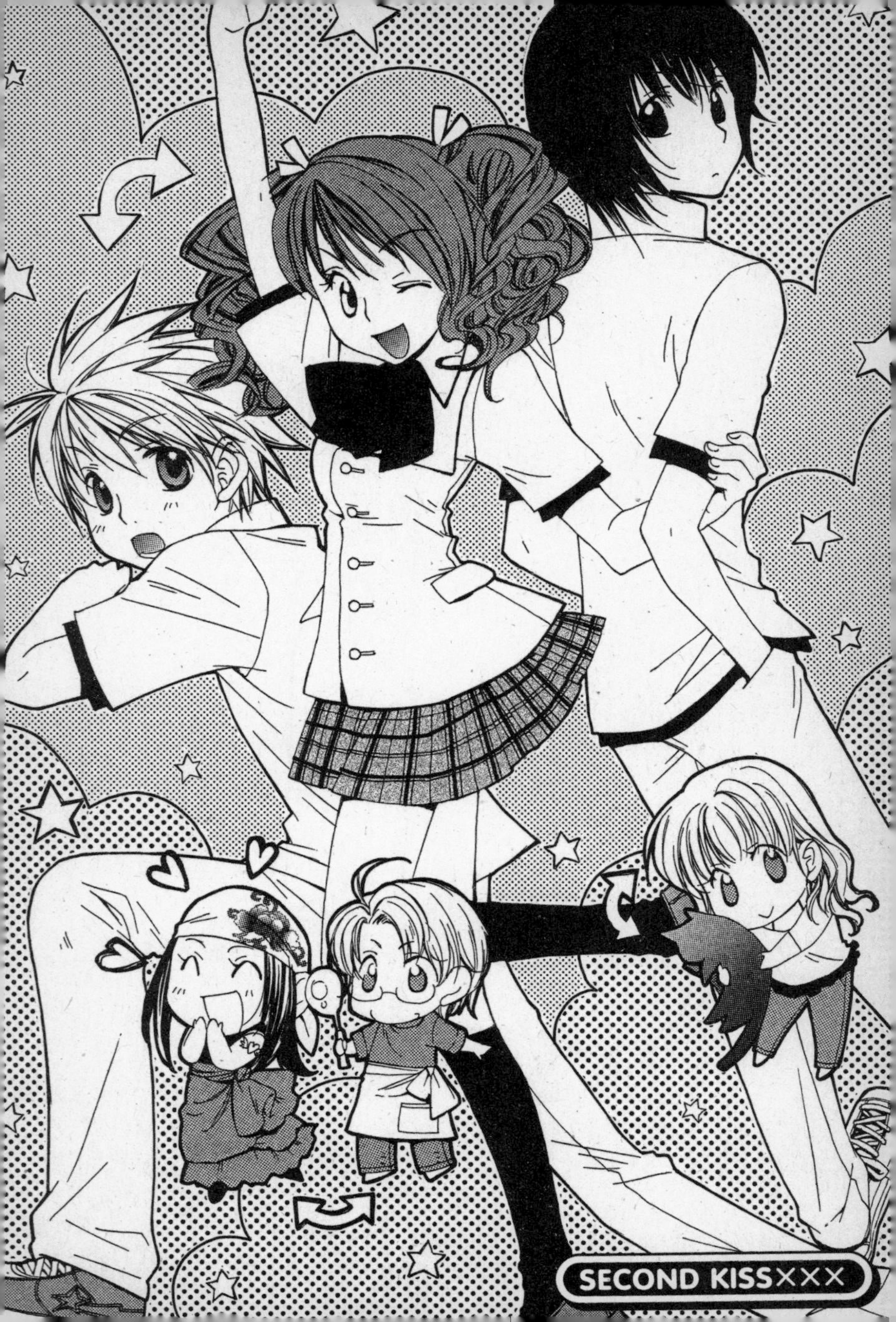
SECOND KISS×××

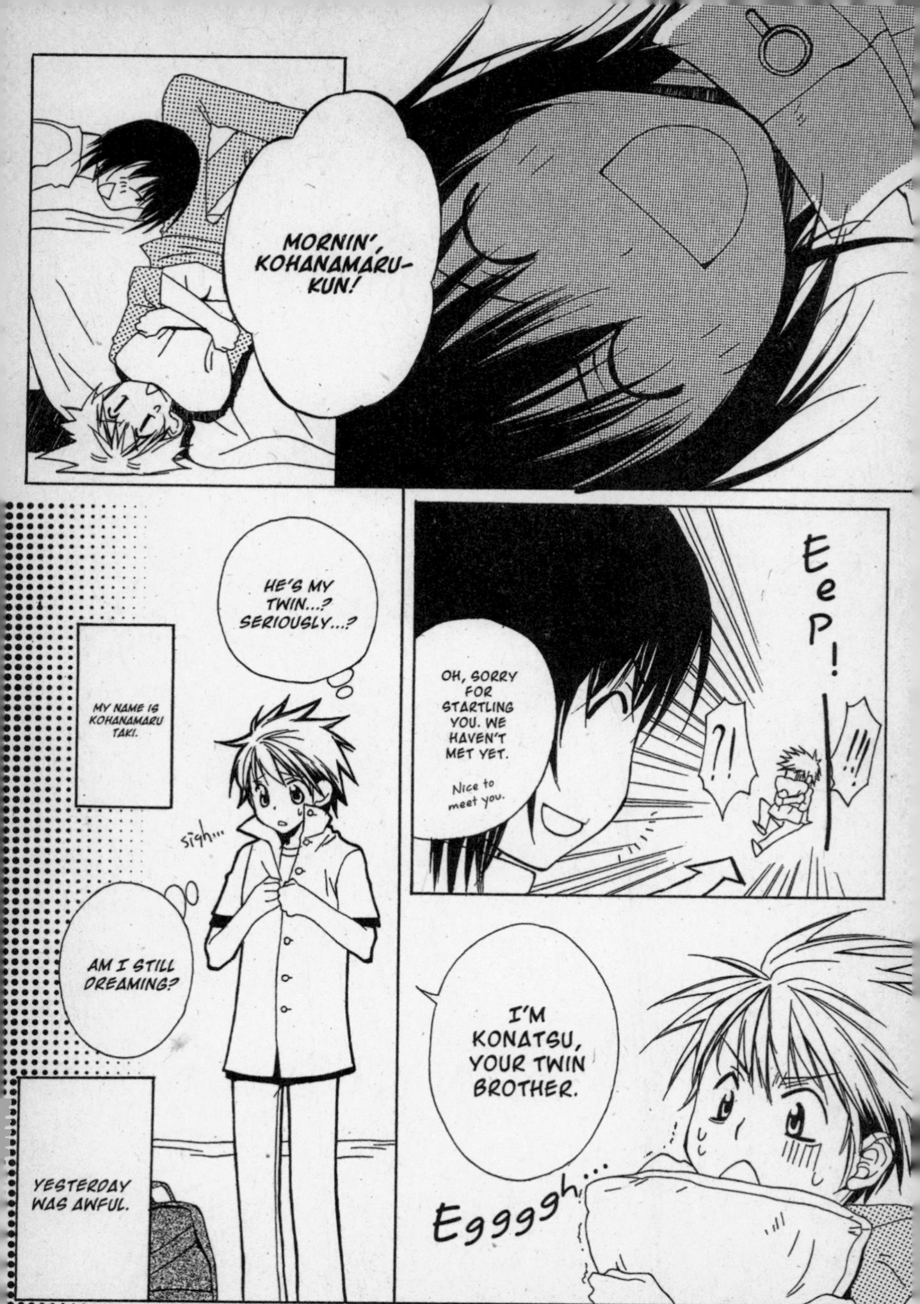
MORNIN', KOHANAMARU-KUN!
Eep!
!!!
?!
OH, SORRY FOR STARTLING YOU. WE HAVEN'T MET YET.
Nice to meet you.
I'M KONATSU, YOUR TWIN BROTHER.
Eggggh...
HE'S MY TWIN...? SERIOUSLY...?
MY NAME IS KOHANAMARU TAKI.
sigh...
AM I STILL DREAMING?
YESTERDAY WAS AWFUL.

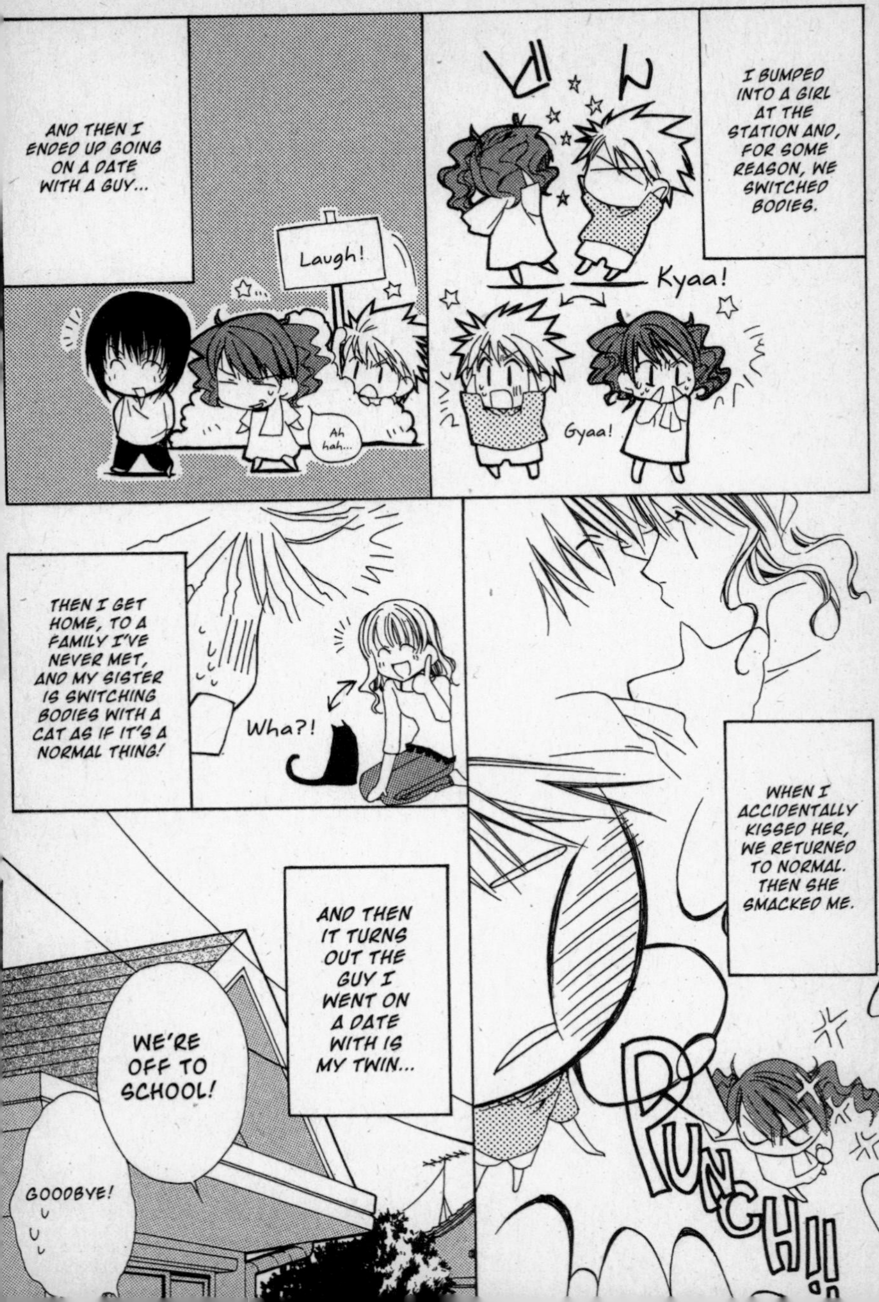
I BUMPED INTO A GIRL AT THE STATION AND, FOR SOME REASON, WE SWITCHED BODIES.
Kyaa!
Gyaa!
AND THEN I ENDED UP GOING ON A DATE WITH A GUY...
Laugh!
Ah hah...
WHEN I ACCIDENTALLY KISSED HER, WE RETURNED TO NORMAL. THEN SHE SMACKED ME.
PUNCH!!
THEN I GET HOME, TO A FAMILY I'VE NEVER MET, AND MY SISTER IS SWITCHING BODIES WITH A CAT AS IF IT'S A NORMAL THING!
Wha?!
AND THEN IT TURNS OUT THE GUY I WENT ON A DATE WITH IS MY TWIN...
WE'RE OFF TO SCHOOL!
GOODBYE!

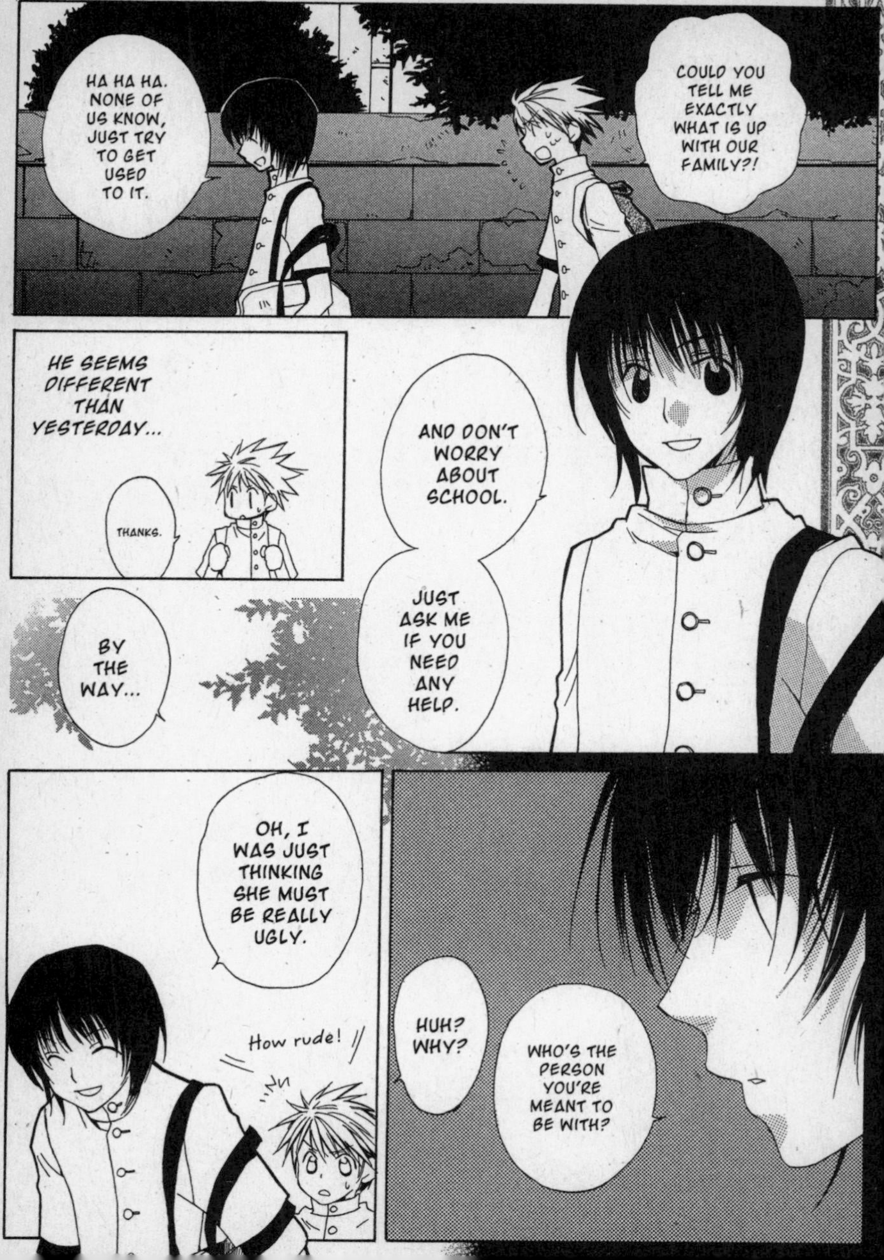
COULD YOU TELL ME EXACTLY WHAT IS UP WITH OUR FAMILY?!
HA HA HA. NONE OF US KNOW, JUST TRY TO GET USED TO IT.
AND DON'T WORRY ABOUT SCHOOL.
JUST ASK ME IF YOU NEED ANY HELP.
HE SEEMS DIFFERENT THAN YESTERDAY...
THANKS.
BY THE WAY...
WHO'S THE PERSON YOU'RE MEANT TO BE WITH?
HUH? WHY?
OH, I WAS JUST THINKING SHE MUST BE REALLY UGLY.
How rude!

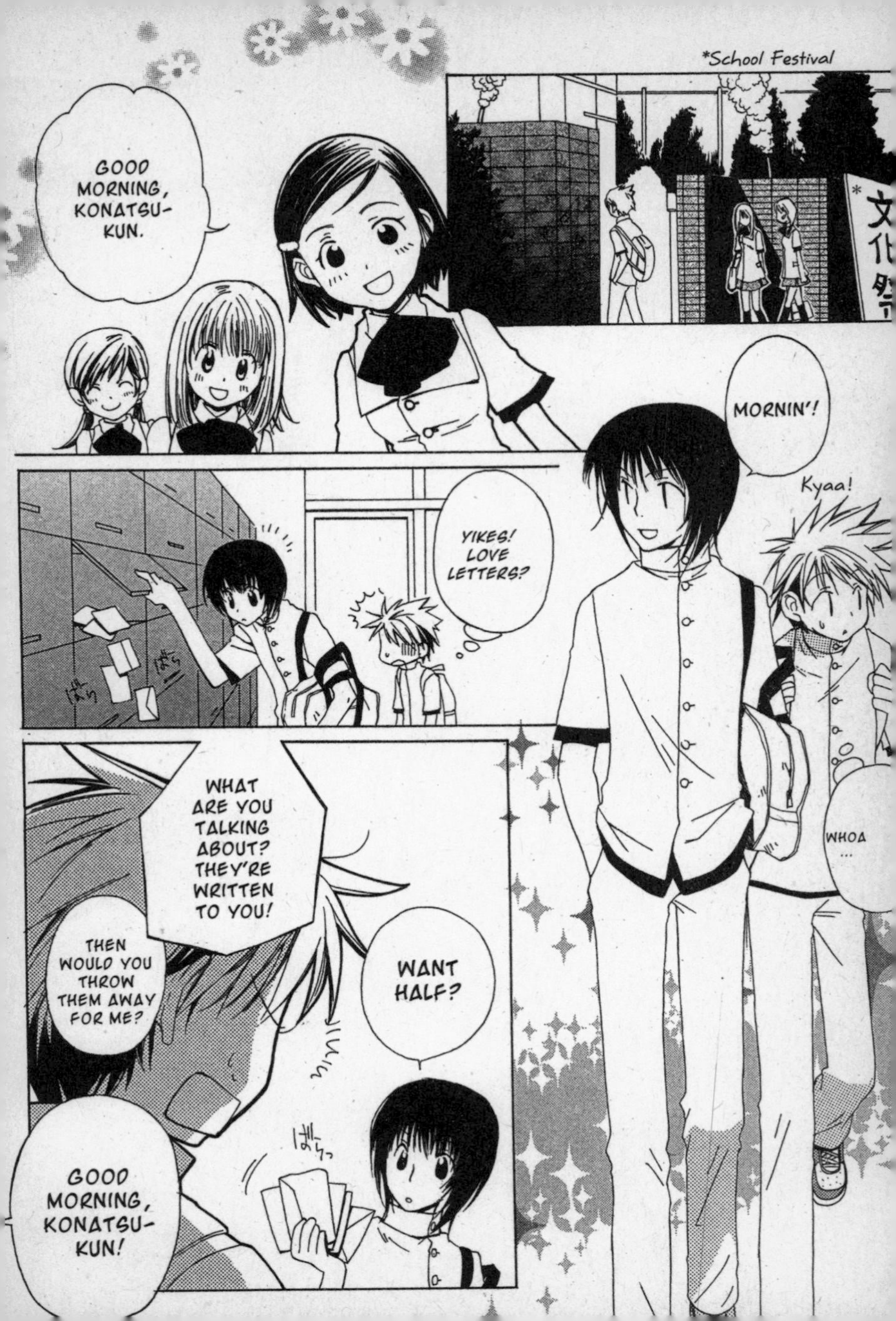
*School Festival
GOOD MORNING, KONATSU-KUN.
MORNIN'!
Kyaa!
WHOA ...
YIKES! LOVE LETTERS?
WHAT ARE YOU TALKING ABOUT? THEY'RE WRITTEN TO YOU!
WANT HALF?
THEN WOULD YOU THROW THEM AWAY FOR ME?
GOOD MORNING, KONATSU-KUN!

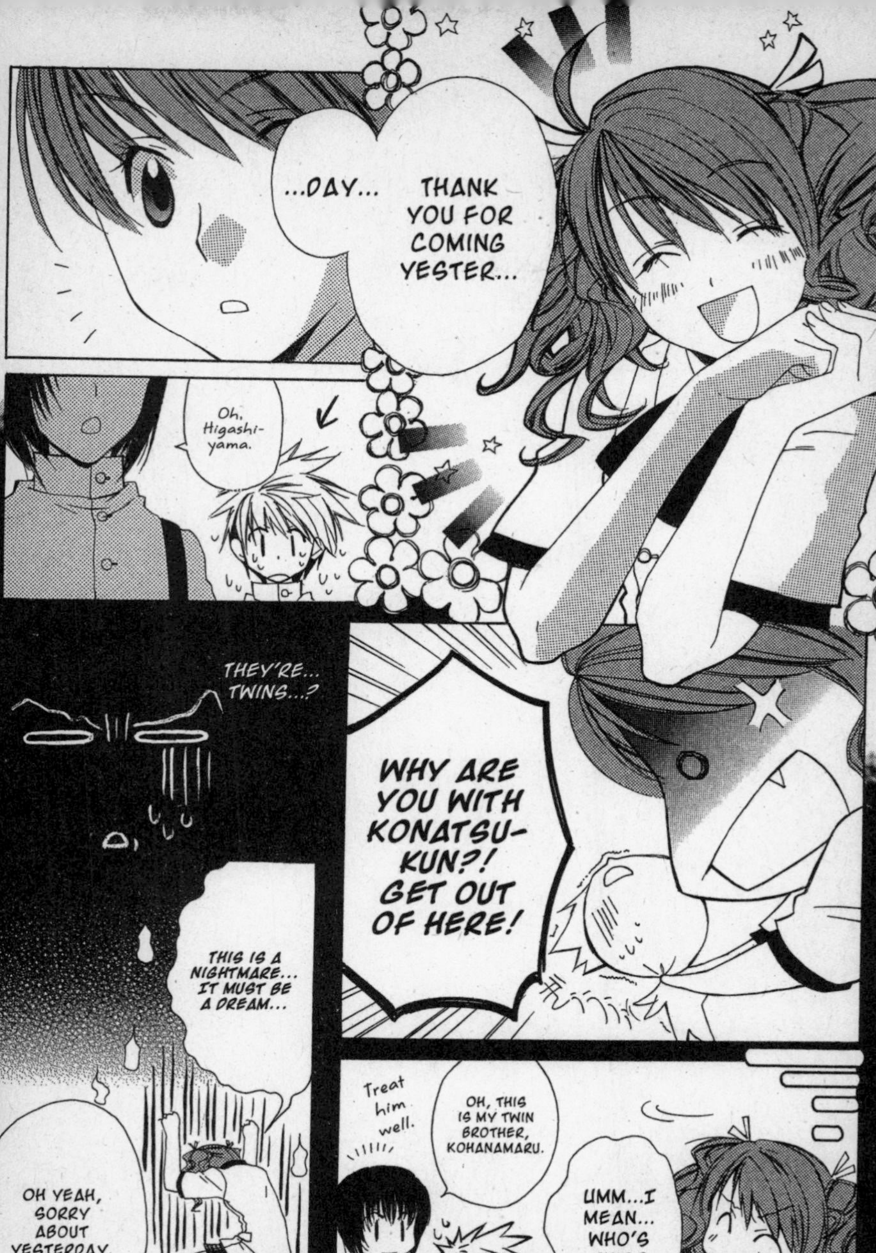
THANK YOU FOR COMING YESTER... ...DAY...
Oh, Higashi-yama.
WHY ARE YOU WITH KONATSU-KUN?! GET OUT OF HERE!
THEY'RE... TWINS...?
THIS IS A NIGHTMARE... IT MUST BE A DREAM...
UMM...I MEAN... WHO'S THIS?
OH, THIS IS MY TWIN BROTHER, KOHANAMARU.
Treat him well.
OH YEAH, SORRY ABOUT YESTERDAY.

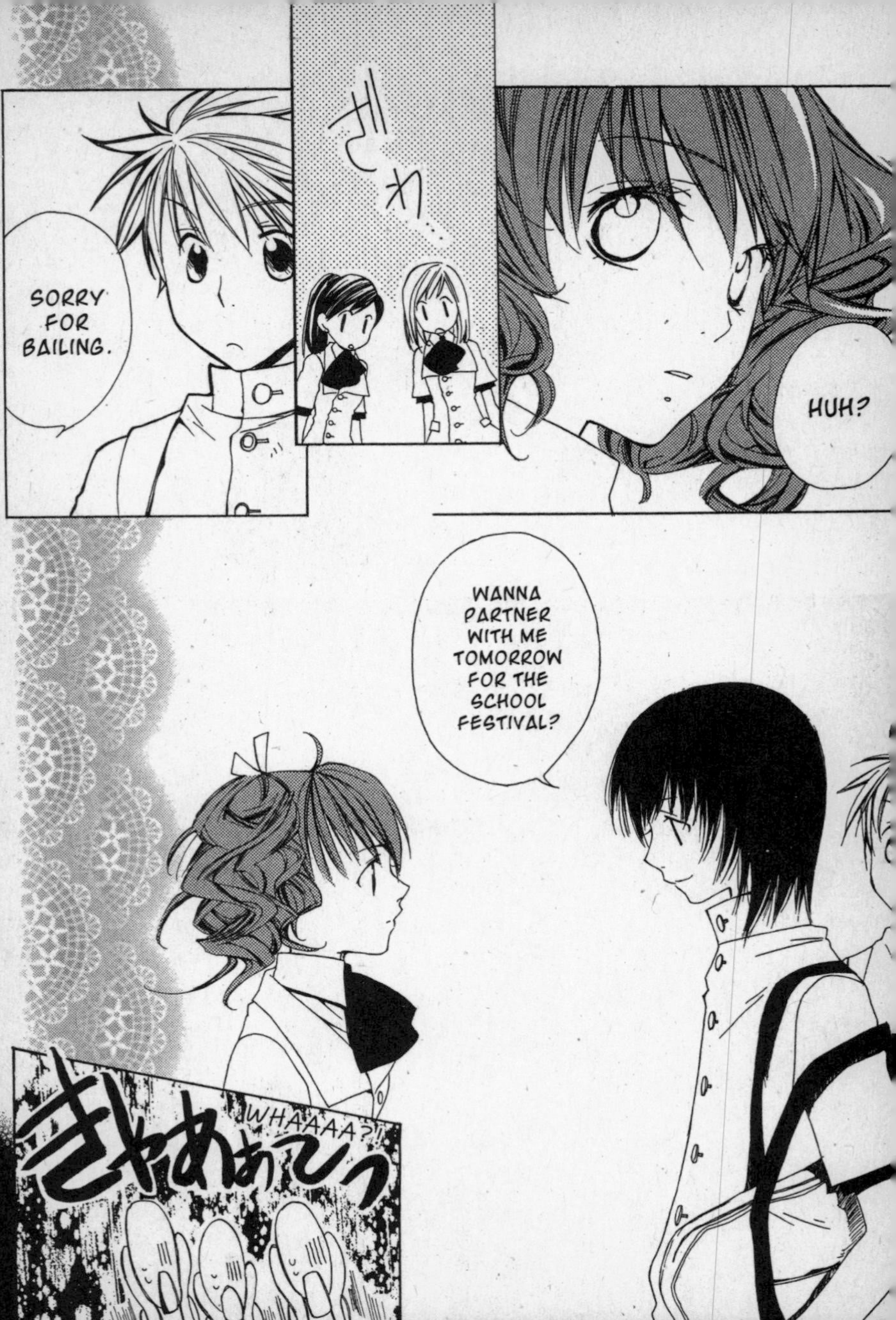
HUH?
ざわ…
SORRY FOR BAILING.
WANNA PARTNER WITH ME TOMORROW FOR THE SCHOOL FESTIVAL?
WHAAAA?!

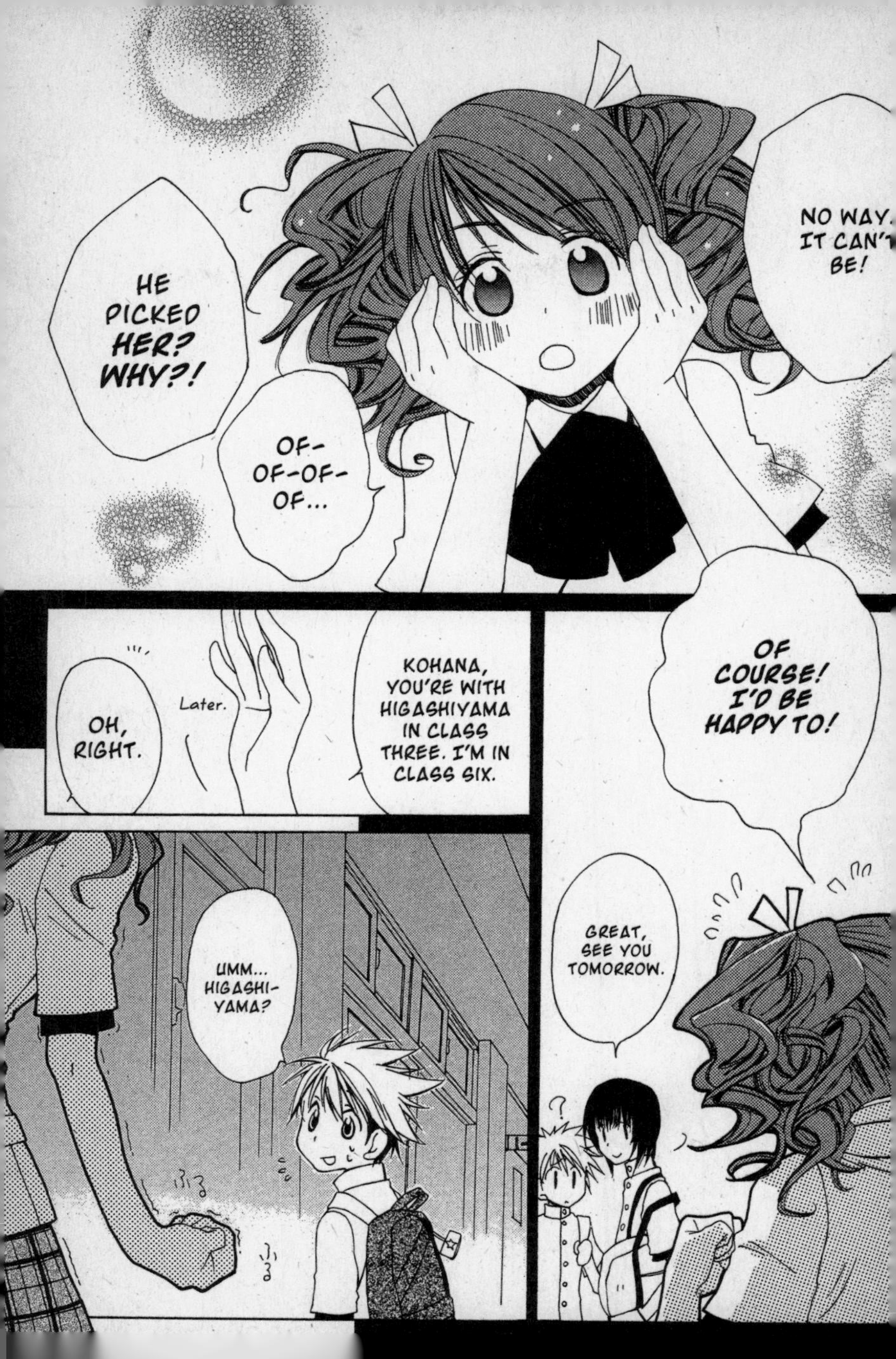
NO WAY. IT CAN'T BE!
HE PICKED HER? WHY?!
OF-OF-OF-OF...
OF COURSE! I'D BE HAPPY TO!
GREAT, SEE YOU TOMORROW.
KOHANA, YOU'RE WITH HIGASHIYAMA IN CLASS THREE. I'M IN CLASS SIX.
Later.
OH, RIGHT.
UMM... HIGASHI-YAMA?
ふる
ふる

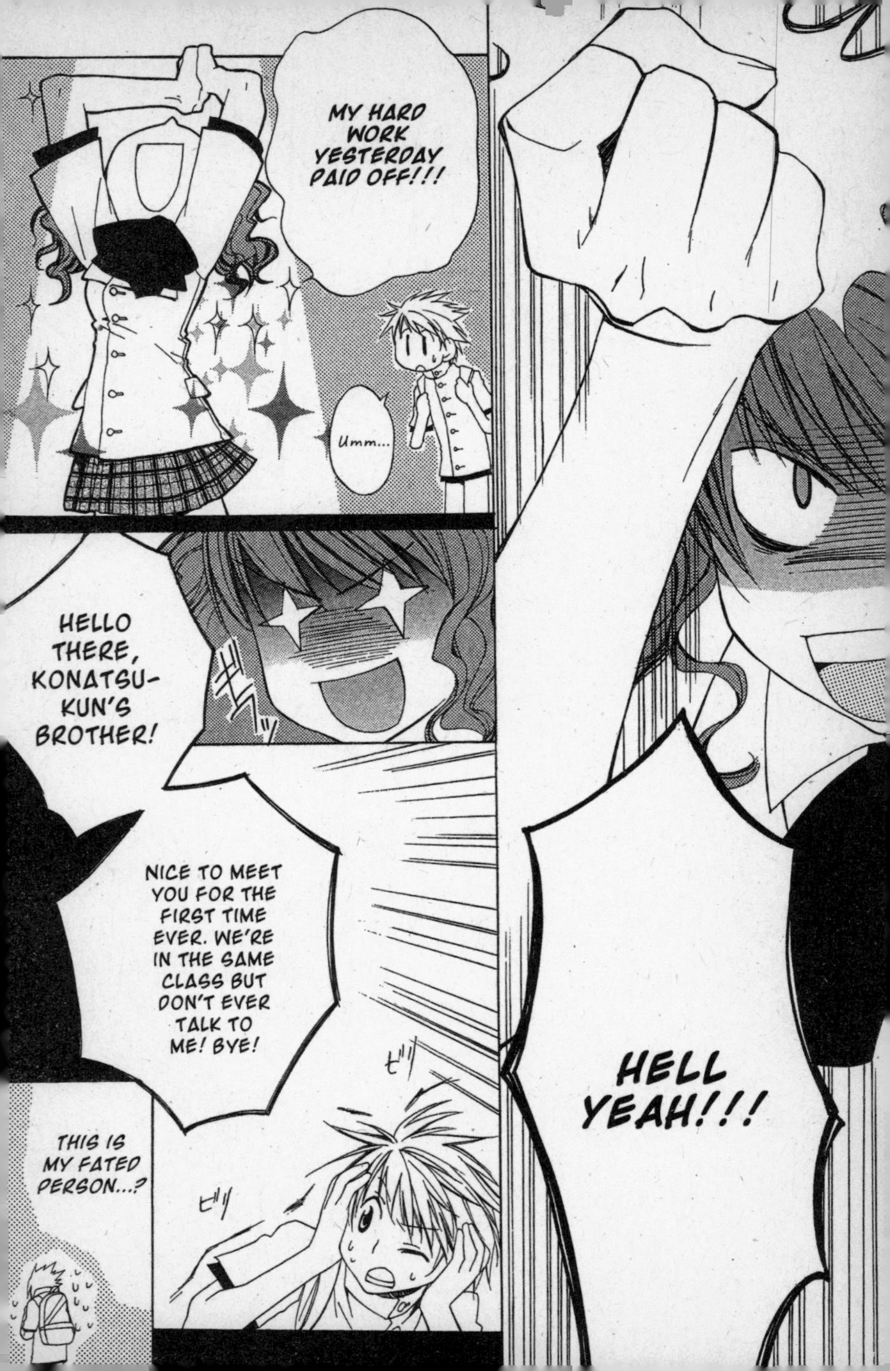
HELL YEAH!!!
MY HARD WORK YESTERDAY PAID OFF!!!
Umm...
HELLO THERE, KONATSU-KUN'S BROTHER!
NICE TO MEET YOU FOR THE FIRST TIME EVER. WE'RE IN THE SAME CLASS BUT DON'T EVER TALK TO ME! BYE!
THIS IS MY FATED PERSON...?

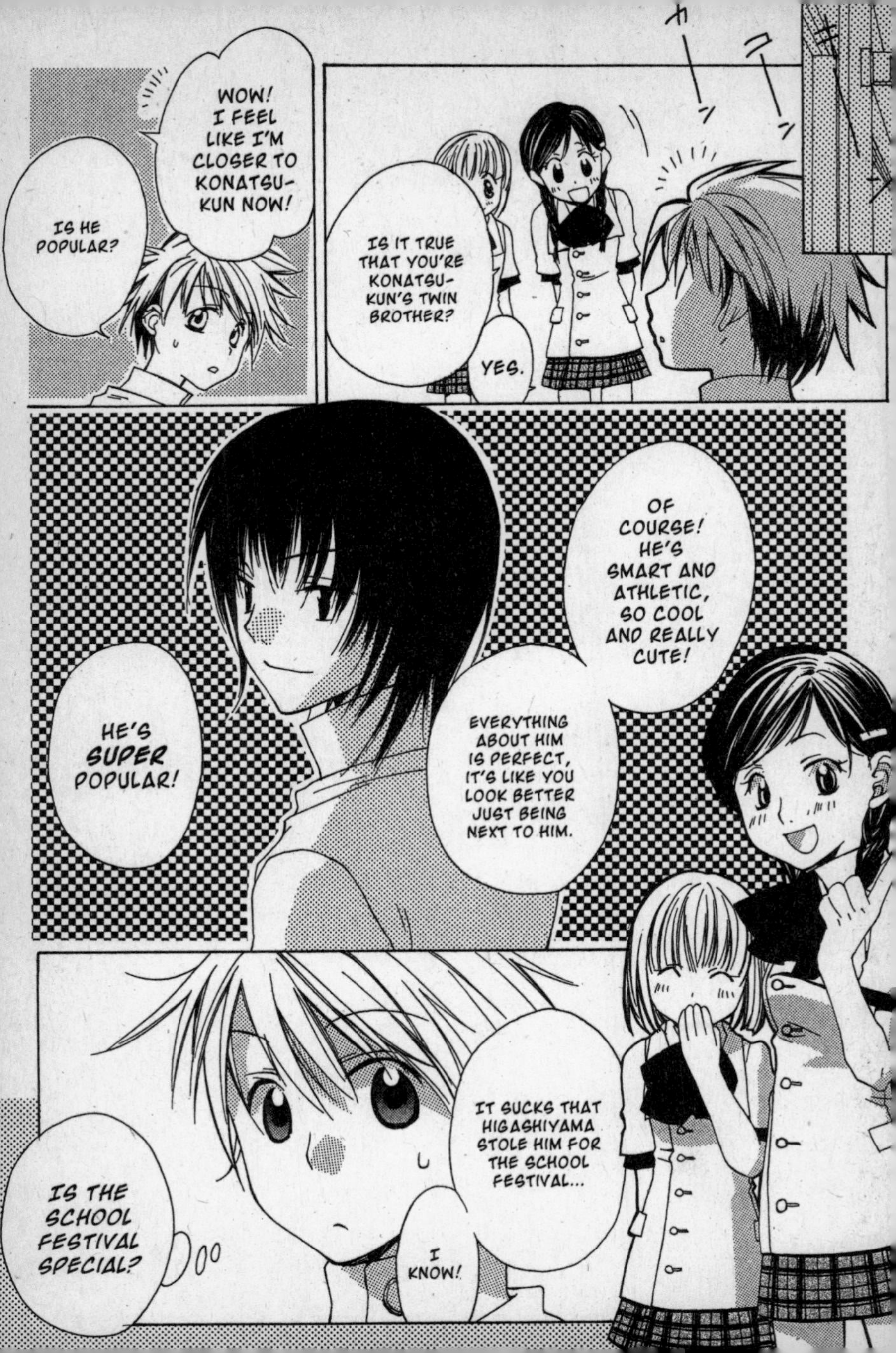
IS IT TRUE THAT YOU'RE KONATSU-KUN'S TWIN BROTHER?
YES.
WOW! I FEEL LIKE I'M CLOSER TO KONATSU-KUN NOW!
IS HE POPULAR?
OF COURSE! HE'S SMART AND ATHLETIC, SO COOL AND REALLY CUTE!
EVERYTHING ABOUT HIM IS PERFECT, IT'S LIKE YOU LOOK BETTER JUST BEING NEXT TO HIM.
HE'S SUPER POPULAR!
IT SUCKS THAT HIGASHIYAMA STOLE HIM FOR THE SCHOOL FESTIVAL...
I KNOW!
IS THE SCHOOL FESTIVAL SPECIAL?

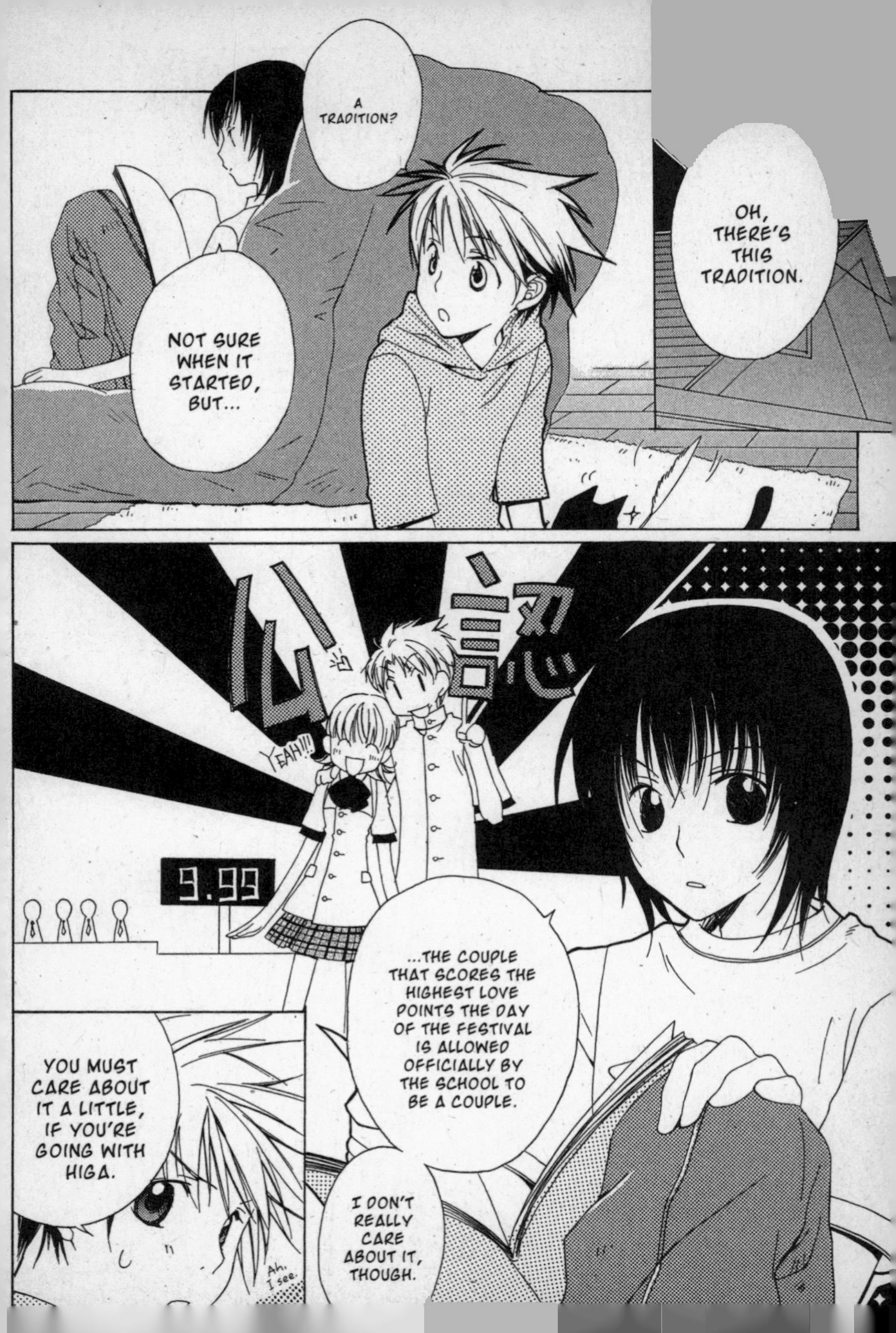
OH, THERE'S THIS TRADITION.
A TRADITION?
NOT SURE WHEN IT STARTED, BUT...
公認
YEAH!!!
9.99
...THE COUPLE THAT SCORES THE HIGHEST LOVE POINTS THE DAY OF THE FESTIVAL IS ALLOWED OFFICIALLY BY THE SCHOOL TO BE A COUPLE.
I DON'T REALLY CARE ABOUT IT, THOUGH.
Ah, I see.
YOU MUST CARE ABOUT IT A LITTLE, IF YOU'RE GOING WITH HIGA.

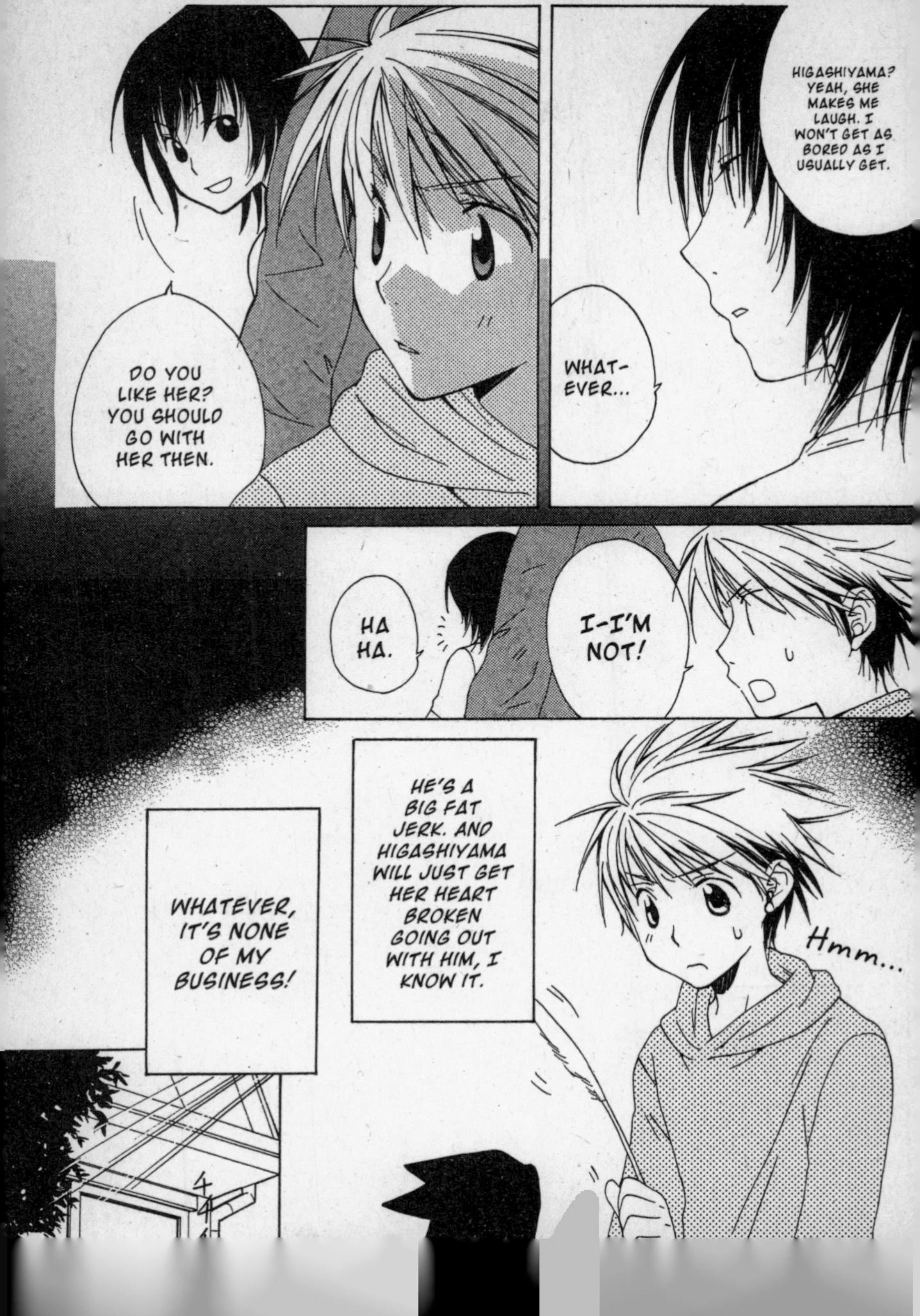
HIGASHIYAMA? YEAH, SHE MAKES ME LAUGH. I WON'T GET AS BORED AS I USUALLY GET.
WHAT-EVER...
DO YOU LIKE HER? YOU SHOULD GO WITH HER THEN.
I-I'M NOT!
HA HA.
Hmm...
HE'S A BIG FAT JERK. AND HIGASHIYAMA WILL JUST GET HER HEART BROKEN GOING OUT WITH HIM, I KNOW IT.
WHATEVER, IT'S NONE OF MY BUSINESS!

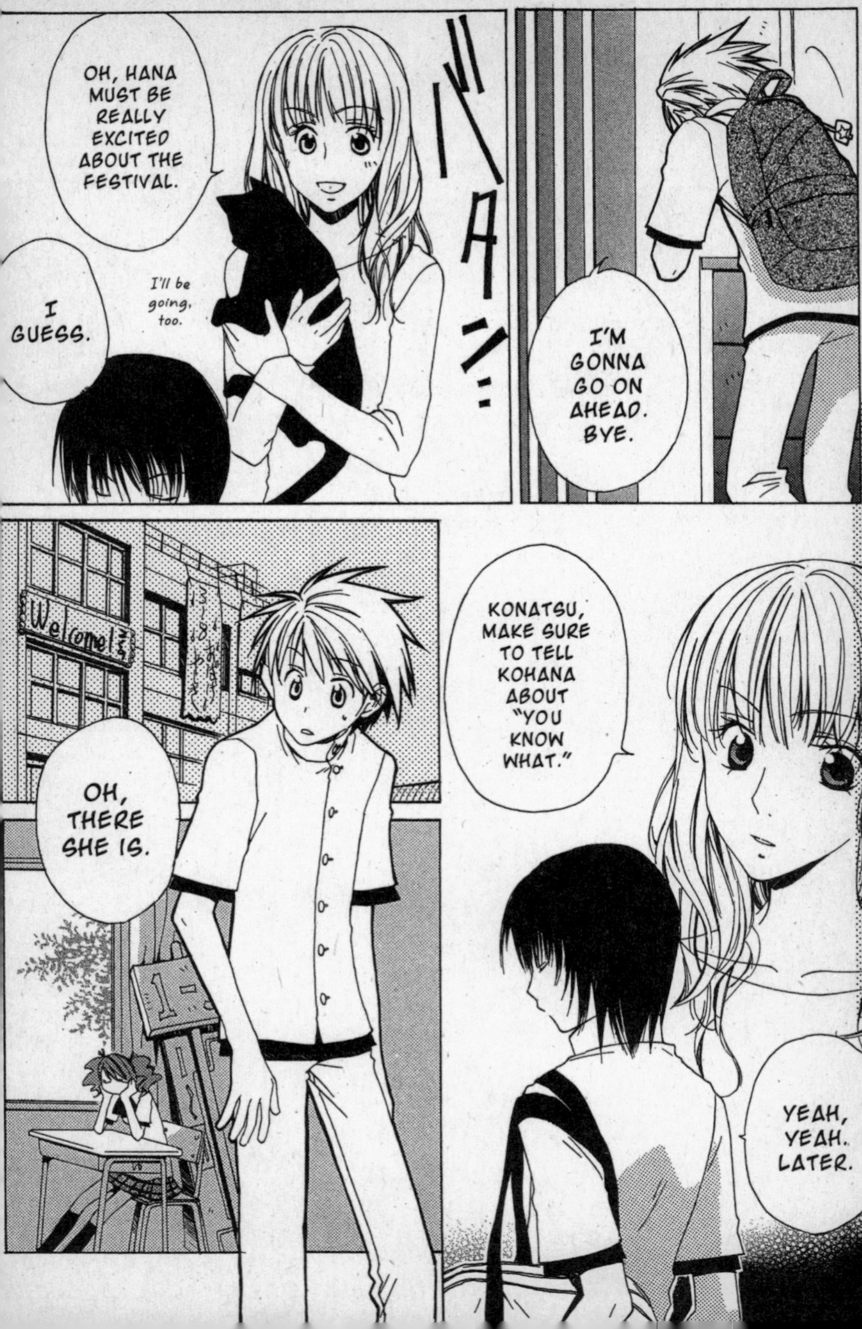

バタン!!
I'M GONNA GO ON AHEAD. BYE.
OH, HANA MUST BE REALLY EXCITED ABOUT THE FESTIVAL.
I'll be going, too.
I GUESS.
KONATSU, MAKE SURE TO TELL KOHANA ABOUT "YOU KNOW WHAT."
YEAH, YEAH. LATER.
Welcome!
OH, THERE SHE IS.

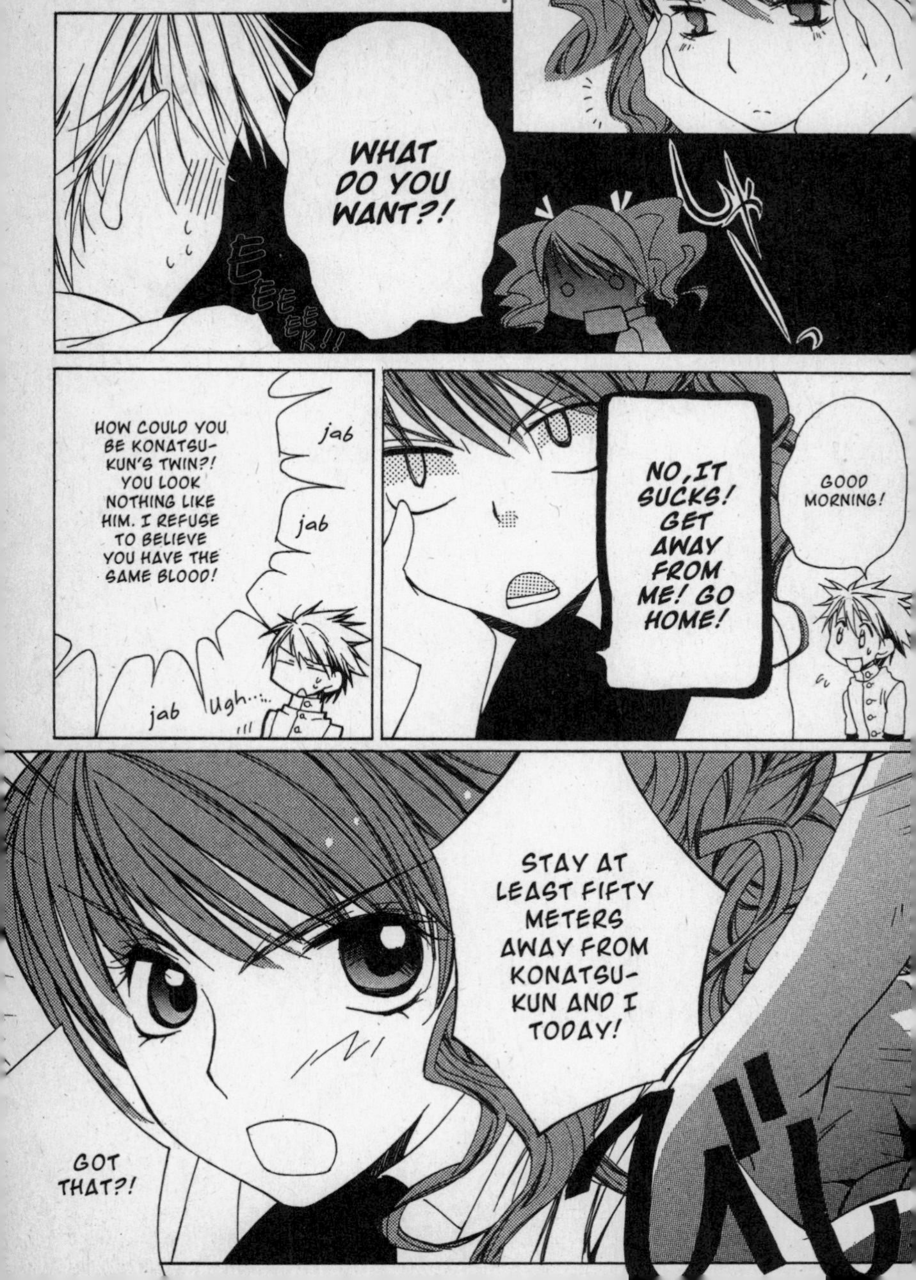
WHAT DO YOU WANT?!
GOOD MORNING!
NO, IT SUCKS! GET AWAY FROM ME! GO HOME!
HOW COULD YOU BE KONATSU-KUN'S TWIN?! YOU LOOK NOTHING LIKE HIM. I REFUSE TO BELIEVE YOU HAVE THE SAME BLOOD!
jab
jab
jab
Ugh...
STAY AT LEAST FIFTY METERS AWAY FROM KONATSU-KUN AND I TODAY!
GOT THAT?!

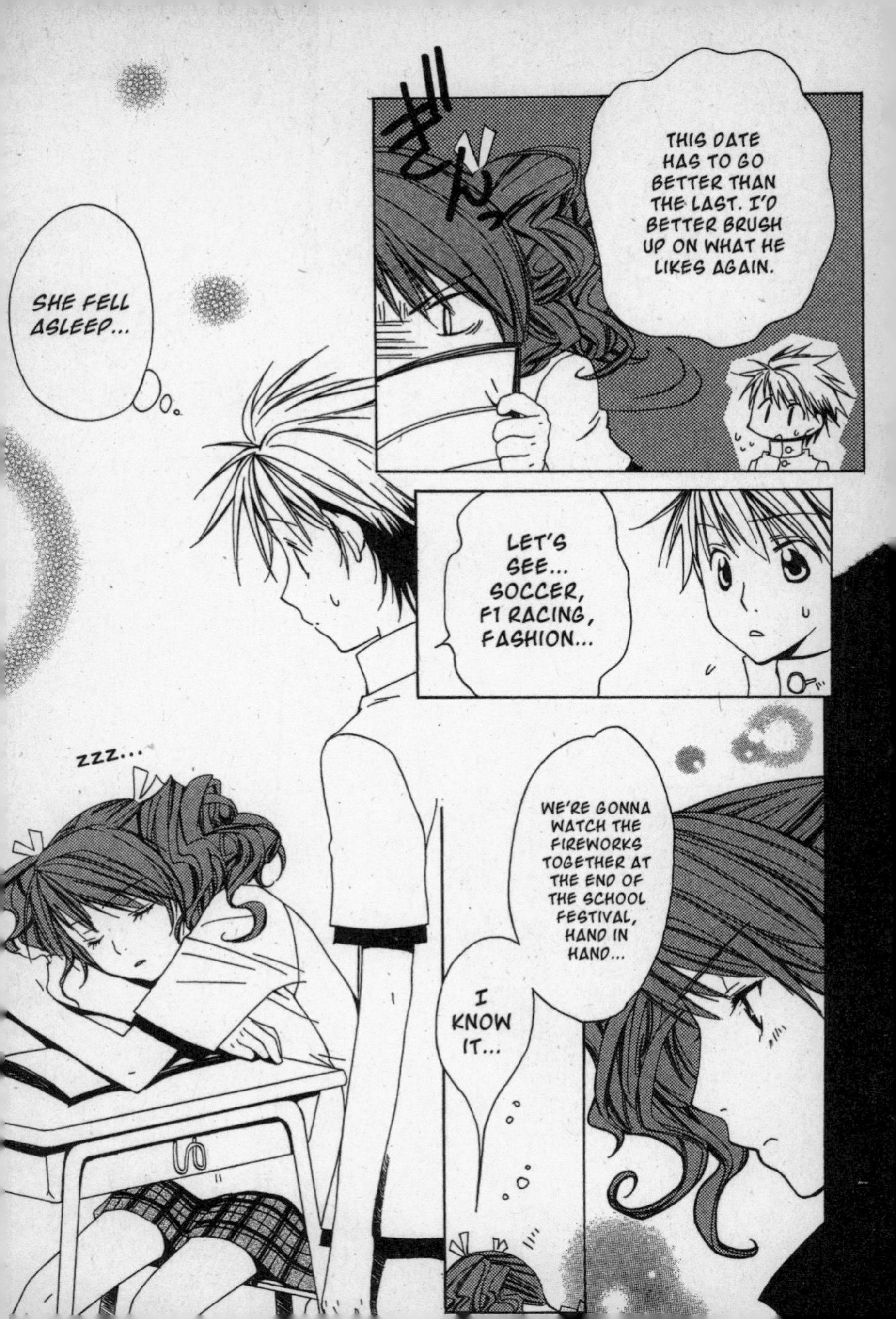
THIS DATE HAS TO GO BETTER THAN THE LAST. I'D BETTER BRUSH UP ON WHAT HE LIKES AGAIN.
LET'S SEE... SOCCER, F1 RACING, FASHION...
WE'RE GONNA WATCH THE FIREWORKS TOGETHER AT THE END OF THE SCHOOL FESTIVAL, HAND IN HAND...
I KNOW IT...
SHE FELL ASLEEP...
ZZZ...

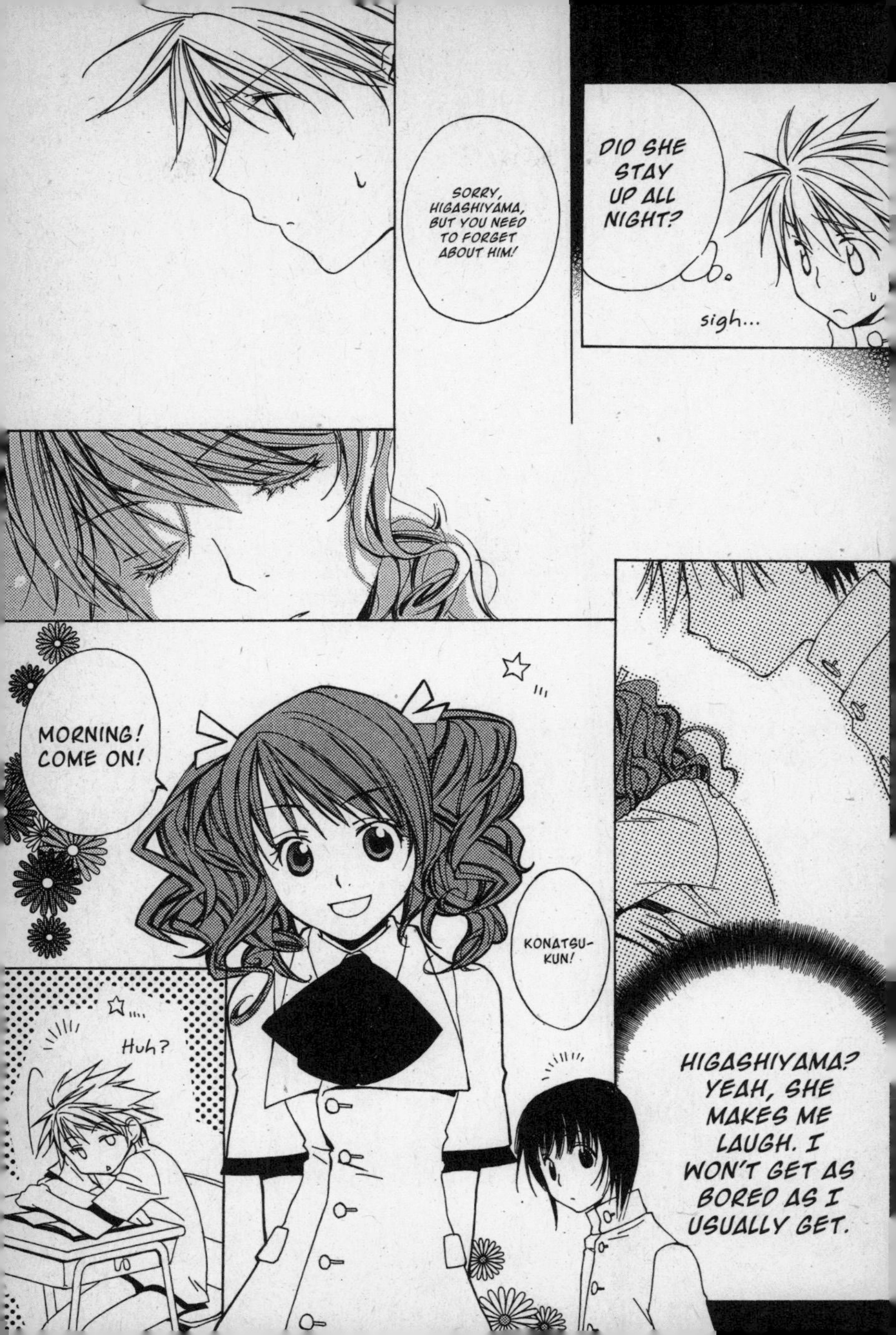
DID SHE STAY UP ALL NIGHT?
sigh...
SORRY, HIGASHIYAMA, BUT YOU NEED TO FORGET ABOUT HIM!
HIGASHIYAMA? YEAH, SHE MAKES ME LAUGH. I WON'T GET AS BORED AS I USUALLY GET.
MORNING! COME ON!
KONATSU-KUN!
Huh?

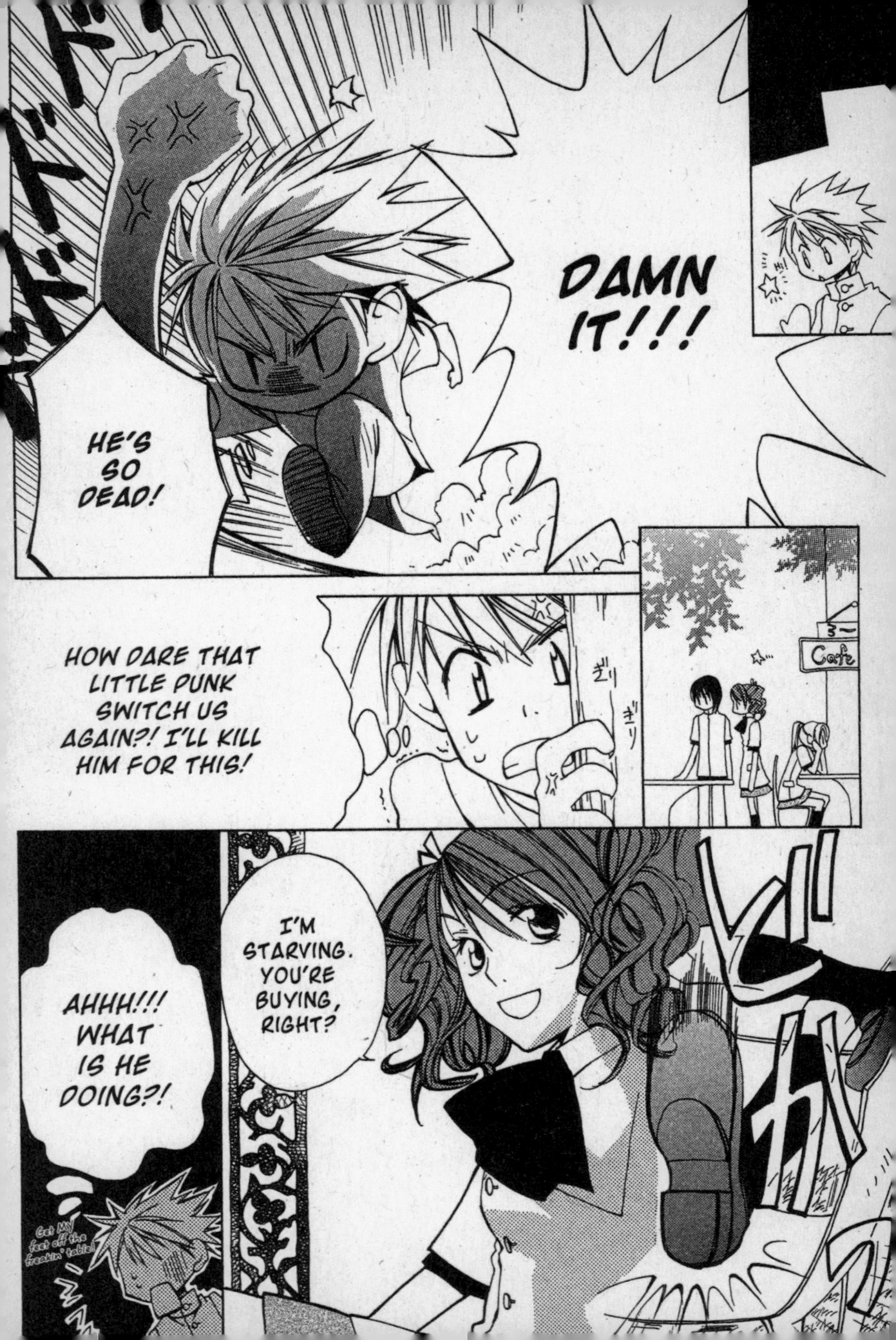
DAMN IT!!!
HE'S SO DEAD!
Cafe
HOW DARE THAT LITTLE PUNK SWITCH US AGAIN?! I'LL KILL HIM FOR THIS!
ギリ
ギリ
I'M STARVING. YOU'RE BUYING, RIGHT?
AHHH!!! WHAT IS HE DOING?!
Get MY feet off the freakin' table!

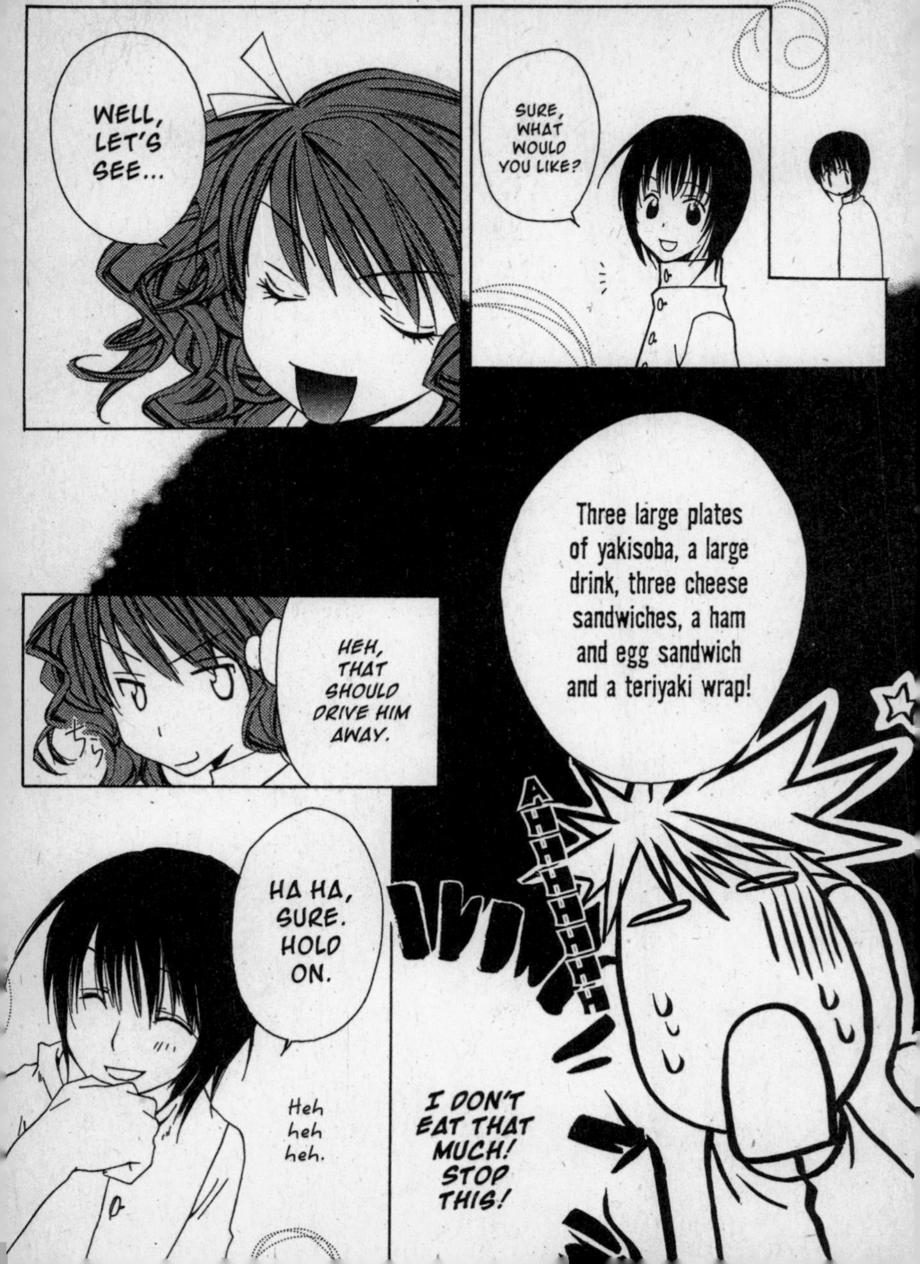
SURE, WHAT WOULD YOU LIKE?
WELL, LET'S SEE...
Three large plates of yakisoba, a large drink, three cheese sandwiches, a ham and egg sandwich and a teriyaki wrap!
HEH, THAT SHOULD DRIVE HIM AWAY.
AHHHHHHHHH
I DON'T EAT THAT MUCH! STOP THIS!
HA HA, SURE. HOLD ON.
Heh heh heh.

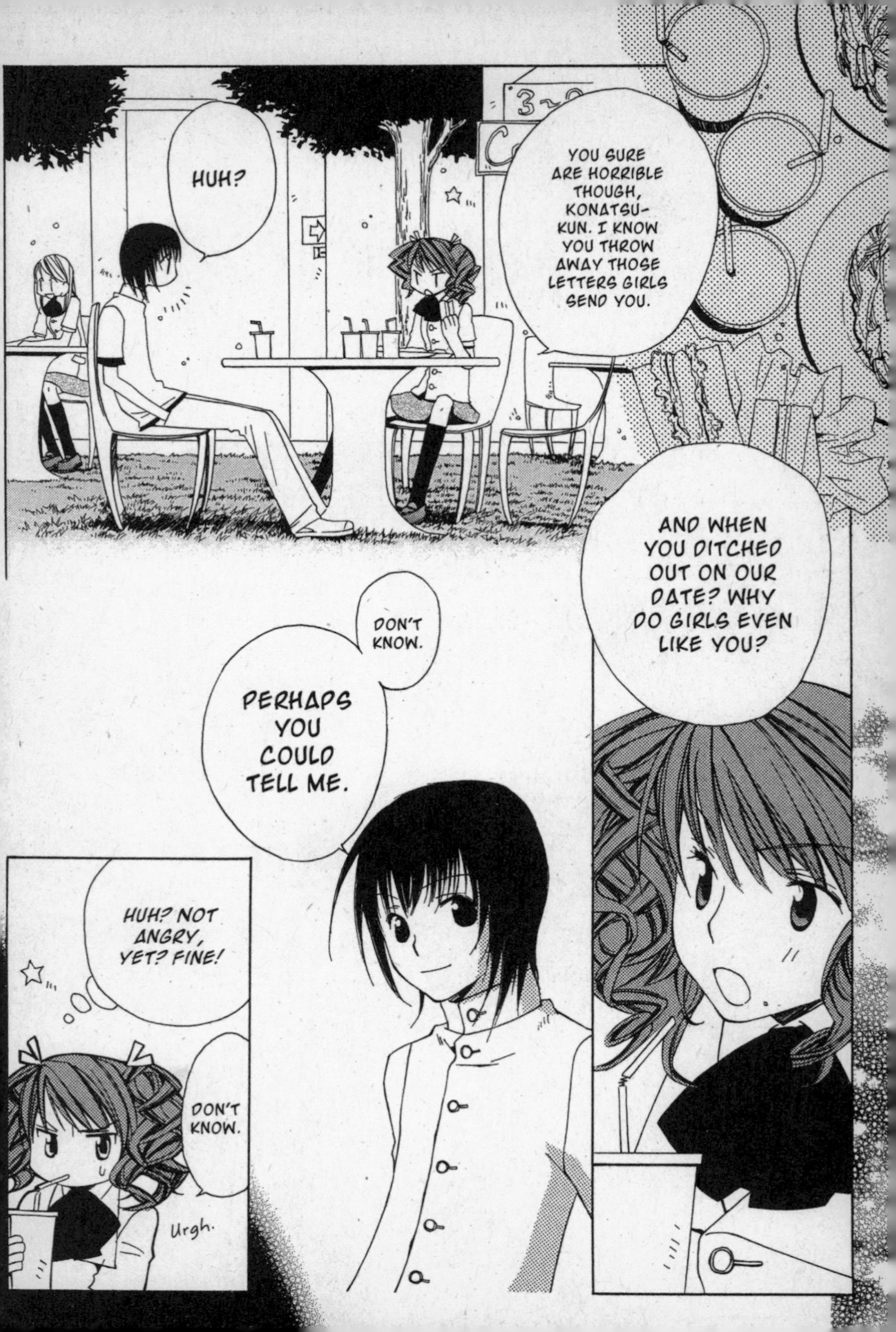
YOU SURE ARE HORRIBLE THOUGH, KONATSU-KUN. I KNOW YOU THROW AWAY THOSE LETTERS GIRLS SEND YOU.
HUH?
AND WHEN YOU DITCHED OUT ON OUR DATE? WHY DO GIRLS EVEN LIKE YOU?
DON'T KNOW.
PERHAPS YOU COULD TELL ME.
HUH? NOT ANGRY, YET? FINE!
DON'T KNOW.
Urgh.

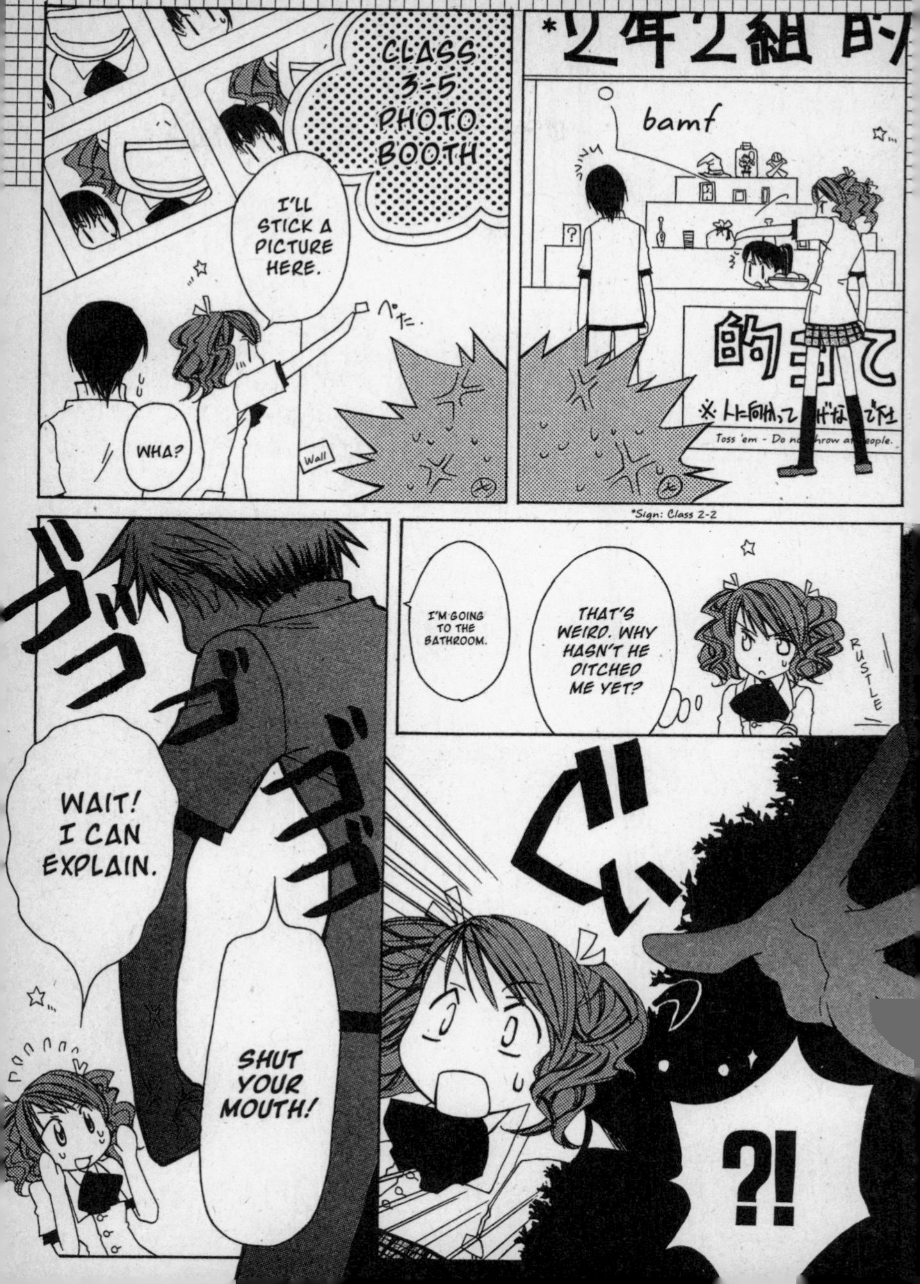
*2年2組 的
bamf
Toss 'em - Do no
hrow at
eople.
CLASS 3-5 PHOTO BOOTH
I'LL STICK A PICTURE HERE.
ぺた
WHA?
Wall
RUSTLE
THAT'S WEIRD. WHY HASN'T HE DITCHED ME YET?
I'M GOING TO THE BATHROOM.
ぐい
?!
ゴゴゴ
WAIT! I CAN EXPLAIN.
SHUT YOUR MOUTH!
*Sign: Class 2-2

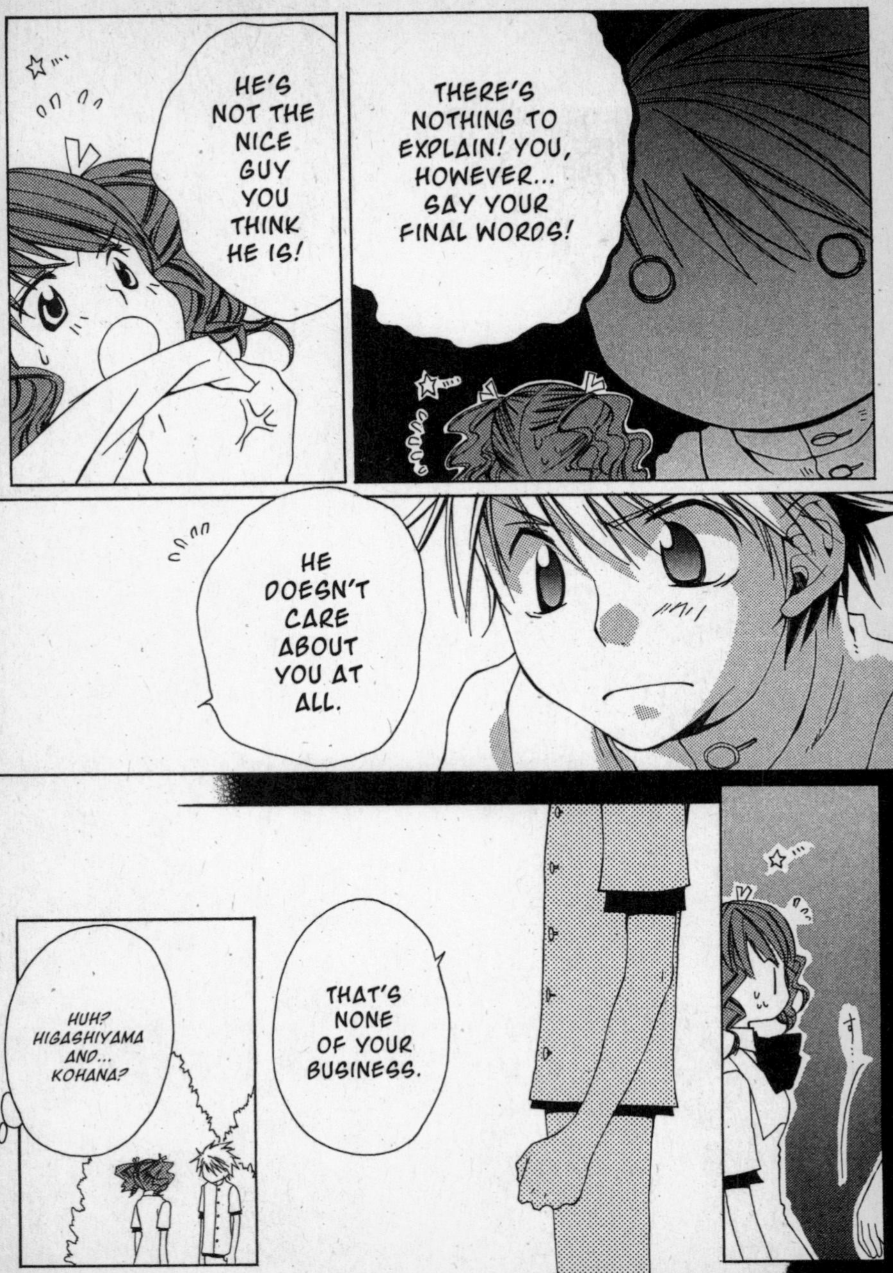
THERE'S NOTHING TO EXPLAIN! YOU, HOWEVER... SAY YOUR FINAL WORDS!
HE'S NOT THE NICE GUY YOU THINK HE IS!
HE DOESN'T CARE ABOUT YOU AT ALL.
す…
THAT'S NONE OF YOUR BUSINESS.
HUH? HIGASHIYAMA AND... KOHANA?

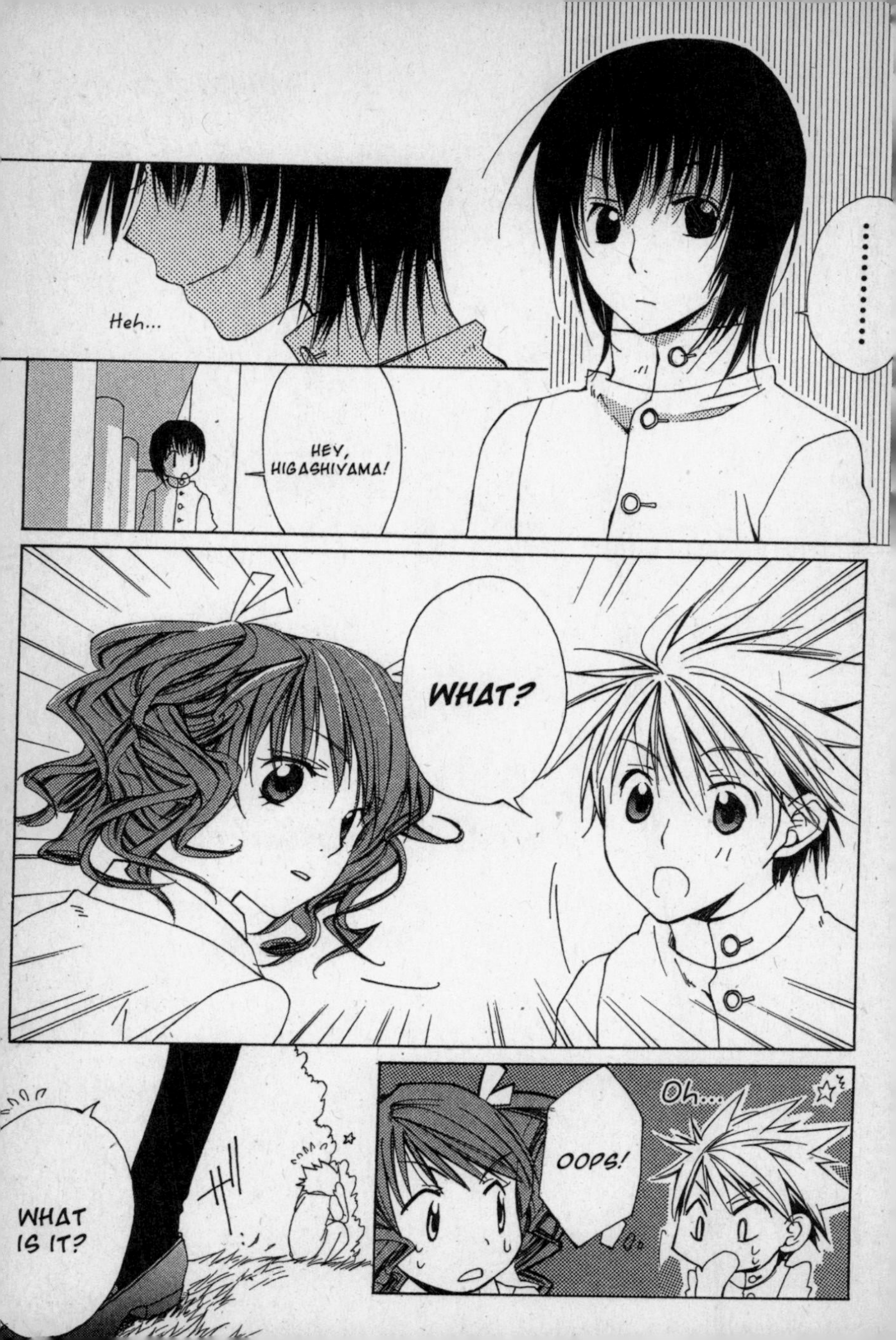
......
Heh...
HEY, HIGASHIYAMA!
WHAT?
Oh...
OOPS!
WHAT IS IT?

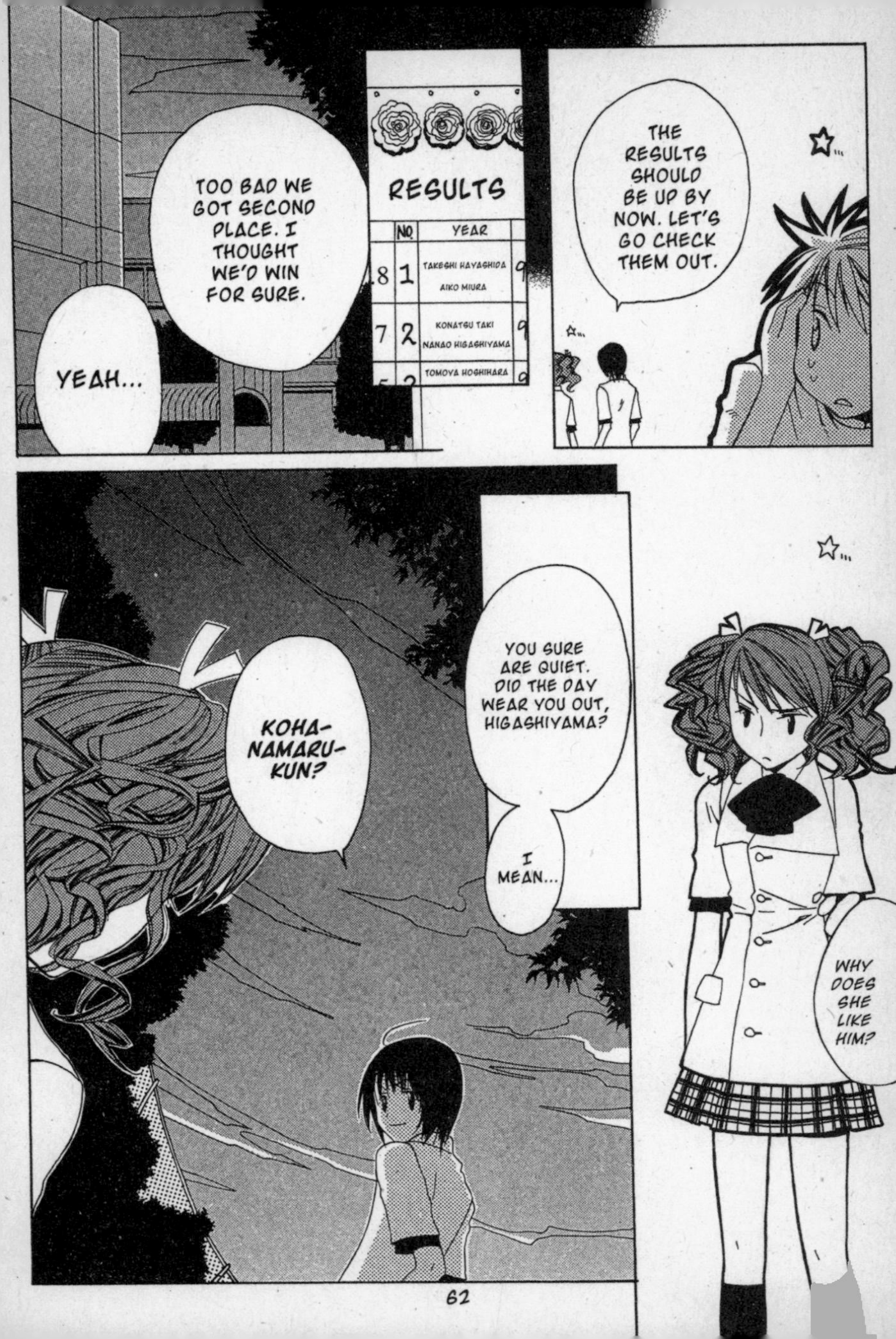
THE RESULTS SHOULD BE UP BY NOW. LET'S GO CHECK THEM OUT.
RESULTS
NO.
YEAR
1 TAKESHI HAYASHIDA AIKO MIURA
2 KONATSU TAKI NANAO HIGASHIYAMA
TOMOYA HOSHIHARA
TOO BAD WE GOT SECOND PLACE. I THOUGHT WE'D WIN FOR SURE.
YEAH...
WHY DOES SHE LIKE HIM?
YOU SURE ARE QUIET. DID THE DAY WEAR YOU OUT, HIGASHIYAMA?
I MEAN...
KOHA-NAMARU-KUN?

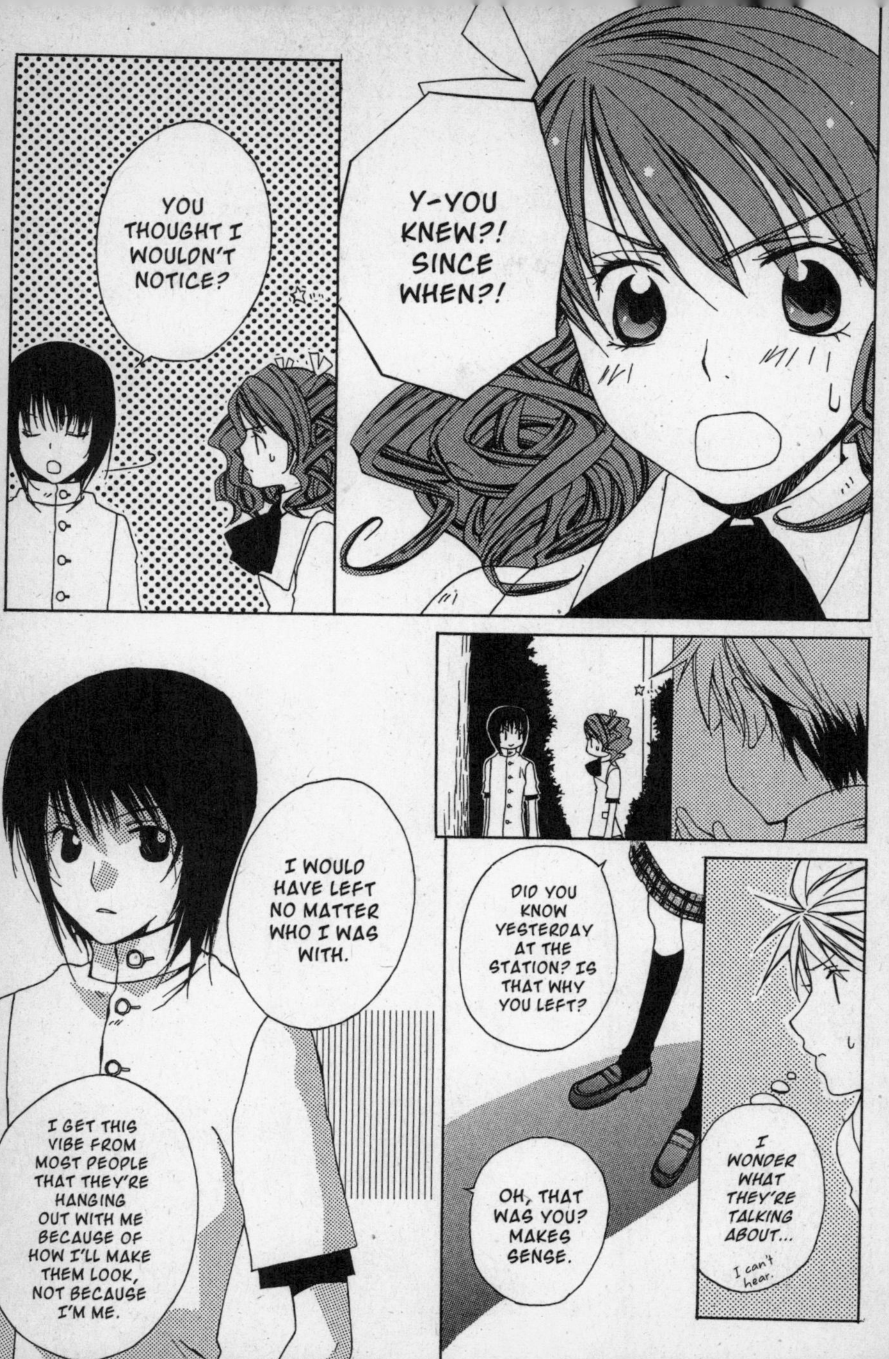
Y-YOU KNEW?! SINCE WHEN?!
YOU THOUGHT I WOULDN'T NOTICE?
I WONDER WHAT THEY'RE TALKING ABOUT...
I can't hear.
DID YOU KNOW YESTERDAY AT THE STATION? IS THAT WHY YOU LEFT?
OH, THAT WAS YOU? MAKES SENSE.
I WOULD HAVE LEFT NO MATTER WHO I WAS WITH.
I GET THIS VIBE FROM MOST PEOPLE THAT THEY'RE HANGING OUT WITH ME BECAUSE OF HOW I'LL MAKE THEM LOOK, NOT BECAUSE I'M ME.

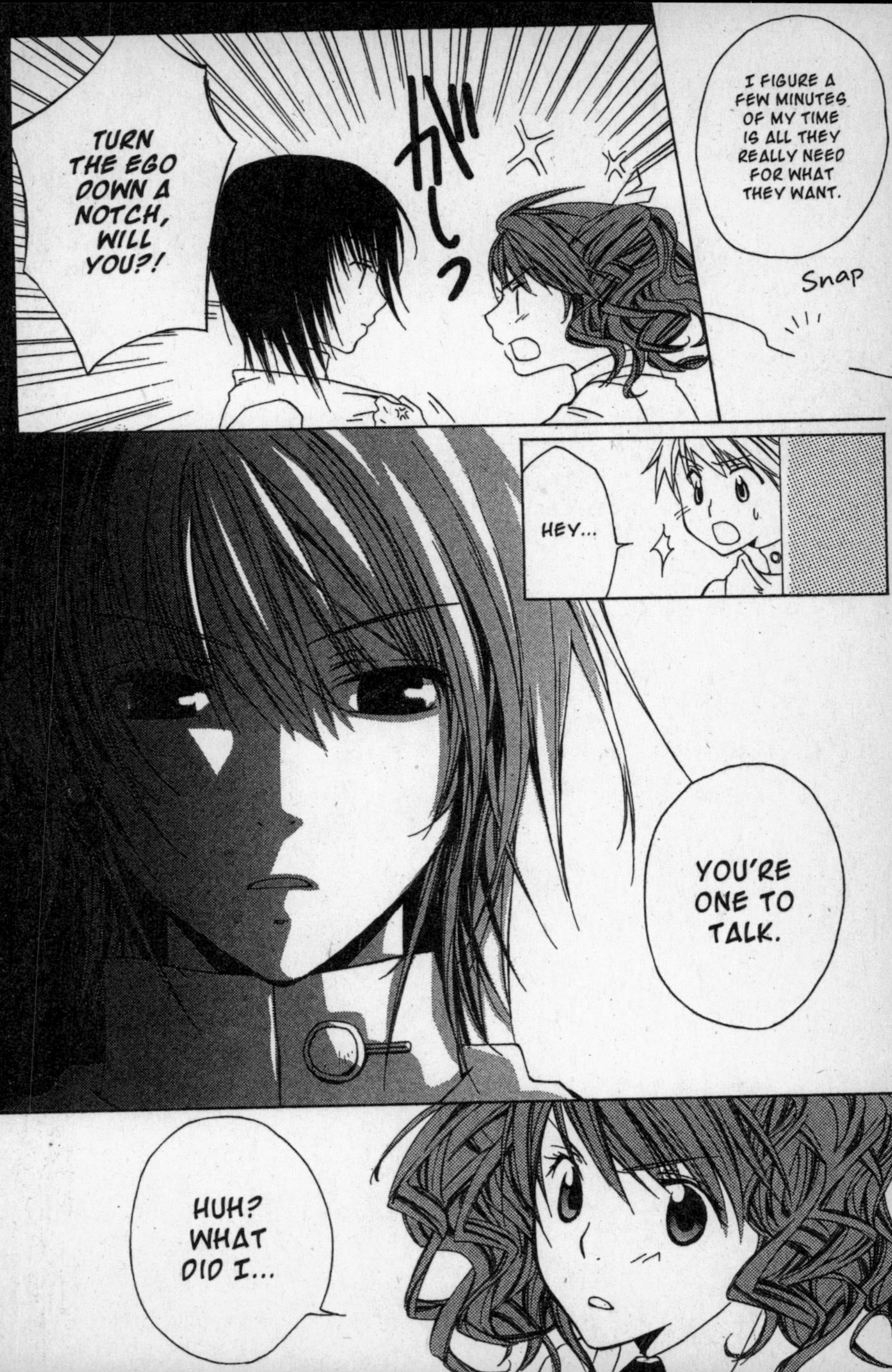

I FIGURE A FEW MINUTES OF MY TIME IS ALL THEY REALLY NEED FOR WHAT THEY WANT.
Snap
がしっ
TURN THE EGO DOWN A NOTCH, WILL YOU?!
HEY...
YOU'RE ONE TO TALK.
HUH? WHAT DID I...

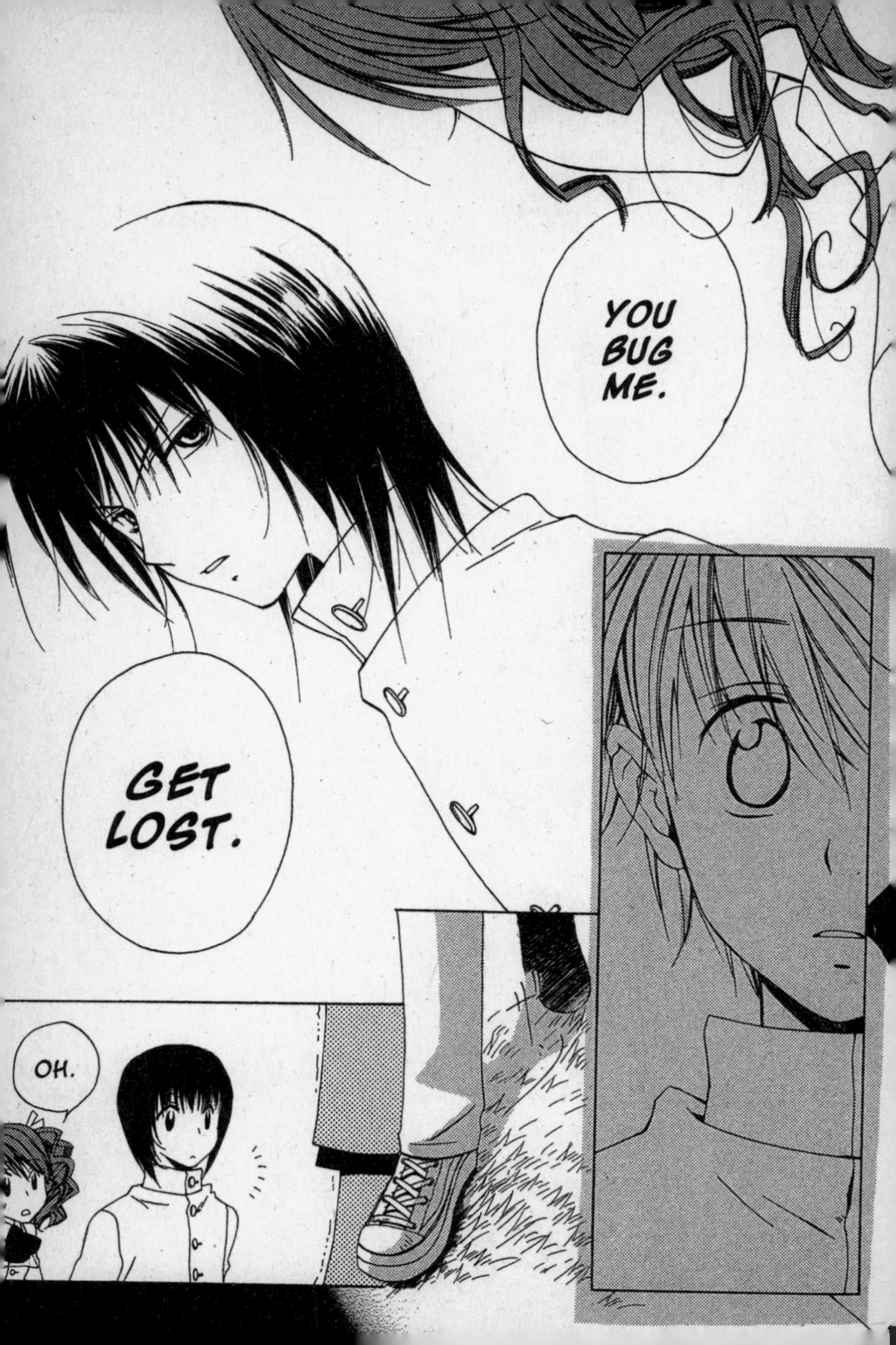
YOU BUG ME.
GET LOST.
OH.

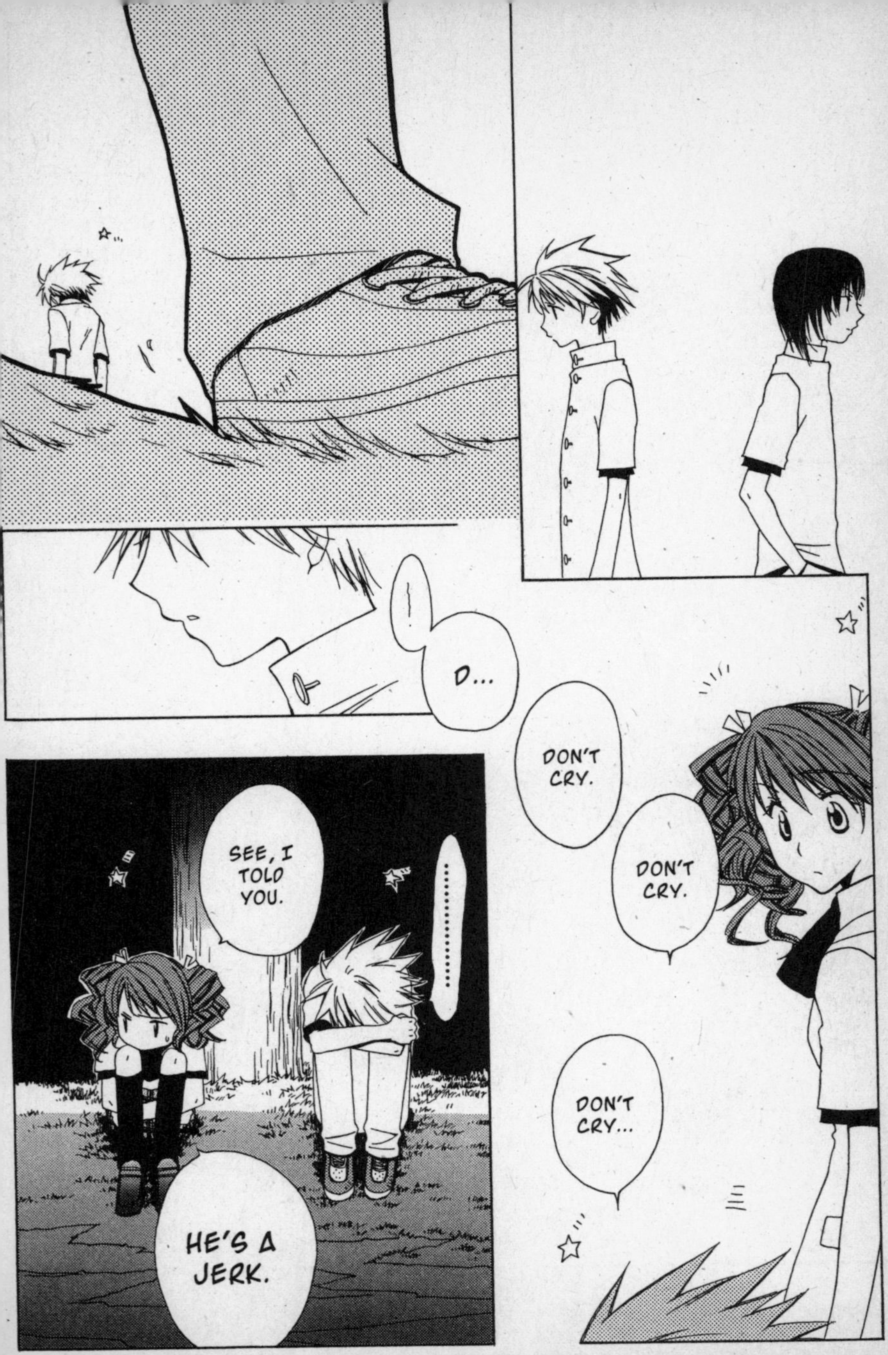

D...
DON'T CRY.
DON'T CRY.
DON'T CRY...
......
SEE, I TOLD YOU.
HE'S A JERK.

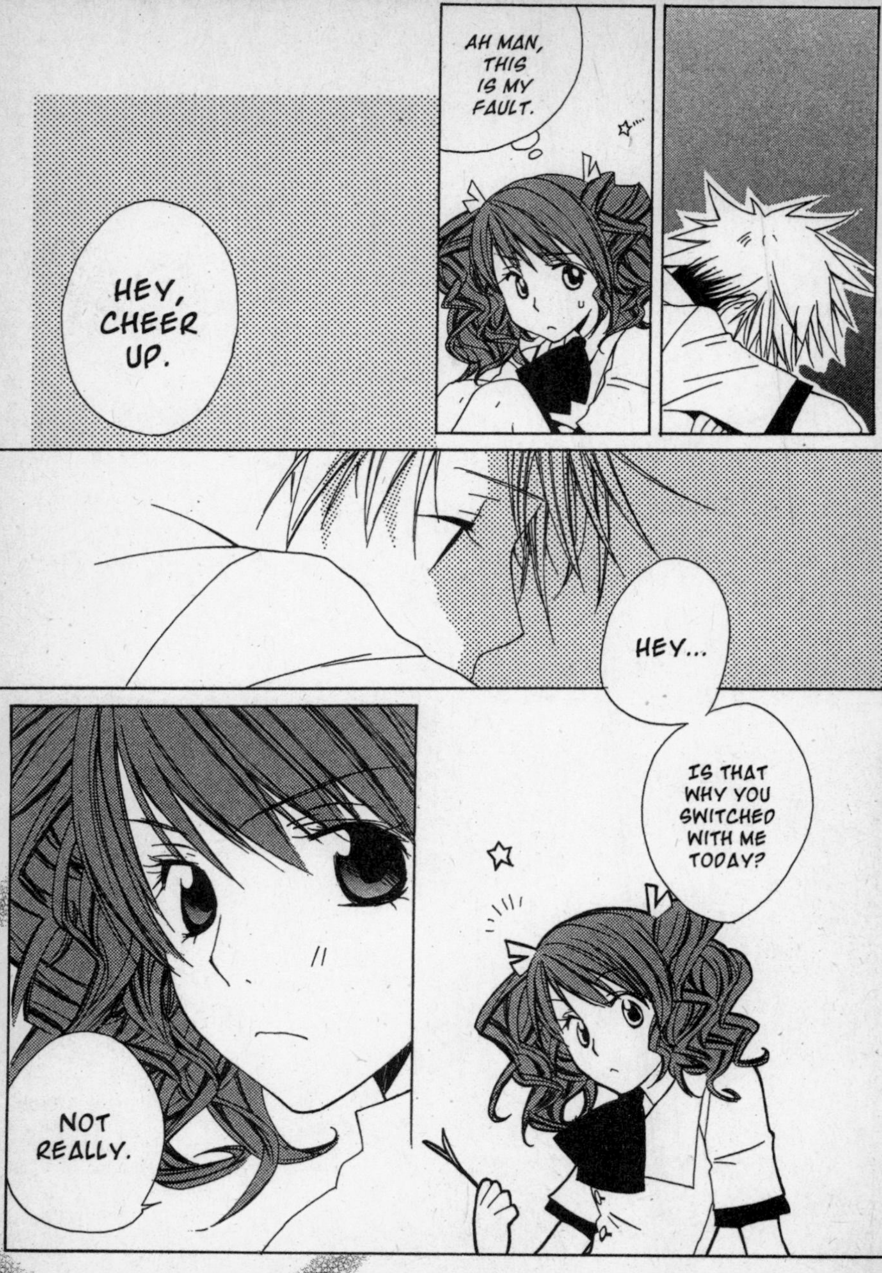
AH MAN, THIS IS MY FAULT.
HEY, CHEER UP.
HEY...
IS THAT WHY YOU SWITCHED WITH ME TODAY?
NOT REALLY.

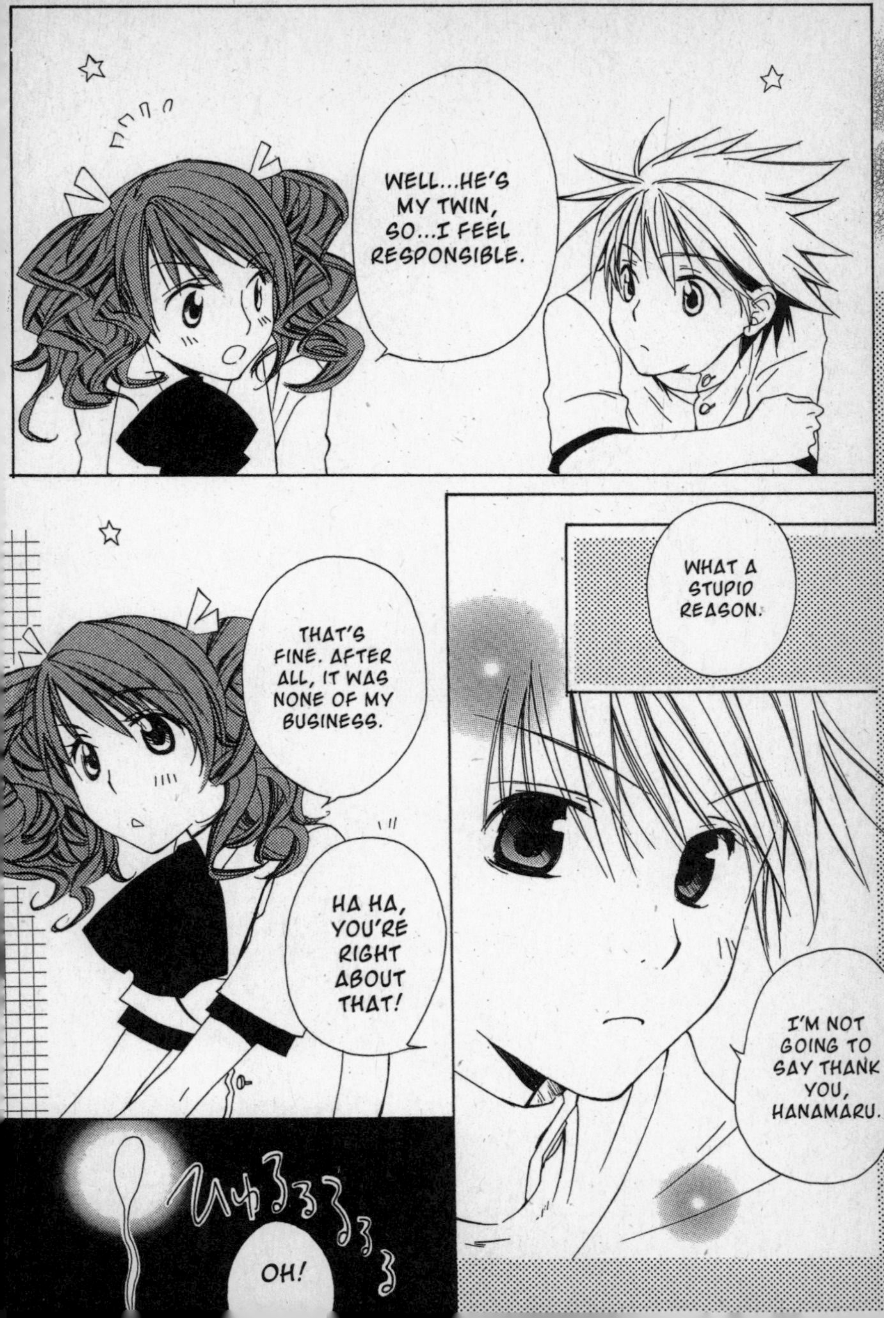
WELL...HE'S MY TWIN, SO...I FEEL RESPONSIBLE.
WHAT A STUPID REASON.
I'M NOT GOING TO SAY THANK YOU, HANAMARU.
THAT'S FINE. AFTER ALL, IT WAS NONE OF MY BUSINESS.
HA HA, YOU'RE RIGHT ABOUT THAT!
OH!

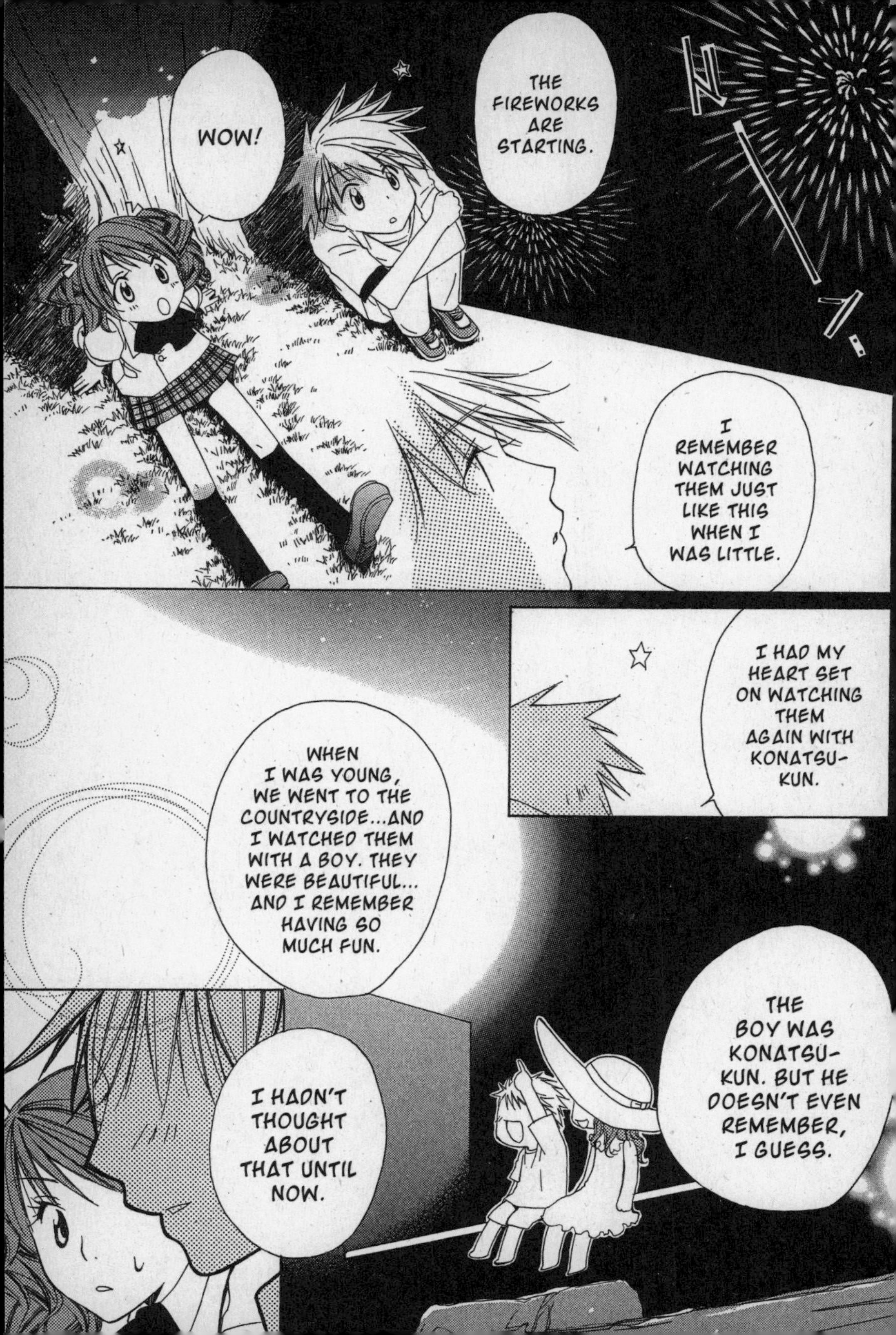
THE FIREWORKS ARE STARTING.
WOW!
I REMEMBER WATCHING THEM JUST LIKE THIS WHEN I WAS LITTLE.
I HAD MY HEART SET ON WATCHING THEM AGAIN WITH KONATSU-KUN.
WHEN I WAS YOUNG, WE WENT TO THE COUNTRYSIDE...AND I WATCHED THEM WITH A BOY. THEY WERE BEAUTIFUL... AND I REMEMBER HAVING SO MUCH FUN.
THE BOY WAS KONATSU-KUN. BUT HE DOESN'T EVEN REMEMBER, I GUESS.
I HADN'T THOUGHT ABOUT THAT UNTIL NOW.

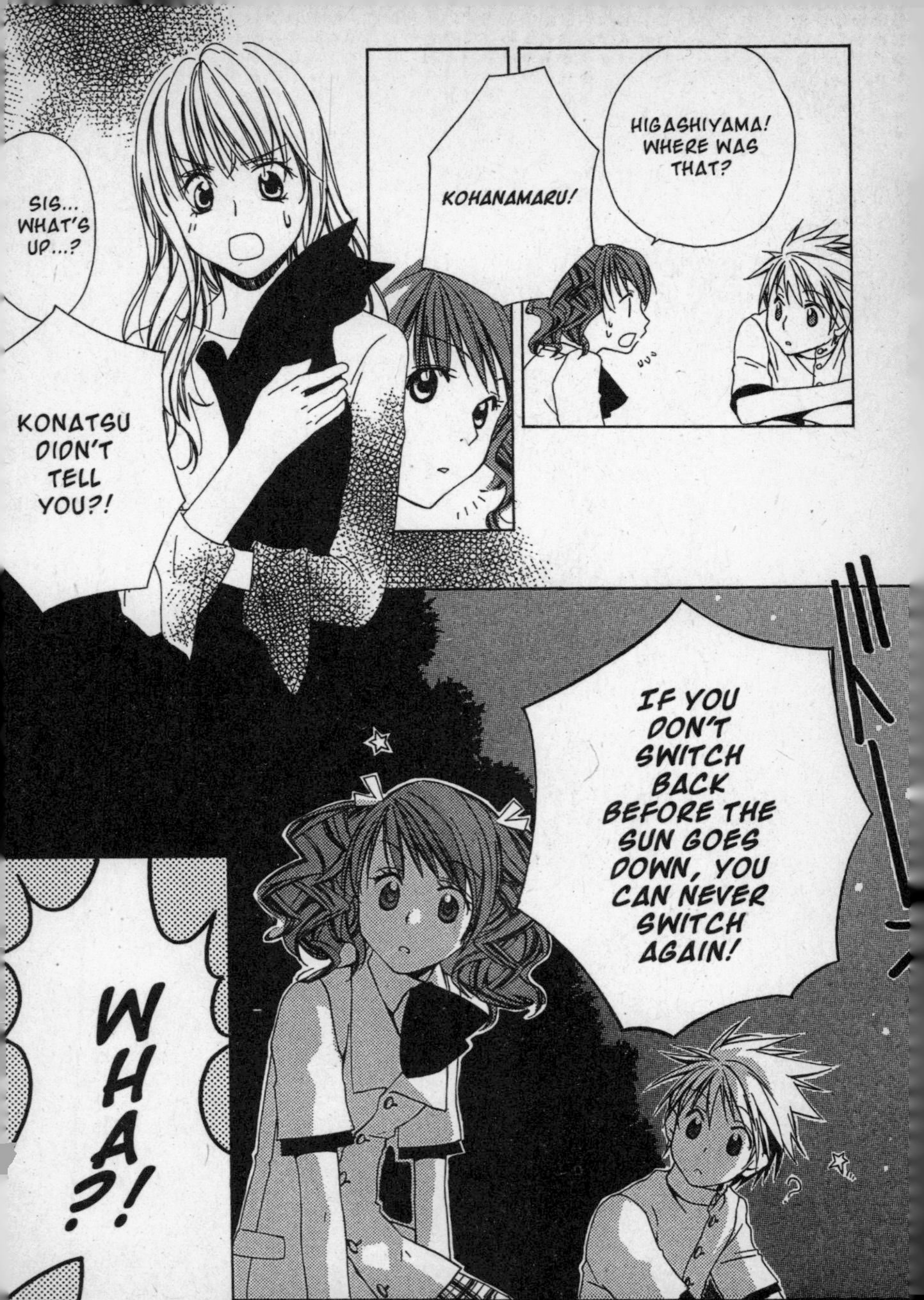
HIGASHIYAMA! WHERE WAS THAT?
KOHANAMARU!
SIS... WHAT'S UP...?
KONATSU DIDN'T TELL YOU?!
IF YOU DON'T SWITCH BACK BEFORE THE SUN GOES DOWN, YOU CAN NEVER SWITCH AGAIN!
WHA?!

★SECOND KISS ××× ★END

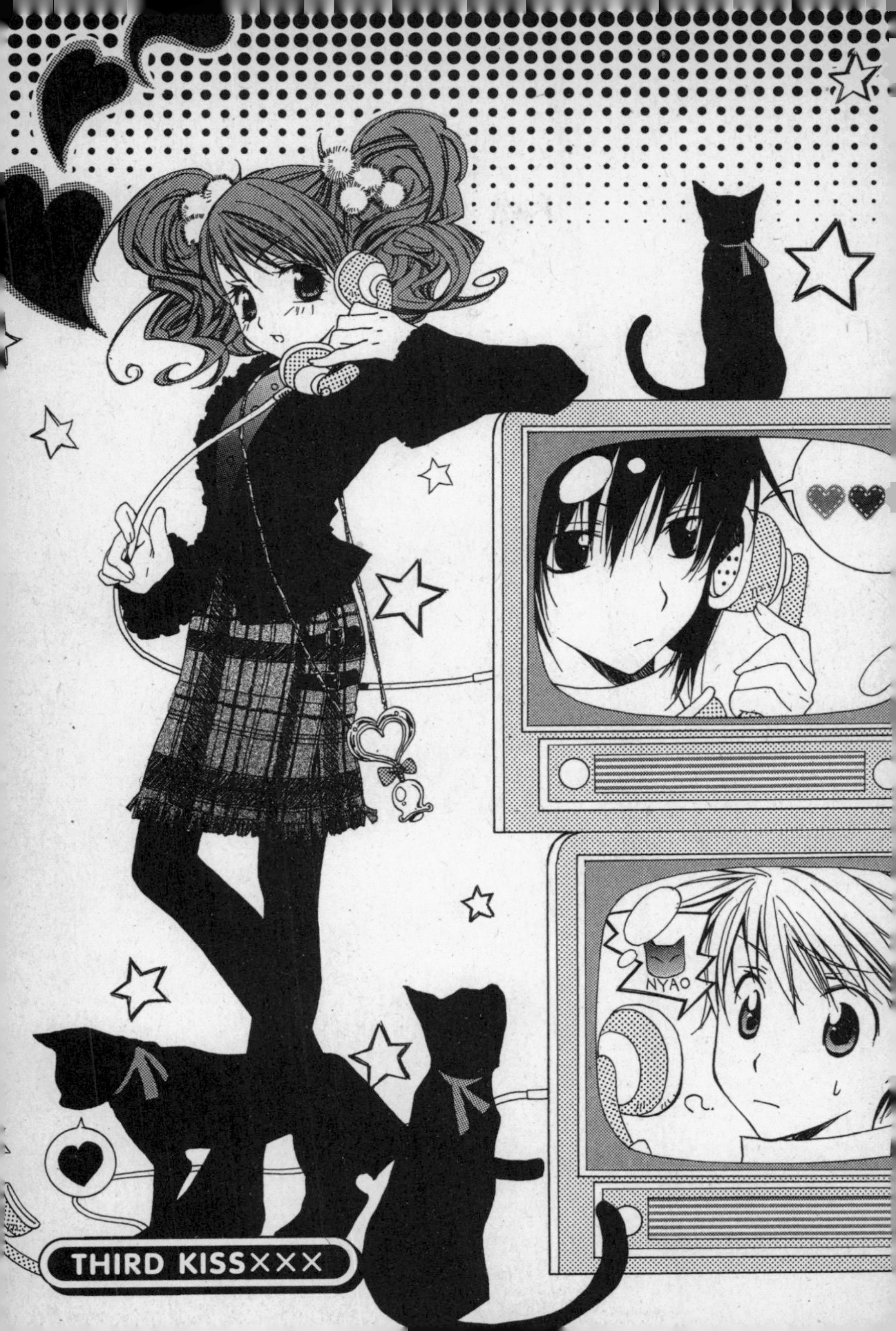
NYAO
THIRD KISS×××

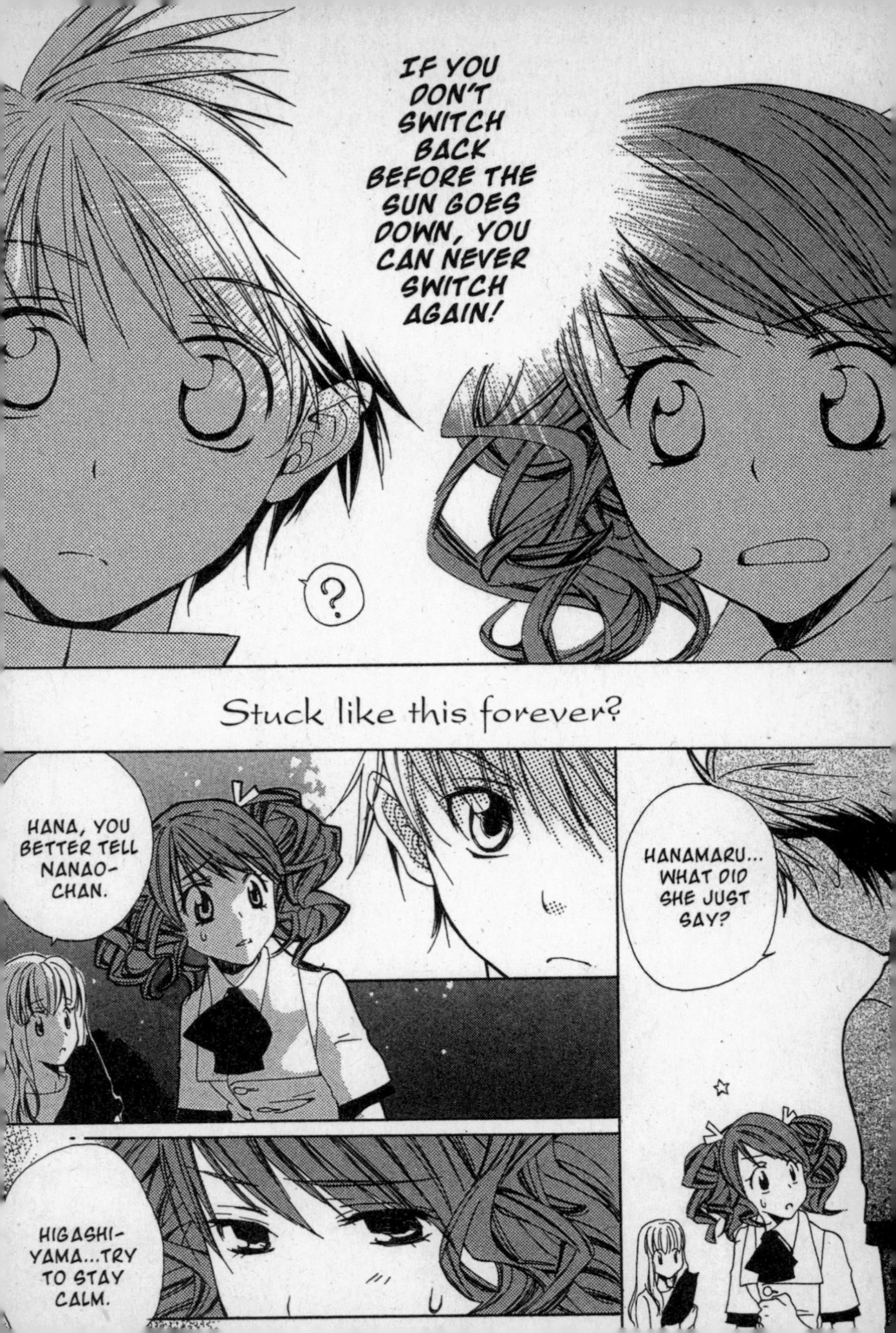
IF YOU DON'T SWITCH BACK BEFORE THE SUN GOES DOWN, YOU CAN NEVER SWITCH AGAIN!
?
Stuck like this forever?
HANAMARU... WHAT DID SHE JUST SAY?
HANA, YOU BETTER TELL NANAO-CHAN.
HIGASHI-YAMA...TRY TO STAY CALM.

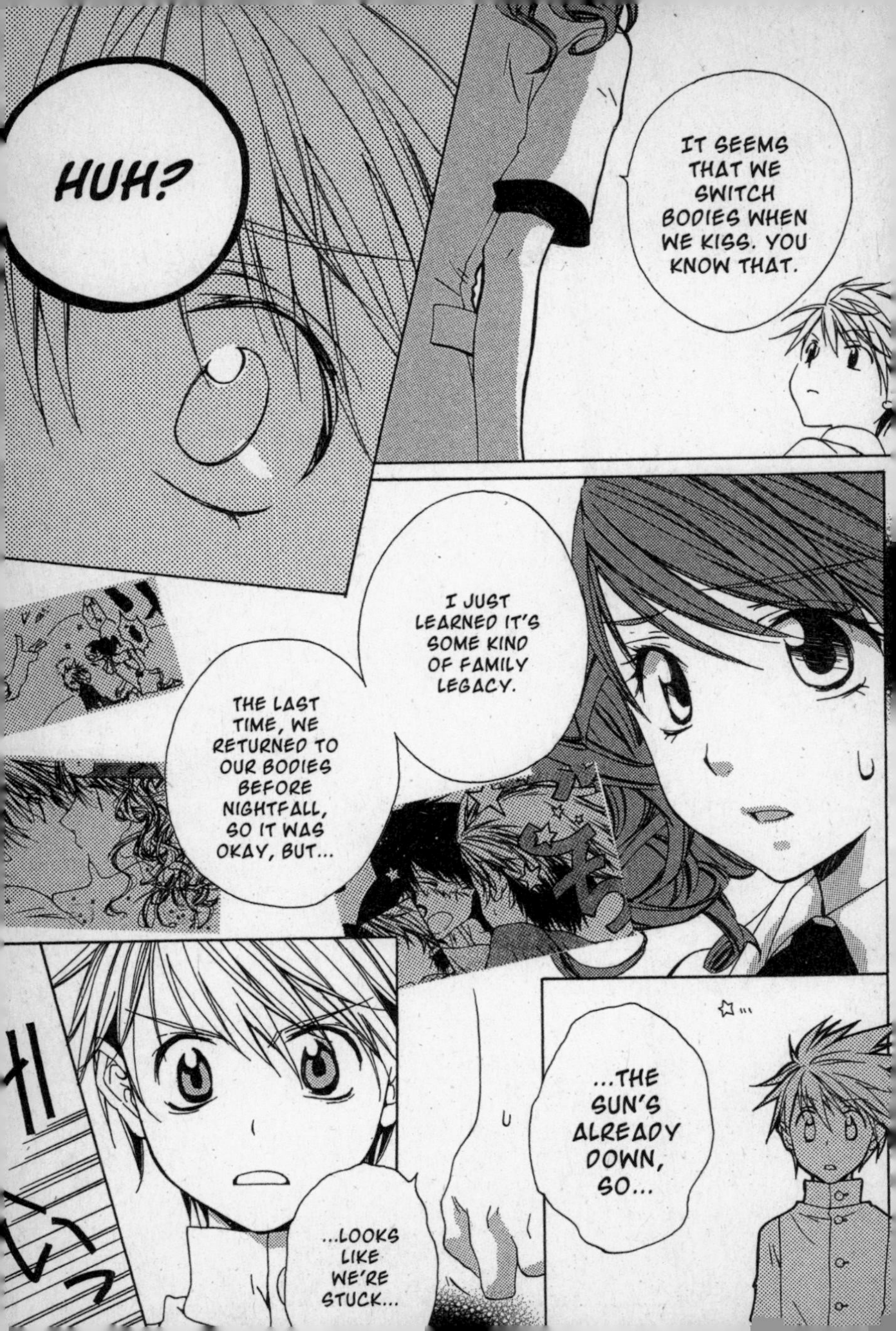
IT SEEMS THAT WE SWITCH BODIES WHEN WE KISS. YOU KNOW THAT.
HUH?
I JUST LEARNED IT'S SOME KIND OF FAMILY LEGACY.
THE LAST TIME, WE RETURNED TO OUR BODIES BEFORE NIGHTFALL, SO IT WAS OKAY, BUT...
...THE SUN'S ALREADY DOWN, SO...
...LOOKS LIKE WE'RE STUCK...

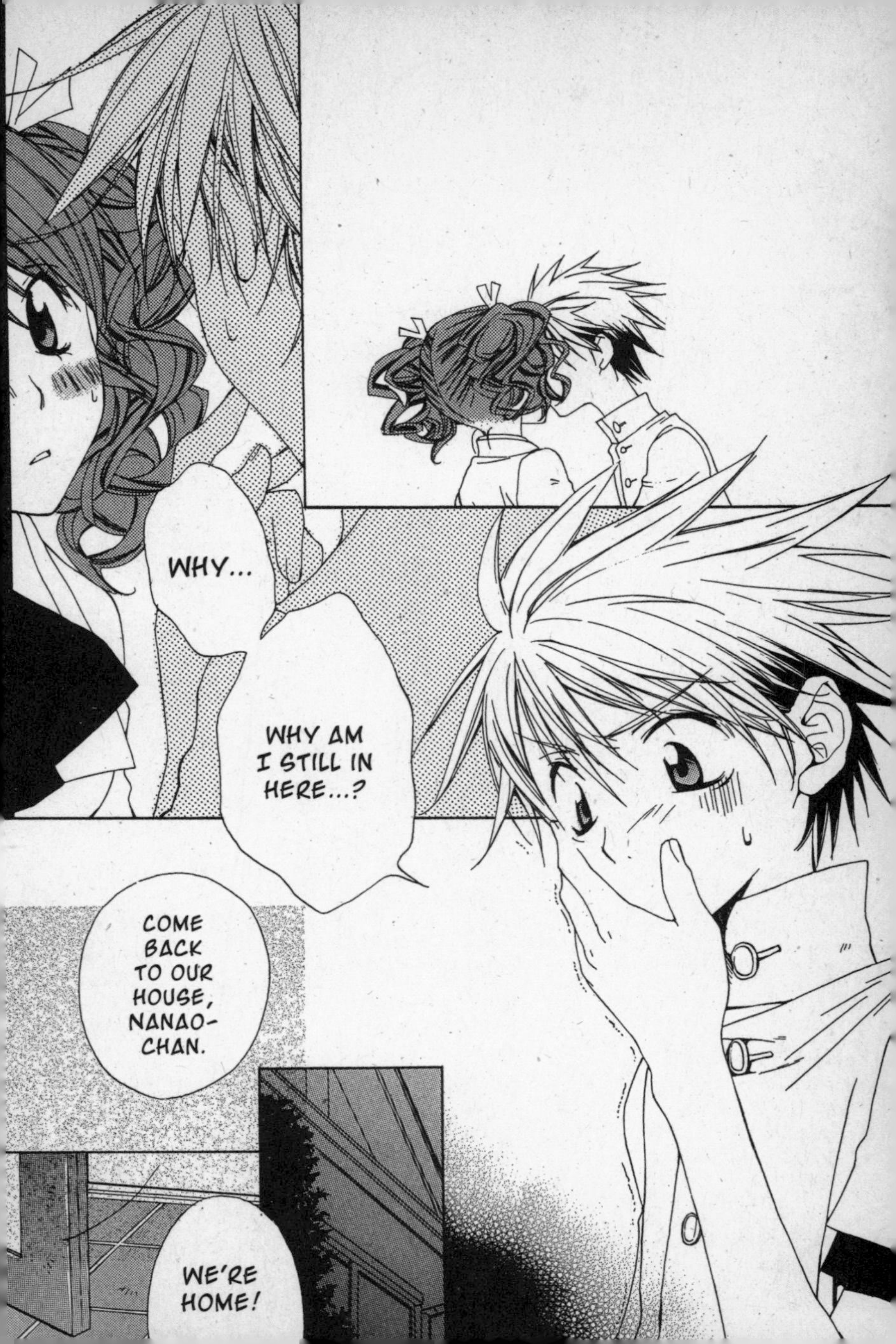
WHY...
WHY AM I STILL IN HERE...?
COME BACK TO OUR HOUSE, NANAO-CHAN.
WE'RE HOME!

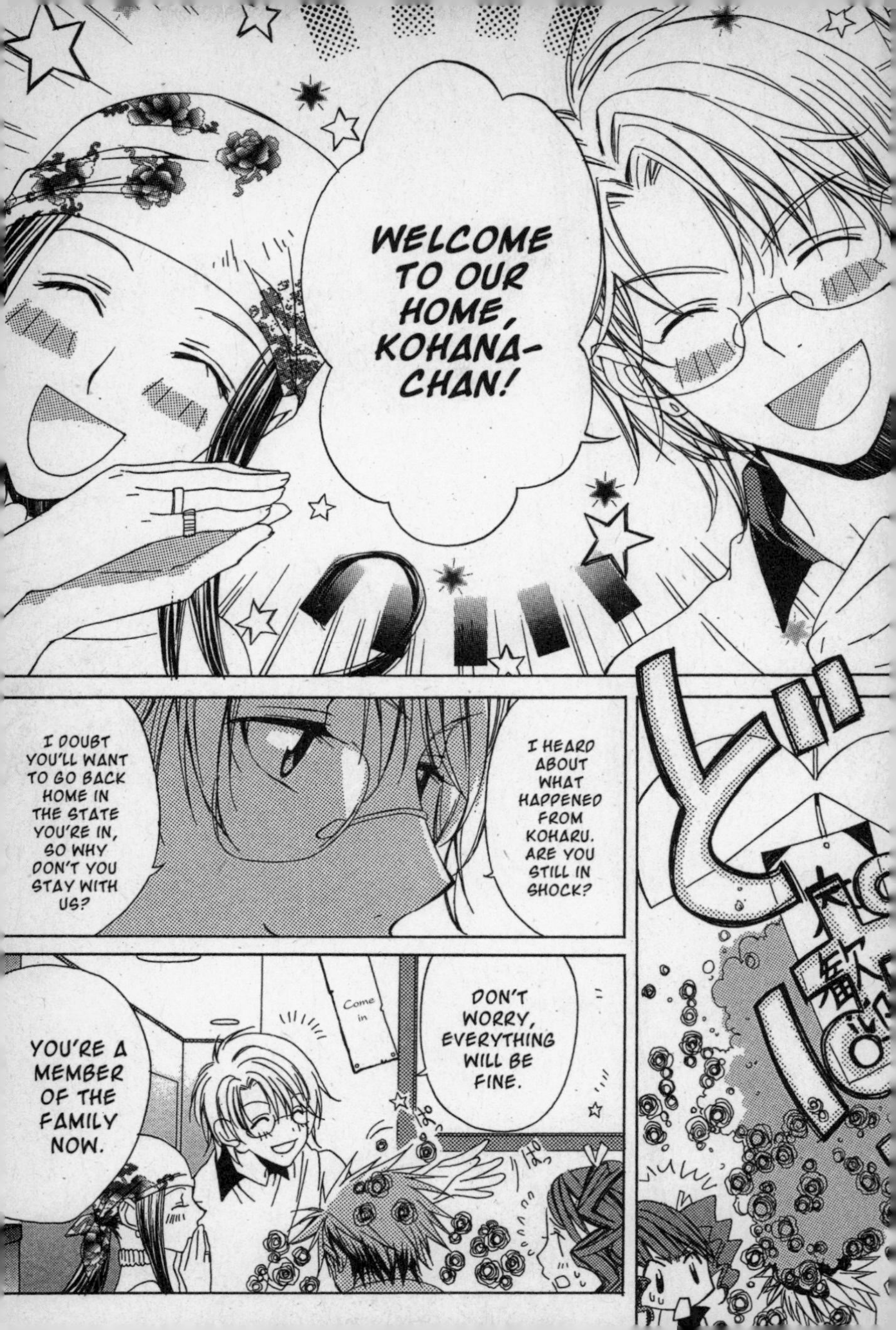
WELCOME TO OUR HOME, KOHANA-CHAN!
I HEARD ABOUT WHAT HAPPENED FROM KOHARU. ARE YOU STILL IN SHOCK?
I DOUBT YOU'LL WANT TO GO BACK HOME IN THE STATE YOU'RE IN, SO WHY DON'T YOU STAY WITH US?
Come in
DON'T WORRY, EVERYTHING WILL BE FINE.
YOU'RE A MEMBER OF THE FAMILY NOW.

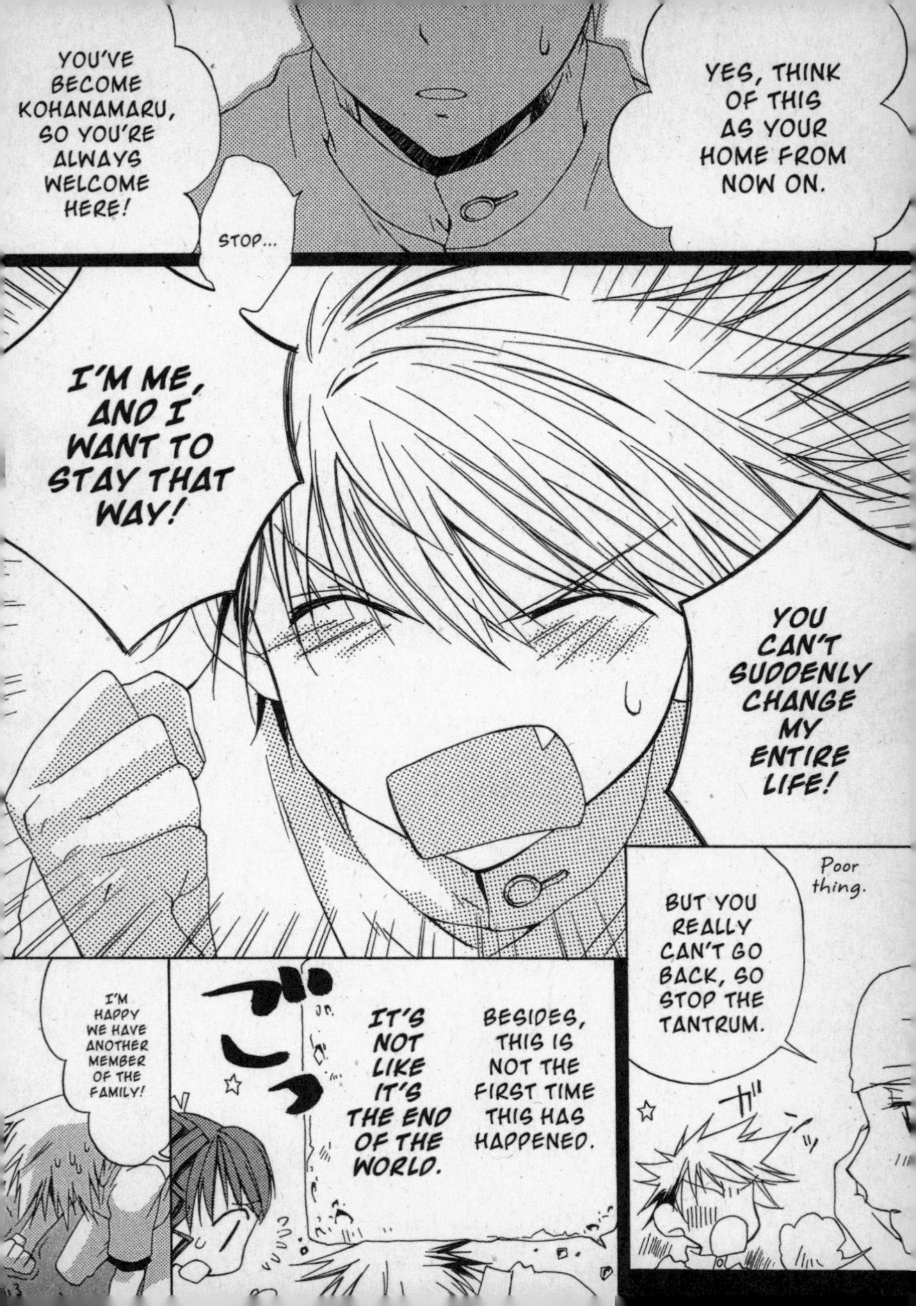
YES, THINK OF THIS AS YOUR HOME FROM NOW ON.
YOU'VE BECOME KOHANAMARU, SO YOU'RE ALWAYS WELCOME HERE!
STOP...
I'M ME, AND I WANT TO STAY THAT WAY!
YOU CAN'T SUDDENLY CHANGE MY ENTIRE LIFE!
Poor thing.
BUT YOU REALLY CAN'T GO BACK, SO STOP THE TANTRUM.
BESIDES, THIS IS NOT THE FIRST TIME THIS HAS HAPPENED.
IT'S NOT LIKE IT'S THE END OF THE WORLD.
I'M HAPPY WE HAVE ANOTHER MEMBER OF THE FAMILY!

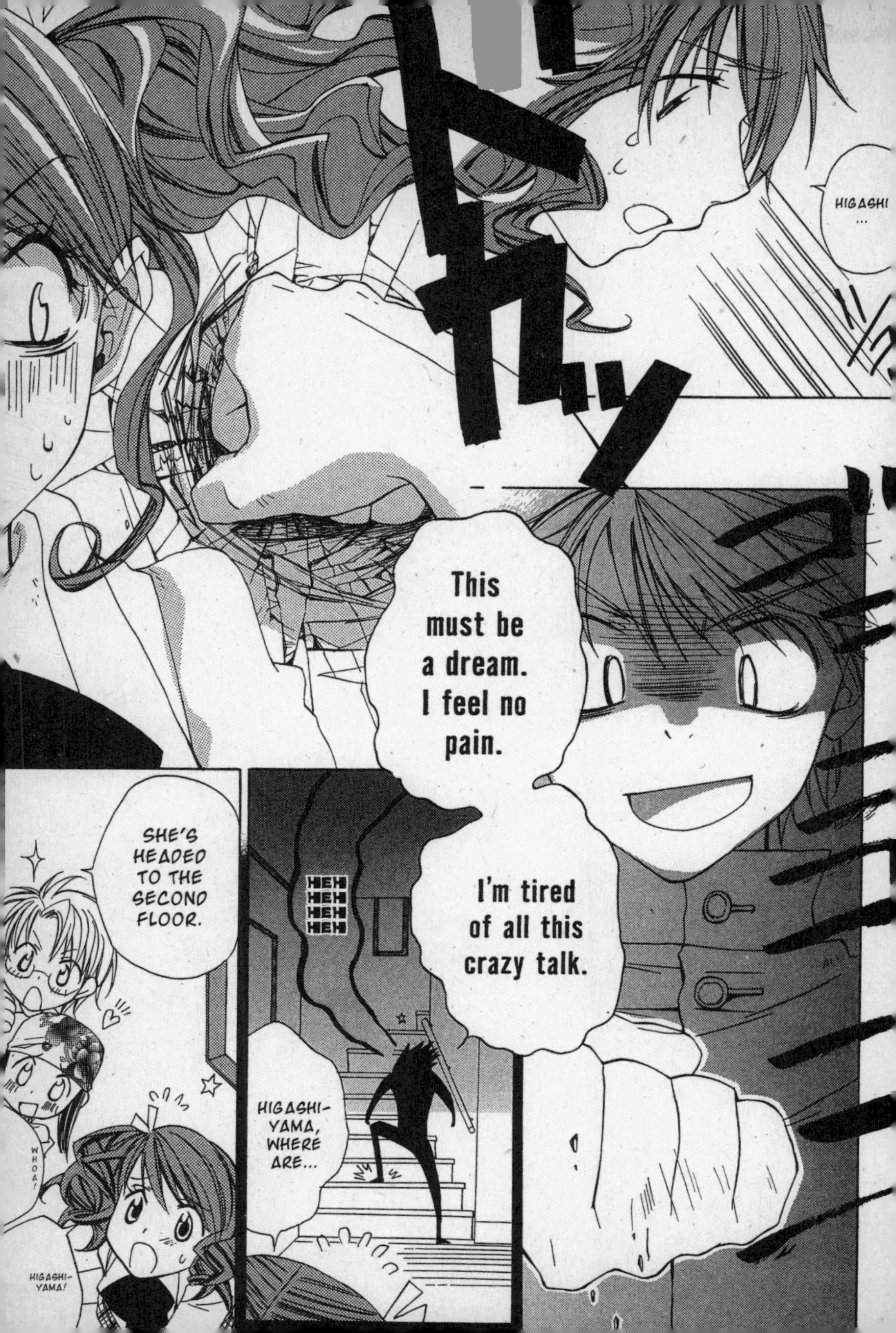
HIGASHI...
This must be a dream. I feel no pain.
I'm tired of all this crazy talk.
HEH HEH HEH HEH
HIGASHI-YAMA, WHERE ARE...
SHE'S HEADED TO THE SECOND FLOOR.
WHOA!
HIGASHI-YAMA!

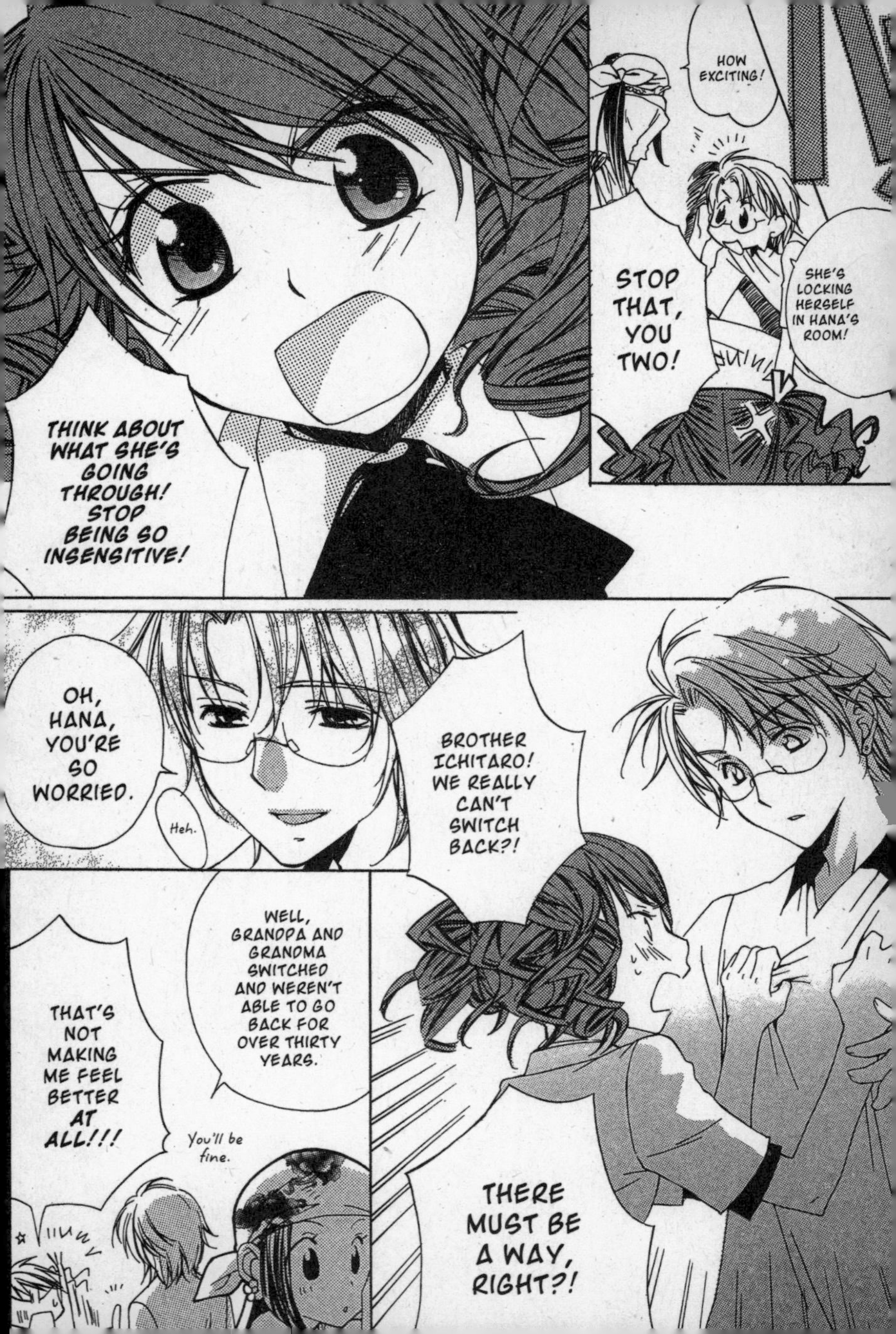
HOW EXCITING!
SHE'S LOCKING HERSELF IN HANA'S ROOM!
STOP THAT, YOU TWO!
THINK ABOUT WHAT SHE'S GOING THROUGH! STOP BEING SO INSENSITIVE!
BROTHER ICHITARO! WE REALLY CAN'T SWITCH BACK?!
THERE MUST BE A WAY, RIGHT?!
OH, HANA, YOU'RE SO WORRIED.
Heh.
WELL, GRANDPA AND GRANDMA SWITCHED AND WEREN'T ABLE TO GO BACK FOR OVER THIRTY YEARS.
THAT'S NOT MAKING ME FEEL BETTER AT ALL!!!
You'll be fine.

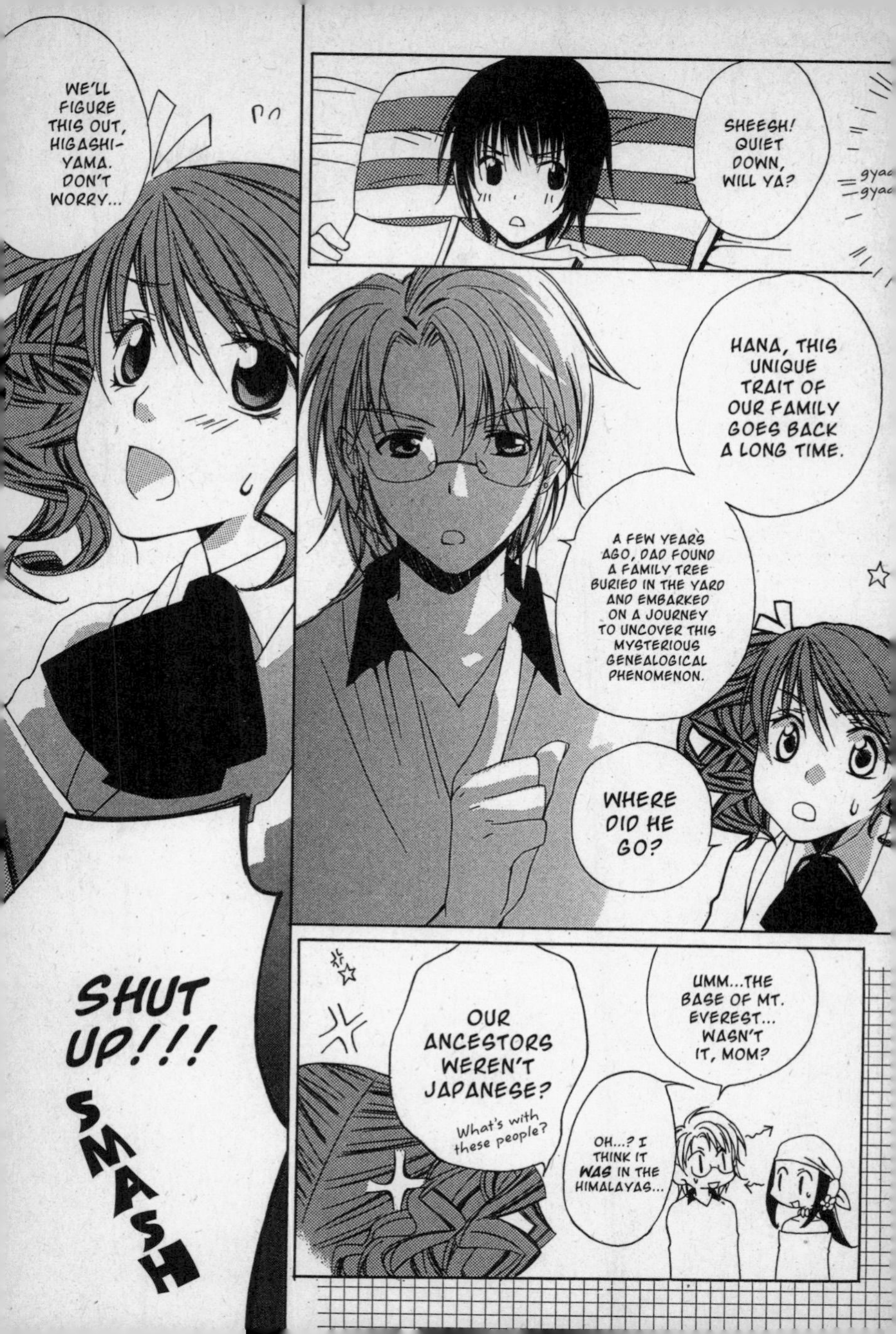
SHEESH! QUIET DOWN, WILL YA?
HANA, THIS UNIQUE TRAIT OF OUR FAMILY GOES BACK A LONG TIME.
A FEW YEARS AGO, DAD FOUND A FAMILY TREE BURIED IN THE YARD AND EMBARKED ON A JOURNEY TO UNCOVER THIS MYSTERIOUS GENEALOGICAL PHENOMENON.
WHERE DID HE GO?
UMM...THE BASE OF MT. EVEREST... WASN'T IT, MOM?
OH...? I THINK IT WAS IN THE HIMALAYAS...
OUR ANCESTORS WEREN'T JAPANESE?
What's with these people?
WE'LL FIGURE THIS OUT, HIGASHI-YAMA. DON'T WORRY...
SHUT UP!!!
SMASH

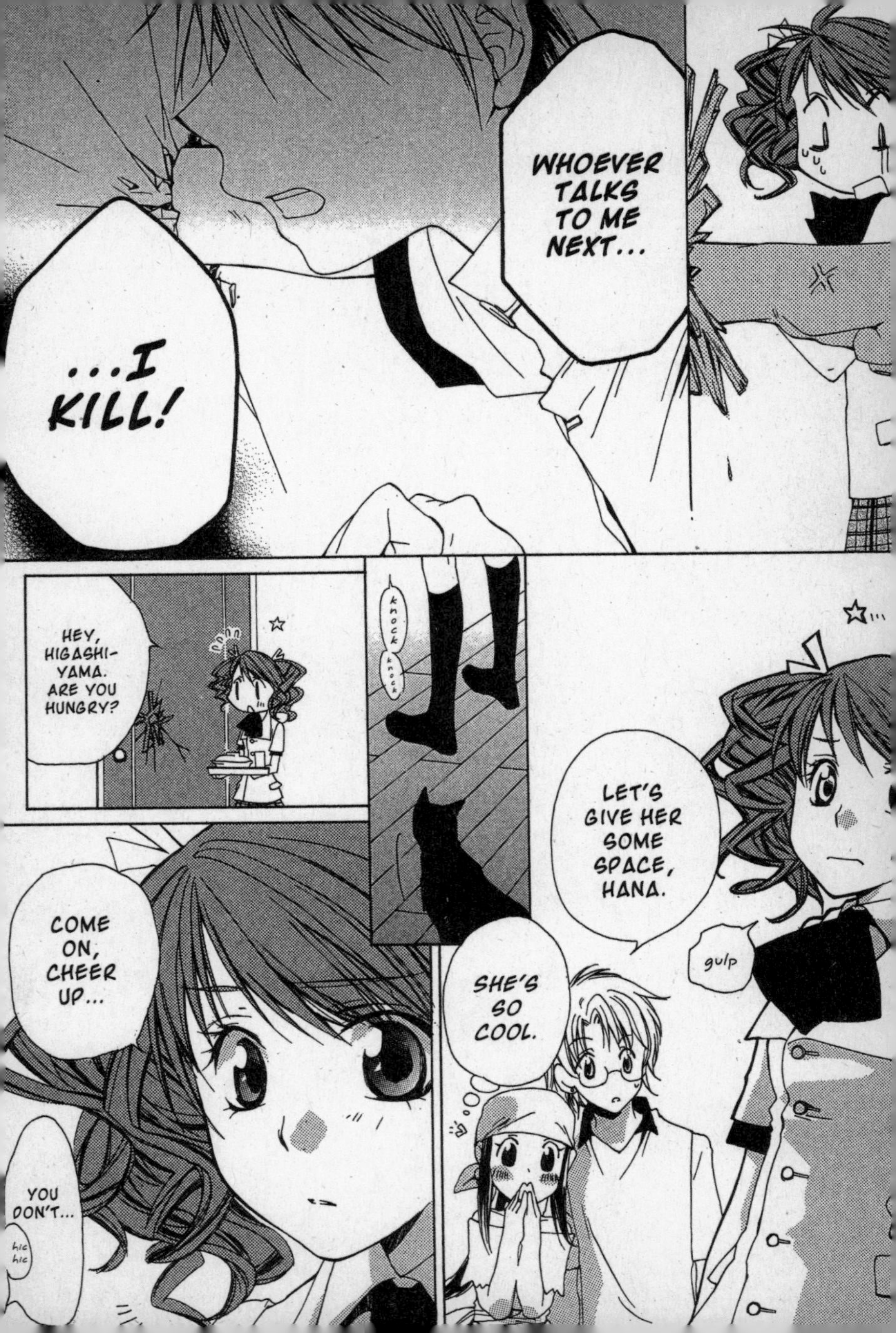
WHOEVER TALKS TO ME NEXT...
...I KILL!
LET'S GIVE HER SOME SPACE, HANA.
gulp
SHE'S SO COOL.
knock knock
HEY, HIGASHI-YAMA. ARE YOU HUNGRY?
COME ON, CHEER UP...
YOU DON'T...
hic hic

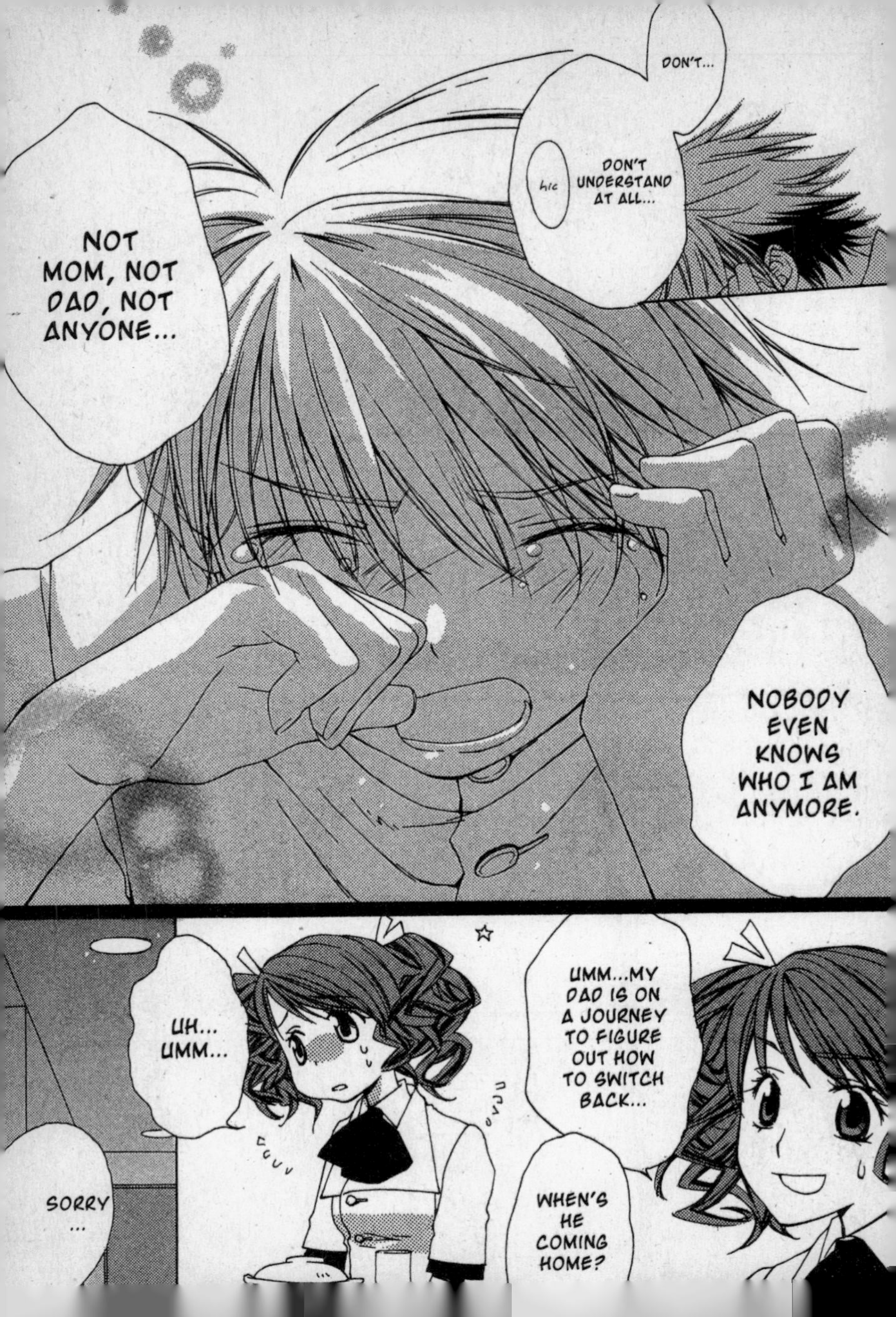
DON'T...
hic
DON'T UNDERSTAND AT ALL...
NOT MOM, NOT DAD, NOT ANYONE...
NOBODY EVEN KNOWS WHO I AM ANYMORE.
UMM...MY DAD IS ON A JOURNEY TO FIGURE OUT HOW TO SWITCH BACK...
WHEN'S HE COMING HOME?
UH... UMM...
SORRY ...

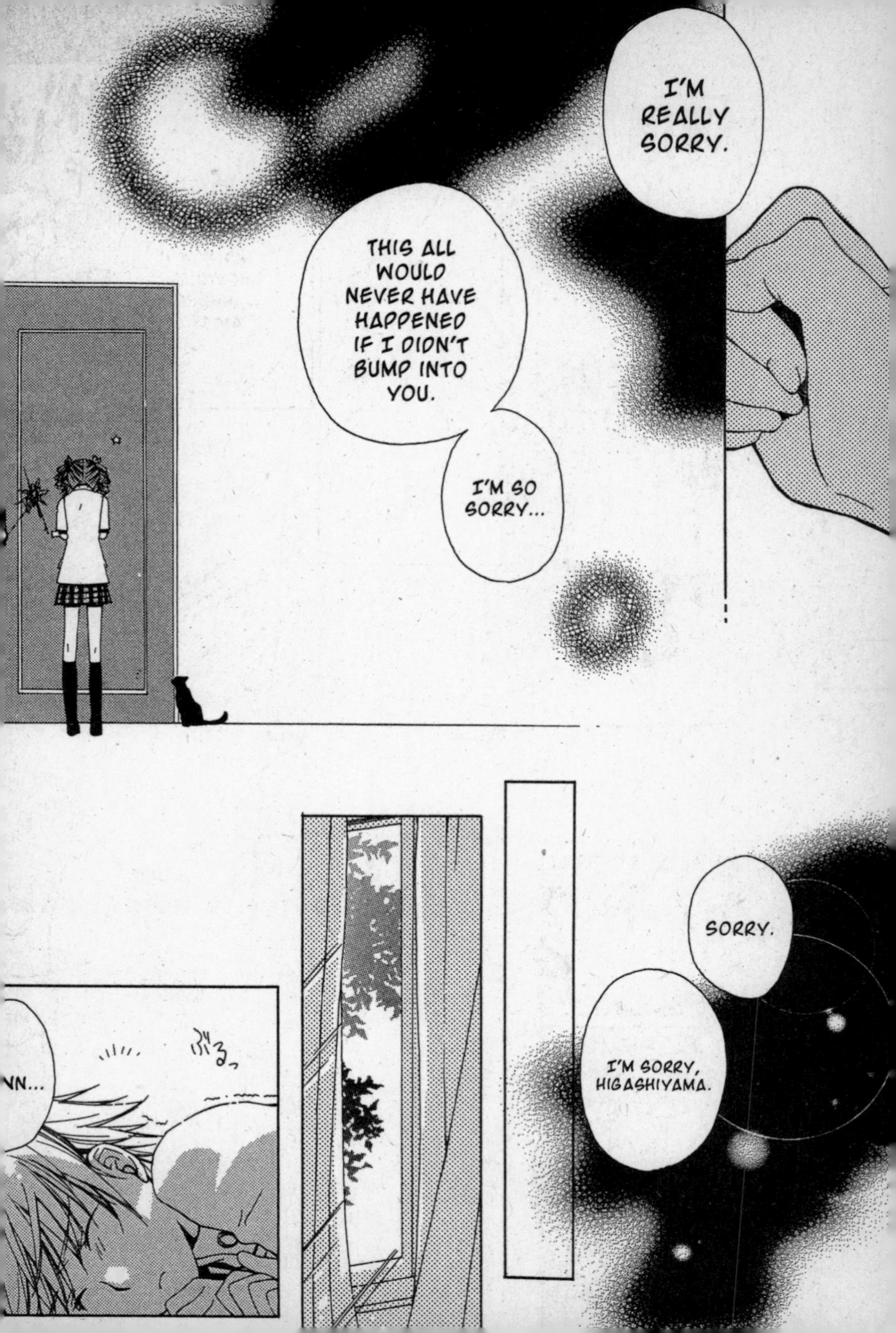
I'M REALLY SORRY.
THIS ALL WOULD NEVER HAVE HAPPENED IF I DIDN'T BUMP INTO YOU.
I'M SO SORRY...
SORRY.
I'M SORRY, HIGASHIYAMA.
NN...

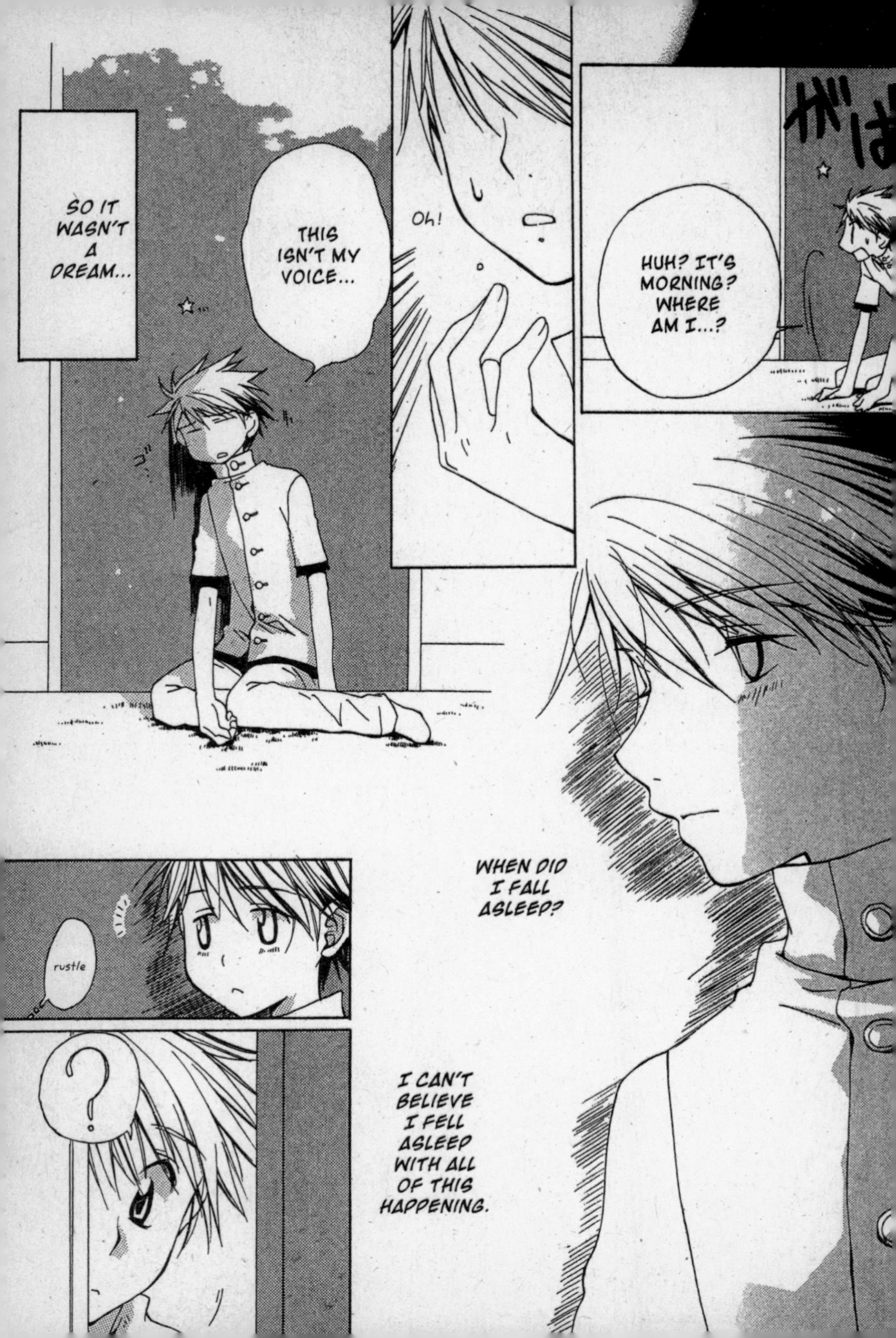

がば
HUH? IT'S MORNING? WHERE AM I...?
Oh!
THIS ISN'T MY VOICE...
SO IT WASN'T A DREAM...
WHEN DID I FALL ASLEEP?
I CAN'T BELIEVE I FELL ASLEEP WITH ALL OF THIS HAPPENING.
rustle
?

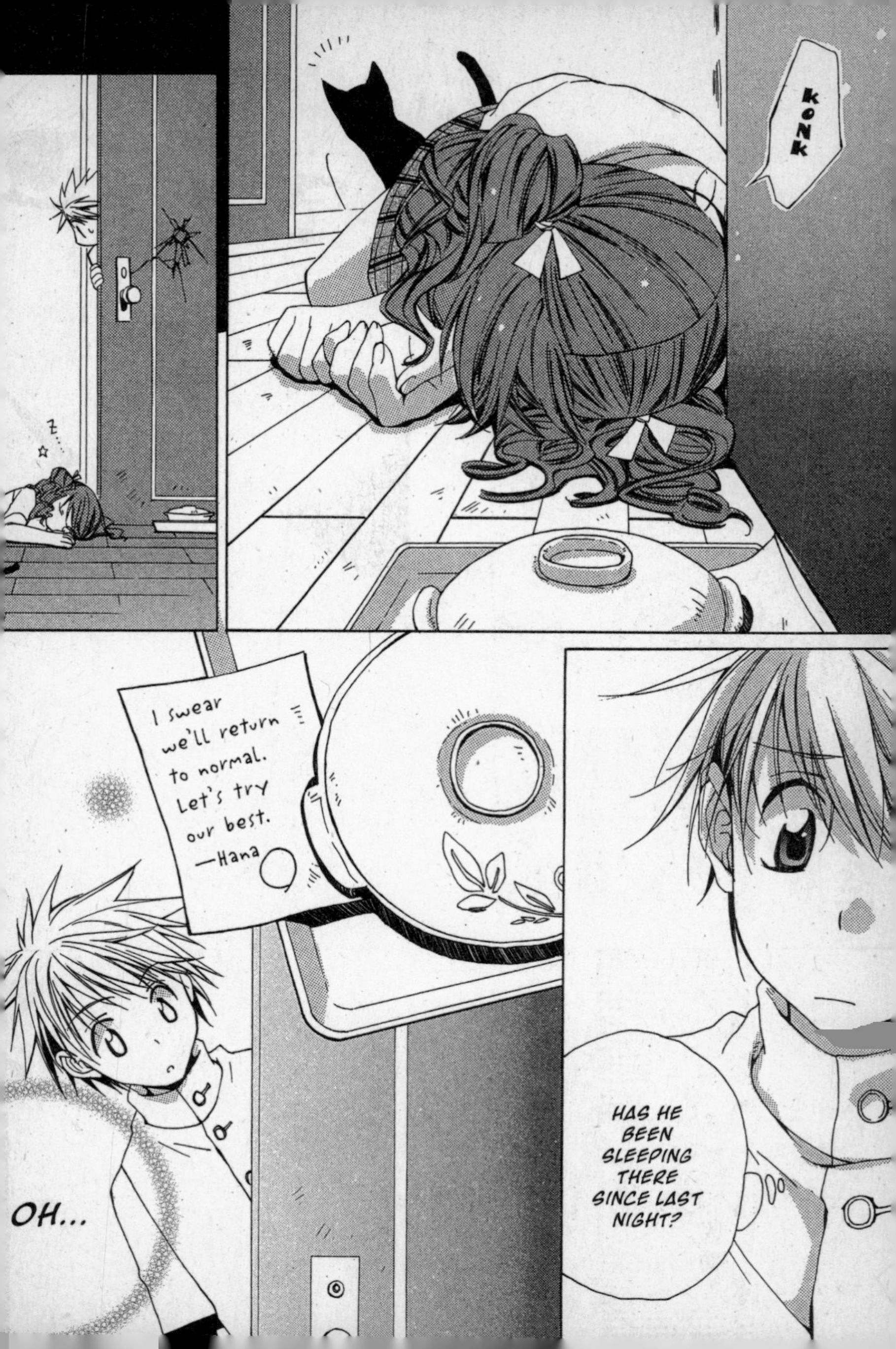
KONK
HAS HE BEEN SLEEPING THERE SINCE LAST NIGHT?
I swear we'll return to normal. Let's try our best. —Hana
OH...

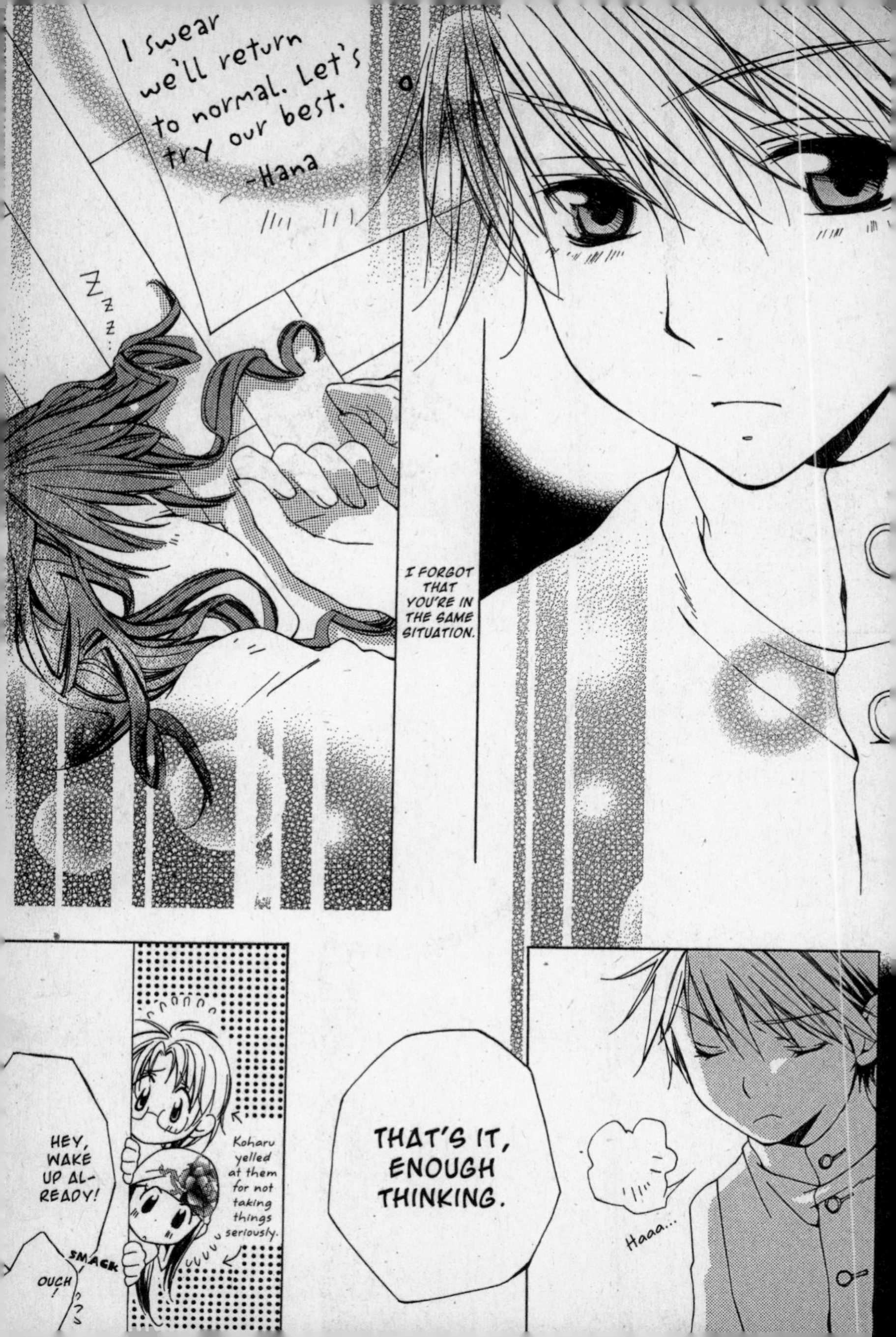
I FORGOT THAT YOU'RE IN THE SAME SITUATION.
I swear we'll return to normal. Let's try our best. -Hana
Zzz...
Haaa...
THAT'S IT, ENOUGH THINKING.
HEY, WAKE UP AL-READY!
Koharu yelled at them for not taking things seriously.
SMACK
OUCH!

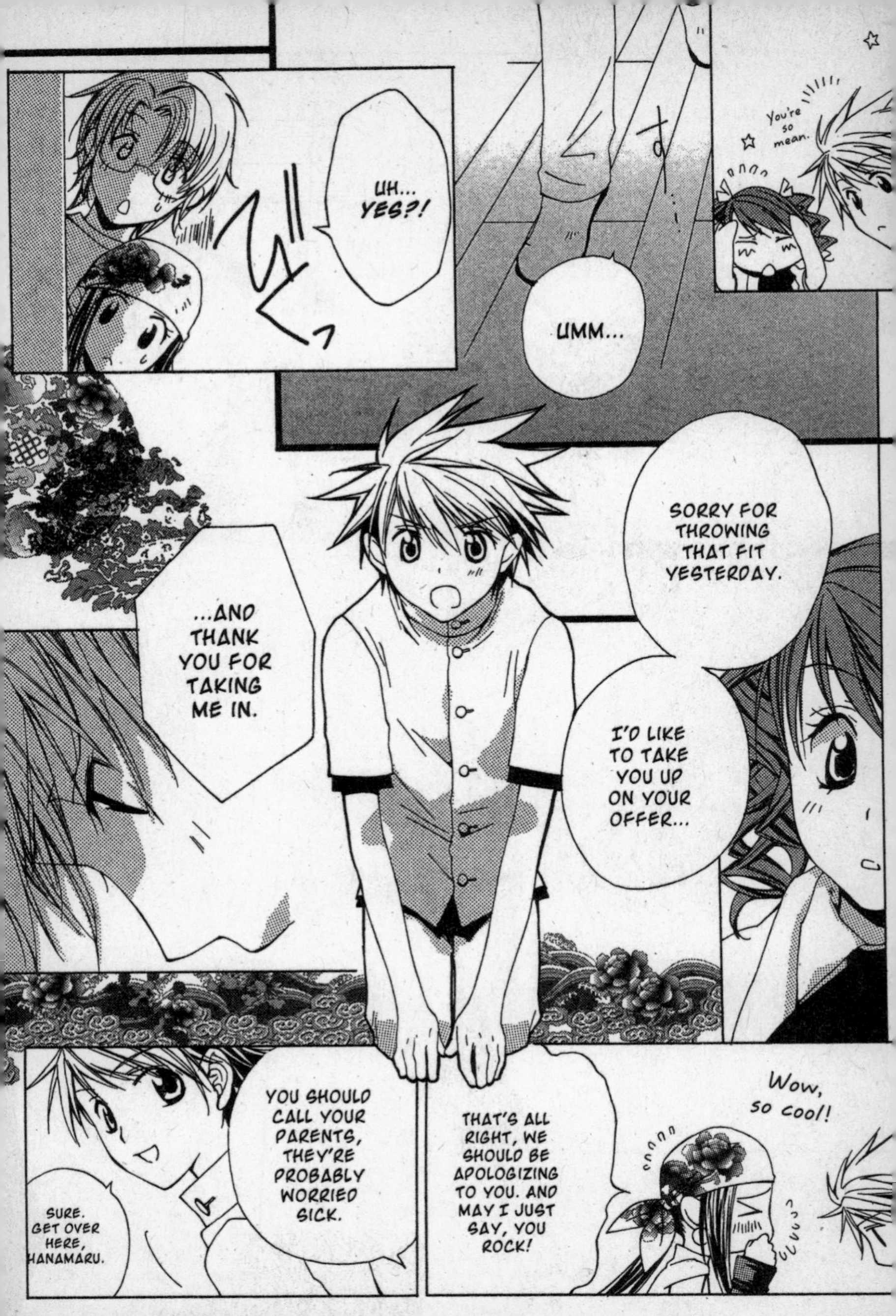
You're so mean.
UMM...
UH... YES?!
SORRY FOR THROWING THAT FIT YESTERDAY.
I'D LIKE TO TAKE YOU UP ON YOUR OFFER...
...AND THANK YOU FOR TAKING ME IN.
Wow, so cool!
THAT'S ALL RIGHT, WE SHOULD BE APOLOGIZING TO YOU. AND MAY I JUST SAY, YOU ROCK!
YOU SHOULD CALL YOUR PARENTS, THEY'RE PROBABLY WORRIED SICK.
SURE. GET OVER HERE, HANAMARU.

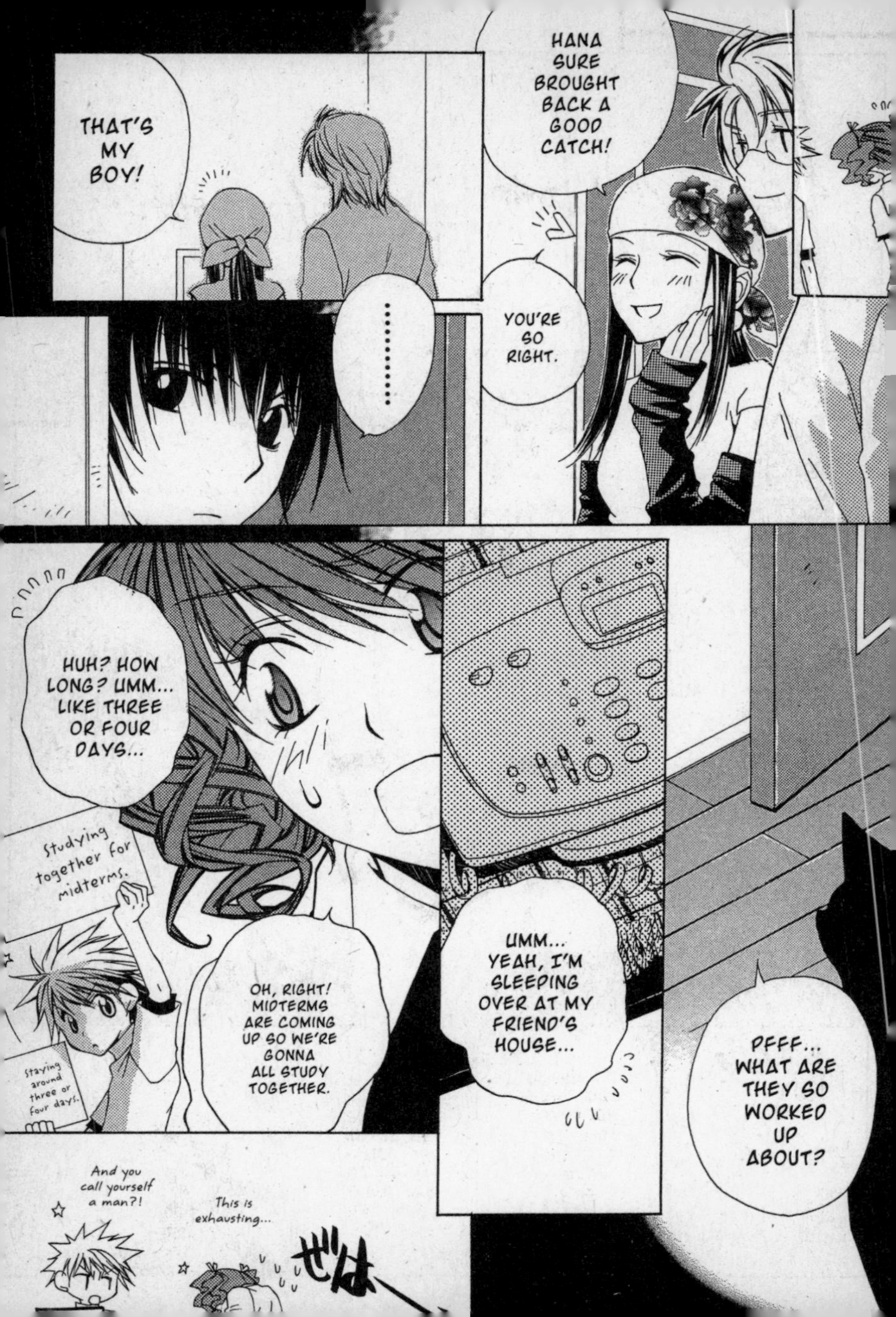
HANA SURE BROUGHT BACK A GOOD CATCH!
YOU'RE SO RIGHT.
THAT'S MY BOY!
....
PFFF... WHAT ARE THEY SO WORKED UP ABOUT?
UMM... YEAH, I'M SLEEPING OVER AT MY FRIEND'S HOUSE...
HUH? HOW LONG? UMM... LIKE THREE OR FOUR DAYS...
Studying together for midterms.
OH, RIGHT! MIDTERMS ARE COMING UP SO WE'RE GONNA ALL STUDY TOGETHER.
Staying around three or four days.
And you call yourself a man?!
This is exhausting...
ぜはー

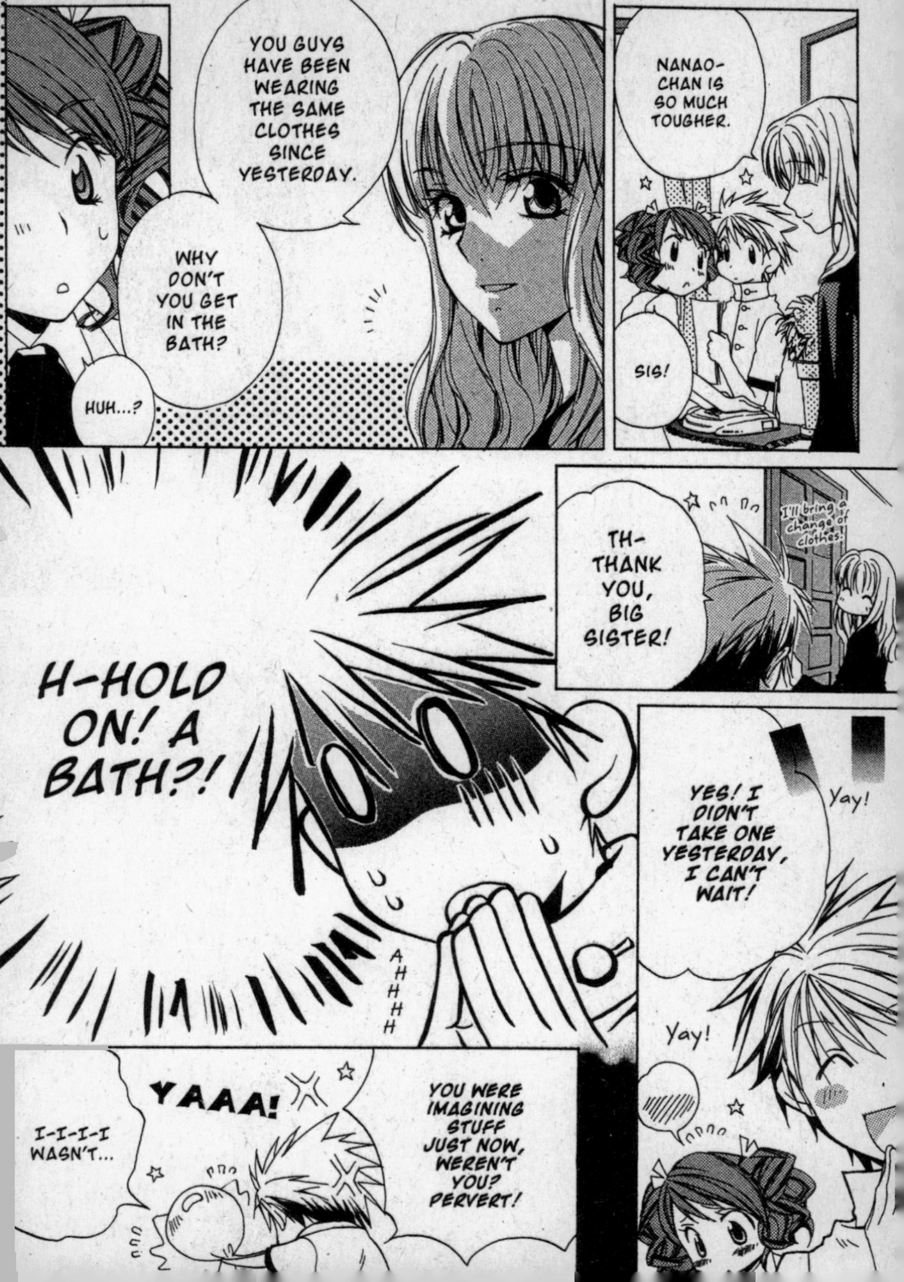
NANAO-CHAN IS SO MUCH TOUGHER.
SIS!
YOU GUYS HAVE BEEN WEARING THE SAME CLOTHES SINCE YESTERDAY.
WHY DON'T YOU GET IN THE BATH?
HUH...?
TH-THANK YOU, BIG SISTER!
I'll bring a change of clothes.
YES! I DIDN'T TAKE ONE YESTERDAY, I CAN'T WAIT!
Yay!
Yay!
H-HOLD ON! A BATH?!
AHHHH
YOU WERE IMAGINING STUFF JUST NOW, WEREN'T YOU? PERVERT!
YAAAA!
I-I-I-I WASN'T...

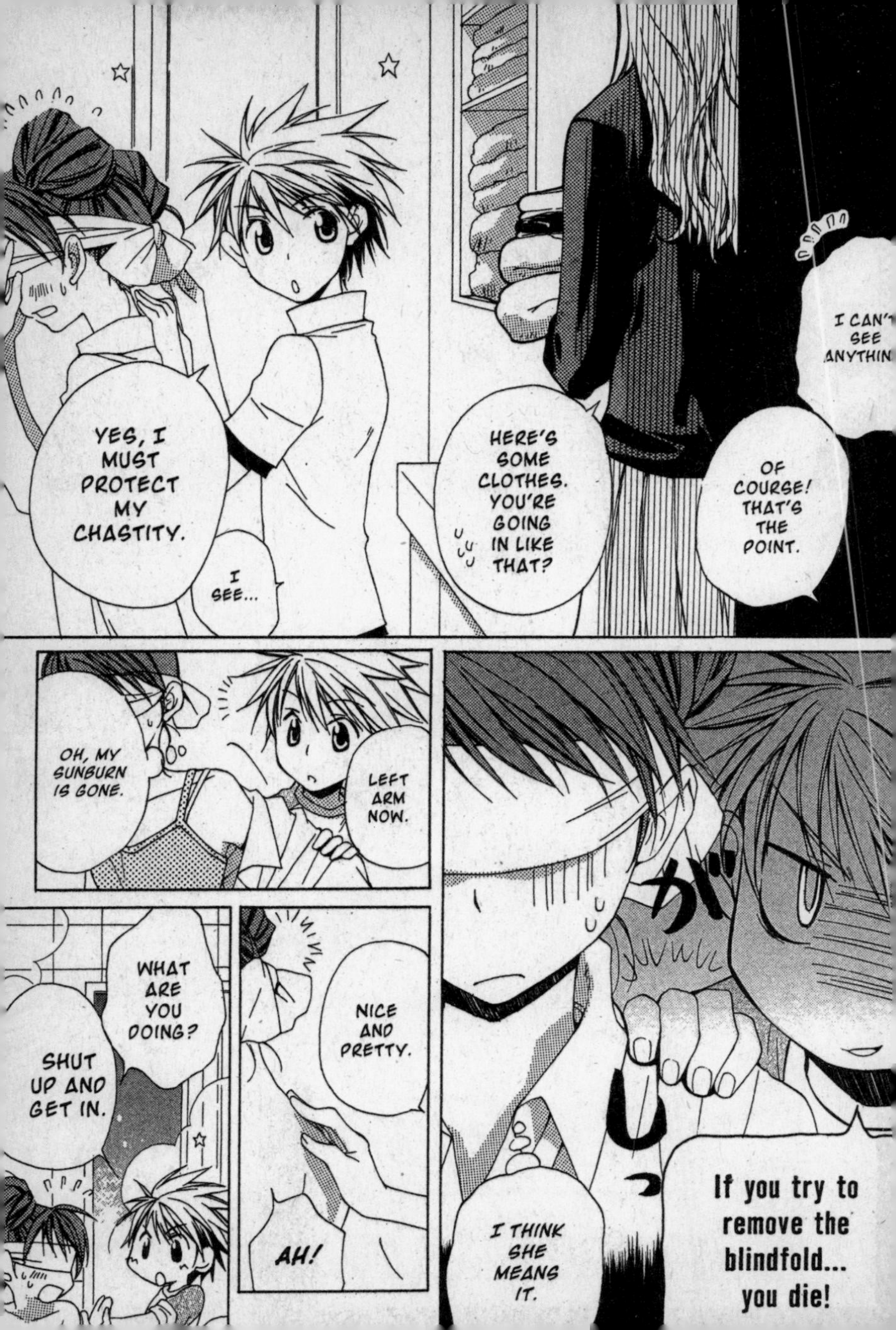
I CAN'T SEE ANYTHIN
OF COURSE! THAT'S THE POINT.
HERE'S SOME CLOTHES. YOU'RE GOING IN LIKE THAT?
YES, I MUST PROTECT MY CHASTITY.
I SEE...
If you try to remove the blindfold... you die!
I THINK SHE MEANS IT.
LEFT ARM NOW.
OH, MY SUNBURN IS GONE.
NICE AND PRETTY.
AH!
WHAT ARE YOU DOING?
SHUT UP AND GET IN.

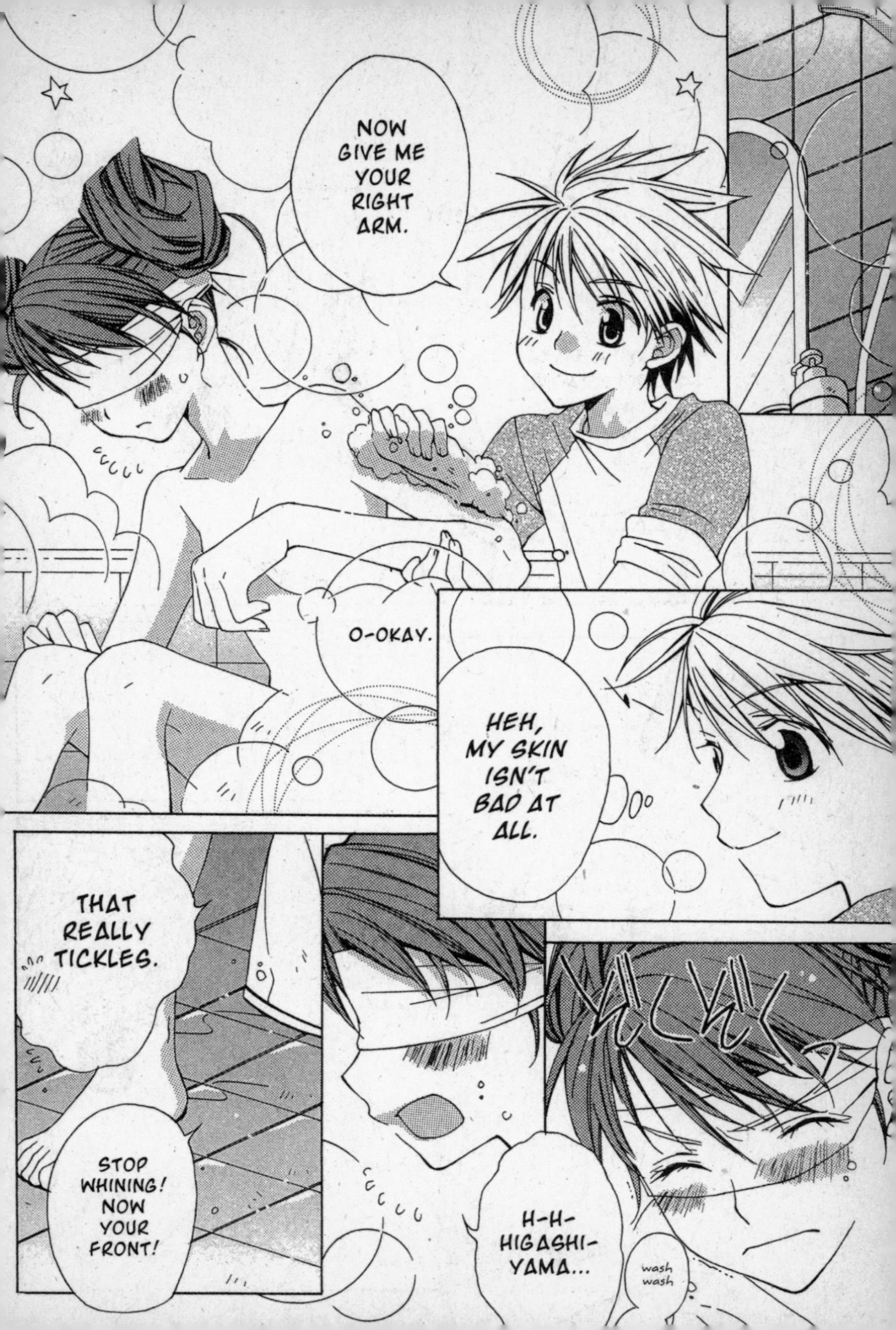
NOW GIVE ME YOUR RIGHT ARM.
O-OKAY.
HEH, MY SKIN ISN'T BAD AT ALL.
H-H-HIGASHI-YAMA...
wash wash
THAT REALLY TICKLES.
STOP WHINING! NOW YOUR FRONT!

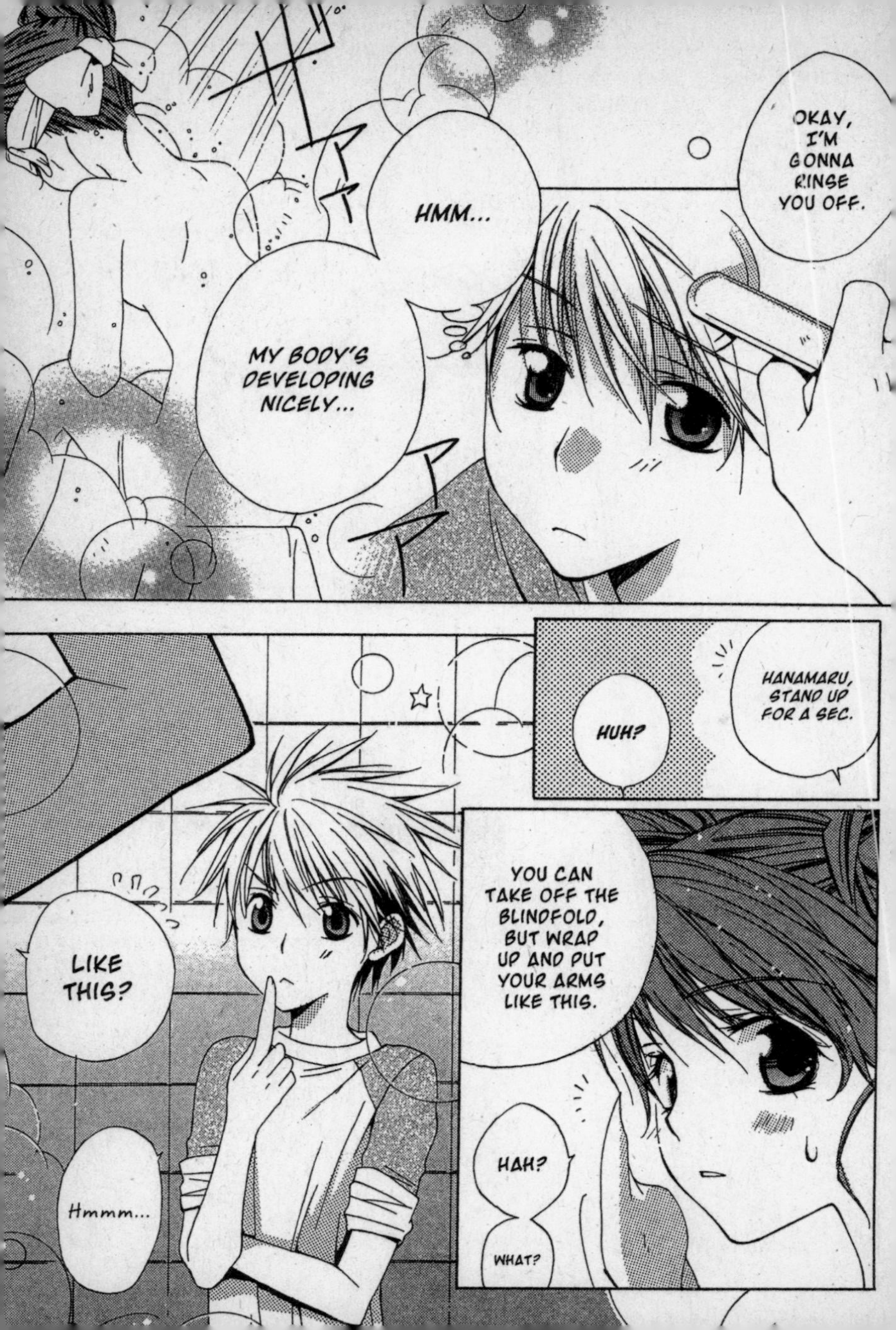
OKAY, I'M GONNA RINSE YOU OFF.
HMM...
MY BODY'S DEVELOPING NICELY...
HANAMARU, STAND UP FOR A SEC.
HUH?
YOU CAN TAKE OFF THE BLINDFOLD, BUT WRAP UP AND PUT YOUR ARMS LIKE THIS.
HAH?
WHAT?
LIKE THIS?
Hmmm...

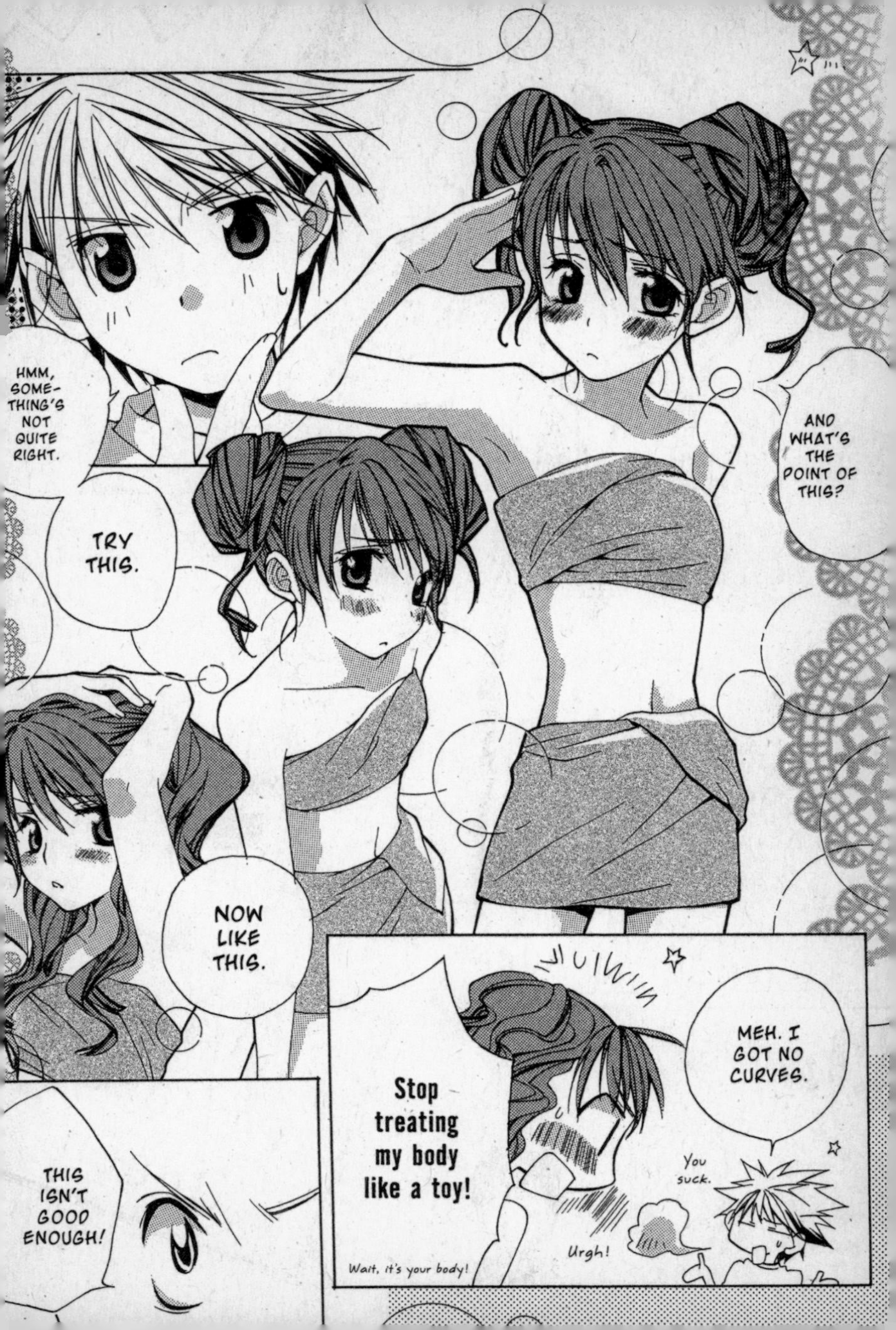
AND WHAT'S THE POINT OF THIS?
HMM, SOME-THING'S NOT QUITE RIGHT.
TRY THIS.
NOW LIKE THIS.
MEH. I GOT NO CURVES.
Stop treating my body like a toy!
You suck.
Urgh!
Wait, it's your body!
THIS ISN'T GOOD ENOUGH!

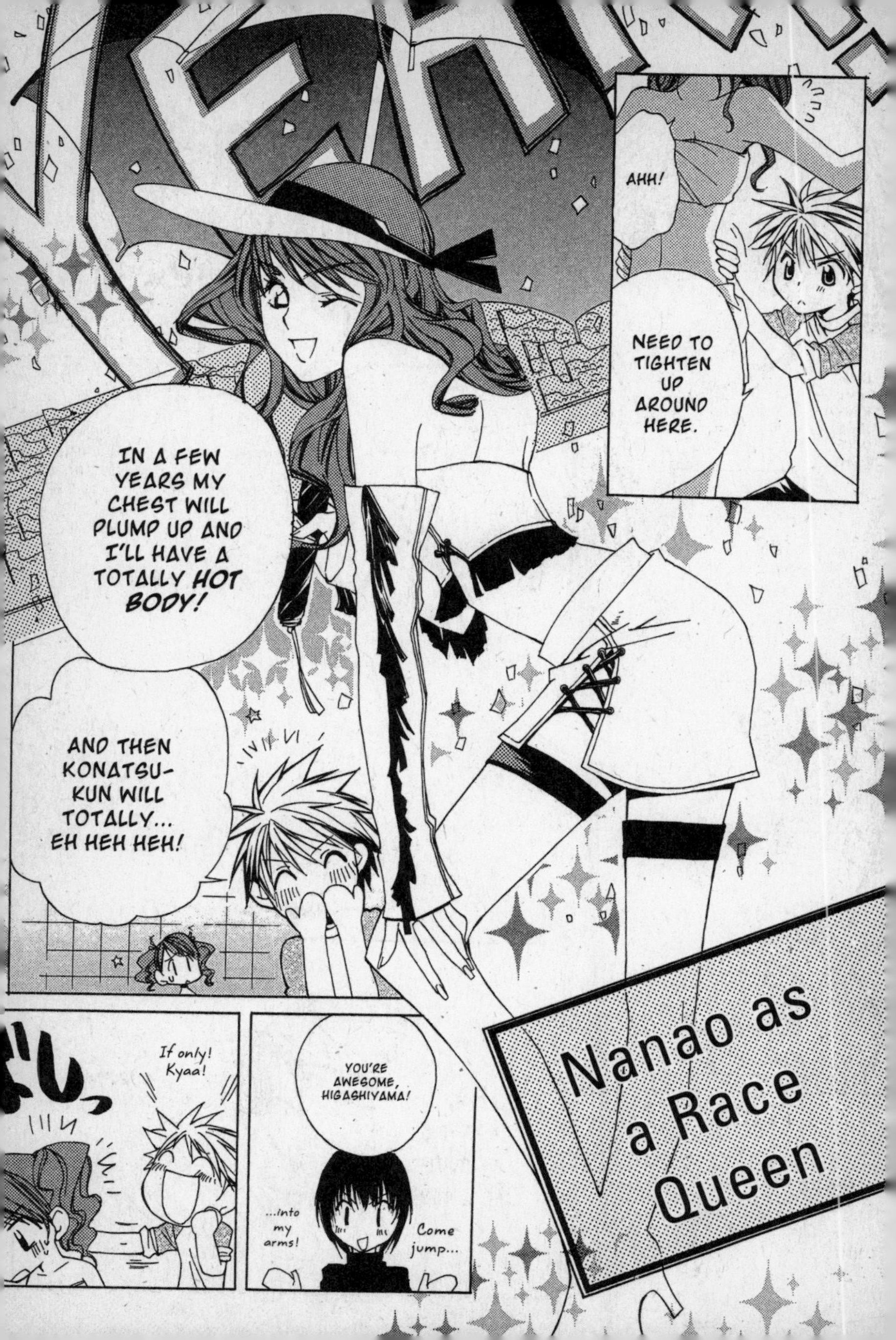
AHH!
NEED TO TIGHTEN UP AROUND HERE.
IN A FEW YEARS MY CHEST WILL PLUMP UP AND I'LL HAVE A TOTALLY HOT BODY!
AND THEN KONATSU-KUN WILL TOTALLY... EH HEH HEH!
Nanao as a Race Queen
YOU'RE AWESOME, HIGASHIYAMA!
Come jump...
...into my arms!
If only! Kyaa!

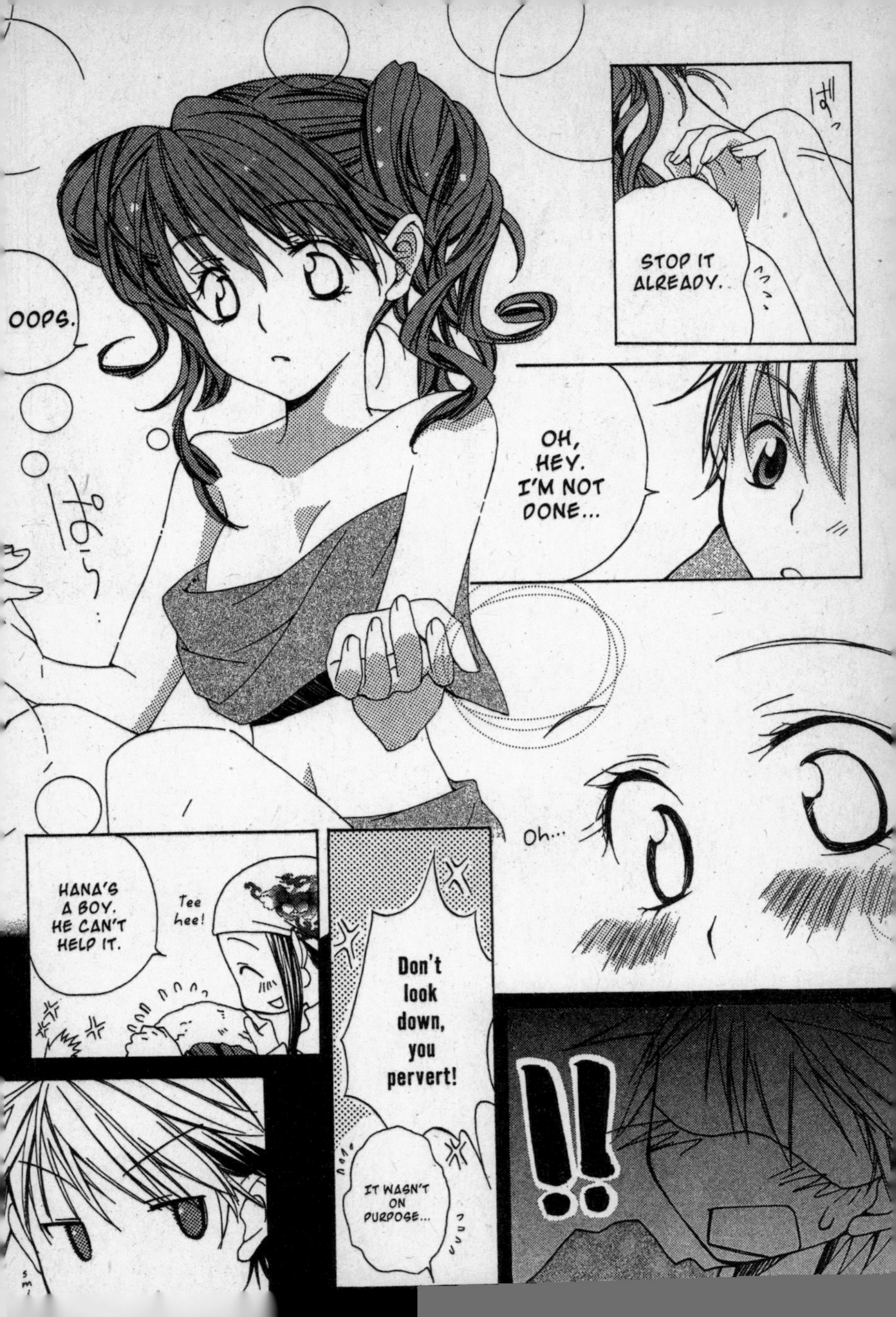
STOP IT ALREADY...
OH, HEY. I'M NOT DONE...
Oh...
OOPS.
!!
Don't look down, you pervert!
IT WASN'T ON PURPOSE...
HANA'S A BOY. HE CAN'T HELP IT.
Tee hee!

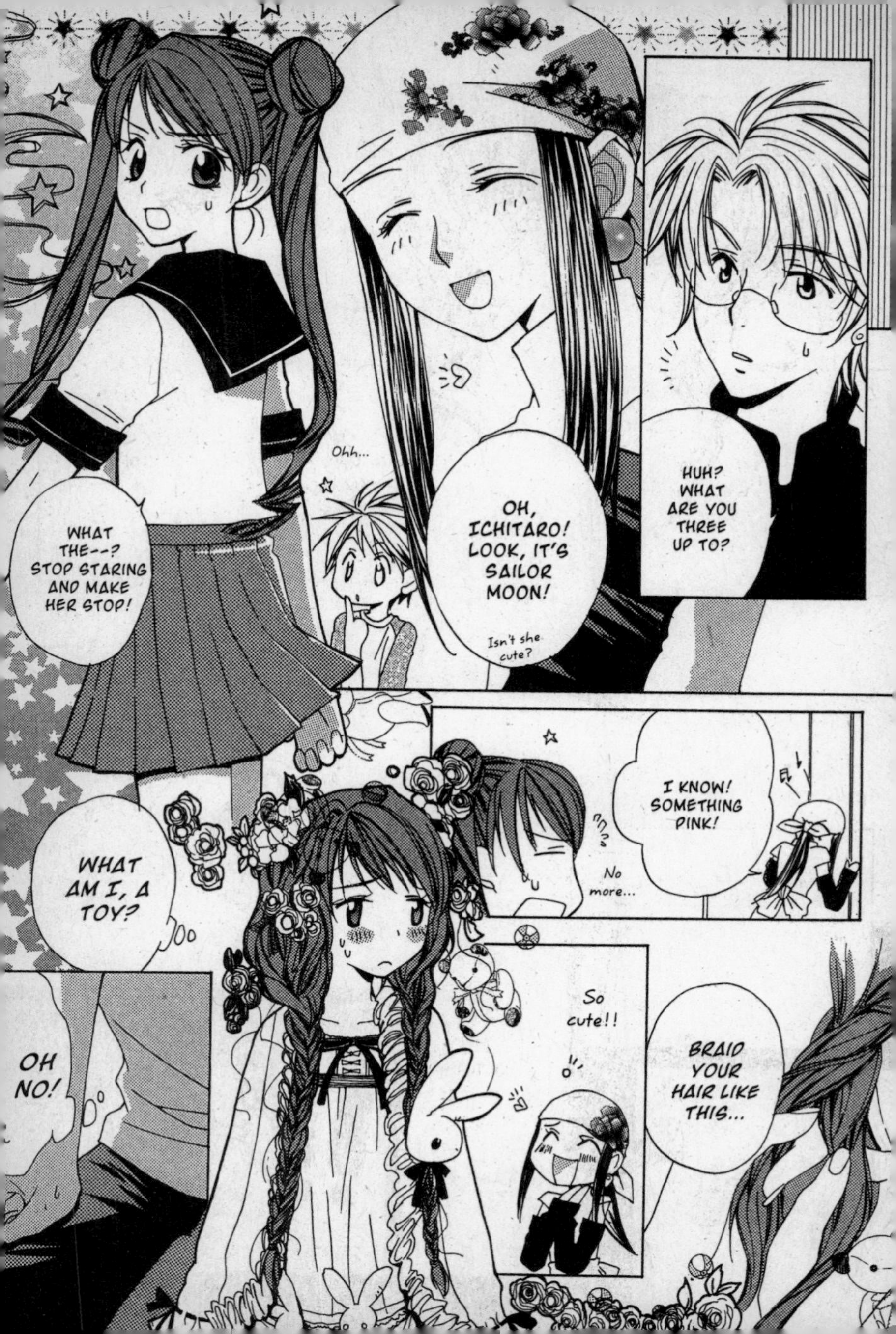
HUH? WHAT ARE YOU THREE UP TO?
OH, ICHITARO! LOOK, IT'S SAILOR MOON!
Isn't she cute?
Ohh...
WHAT THE--? STOP STARING AND MAKE HER STOP!
I KNOW! SOMETHING PINK!
No more...
WHAT AM I, A TOY?
BRAID YOUR HAIR LIKE THIS...
So cute!!
OH NO!

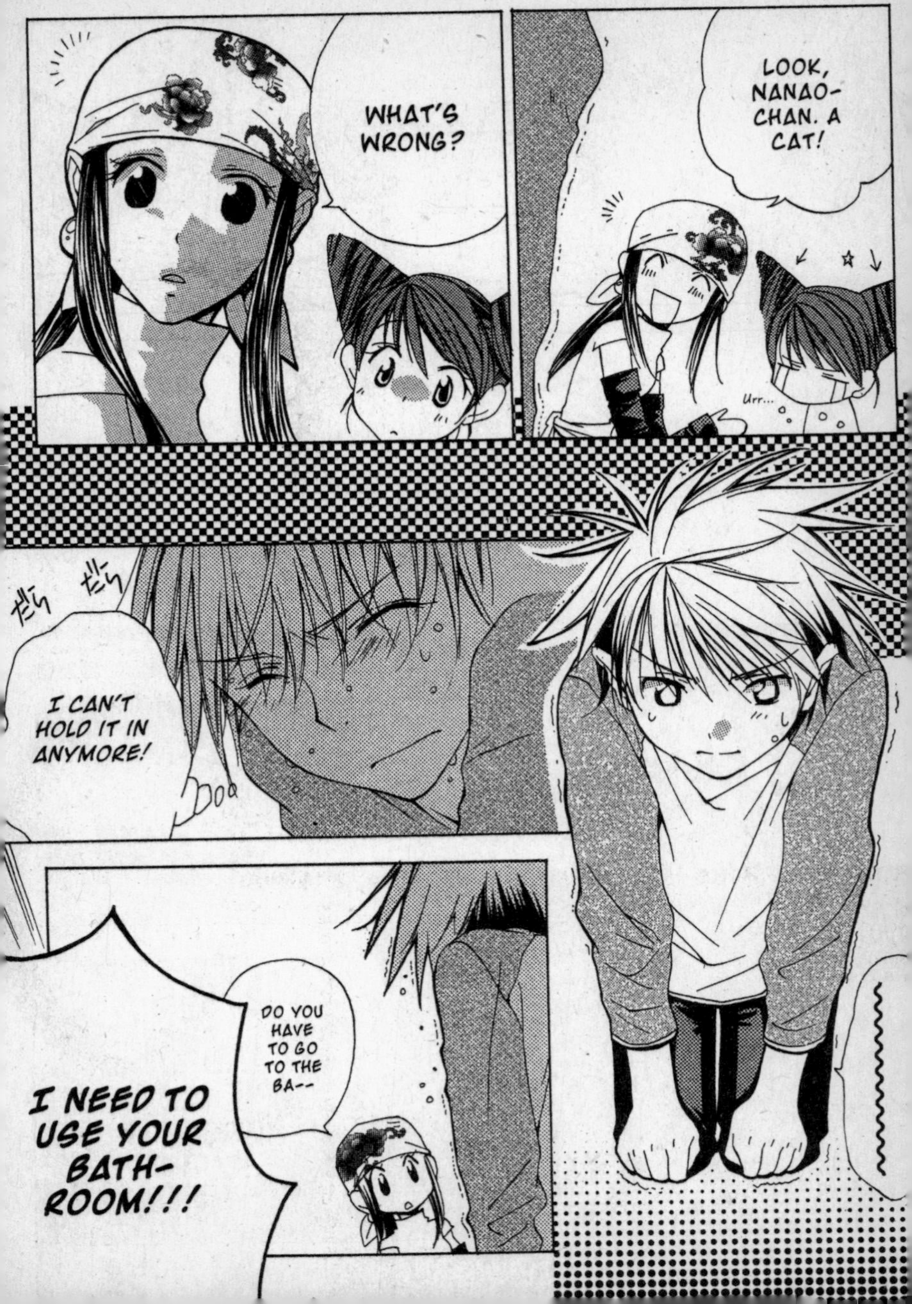
LOOK, NANAO-CHAN. A CAT!
Urr...
WHAT'S WRONG?
I CAN'T HOLD IT IN ANYMORE!
DO YOU HAVE TO GO TO THE BA--
I NEED TO USE YOUR BATH-ROOM!!!

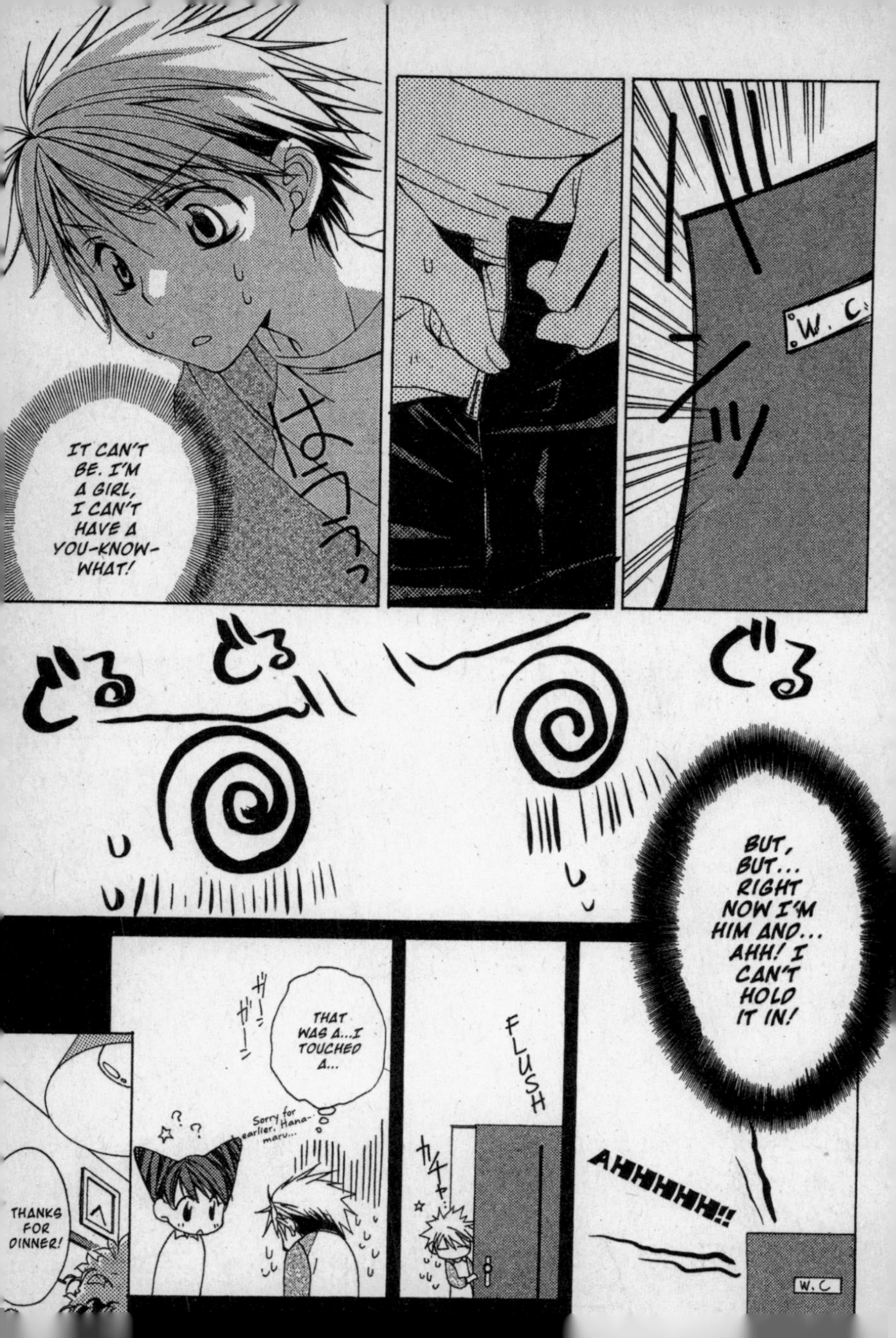
W. C
IT CAN'T BE. I'M A GIRL, I CAN'T HAVE A YOU-KNOW-WHAT!
BUT, BUT... RIGHT NOW I'M HIM AND... AHH! I CAN'T HOLD IT IN!
AHHHHHH!!
W. C
FLUSH
THAT WAS A...I TOUCHED A...
Sorry for earlier, Hana-maru...
THANKS FOR DINNER!

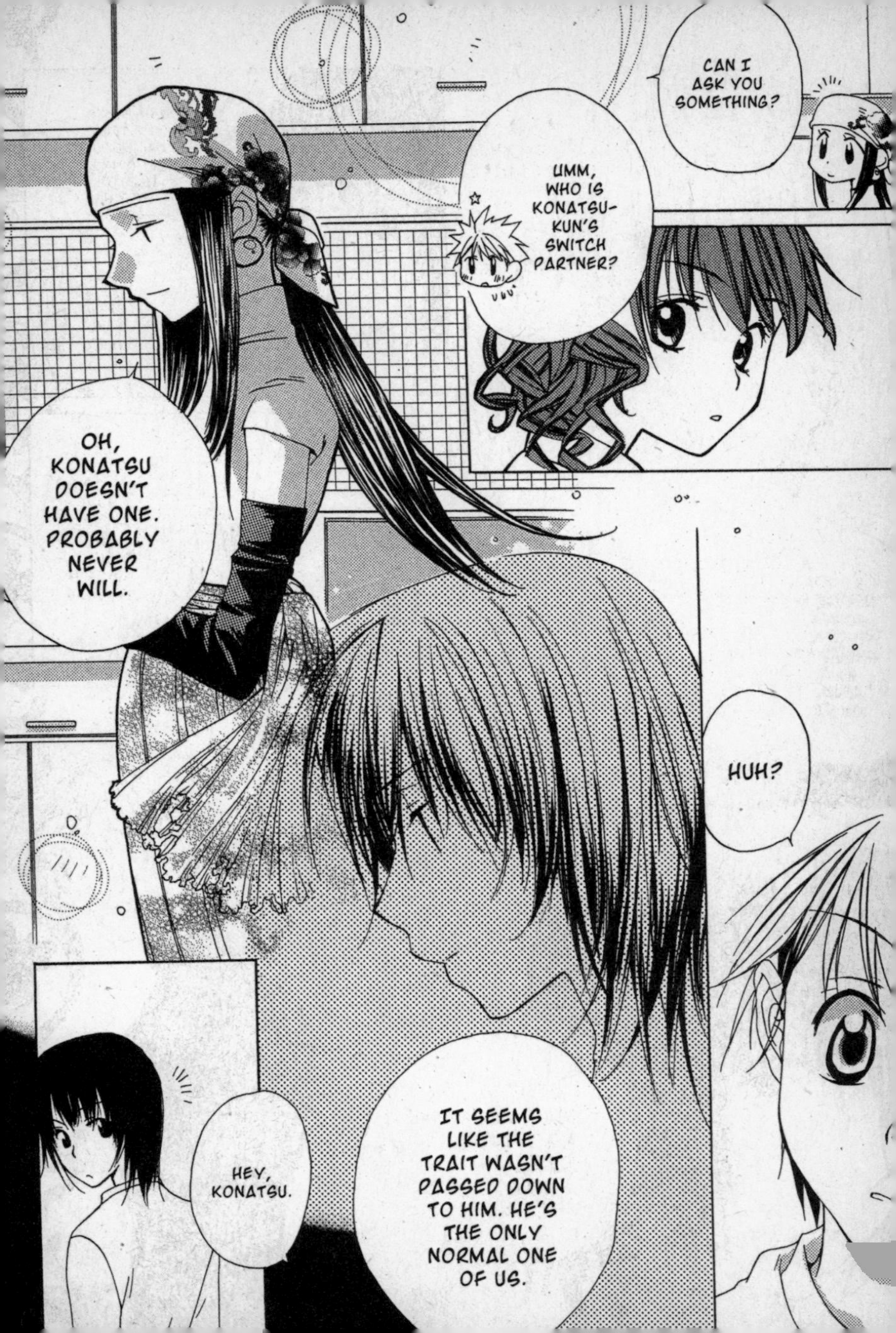
CAN I ASK YOU SOMETHING?
UMM, WHO IS KONATSU-KUN'S SWITCH PARTNER?
OH, KONATSU DOESN'T HAVE ONE. PROBABLY NEVER WILL.
HUH?
IT SEEMS LIKE THE TRAIT WASN'T PASSED DOWN TO HIM. HE'S THE ONLY NORMAL ONE OF US.
HEY, KONATSU.

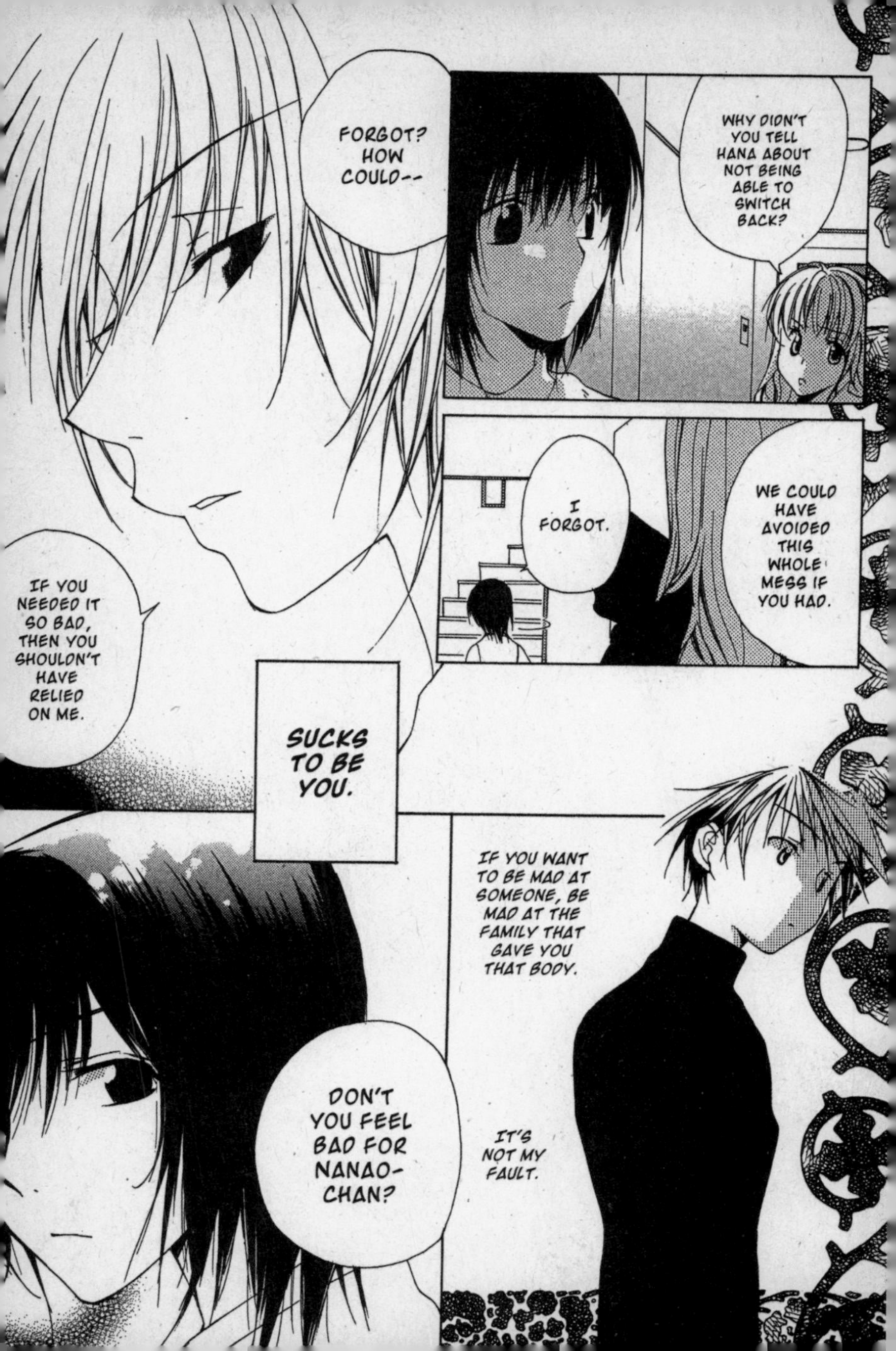
WHY DIDN'T YOU TELL HANA ABOUT NOT BEING ABLE TO SWITCH BACK?
WE COULD HAVE AVOIDED THIS WHOLE MESS IF YOU HAD.
I FORGOT.
FORGOT? HOW COULD--
IF YOU NEEDED IT SO BAD, THEN YOU SHOULDN'T HAVE RELIED ON ME.
SUCKS TO BE YOU.
IF YOU WANT TO BE MAD AT SOMEONE, BE MAD AT THE FAMILY THAT GAVE YOU THAT BODY.
IT'S NOT MY FAULT.
DON'T YOU FEEL BAD FOR NANAO-CHAN?

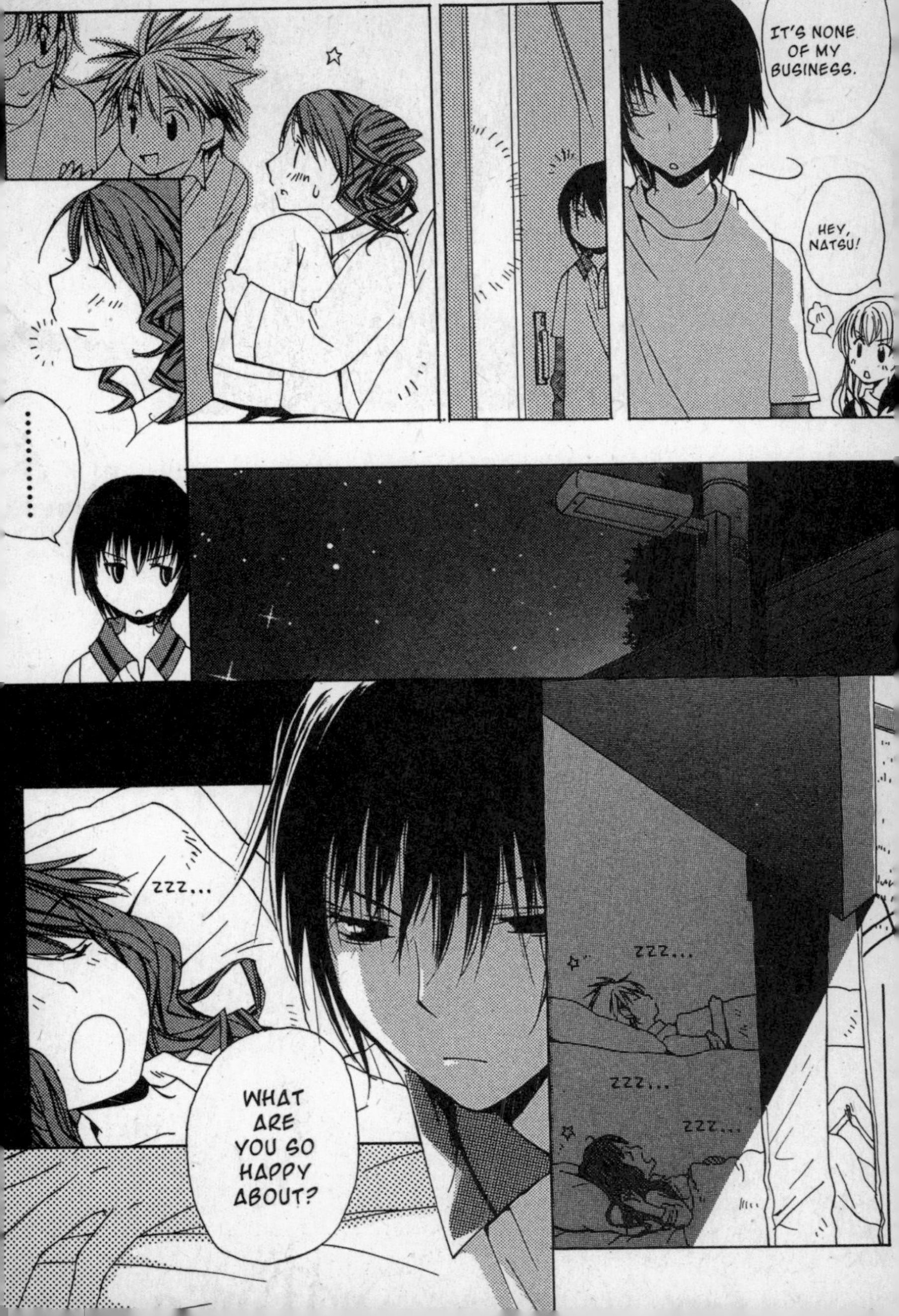
IT'S NONE OF MY BUSINESS.
HEY, NATSU!
......
ZZZ...
ZZZ...
ZZZ...
ZZZ...
WHAT ARE YOU SO HAPPY ABOUT?

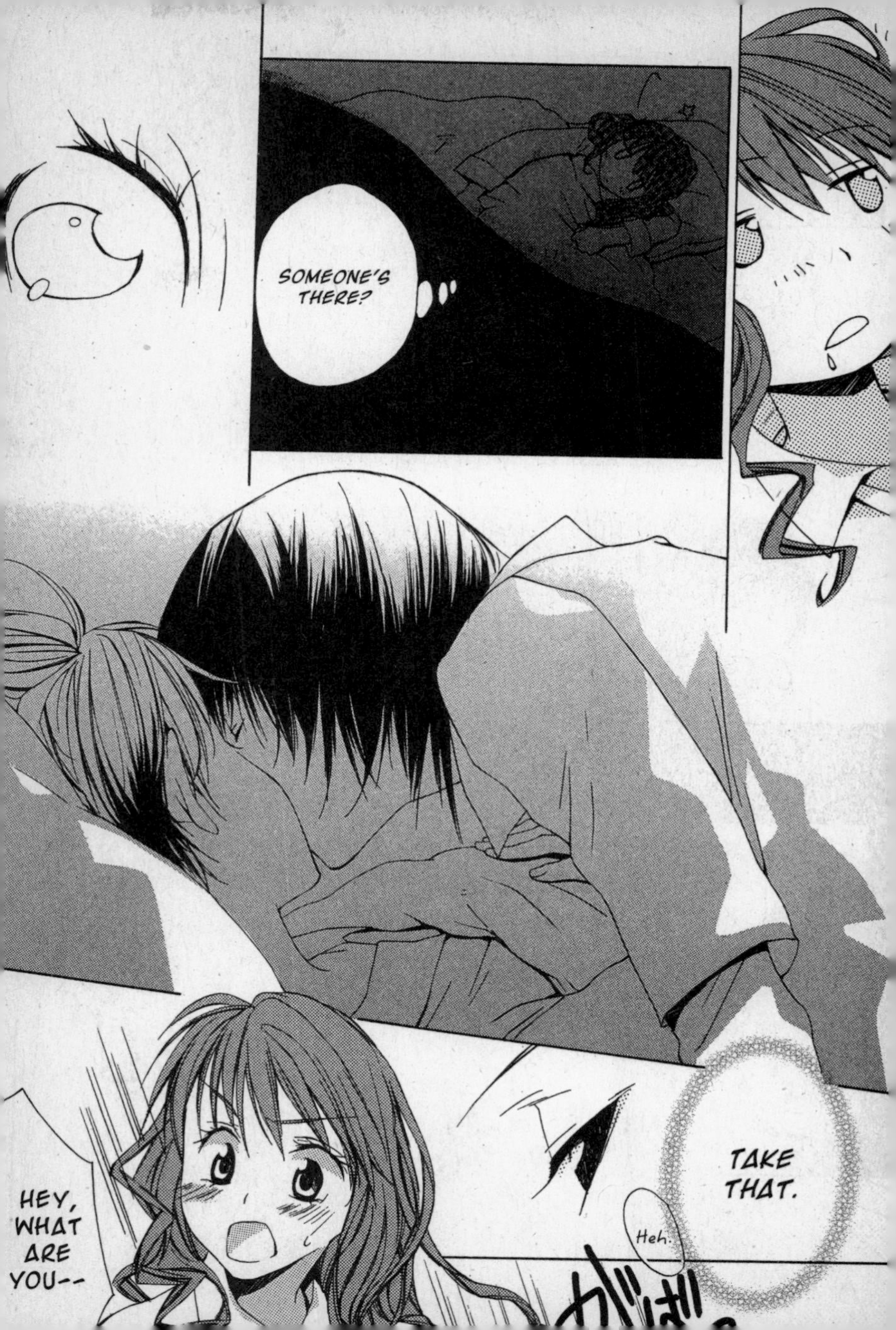
SOMEONE'S THERE?
TAKE THAT.
Heh.
HEY, WHAT ARE YOU--

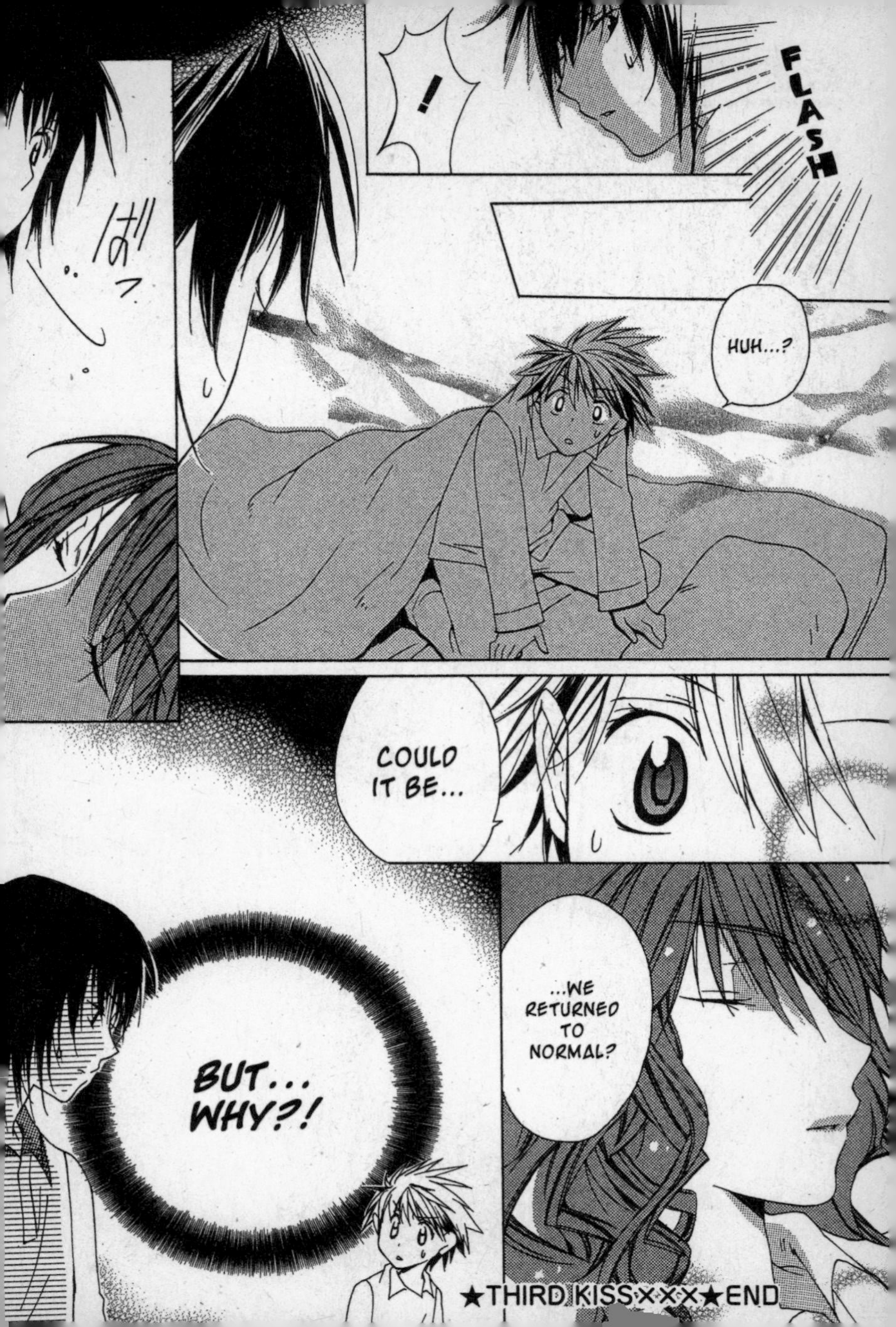
!
FLASH
ぱのっ
HUH...?
COULD IT BE...
...WE RETURNED TO NORMAL?
BUT... WHY?!
★THIRD KISS×××★END

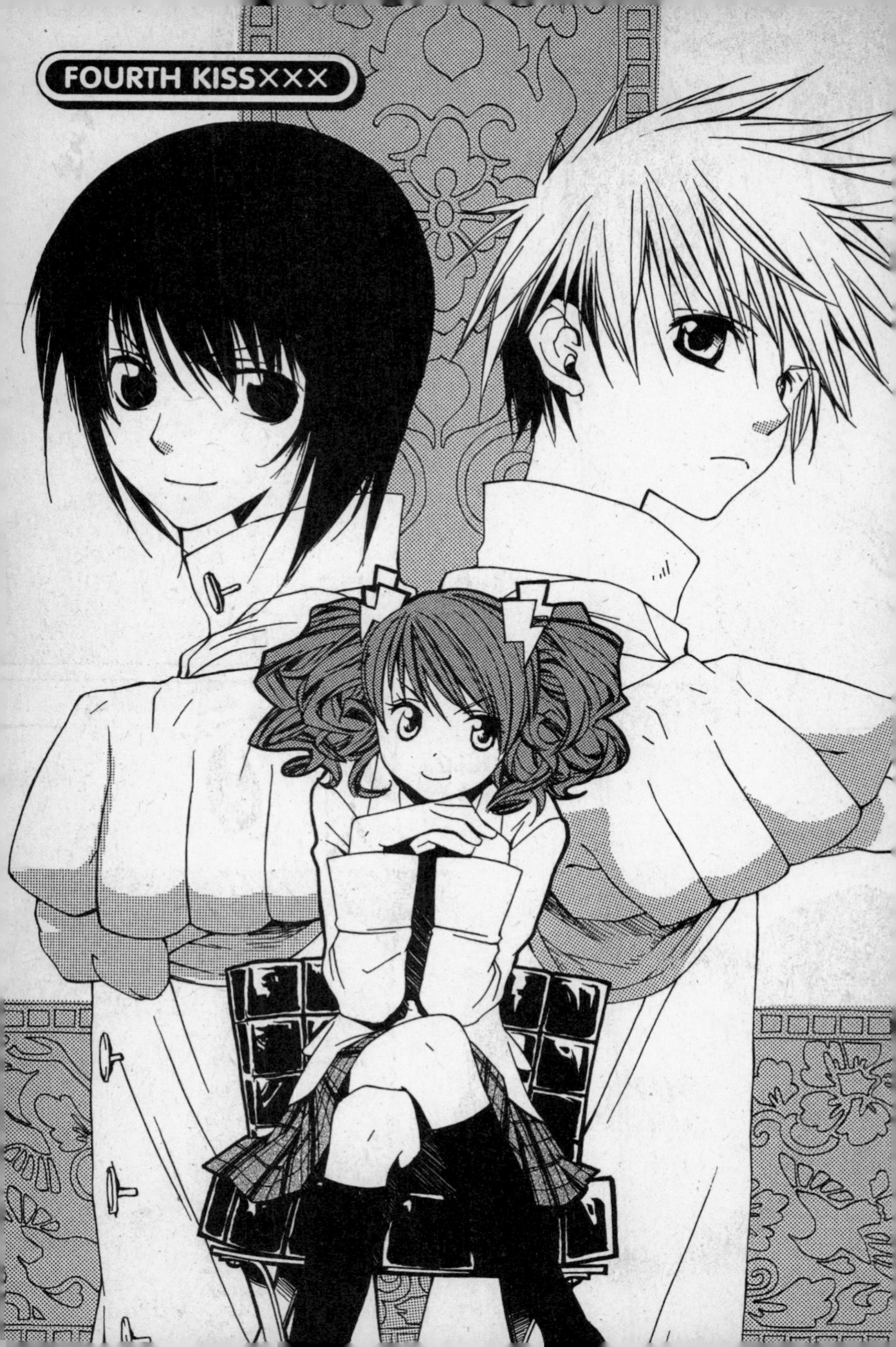
FOURTH KISS×××

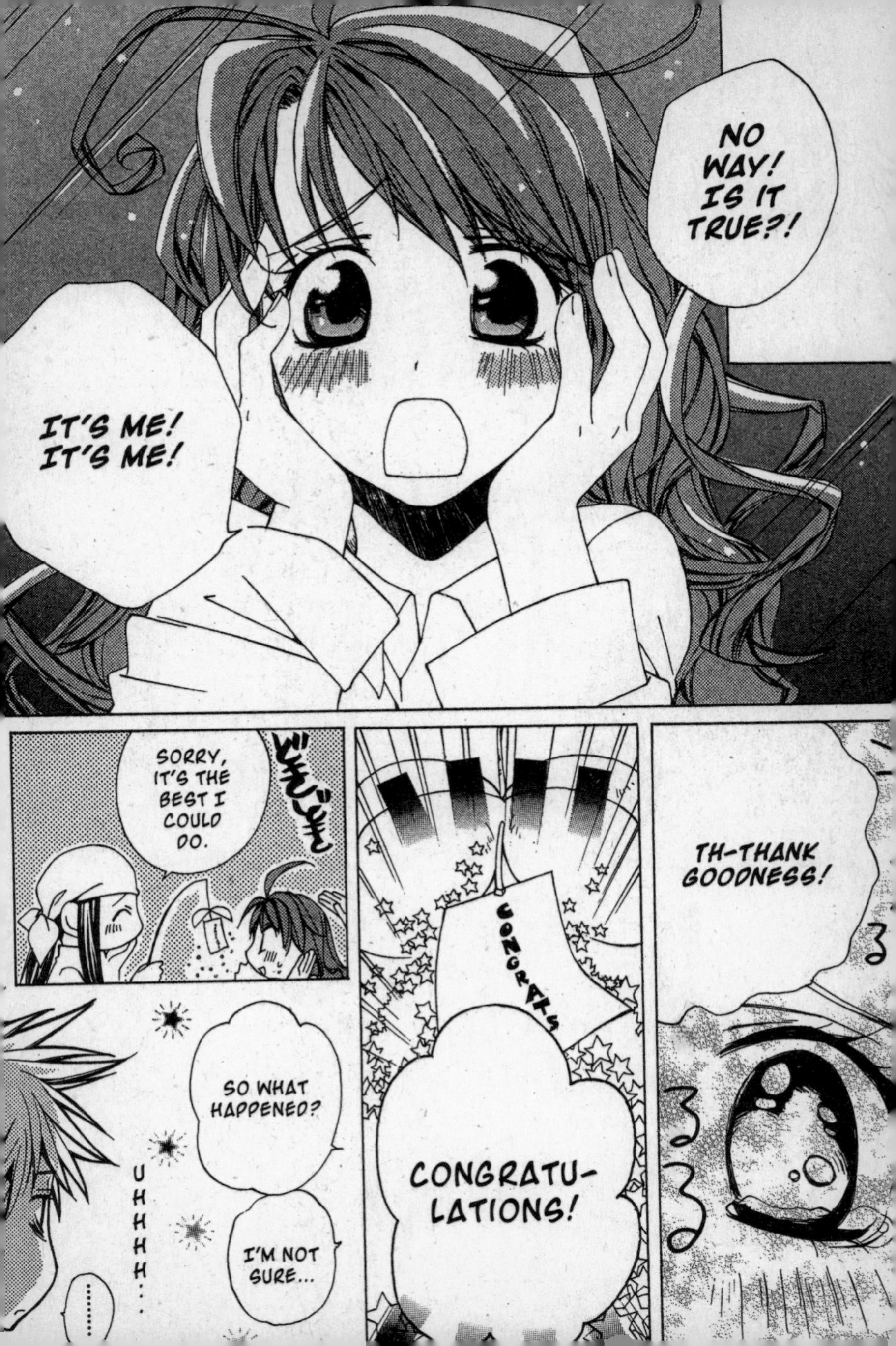
NO WAY! IS IT TRUE?!
IT'S ME! IT'S ME!
TH-THANK GOODNESS!
CONGRATS
CONGRATU-LATIONS!
SORRY, IT'S THE BEST I COULD DO.
SO WHAT HAPPENED?
I'M NOT SURE...
UHHHH...
......

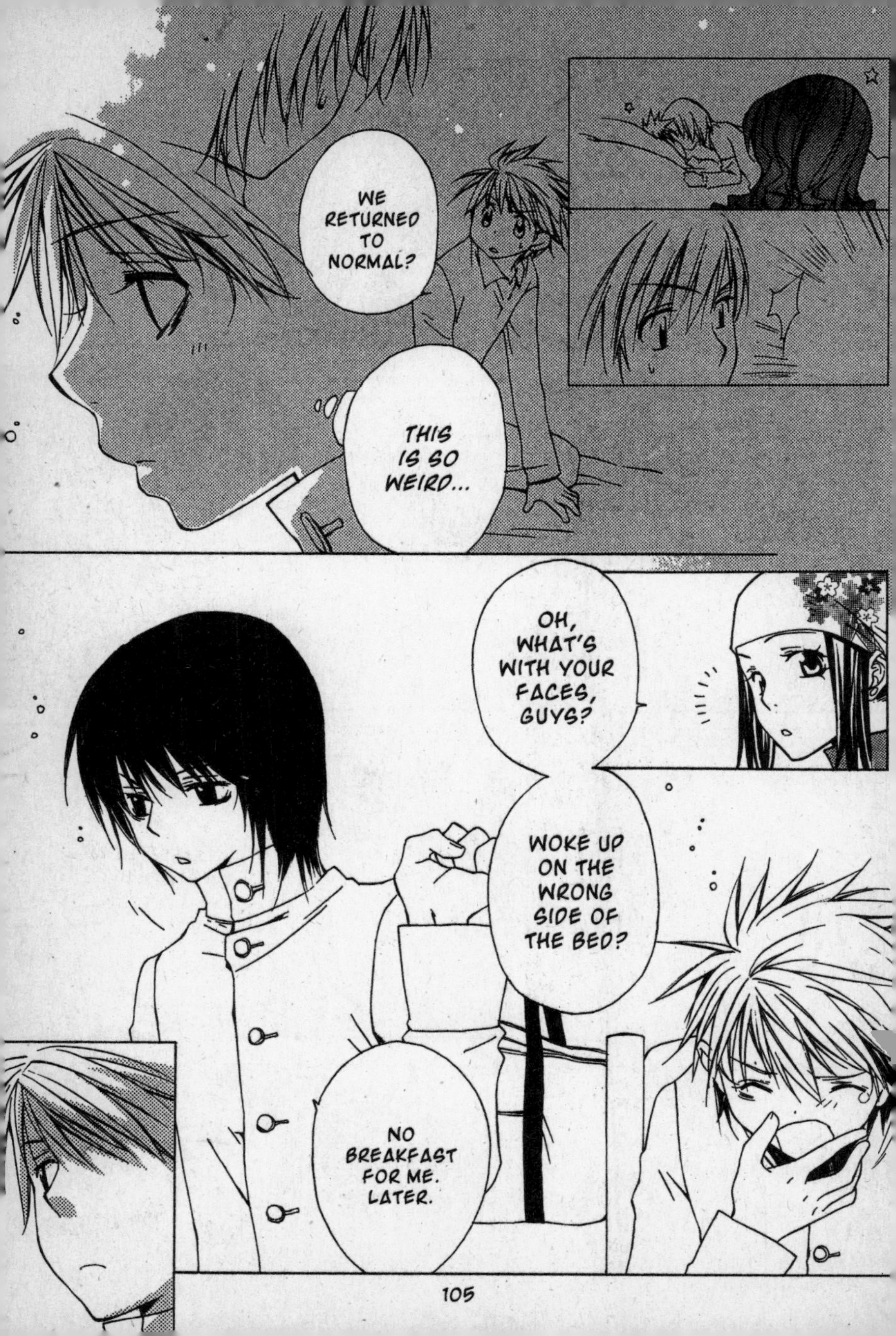
WE RETURNED TO NORMAL?
THIS IS SO WEIRD...
OH, WHAT'S WITH YOUR FACES, GUYS?
WOKE UP ON THE WRONG SIDE OF THE BED?
NO BREAKFAST FOR ME. LATER.

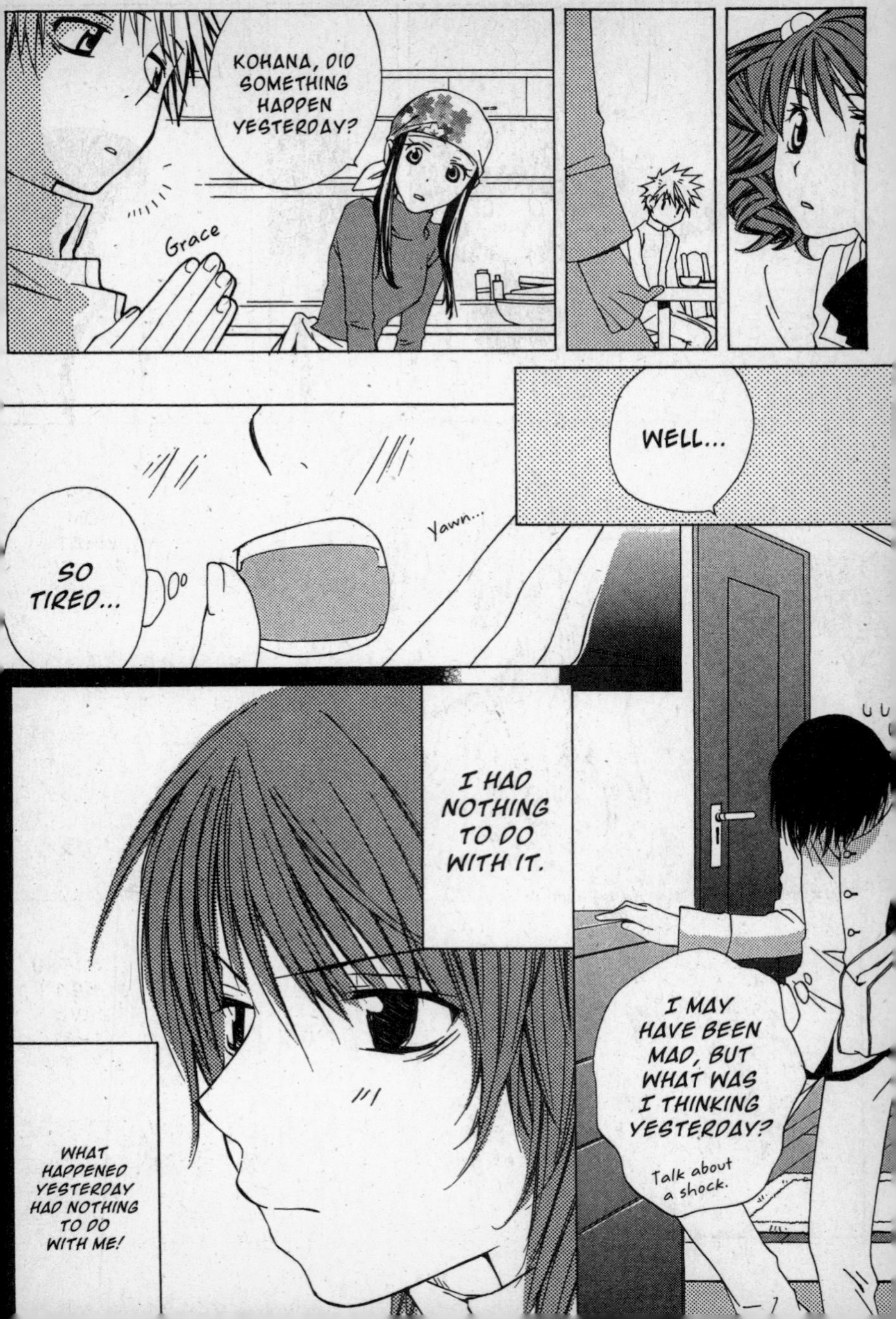
KOHANA, DID SOMETHING HAPPEN YESTERDAY?
Grace
WELL...
Yawn...
SO TIRED...
I MAY HAVE BEEN MAD, BUT WHAT WAS I THINKING YESTERDAY?
Talk about a shock.
I HAD NOTHING TO DO WITH IT.
WHAT HAPPENED YESTERDAY HAD NOTHING TO DO WITH ME!

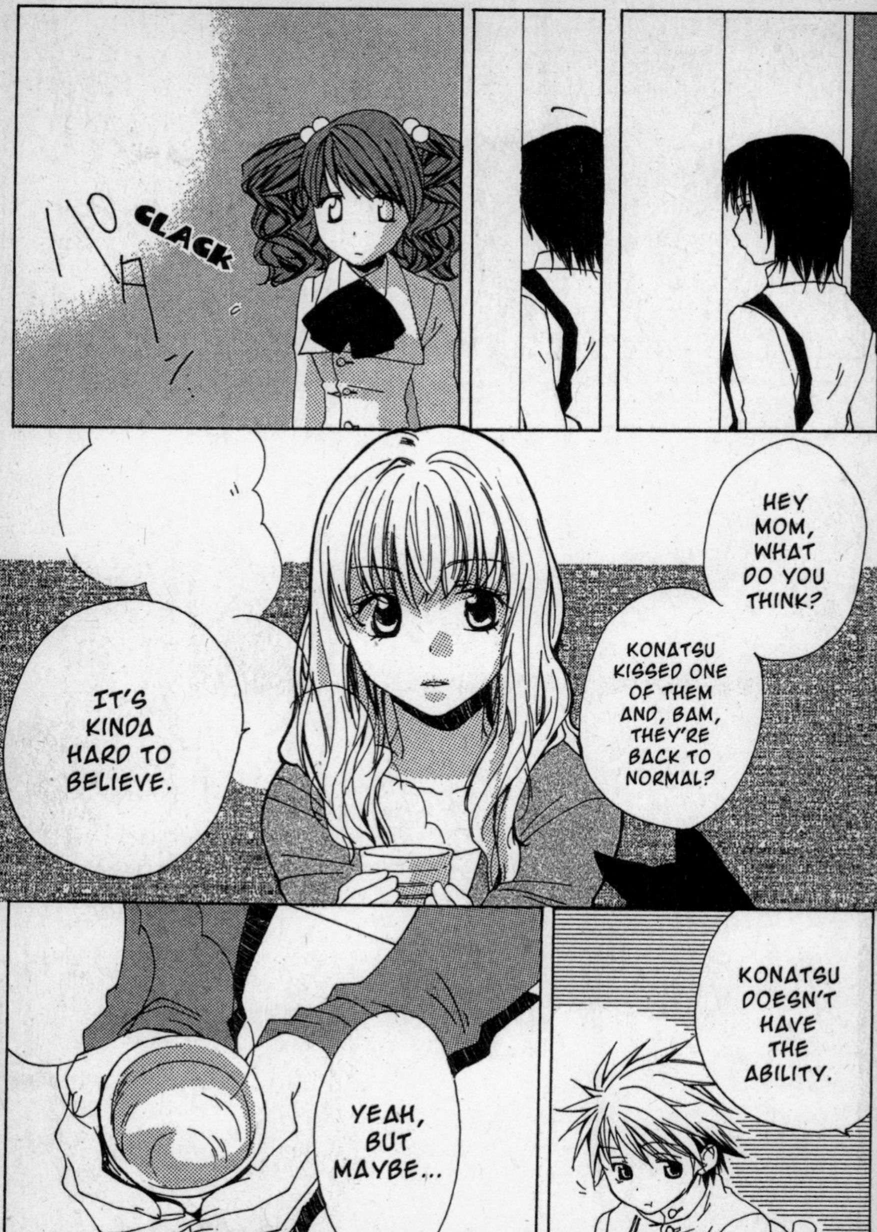
CLACK
HEY MOM, WHAT DO YOU THINK?
KONATSU KISSED ONE OF THEM AND, BAM, THEY'RE BACK TO NORMAL?
IT'S KINDA HARD TO BELIEVE.
KONATSU DOESN'T HAVE THE ABILITY.
YEAH, BUT MAYBE...

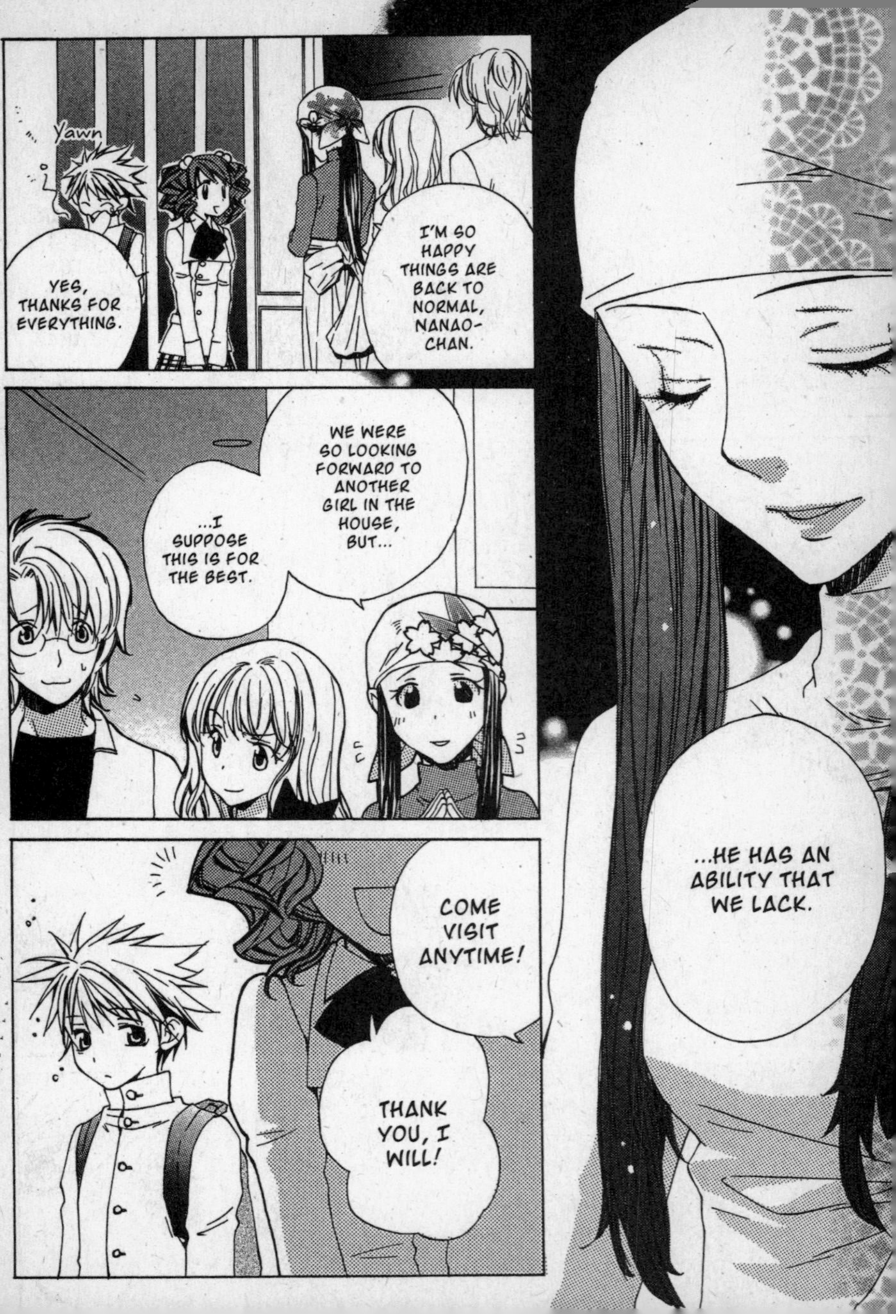
...HE HAS AN ABILITY THAT WE LACK.
I'M SO HAPPY THINGS ARE BACK TO NORMAL, NANAO-CHAN.
Yawn
YES, THANKS FOR EVERYTHING.
WE WERE SO LOOKING FORWARD TO ANOTHER GIRL IN THE HOUSE, BUT...
...I SUPPOSE THIS IS FOR THE BEST.
COME VISIT ANYTIME!
THANK YOU, I WILL!

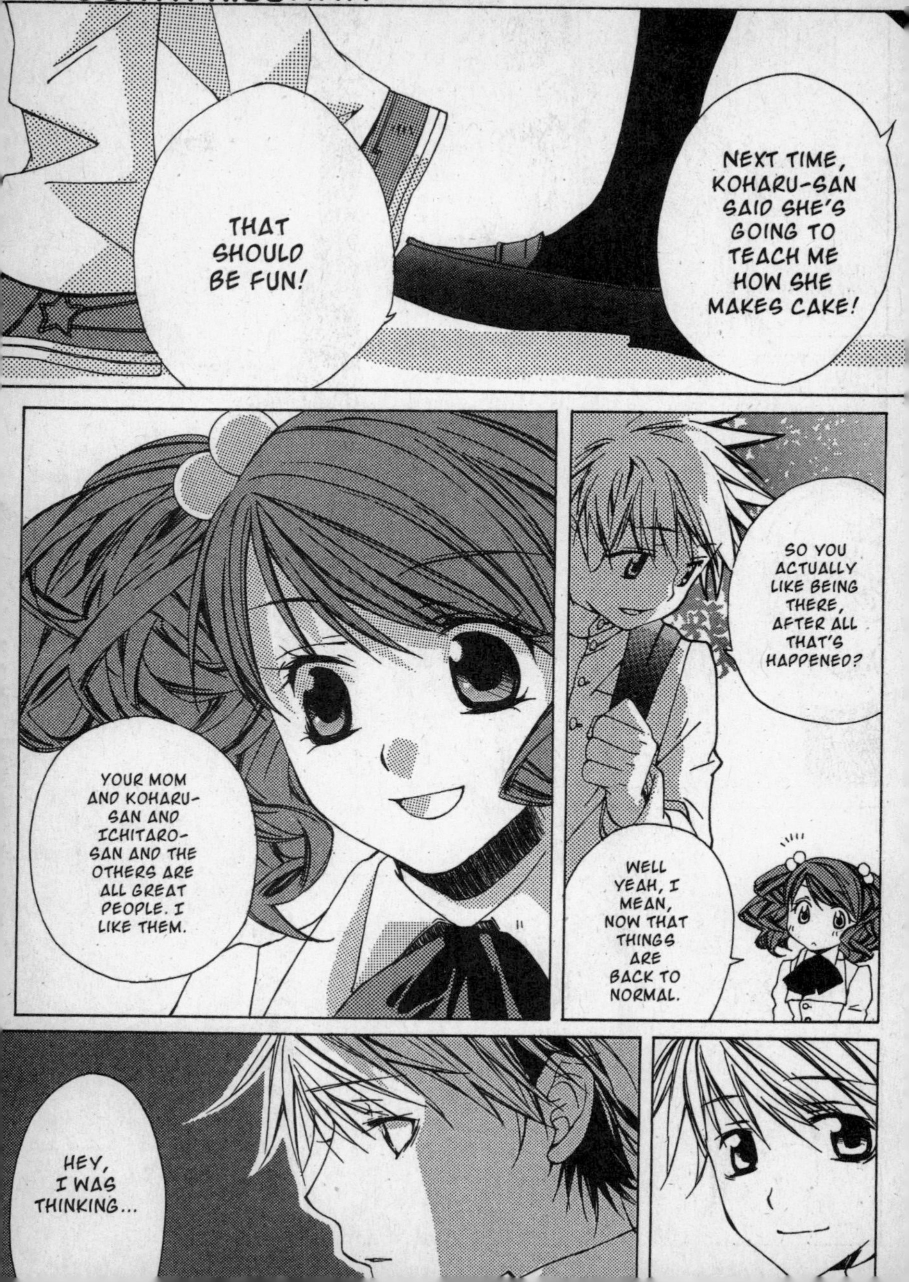
NEXT TIME, KOHARU-SAN SAID SHE'S GOING TO TEACH ME HOW SHE MAKES CAKE!
THAT SHOULD BE FUN!
SO YOU ACTUALLY LIKE BEING THERE, AFTER ALL THAT'S HAPPENED?
WELL YEAH, I MEAN, NOW THAT THINGS ARE BACK TO NORMAL.
YOUR MOM AND KOHARU-SAN AND ICHITARO-SAN AND THE OTHERS ARE ALL GREAT PEOPLE. I LIKE THEM.
HEY, I WAS THINKING...

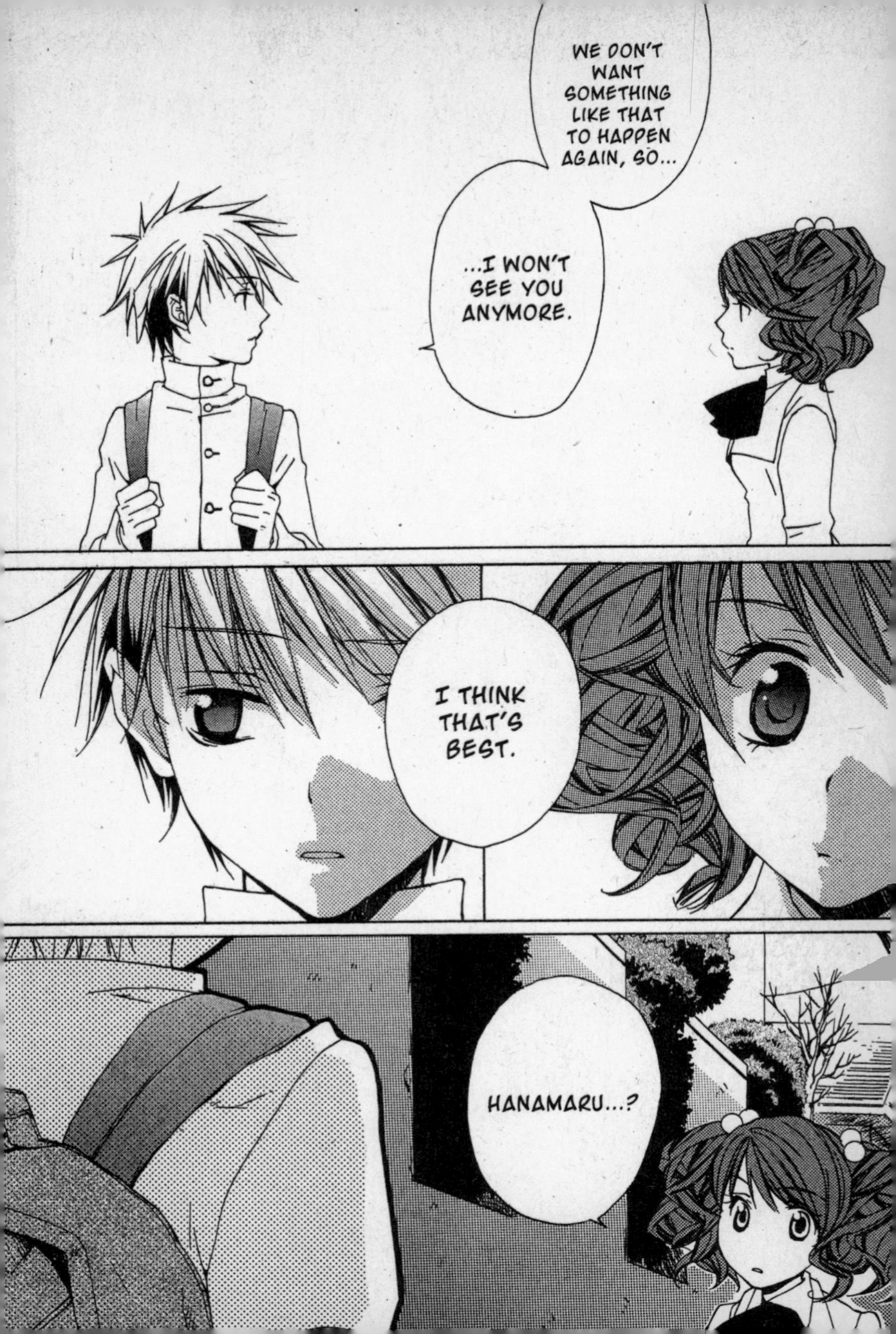
WE DON'T WANT SOMETHING LIKE THAT TO HAPPEN AGAIN, SO...
...I WON'T SEE YOU ANYMORE.
I THINK THAT'S BEST.
HANAMARU...?

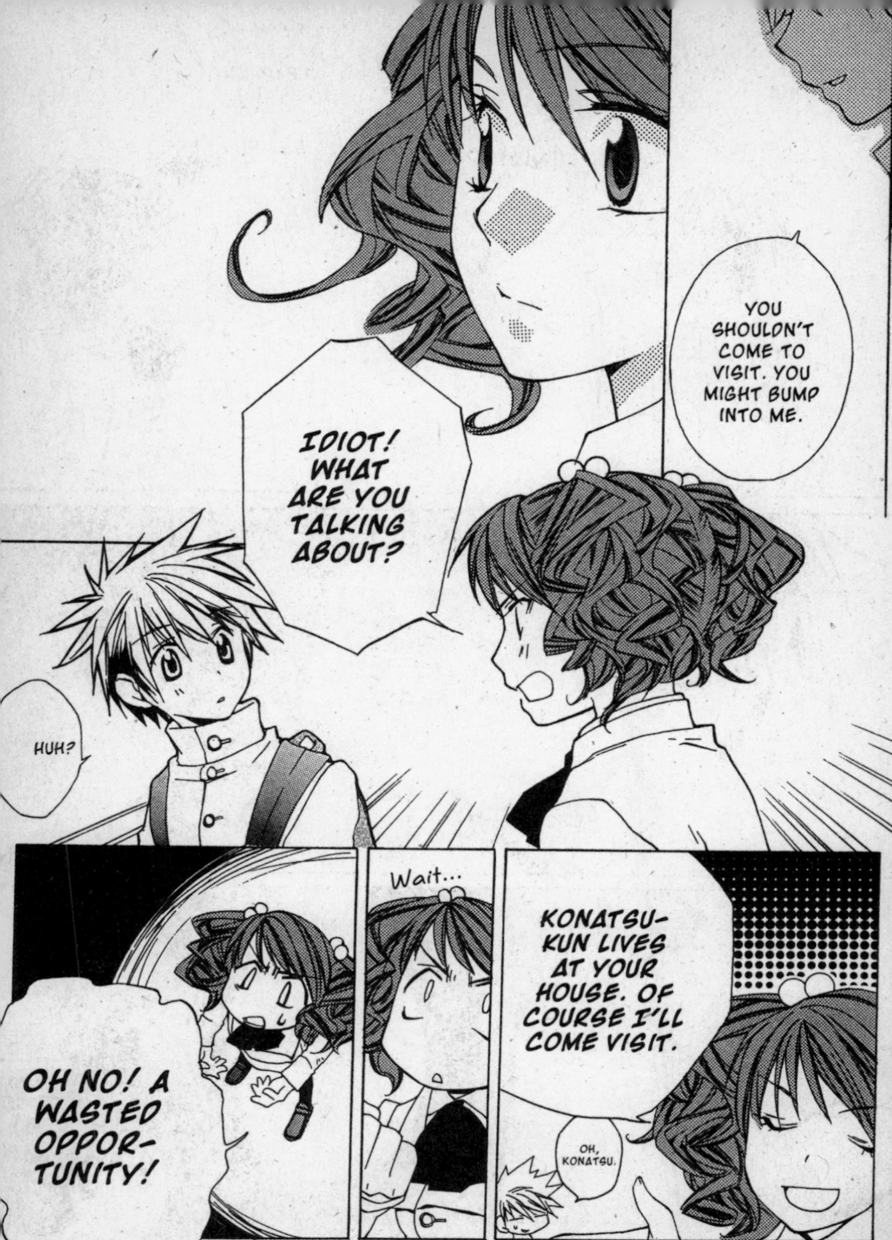
YOU SHOULDN'T COME TO VISIT. YOU MIGHT BUMP INTO ME.
IDIOT! WHAT ARE YOU TALKING ABOUT?
HUH?
KONATSU-KUN LIVES AT YOUR HOUSE. OF COURSE I'LL COME VISIT.
OH, KONATSU.
Wait...
OH NO! A WASTED OPPOR-TUNITY!

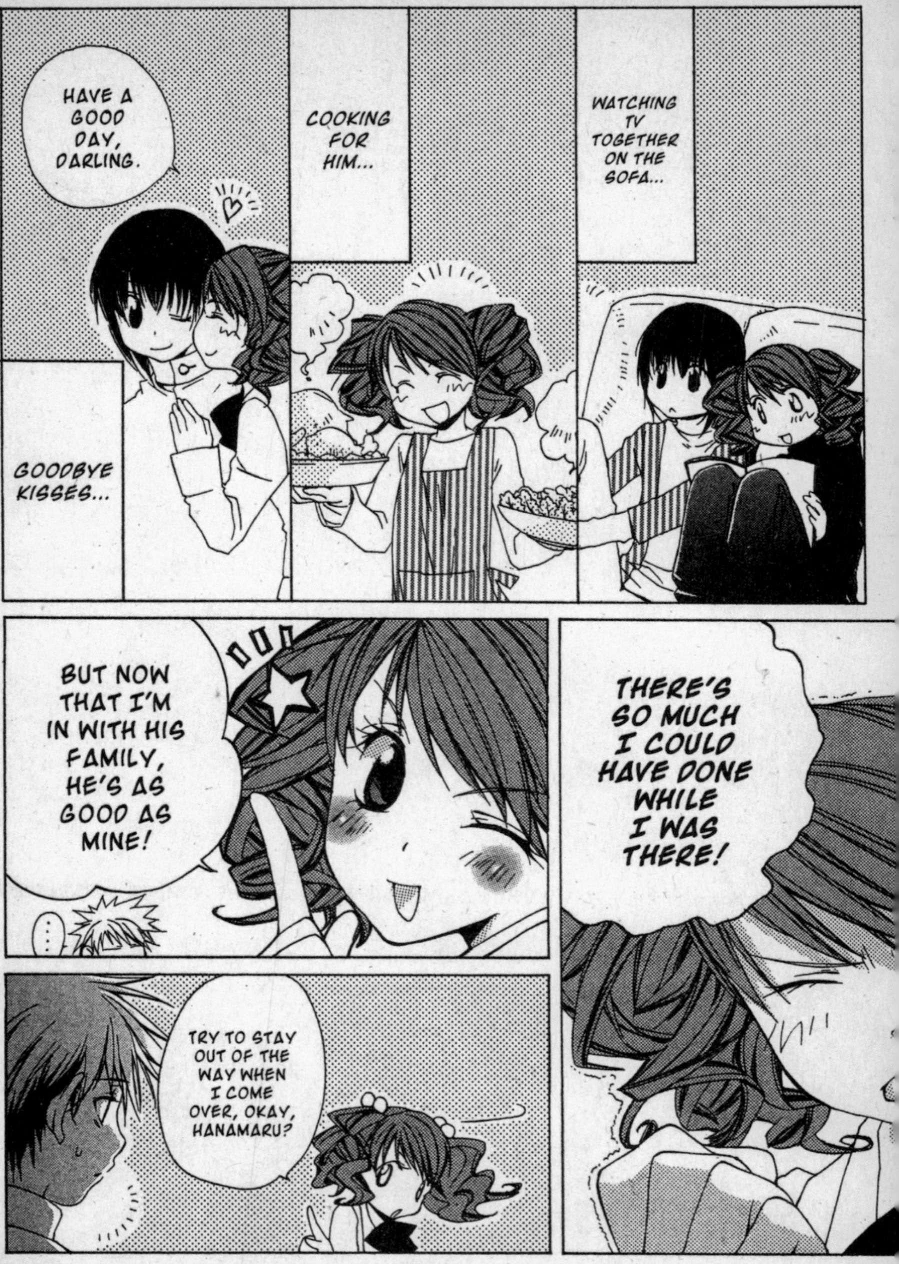
WATCHING TV TOGETHER ON THE SOFA...
COOKING FOR HIM...
HAVE A GOOD DAY, DARLING.
GOODBYE KISSES...
THERE'S SO MUCH I COULD HAVE DONE WHILE I WAS THERE!
BUT NOW THAT I'M IN WITH HIS FAMILY, HE'S AS GOOD AS MINE!
...
TRY TO STAY OUT OF THE WAY WHEN I COME OVER, OKAY, HANAMARU?

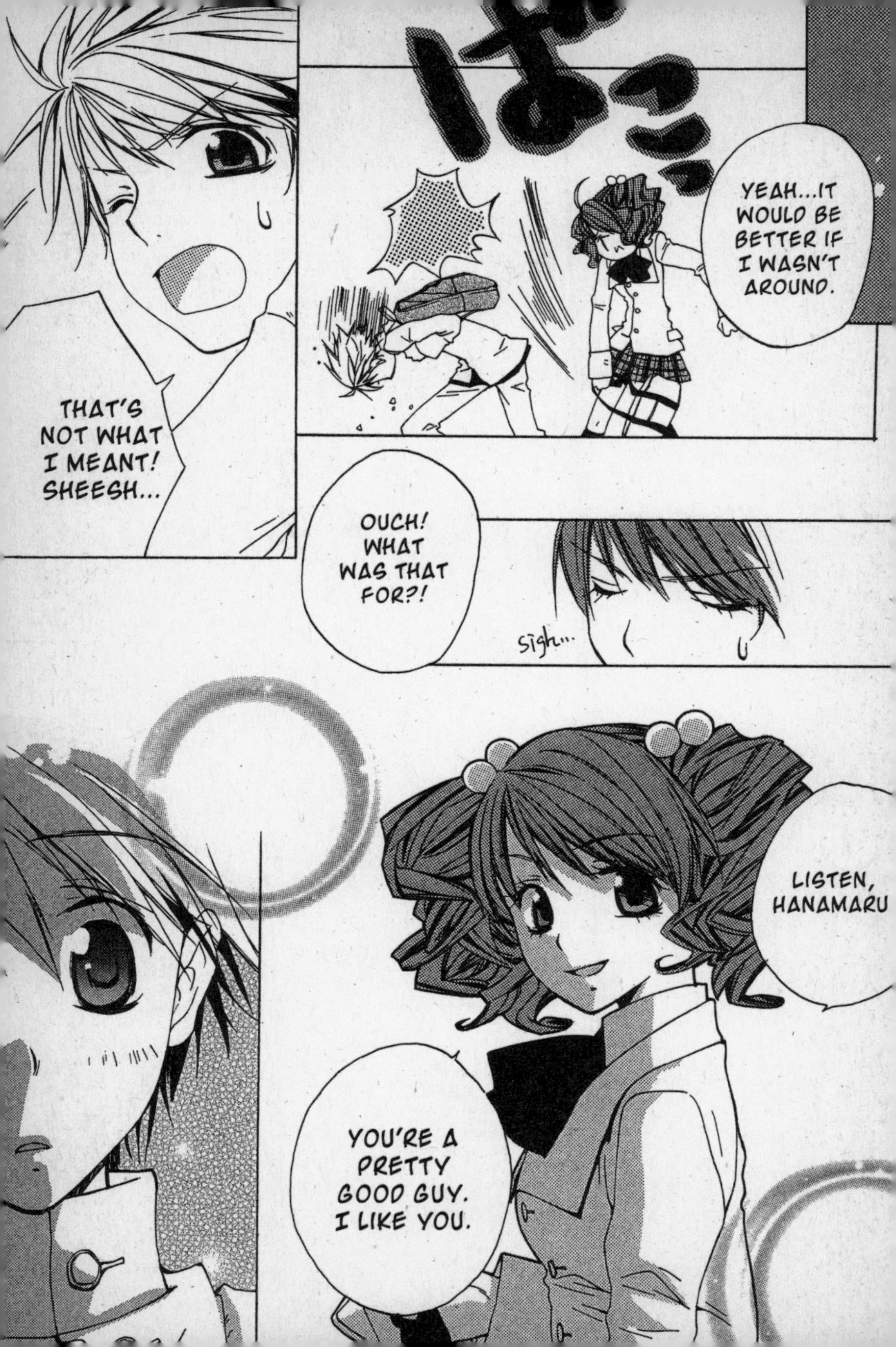

ぼこっ
YEAH...IT WOULD BE BETTER IF I WASN'T AROUND.
OUCH! WHAT WAS THAT FOR?!
Sigh...
THAT'S NOT WHAT I MEANT! SHEESH...
LISTEN, HANAMARU
YOU'RE A PRETTY GOOD GUY. I LIKE YOU.

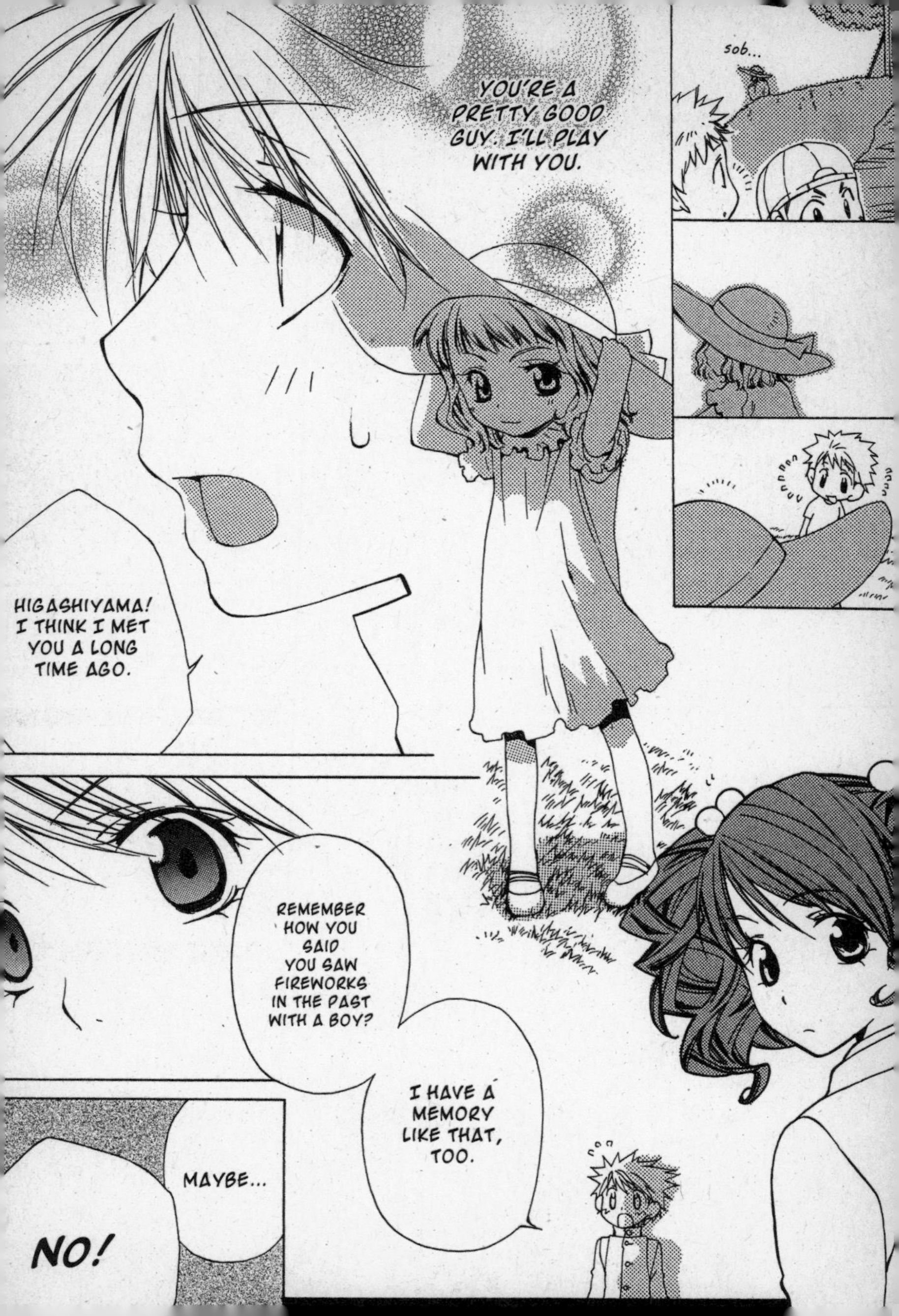

sob...
YOU'RE A PRETTY GOOD GUY. I'LL PLAY WITH YOU.
HIGASHIYAMA! I THINK I MET YOU A LONG TIME AGO.
REMEMBER HOW YOU SAID YOU SAW FIREWORKS IN THE PAST WITH A BOY?
I HAVE A MEMORY LIKE THAT, TOO.
MAYBE...
NO!

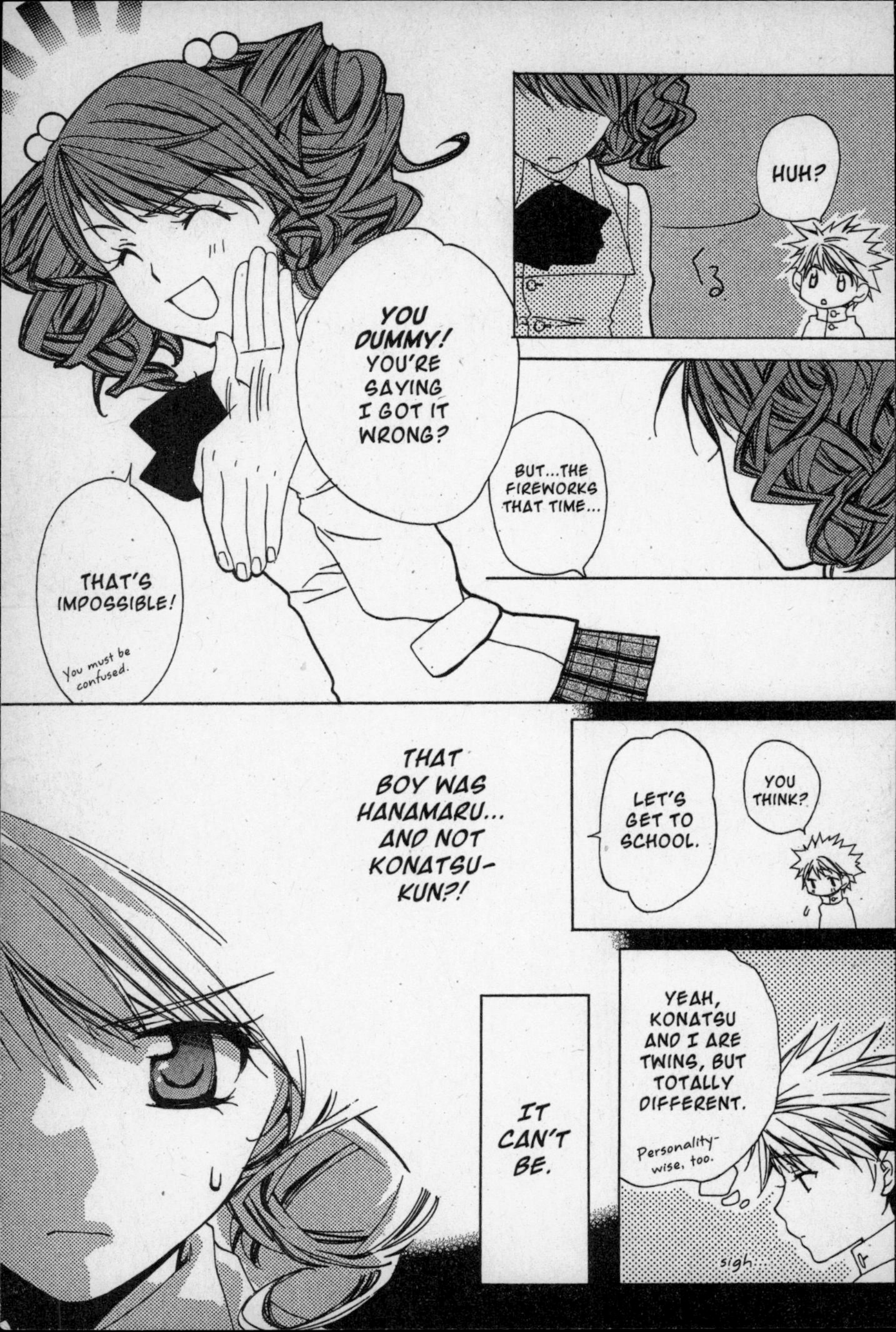
HUH?
BUT...THE FIREWORKS THAT TIME...
YOU DUMMY! YOU'RE SAYING I GOT IT WRONG?
THAT'S IMPOSSIBLE!
You must be confused.
YOU THINK?
LET'S GET TO SCHOOL.
YEAH, KONATSU AND I ARE TWINS, BUT TOTALLY DIFFERENT.
Personality-wise, too.
sigh
THAT BOY WAS HANAMARU... AND NOT KONATSU-KUN?!
IT CAN'T BE.

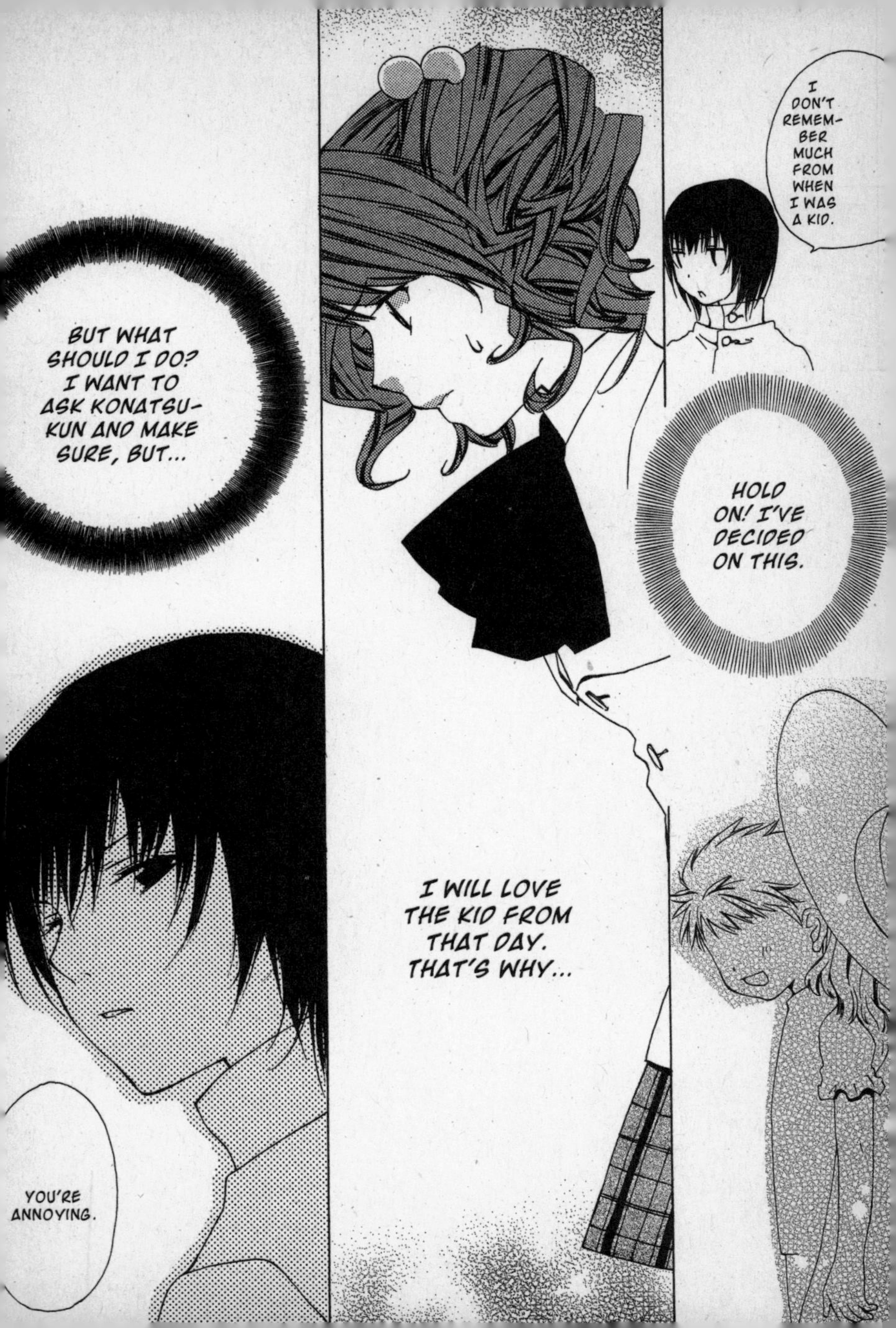
I DON'T REMEMBER MUCH FROM WHEN I WAS A KID.
HOLD ON! I'VE DECIDED ON THIS.
I WILL LOVE THE KID FROM THAT DAY. THAT'S WHY...
BUT WHAT SHOULD I DO? I WANT TO ASK KONATSU-KUN AND MAKE SURE, BUT...
YOU'RE ANNOYING.

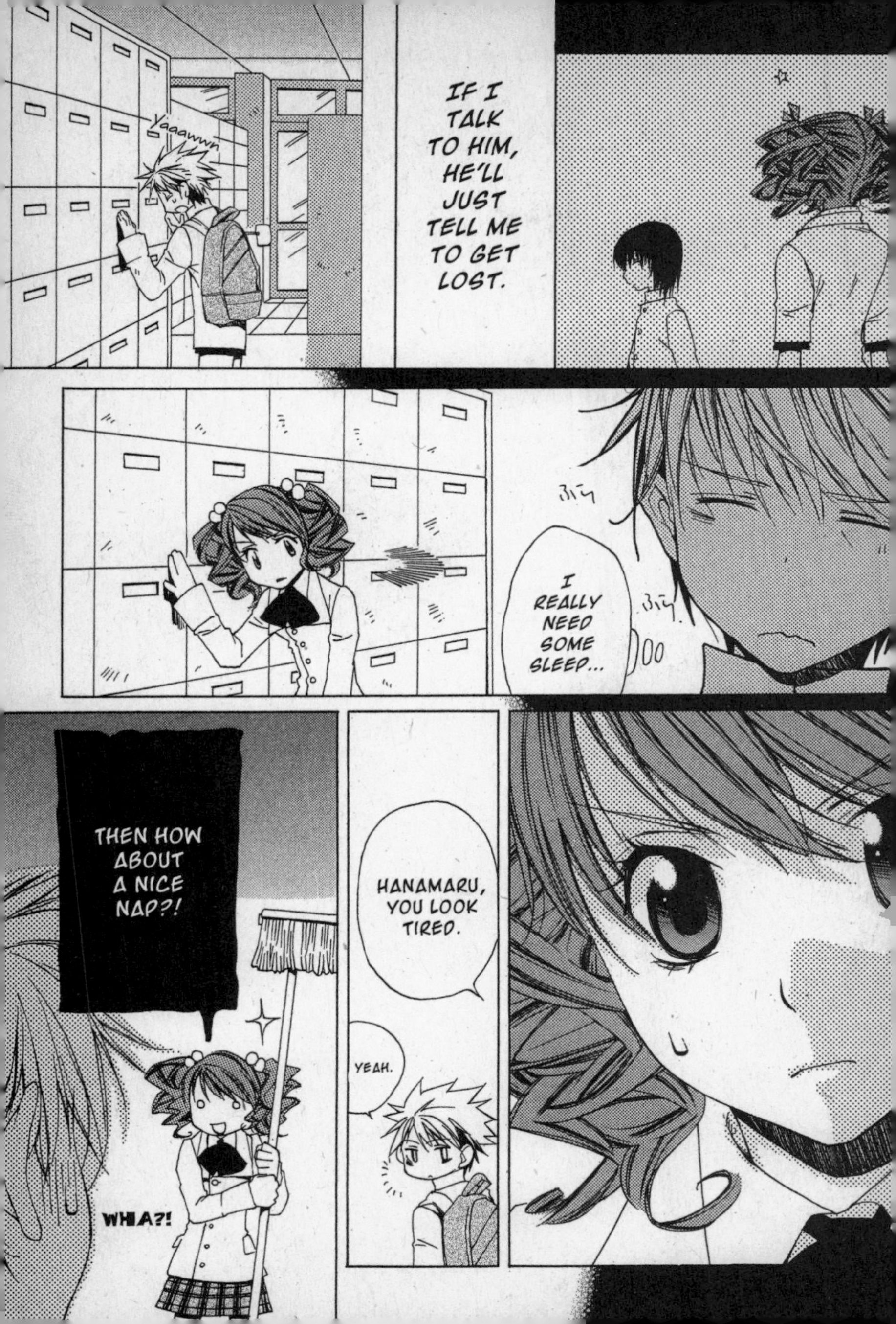
IF I TALK TO HIM, HE'LL JUST TELL ME TO GET LOST.
Yaaawwn
I REALLY NEED SOME SLEEP...
HANAMARU, YOU LOOK TIRED.
YEAH.
THEN HOW ABOUT A NICE NAP?!
WHA?!

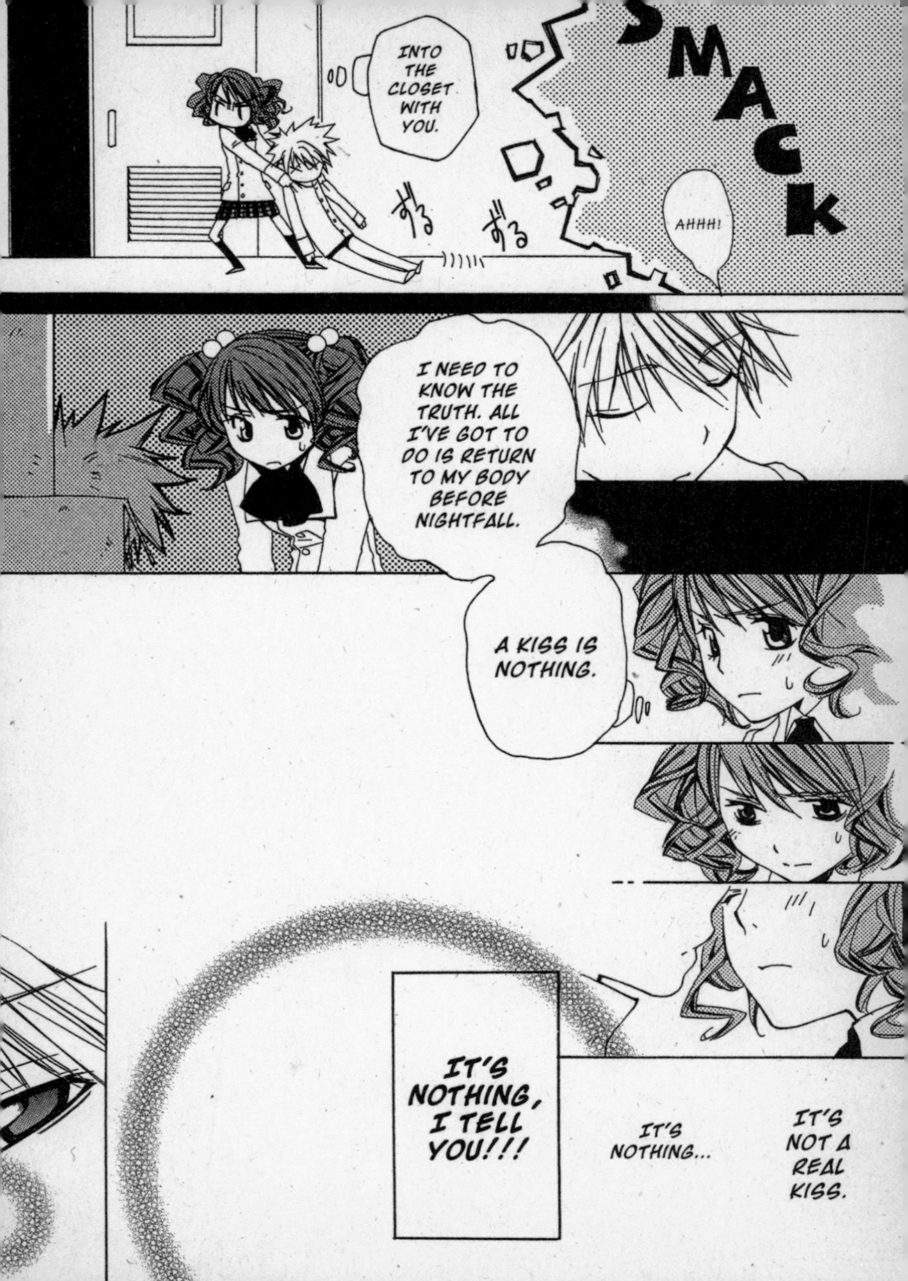
SMACK
AHHH!
INTO THE CLOSET WITH YOU.
ずる
ずる
I NEED TO KNOW THE TRUTH. ALL I'VE GOT TO DO IS RETURN TO MY BODY BEFORE NIGHTFALL.
A KISS IS NOTHING.
IT'S NOT A REAL KISS.
IT'S NOTHING...
IT'S NOTHING, I TELL YOU!!!

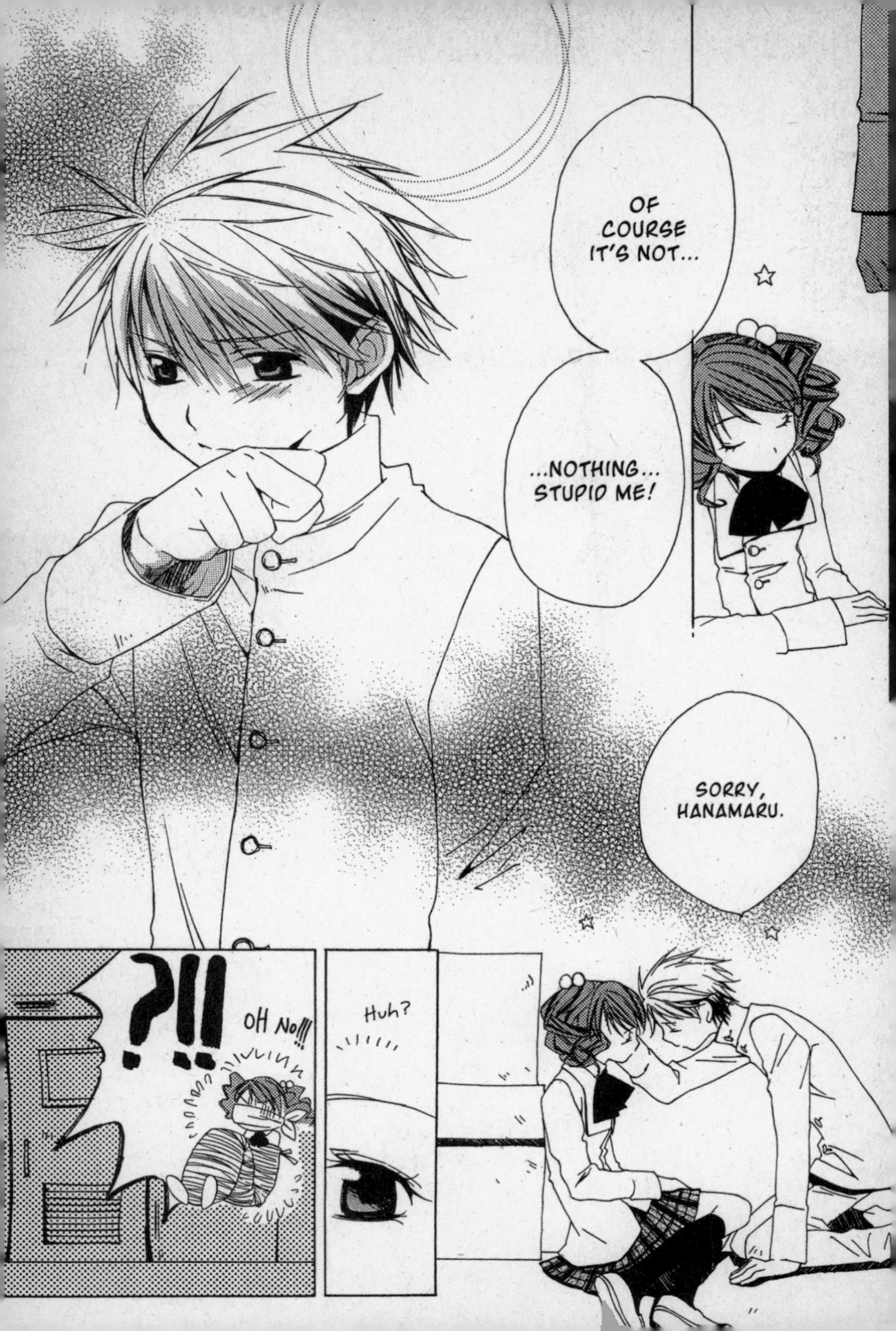
OF COURSE IT'S NOT...
...NOTHING... STUPID ME!
SORRY, HANAMARU.
Huh?
?!!
OH NO!!!

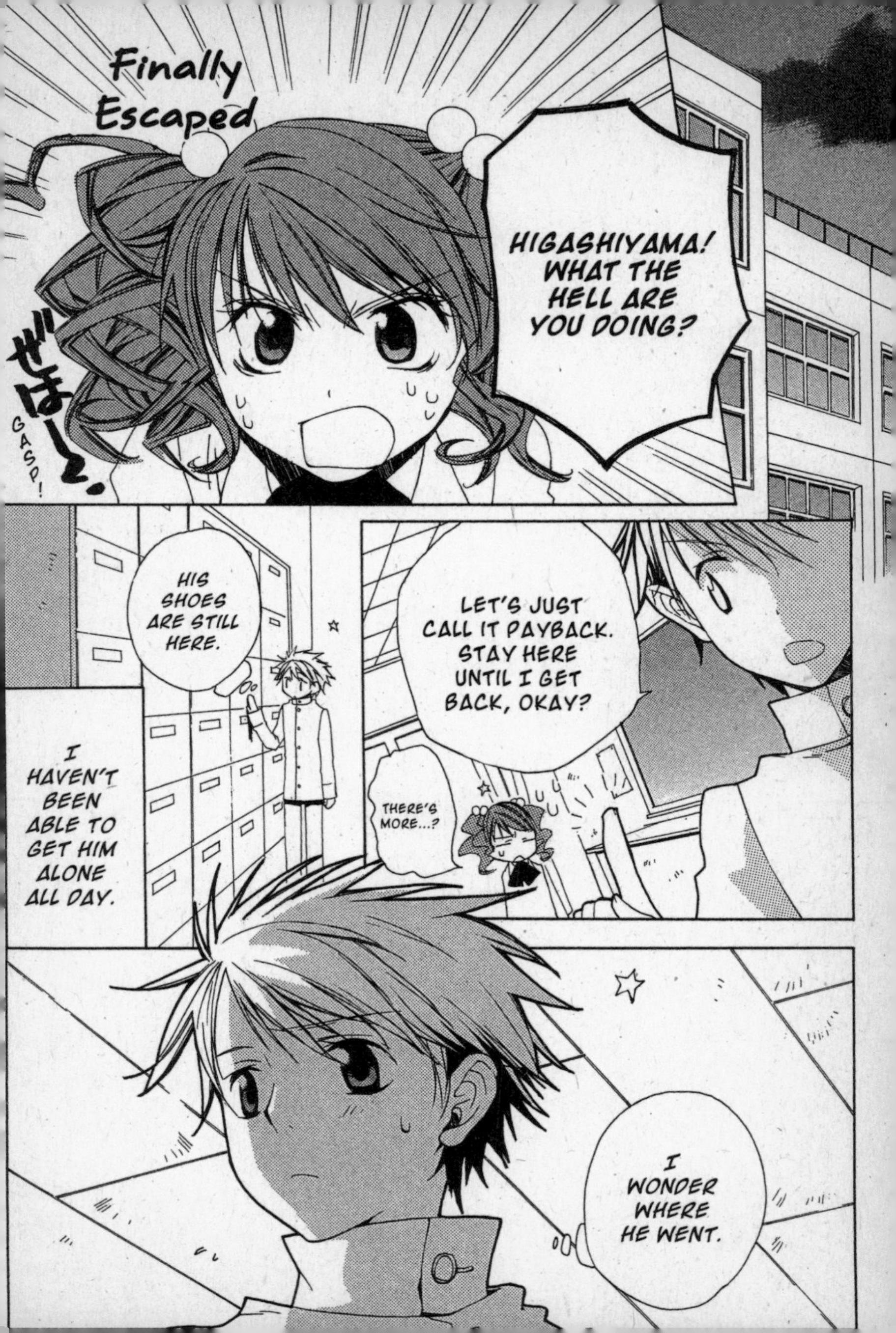
HIGASHIYAMA! WHAT THE HELL ARE YOU DOING?
Finally Escaped
ぜはーっ
GASP!
LET'S JUST CALL IT PAYBACK. STAY HERE UNTIL I GET BACK, OKAY?
THERE'S MORE...?
HIS SHOES ARE STILL HERE.
I HAVEN'T BEEN ABLE TO GET HIM ALONE ALL DAY.
I WONDER WHERE HE WENT.

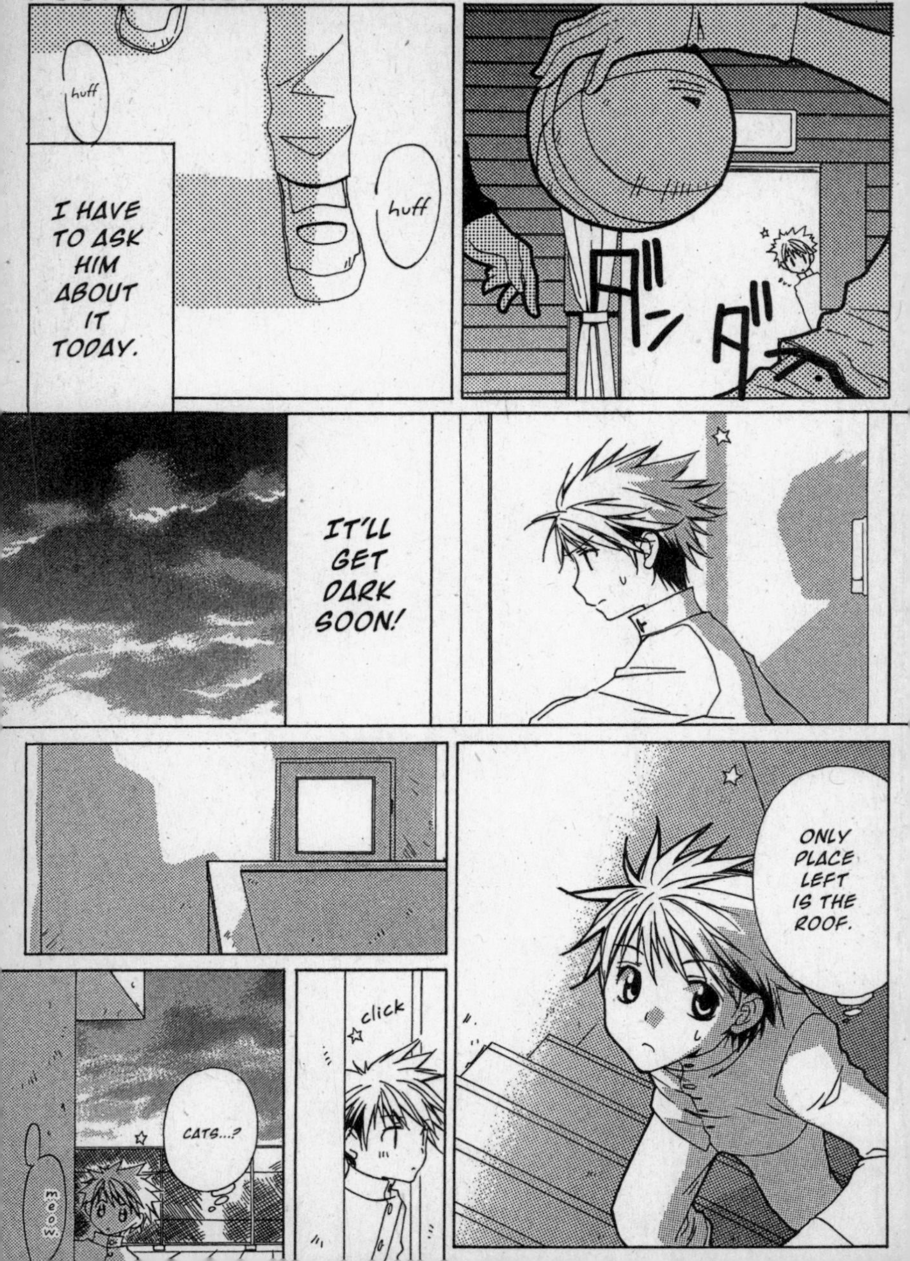
ダンダッ
huff
huff
I HAVE TO ASK HIM ABOUT IT TODAY.
IT'LL GET DARK SOON!
ONLY PLACE LEFT IS THE ROOF.
click
CATS...?
meow.

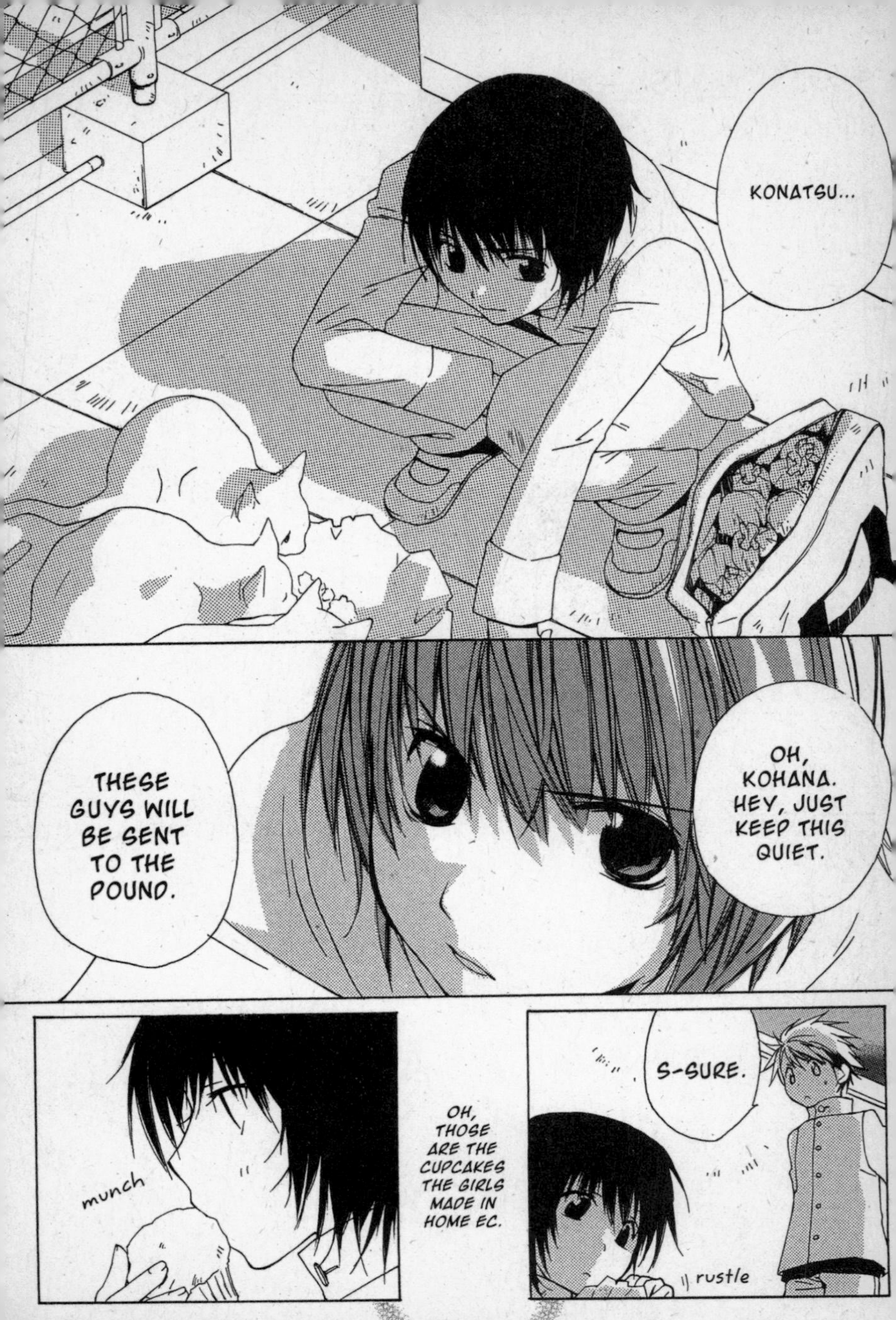
KONATSU...
OH, KOHANA. HEY, JUST KEEP THIS QUIET.
THESE GUYS WILL BE SENT TO THE POUND.
S-SURE.
rustle
OH, THOSE ARE THE CUPCAKES THE GIRLS MADE IN HOME EC.
munch

FOURTH KISS×××

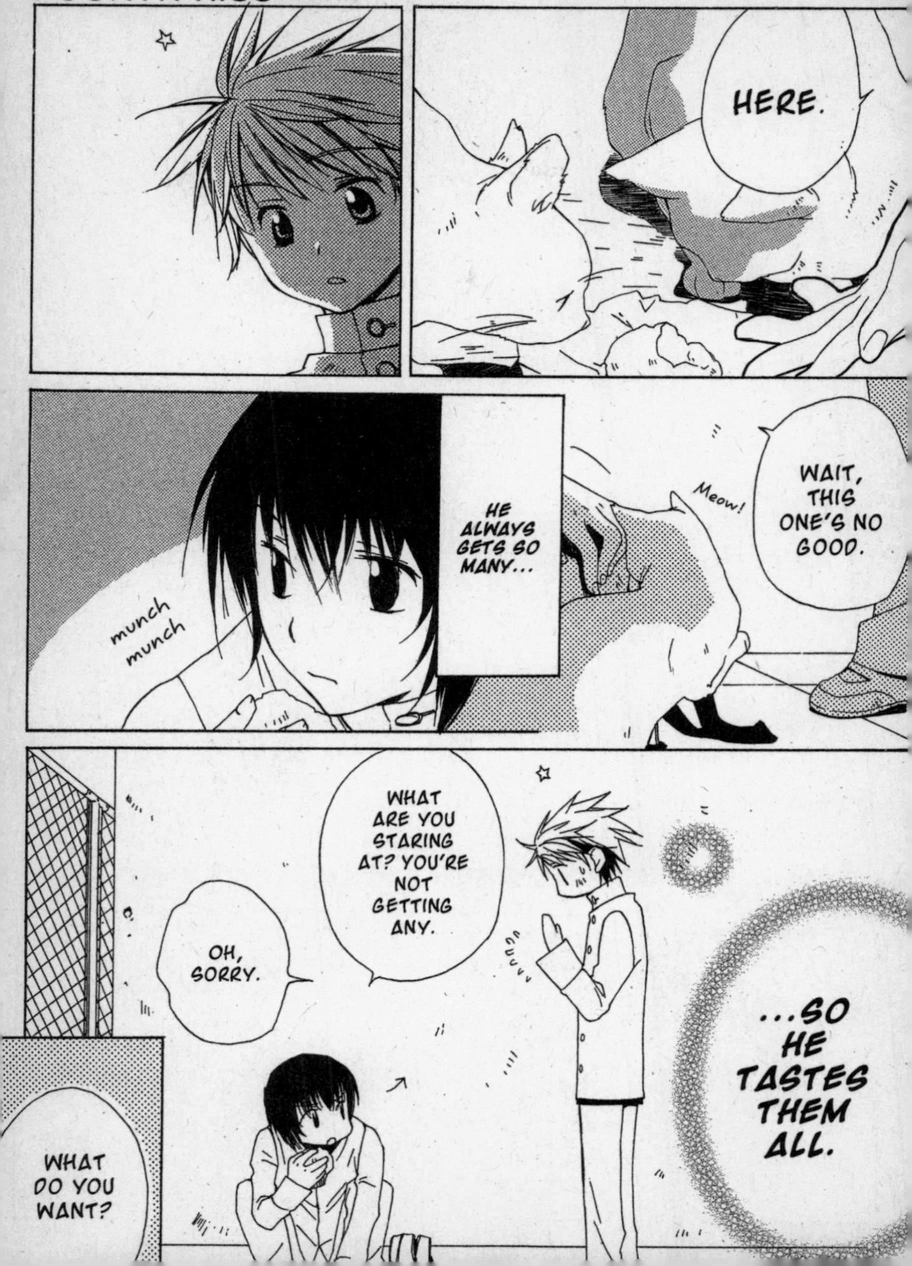
HERE.
WAIT, THIS ONE'S NO GOOD.
Meow!
HE ALWAYS GETS SO MANY...
munch munch
...SO HE TASTES THEM ALL.
WHAT ARE YOU STARING AT? YOU'RE NOT GETTING ANY.
OH, SORRY.
WHAT DO YOU WANT?

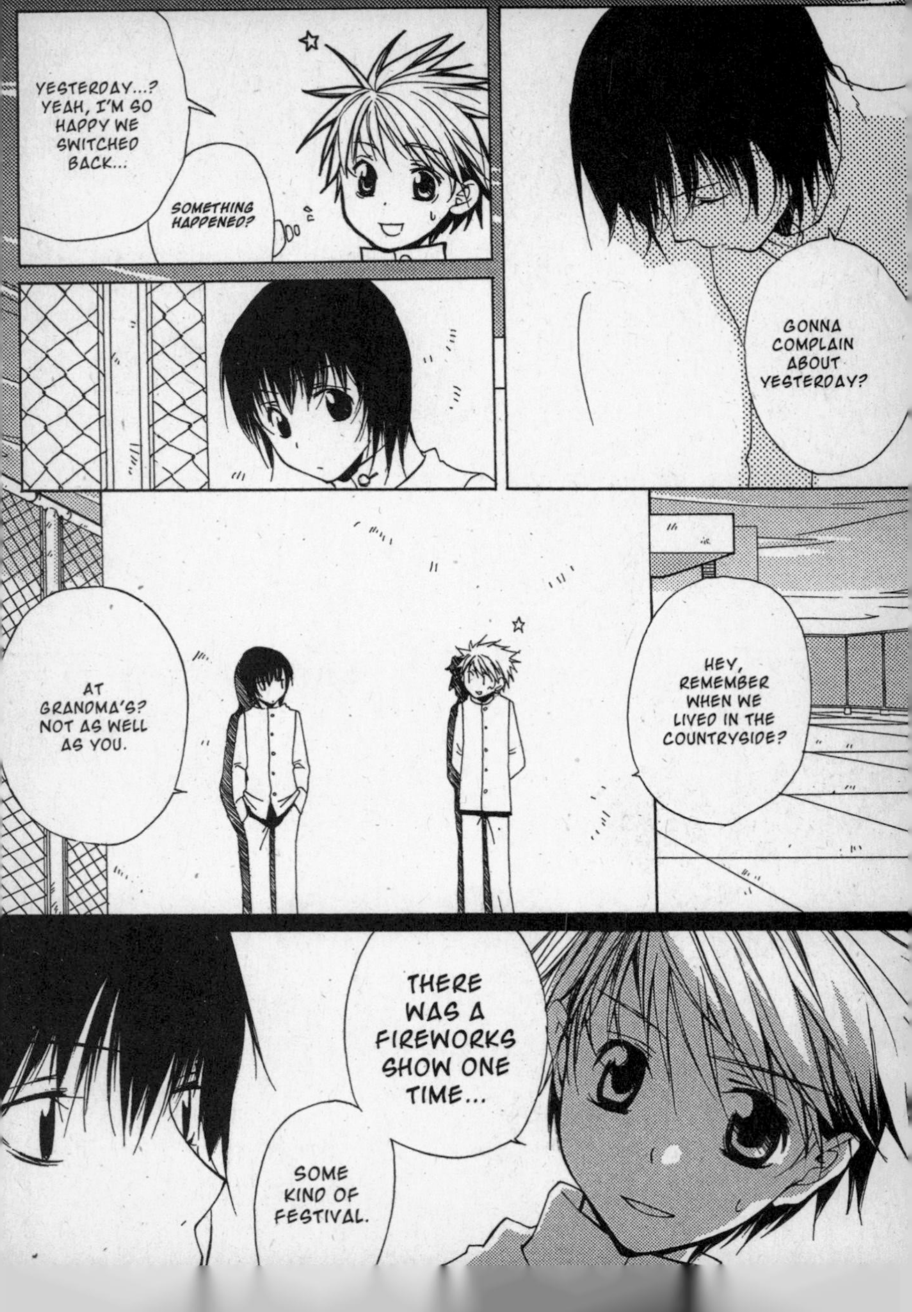
GONNA COMPLAIN ABOUT YESTERDAY?
SOMETHING HAPPENED?
YESTERDAY...? YEAH, I'M SO HAPPY WE SWITCHED BACK...
HEY, REMEMBER WHEN WE LIVED IN THE COUNTRYSIDE?
AT GRANDMA'S? NOT AS WELL AS YOU.
THERE WAS A FIREWORKS SHOW ONE TIME...
SOME KIND OF FESTIVAL.

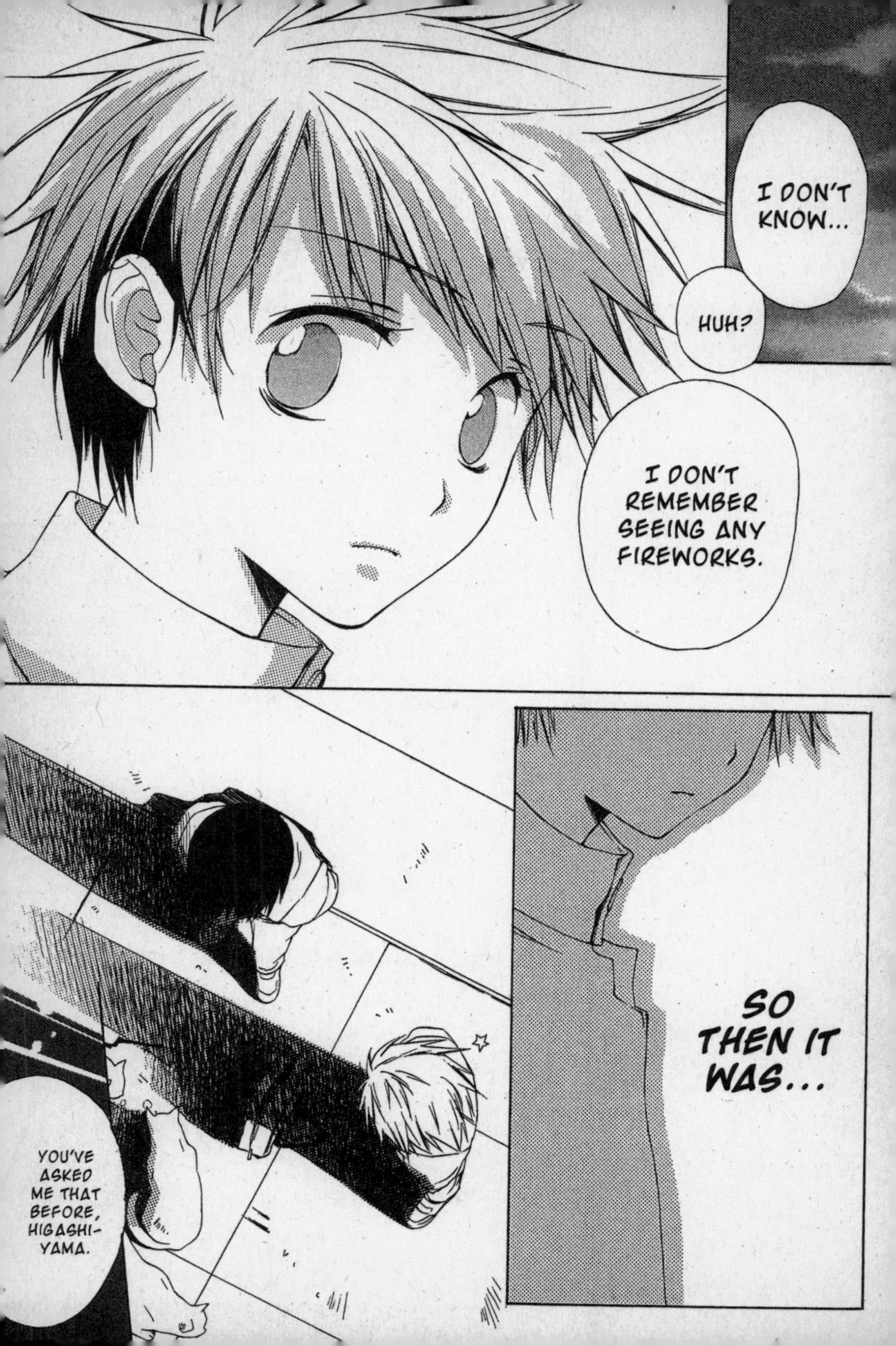
I DON'T KNOW...
HUH?
I DON'T REMEMBER SEEING ANY FIREWORKS.
SO THEN IT WAS...
YOU'VE ASKED ME THAT BEFORE, HIGASHIYAMA.

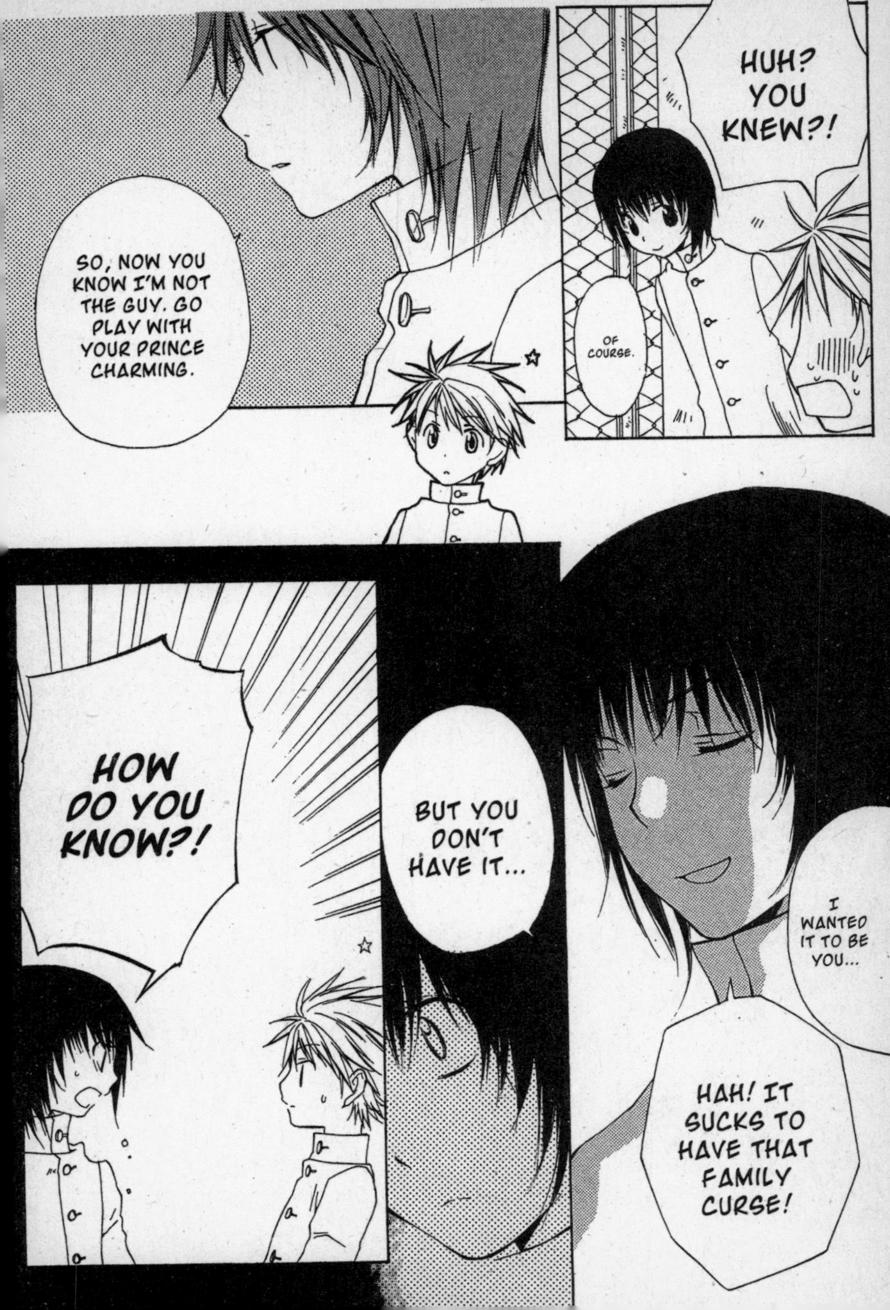
HUH? YOU KNEW?!
OF COURSE.
SO, NOW YOU KNOW I'M NOT THE GUY. GO PLAY WITH YOUR PRINCE CHARMING.
I WANTED IT TO BE YOU...
HAH! IT SUCKS TO HAVE THAT FAMILY CURSE!
BUT YOU DON'T HAVE IT...
HOW DO YOU KNOW?!

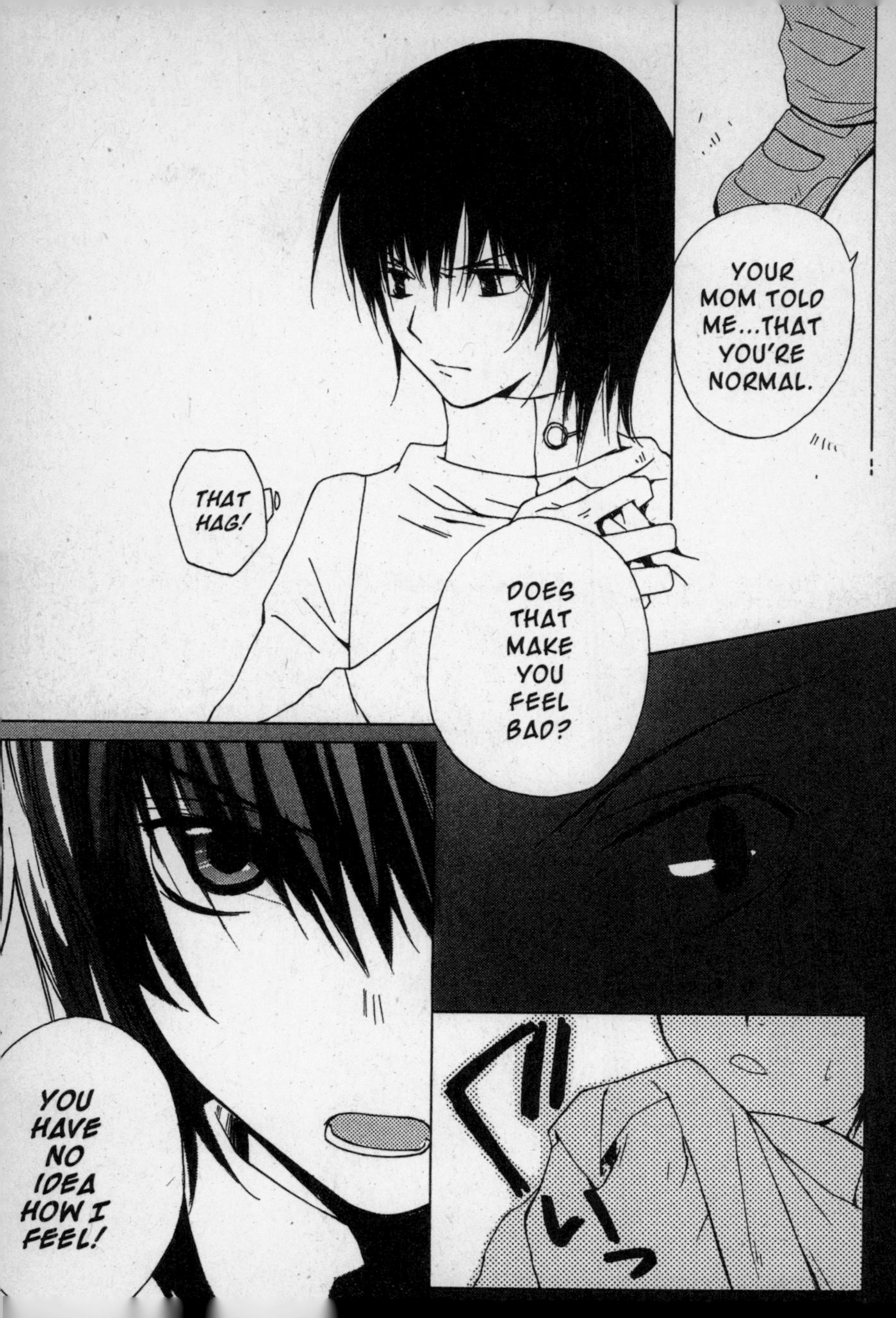
YOUR MOM TOLD ME...THAT YOU'RE NORMAL.
THAT HAG!
DOES THAT MAKE YOU FEEL BAD?
YOU HAVE NO IDEA HOW I FEEL!

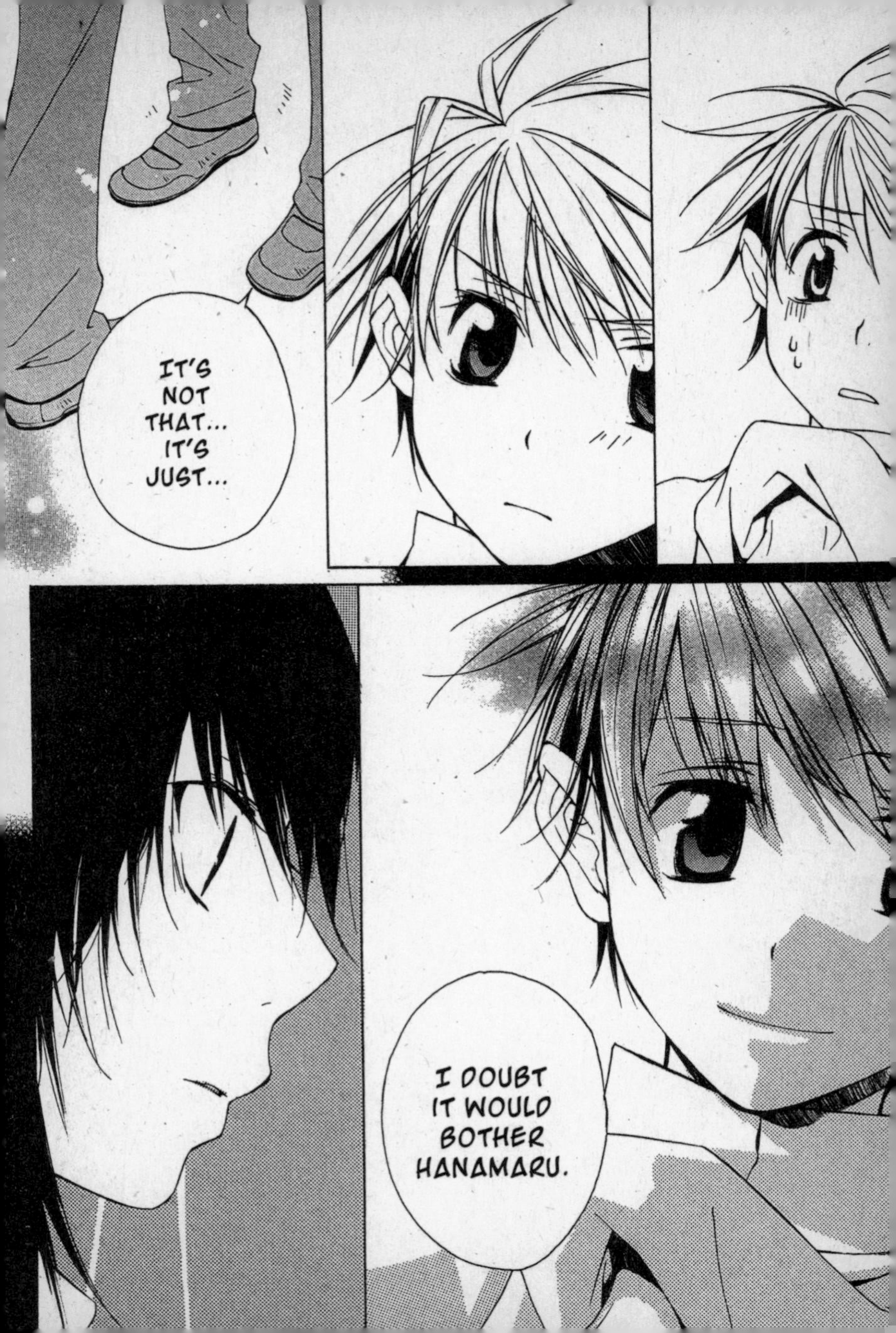
IT'S NOT THAT... IT'S JUST...
I DOUBT IT WOULD BOTHER HANAMARU.

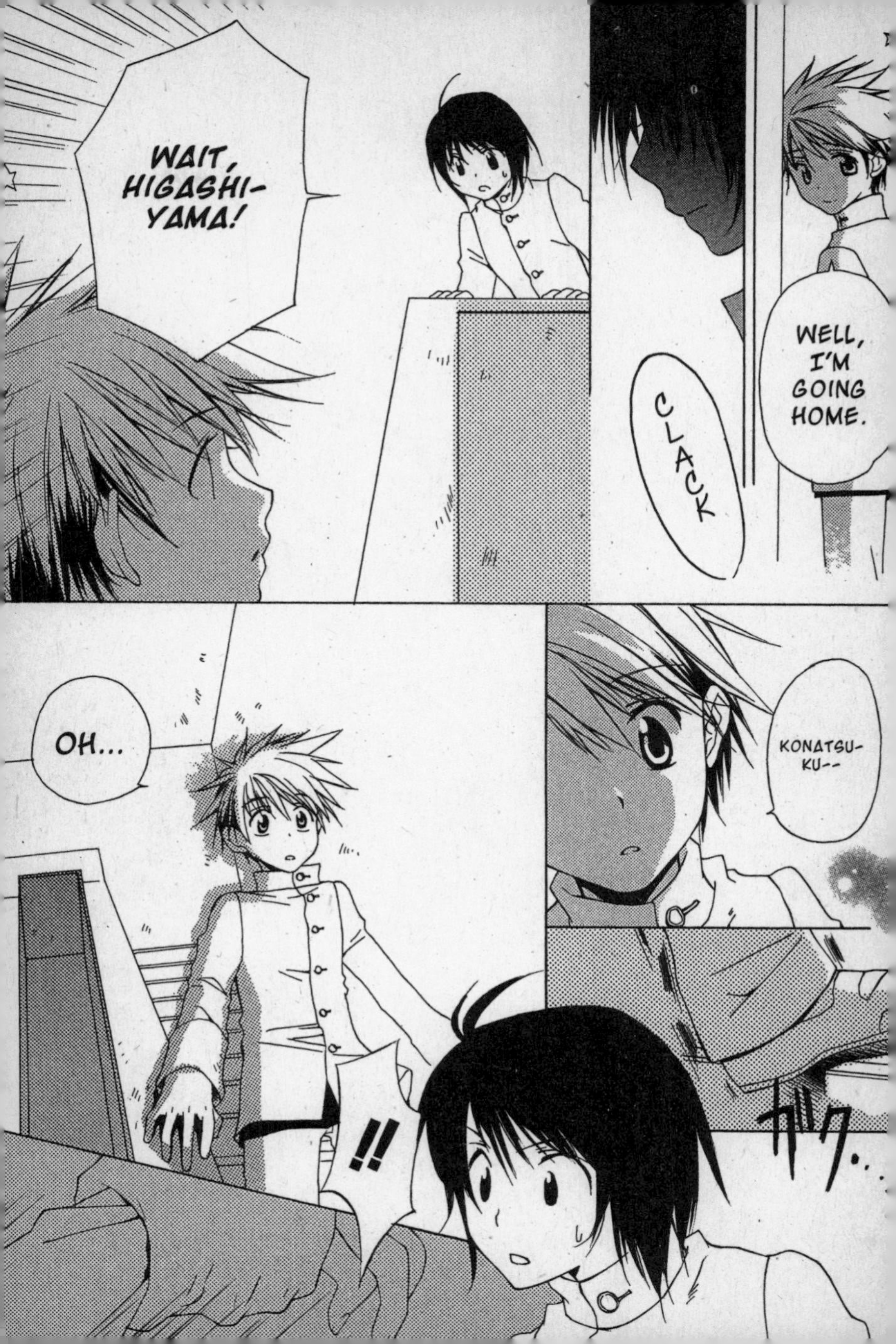
WELL, I'M GOING HOME.
CLACK
WAIT, HIGASHI-YAMA!
KONATSU-KU--
ガク...
OH...
!!

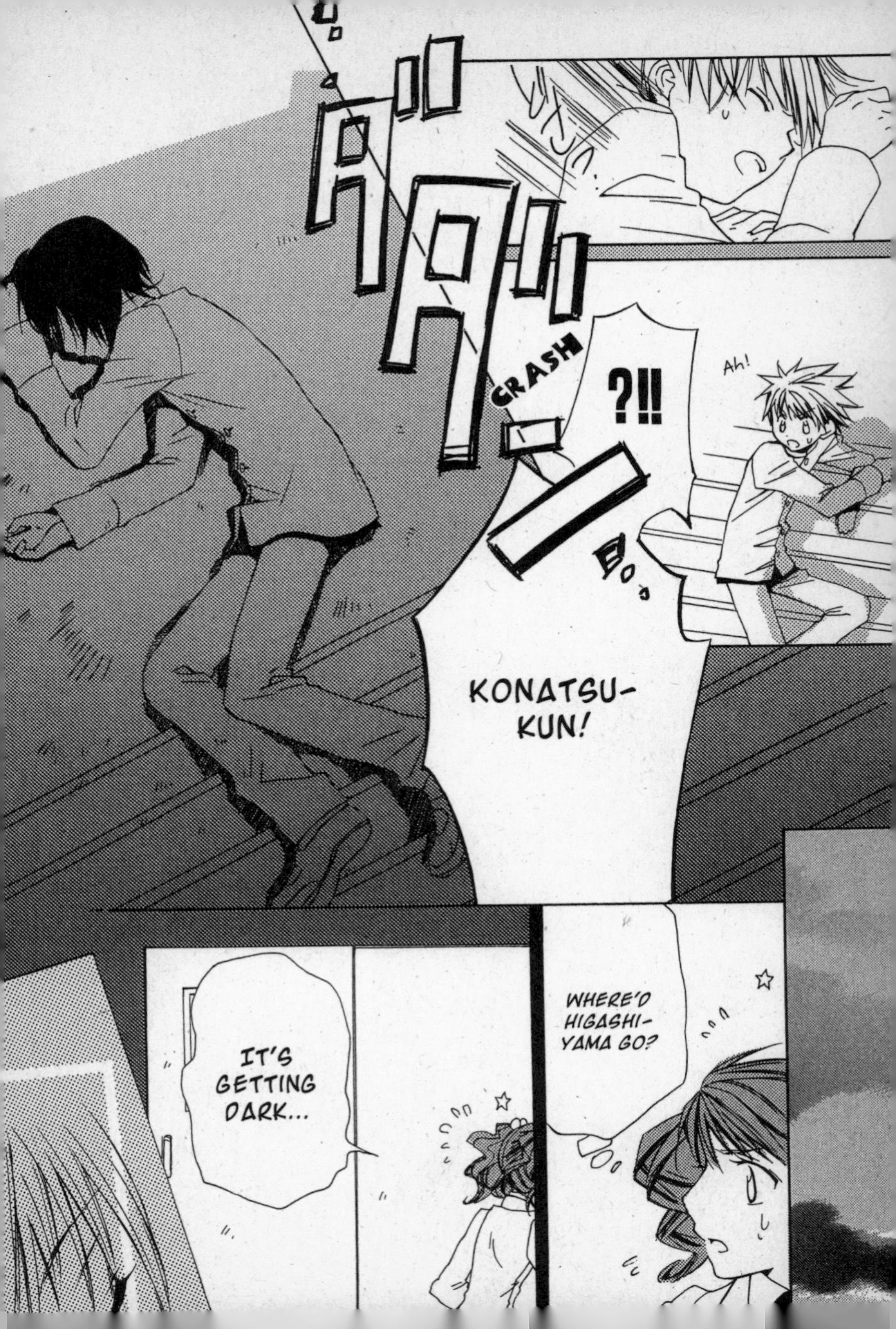
CRASH
?!!
Ah!
KONATSU-KUN!
WHERE'D HIGASHI-YAMA GO?
IT'S GETTING DARK...

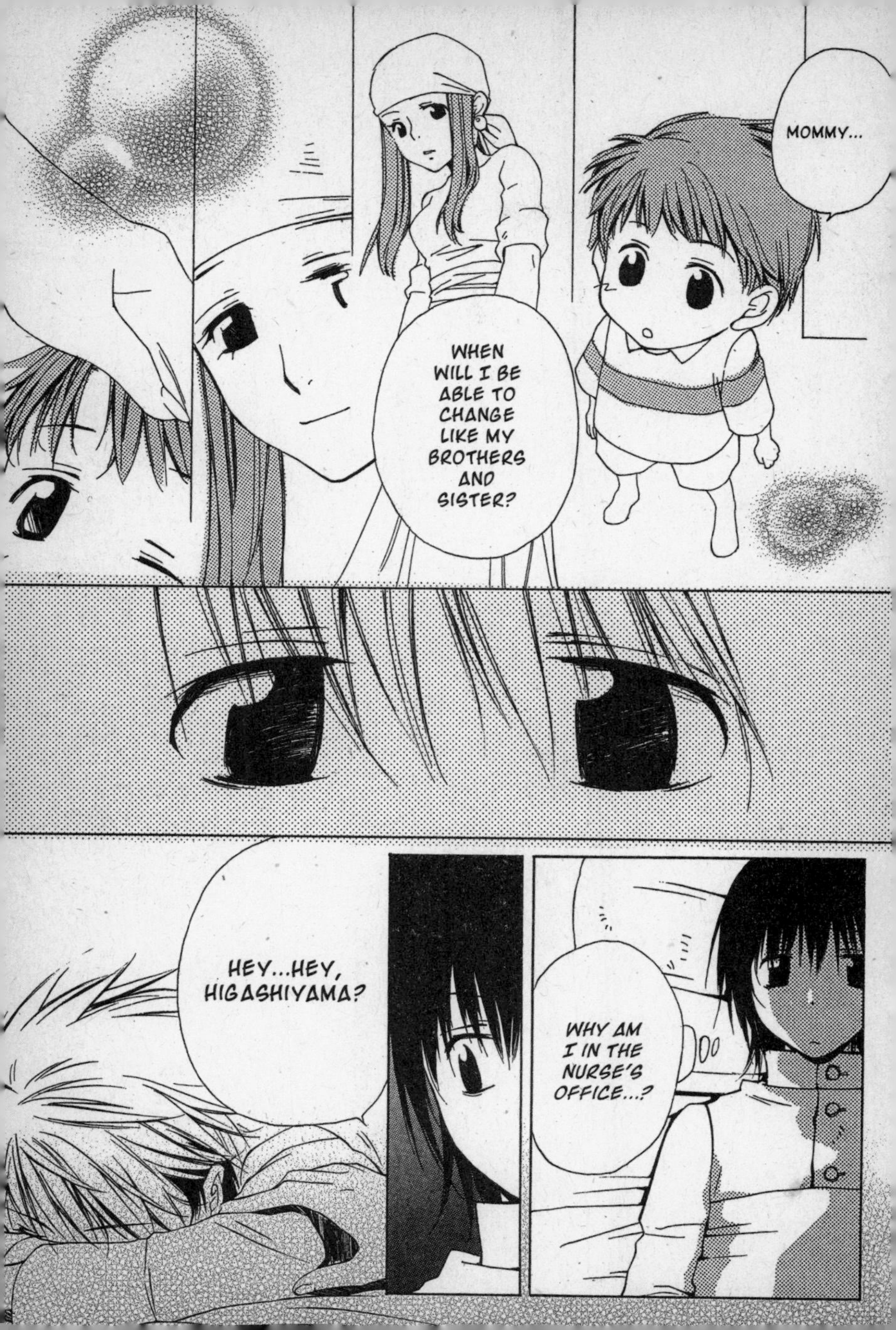
MOMMY...
WHEN WILL I BE ABLE TO CHANGE LIKE MY BROTHERS AND SISTER?
WHY AM I IN THE NURSE'S OFFICE...?
HEY...HEY, HIGASHIYAMA?

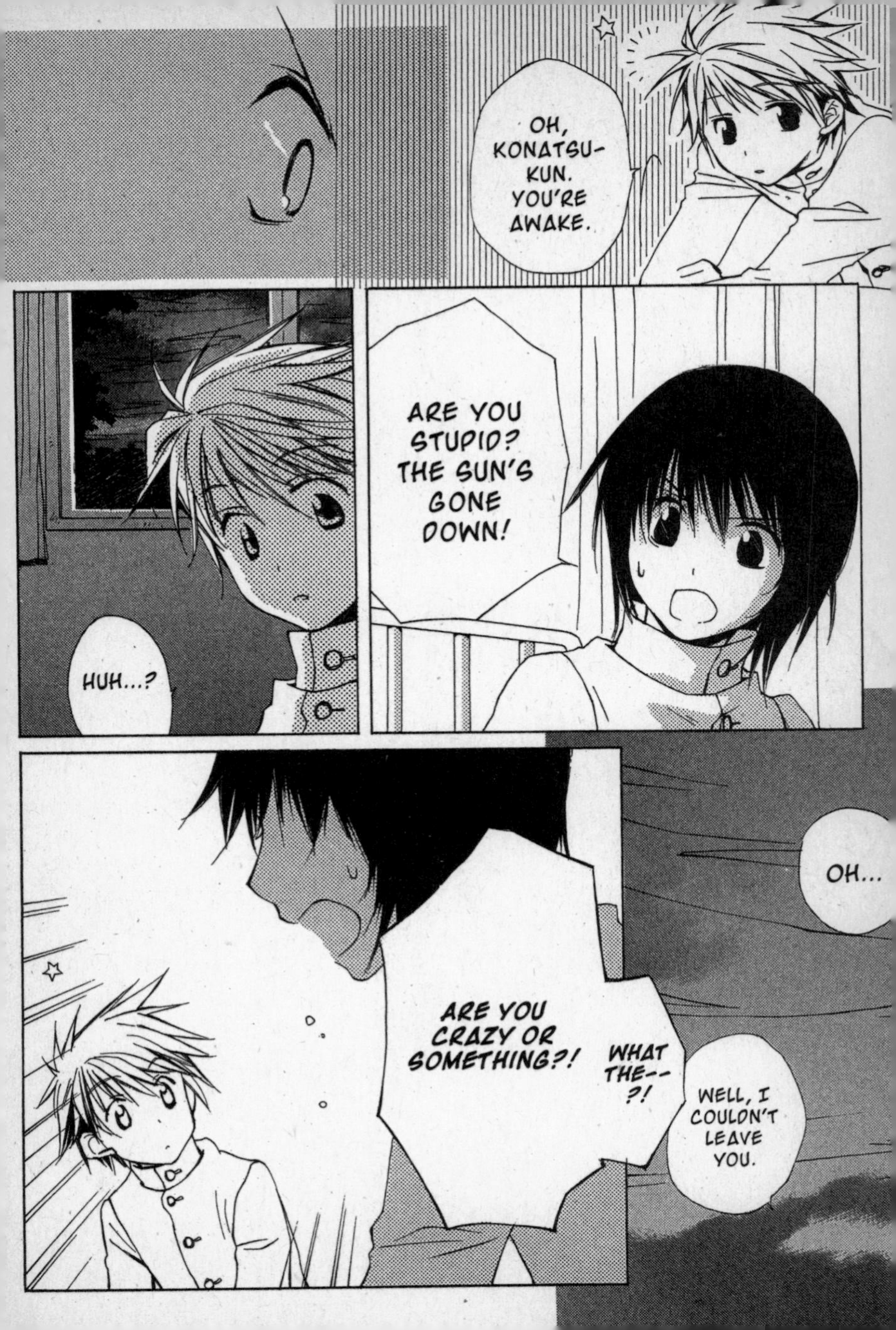
OH, KONATSU-KUN. YOU'RE AWAKE.
ARE YOU STUPID? THE SUN'S GONE DOWN!
HUH...?
OH...
WELL, I COULDN'T LEAVE YOU.
WHAT THE-- ?!
ARE YOU CRAZY OR SOMETHING?!

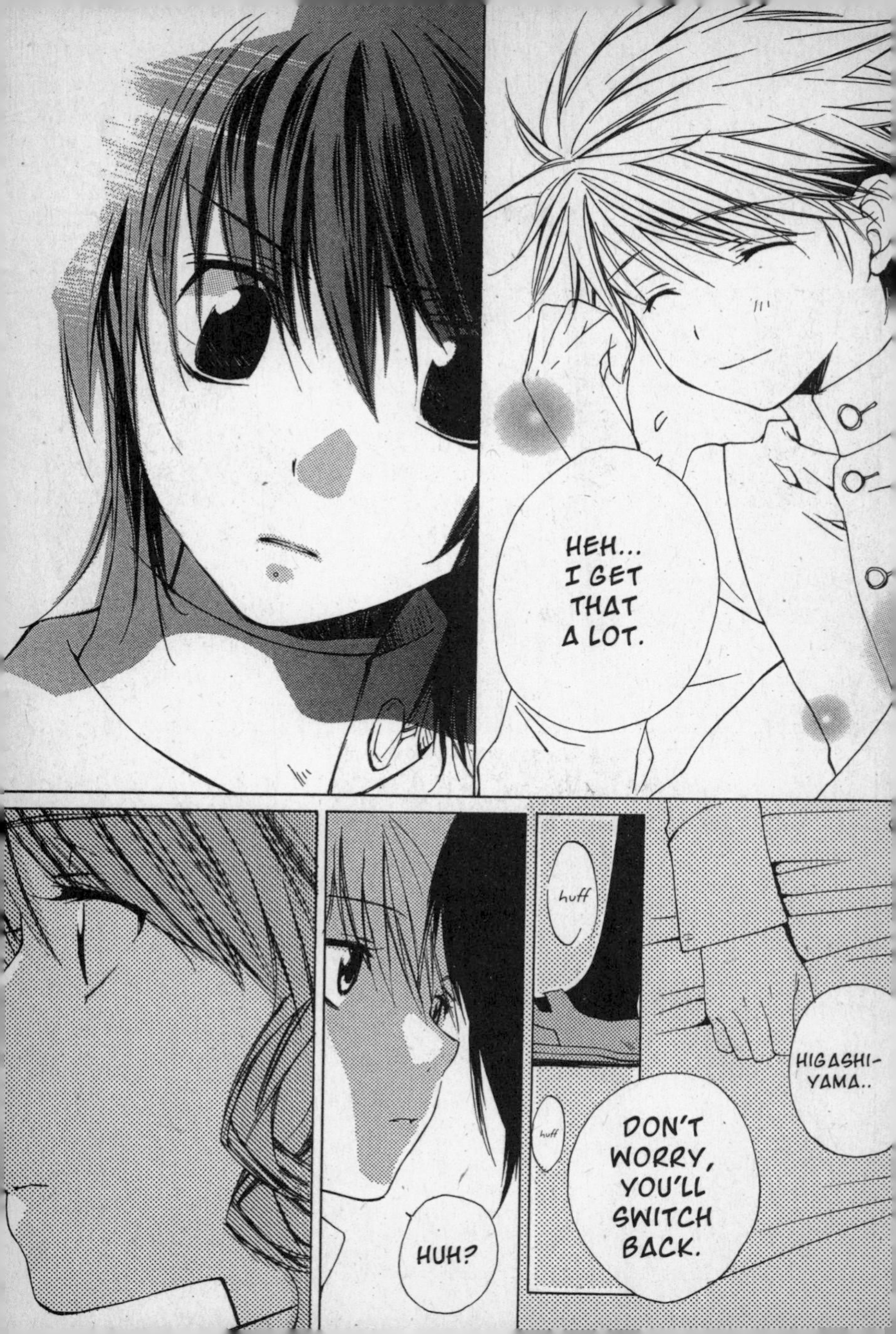
HEH... I GET THAT A LOT.
huff
HIGASHI-YAMA..
huff
DON'T WORRY, YOU'LL SWITCH BACK.
HUH?

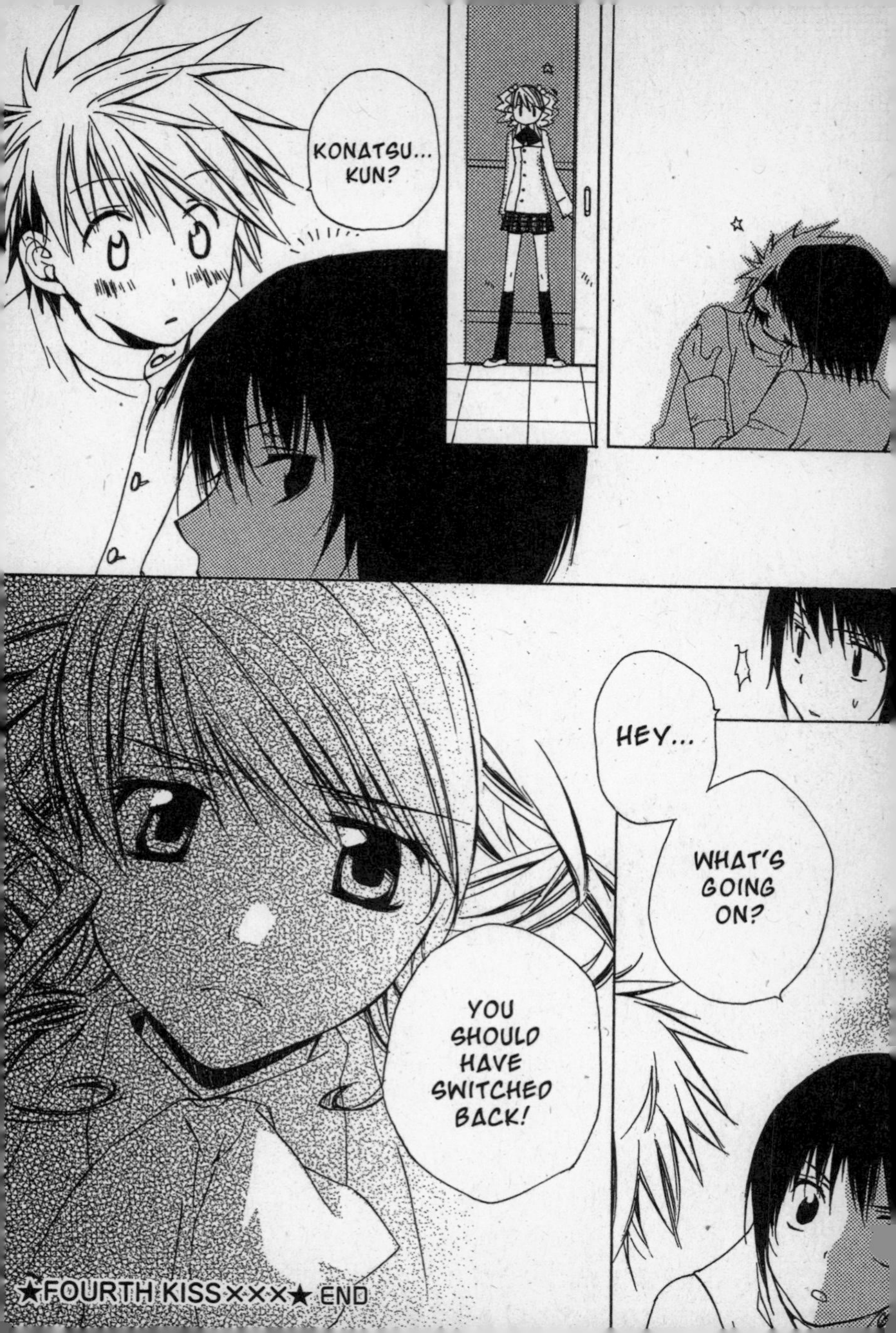
KONATSU... KUN?
HEY...
WHAT'S GOING ON?
YOU SHOULD HAVE SWITCHED BACK!
★FOURTH KISS×××★ END

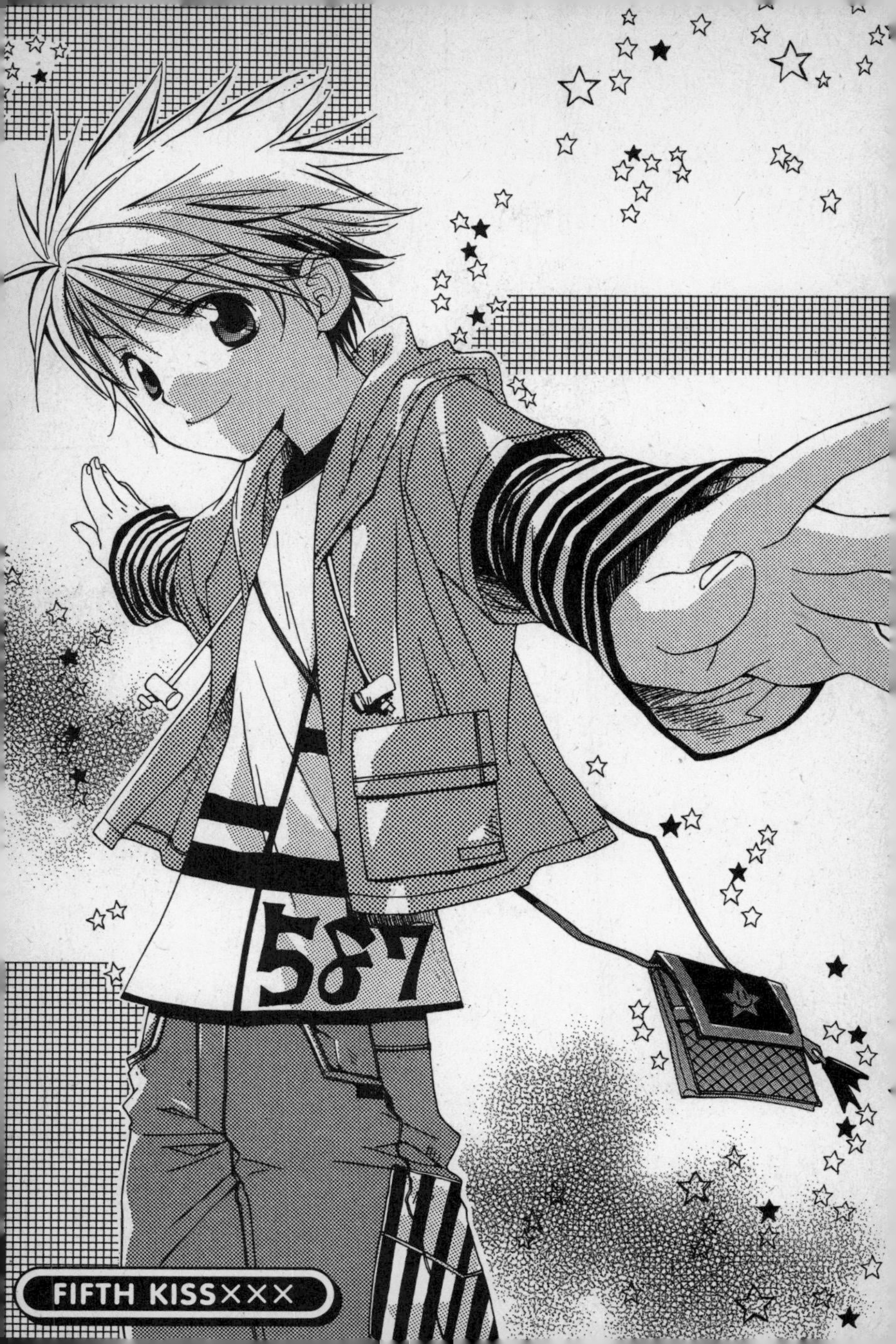
587

FIFTH KISS×××

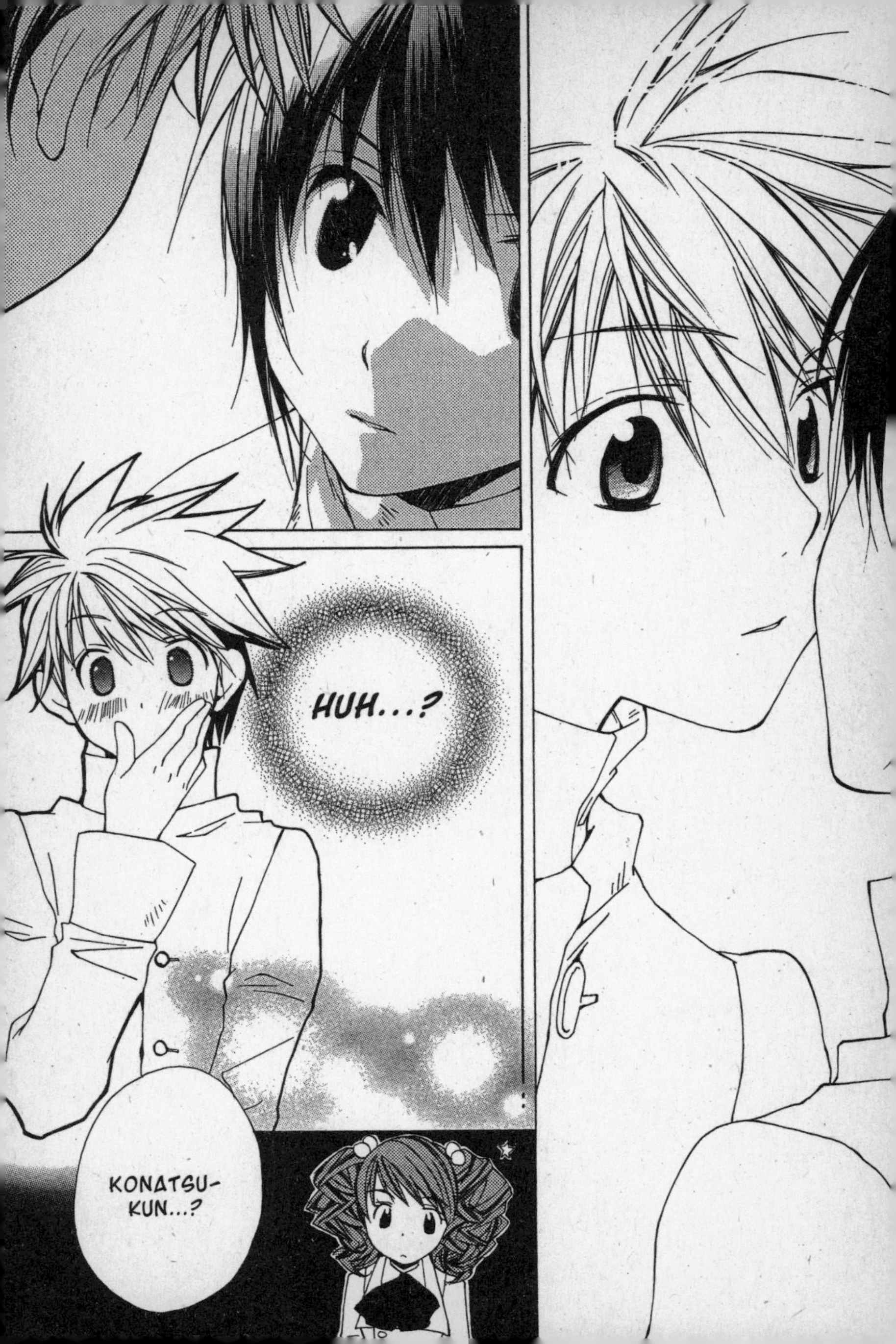
HUH...?
KONATSU-KUN...?

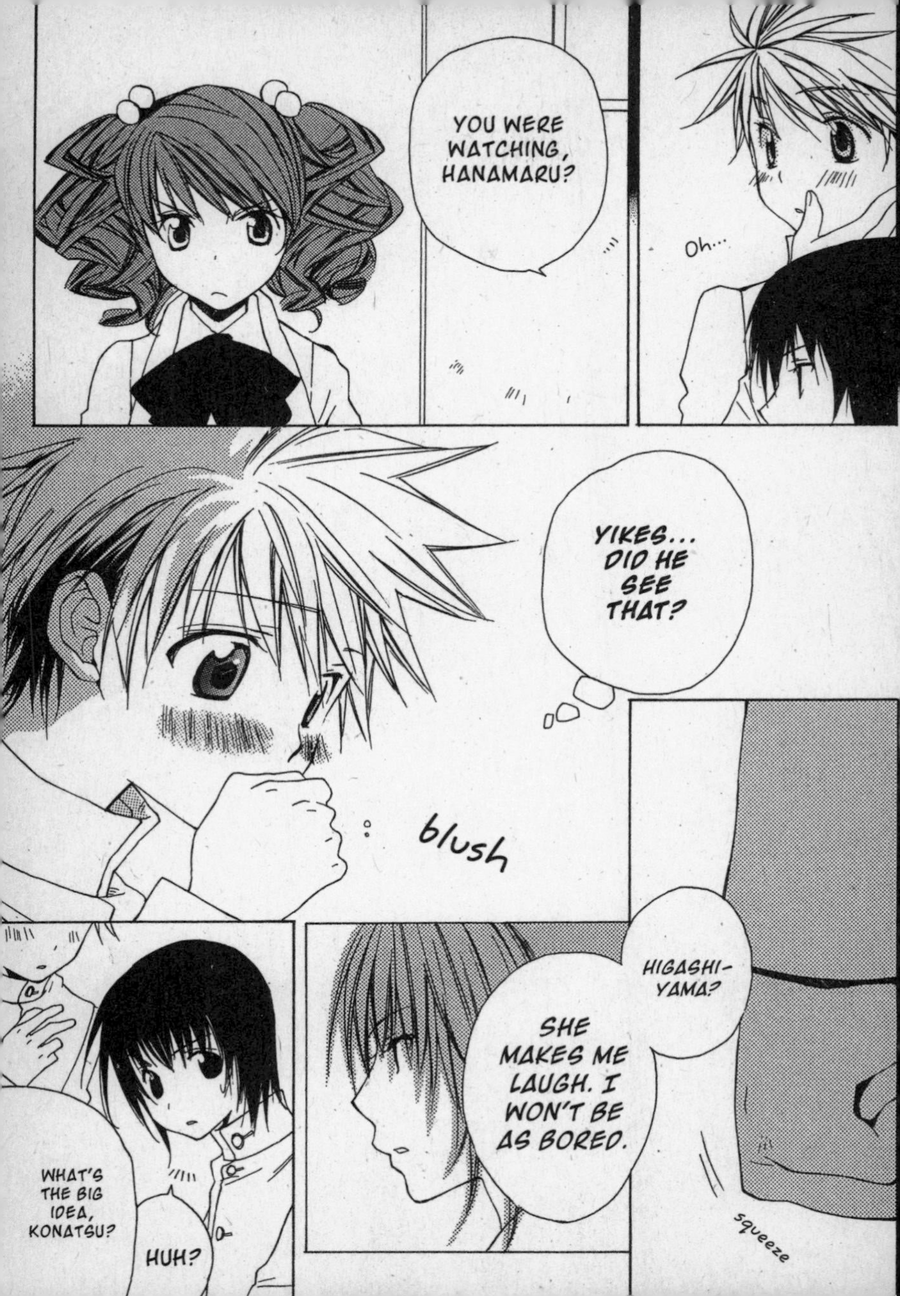
Oh...
YOU WERE WATCHING, HANAMARU?
YIKES... DID HE SEE THAT?
blush
HIGASHI-YAMA?
squeeze
SHE MAKES ME LAUGH. I WON'T BE AS BORED.
WHAT'S THE BIG IDEA, KONATSU?
HUH?

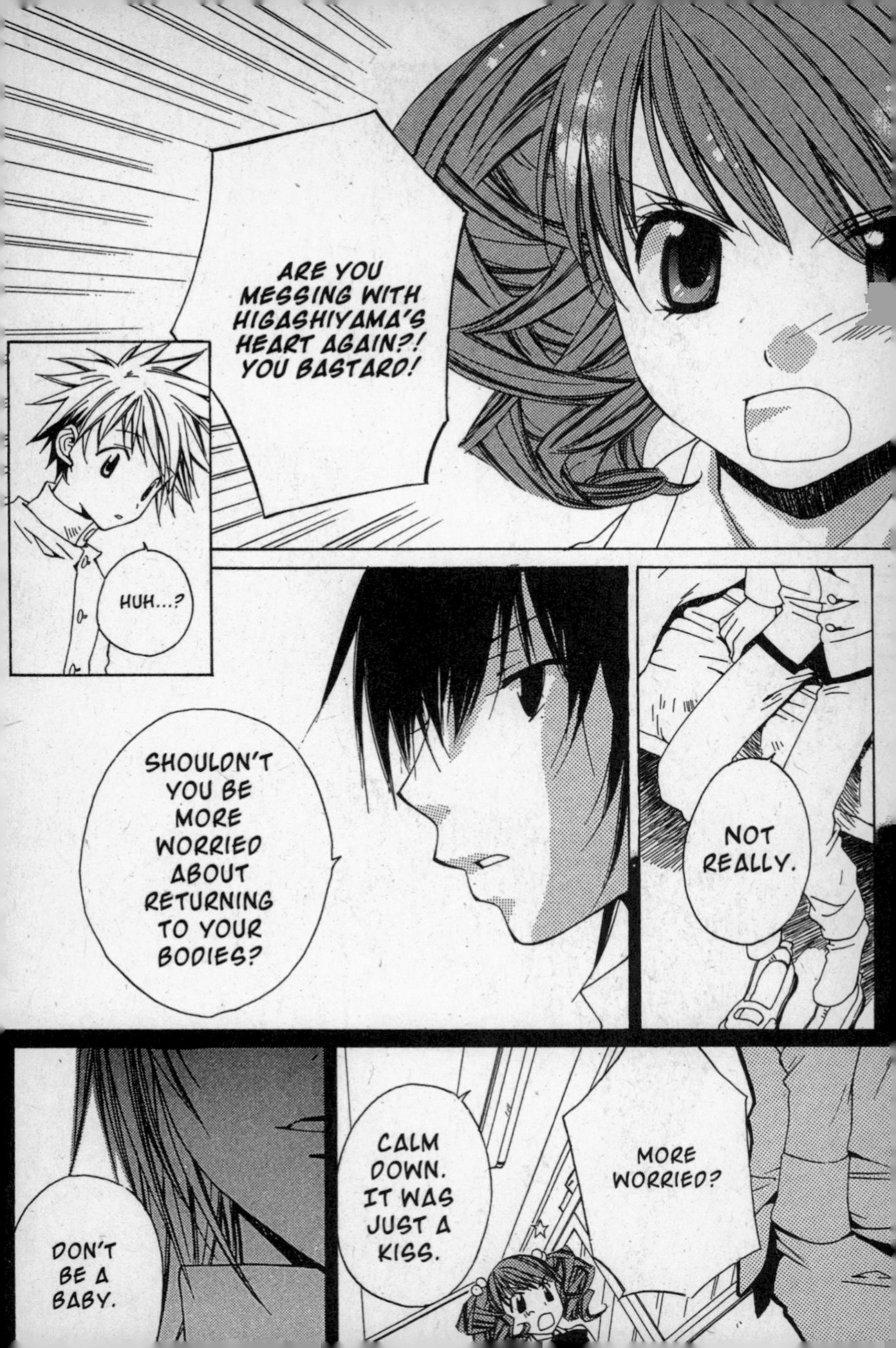
ARE YOU MESSING WITH HIGASHIYAMA'S HEART AGAIN?! YOU BASTARD!
HUH...?
NOT REALLY.
SHOULDN'T YOU BE MORE WORRIED ABOUT RETURNING TO YOUR BODIES?
MORE WORRIED?
CALM DOWN. IT WAS JUST A KISS.
DON'T BE A BABY.

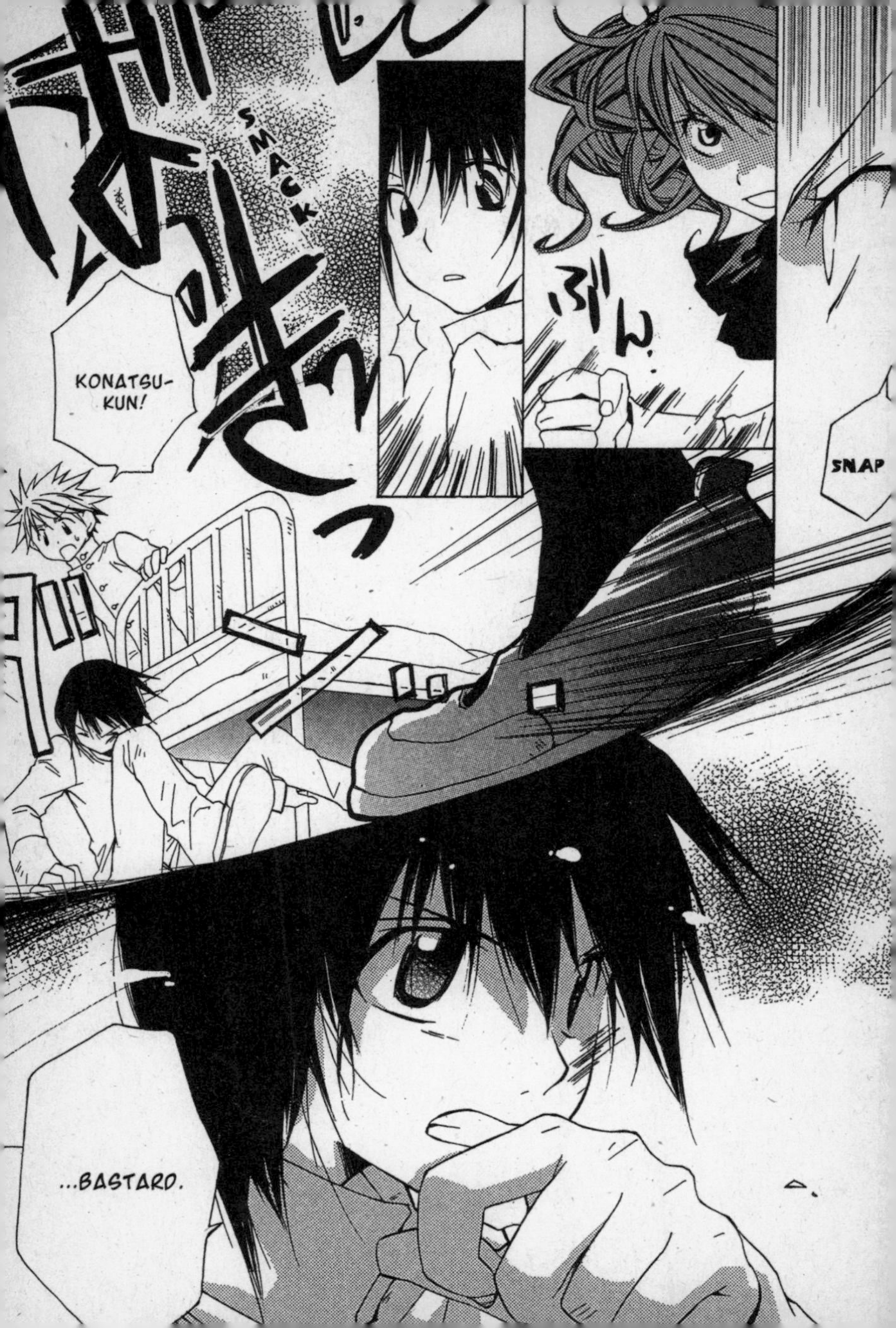
SNAP
SMACK
KONATSU-KUN!
...BASTARD.

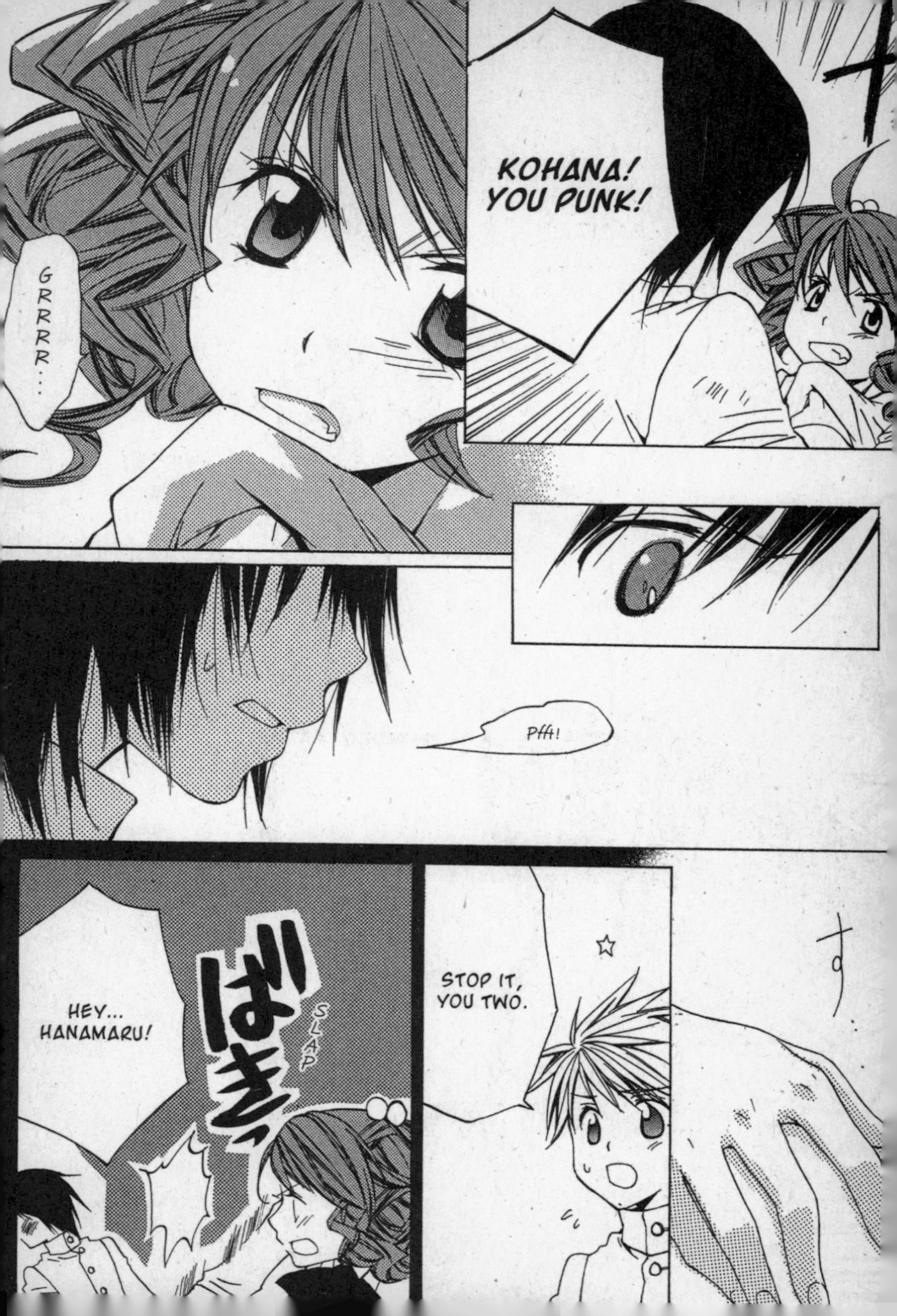
KOHANA! YOU PUNK!
GRRRR...
Pfft!
す
STOP IT, YOU TWO.
ばきっ
SLAP
HEY... HANAMARU!

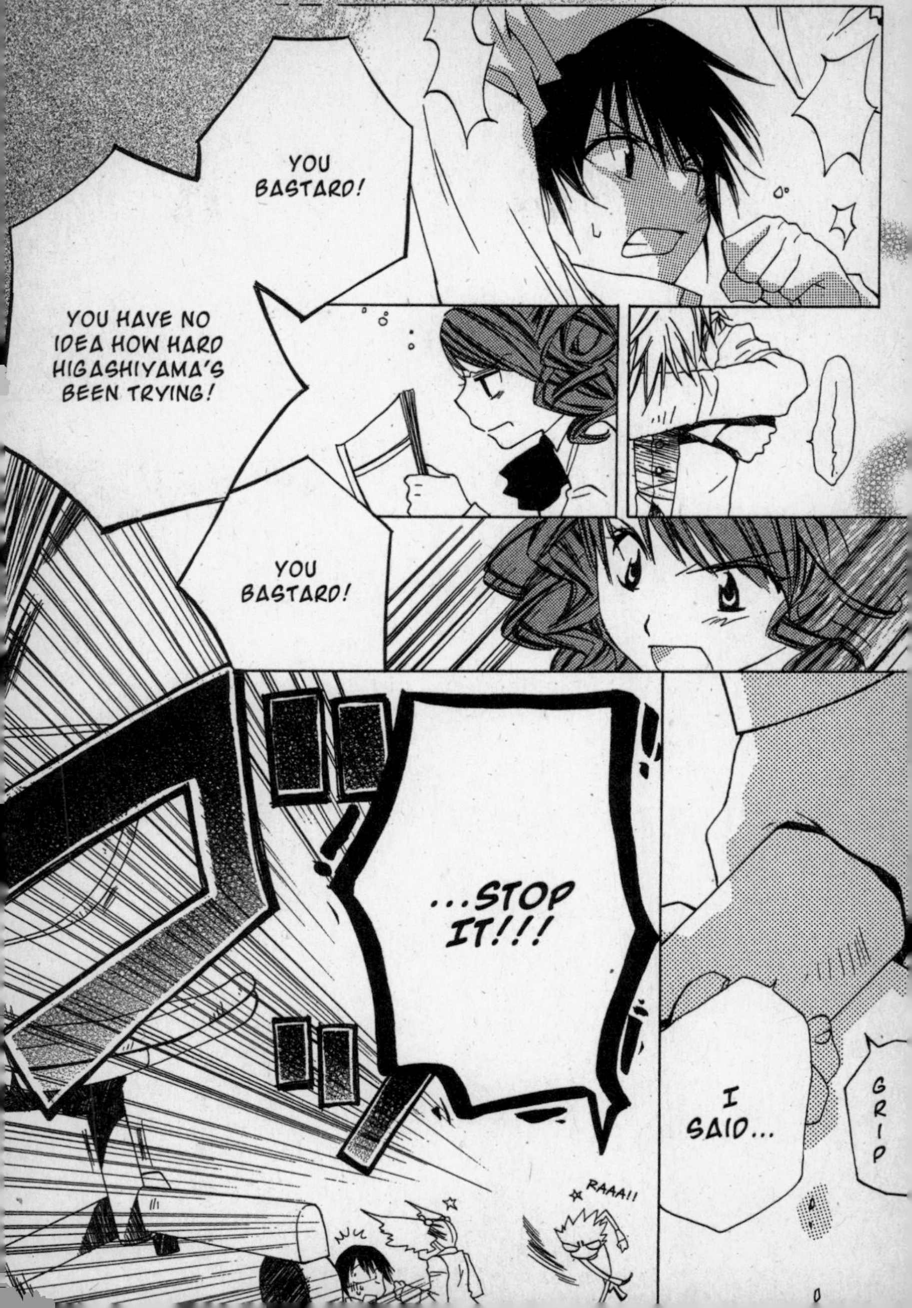
YOU BASTARD!
YOU HAVE NO IDEA HOW HARD HIGASHIYAMA'S BEEN TRYING!
YOU BASTARD!
GRIP
I SAID...
...STOP IT!!!
RAAA!!

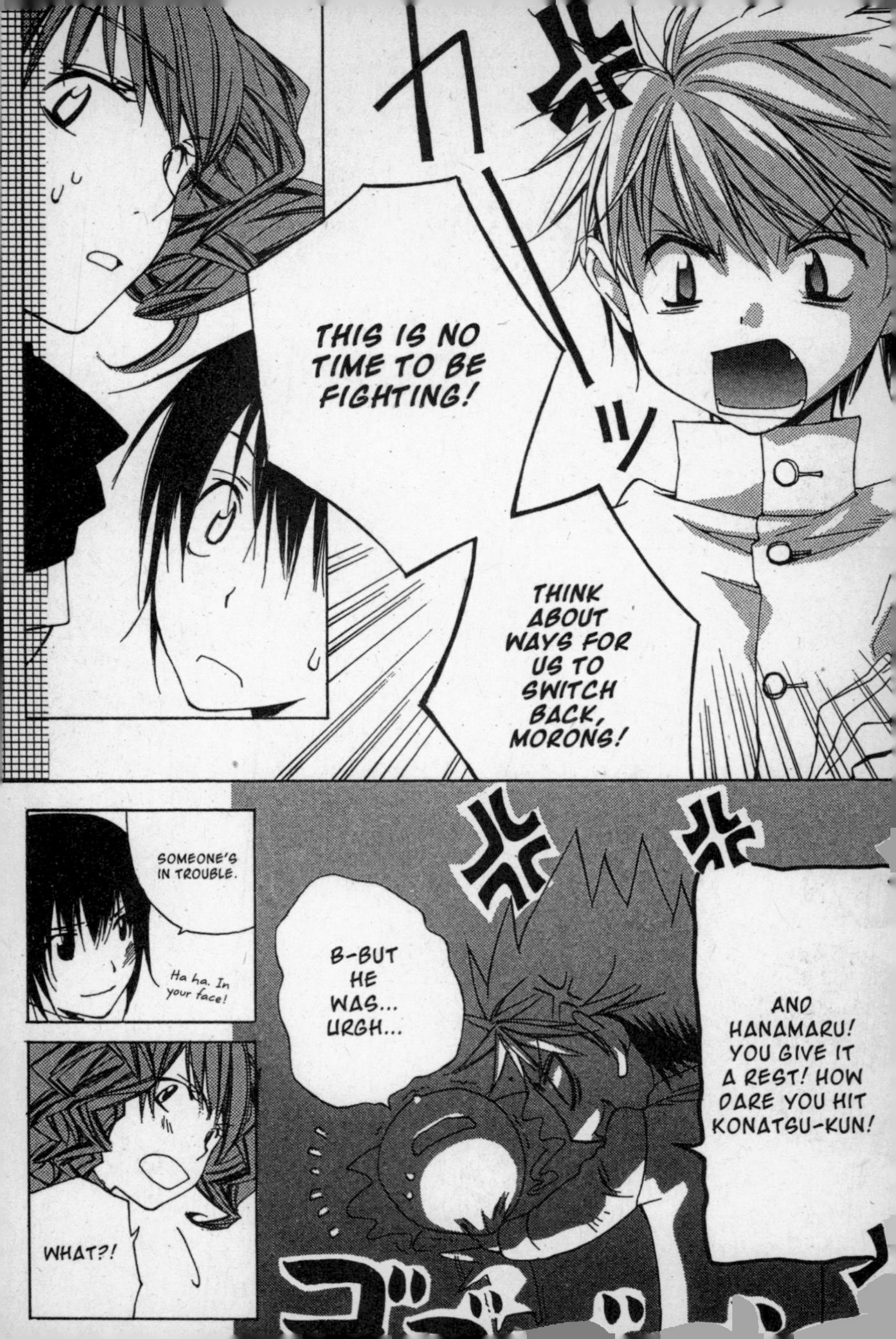
THIS IS NO TIME TO BE FIGHTING!
THINK ABOUT WAYS FOR US TO SWITCH BACK, MORONS!
AND HANAMARU! YOU GIVE IT A REST! HOW DARE YOU HIT KONATSU-KUN!
B-BUT HE WAS... URGH...
SOMEONE'S IN TROUBLE.
Ha ha. In your face!
WHAT?!

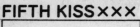

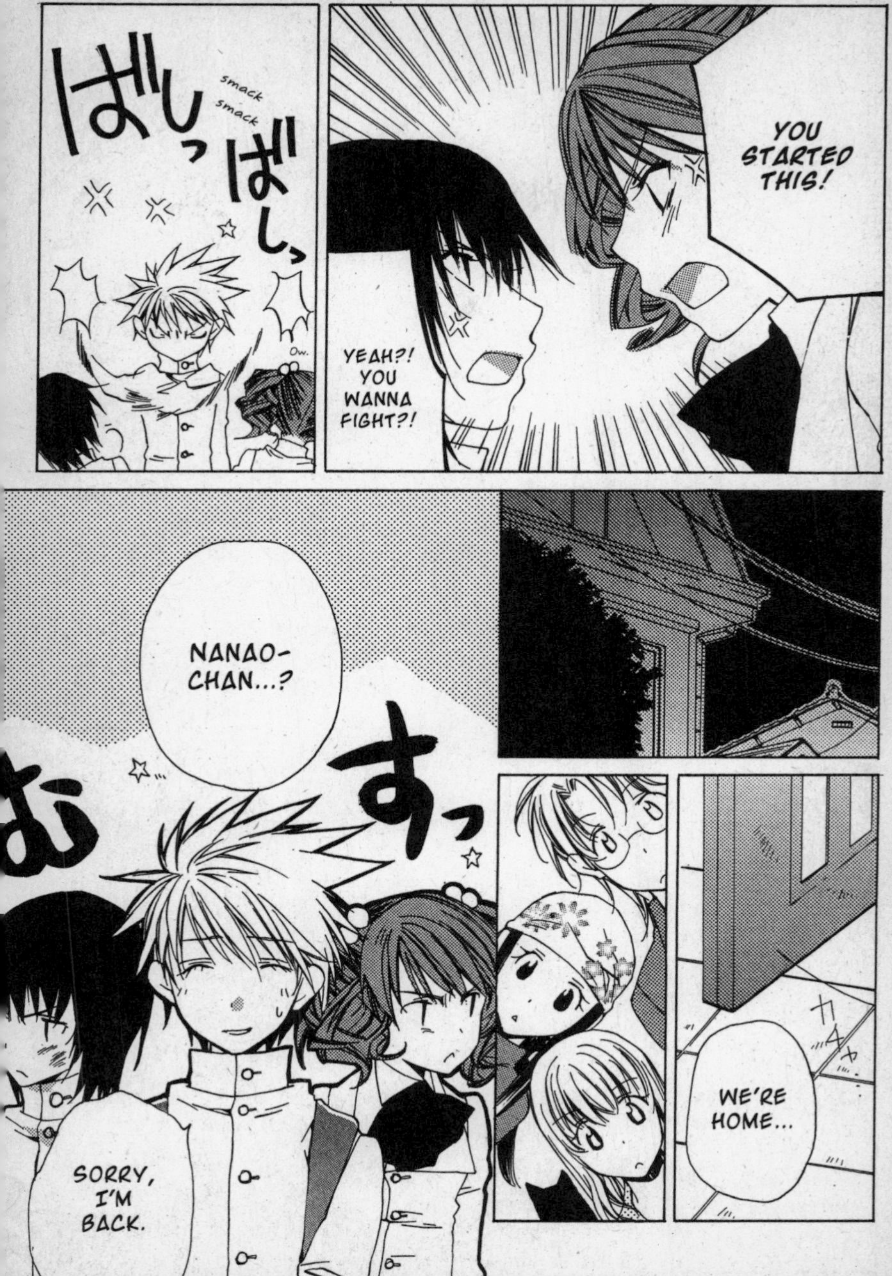
YOU STARTED THIS!
YEAH?! YOU WANNA FIGHT?!
ばしっばしっ
smack smack
Ow.
カチャ
WE'RE HOME...
NANAO-CHAN...?
すっ
SORRY, I'M BACK.

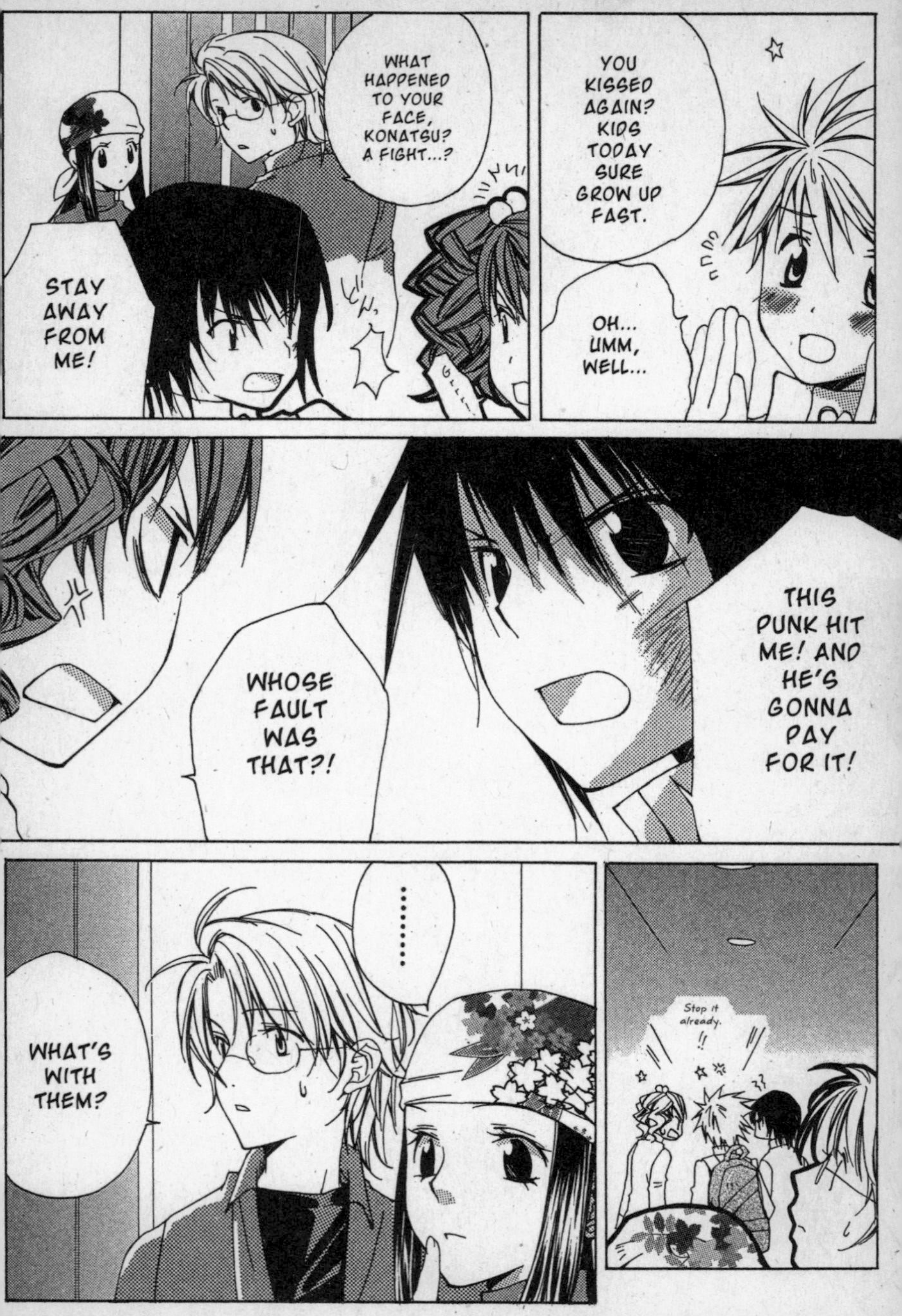
YOU KISSED AGAIN? KIDS TODAY SURE GROW UP FAST.
OH... UMM, WELL...
WHAT HAPPENED TO YOUR FACE, KONATSU? A FIGHT...?
STAY AWAY FROM ME!
THIS PUNK HIT ME! AND HE'S GONNA PAY FOR IT!
WHOSE FAULT WAS THAT?!
Stop it already. !!
....
WHAT'S WITH THEM?

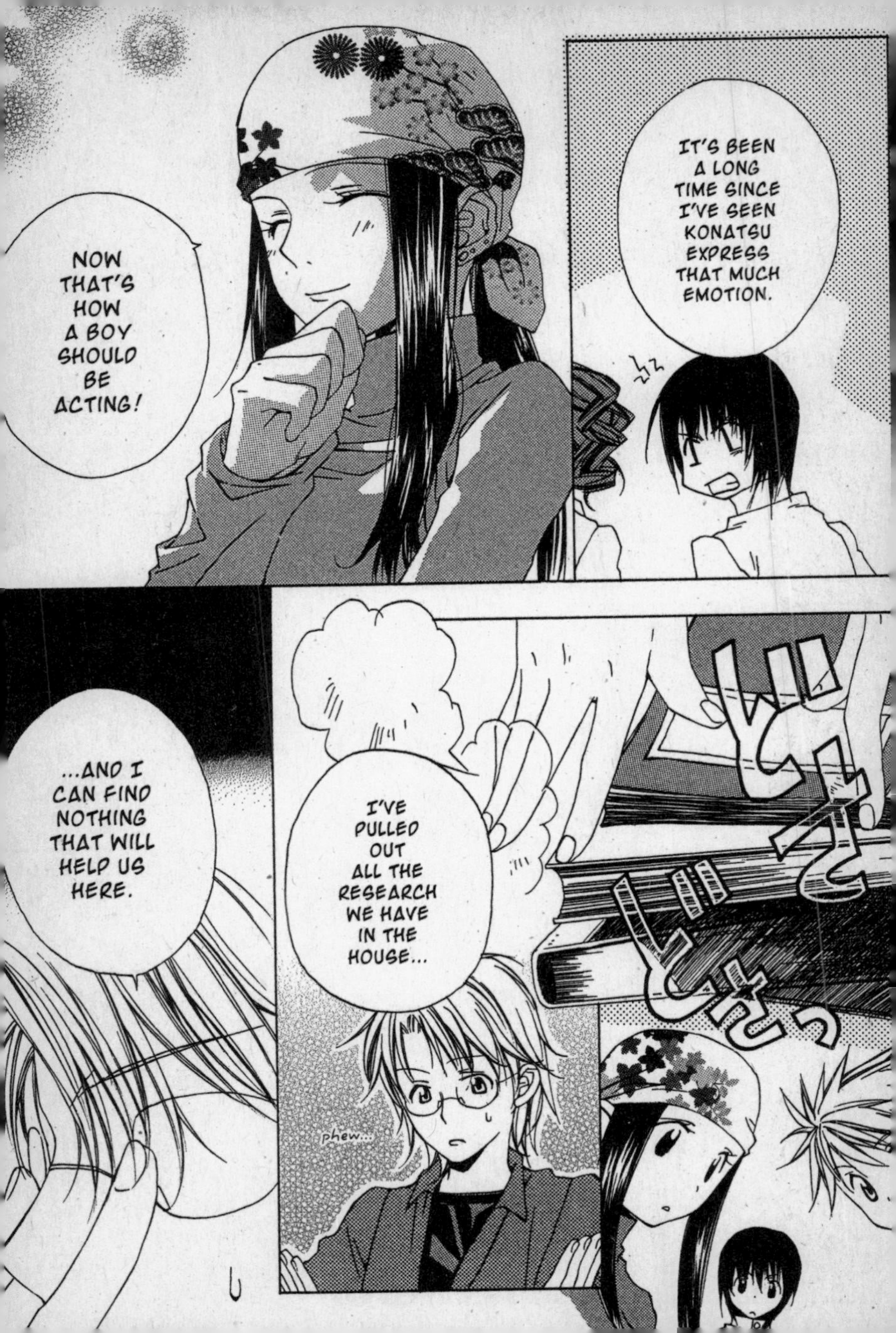
IT'S BEEN A LONG TIME SINCE I'VE SEEN KONATSU EXPRESS THAT MUCH EMOTION.
NOW THAT'S HOW A BOY SHOULD BE ACTING!
I'VE PULLED OUT ALL THE RESEARCH WE HAVE IN THE HOUSE...
phew...
...AND I CAN FIND NOTHING THAT WILL HELP US HERE.

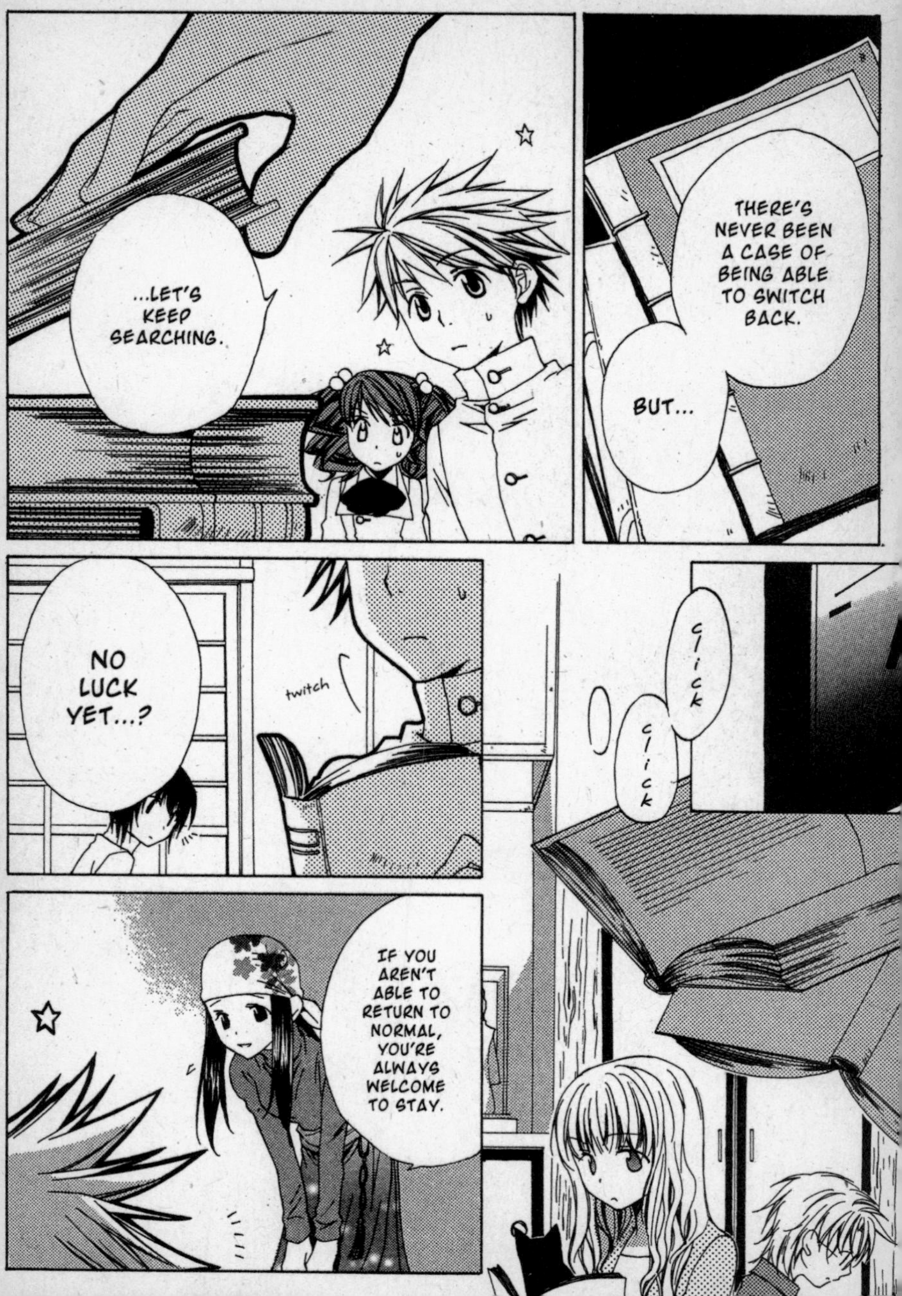

THERE'S NEVER BEEN A CASE OF BEING ABLE TO SWITCH BACK.
BUT...
...LET'S KEEP SEARCHING.
click
click
NO LUCK YET...?
twitch
IF YOU AREN'T ABLE TO RETURN TO NORMAL, YOU'RE ALWAYS WELCOME TO STAY.

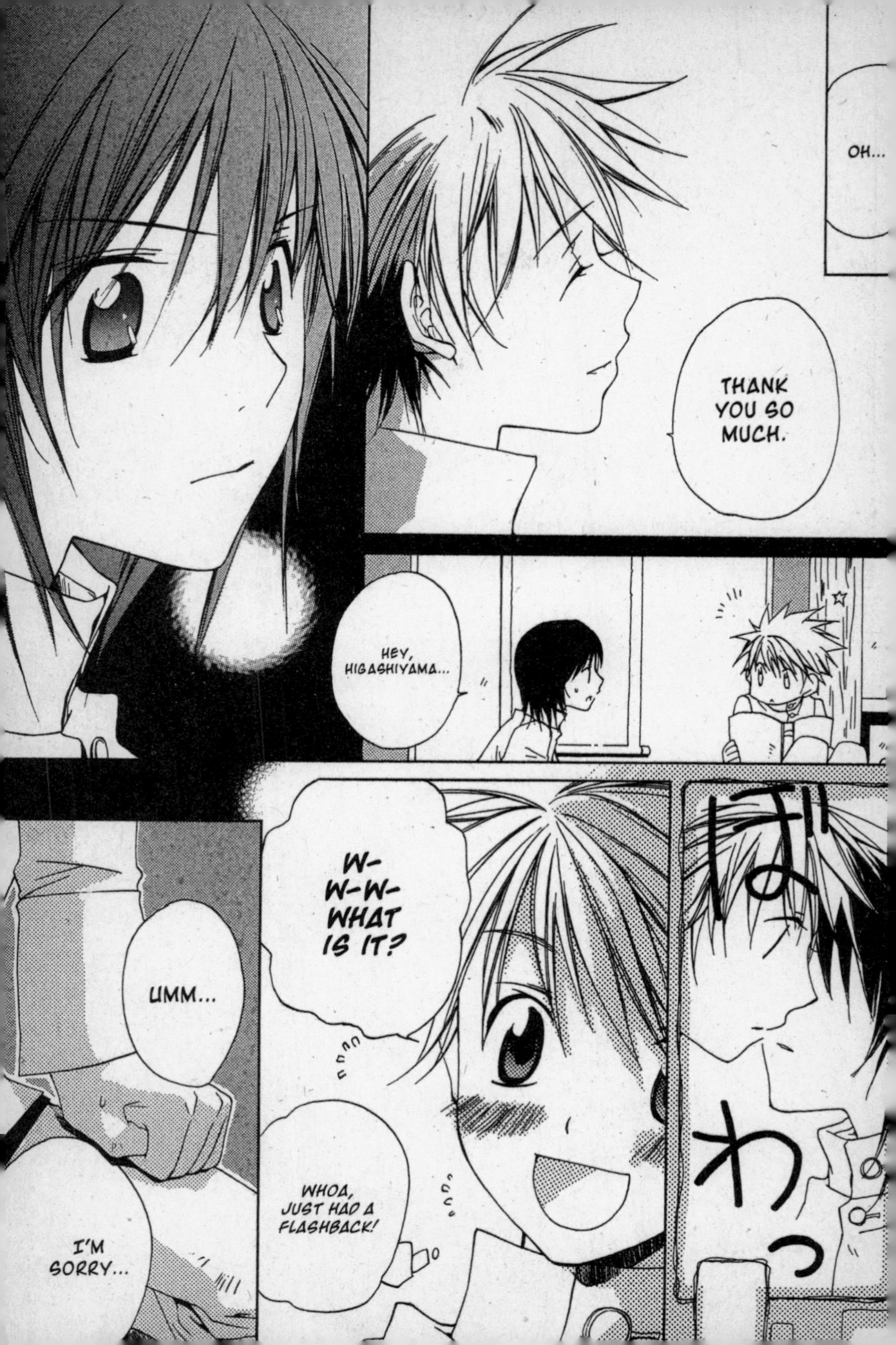
OH...
THANK YOU SO MUCH.
HEY, HIGASHIYAMA...
ばわっ
W-W-W-WHAT IS IT?
WHOA, JUST HAD A FLASHBACK!
UMM...
I'M SORRY...

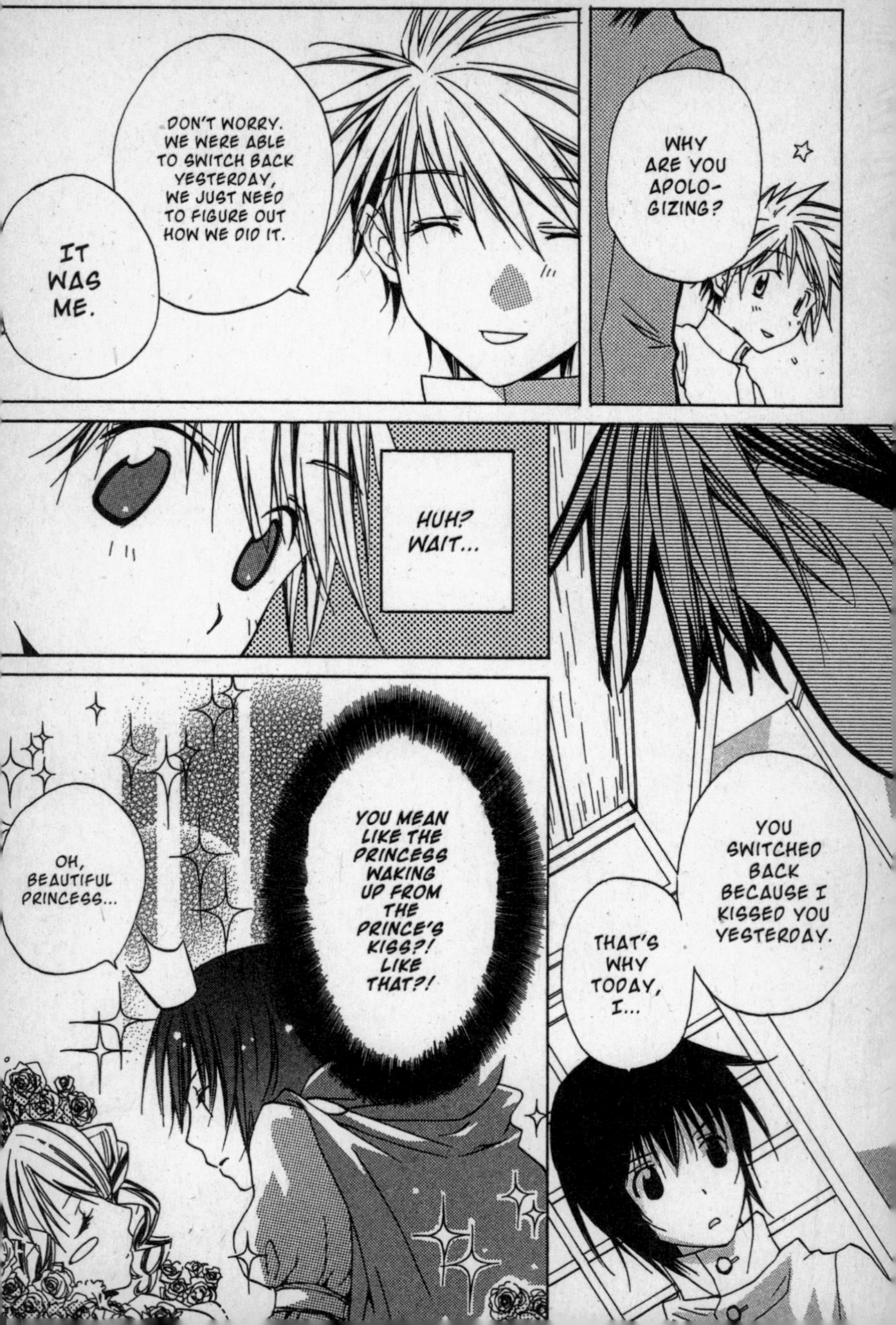
WHY ARE YOU APOLO-GIZING?
DON'T WORRY. WE WERE ABLE TO SWITCH BACK YESTERDAY, WE JUST NEED TO FIGURE OUT HOW WE DID IT.
IT WAS ME.
YOU SWITCHED BACK BECAUSE I KISSED YOU YESTERDAY.
THAT'S WHY TODAY, I...
HUH? WAIT...
YOU MEAN LIKE THE PRINCESS WAKING UP FROM THE PRINCE'S KISS?! LIKE THAT?!
OH, BEAUTIFUL PRINCESS...

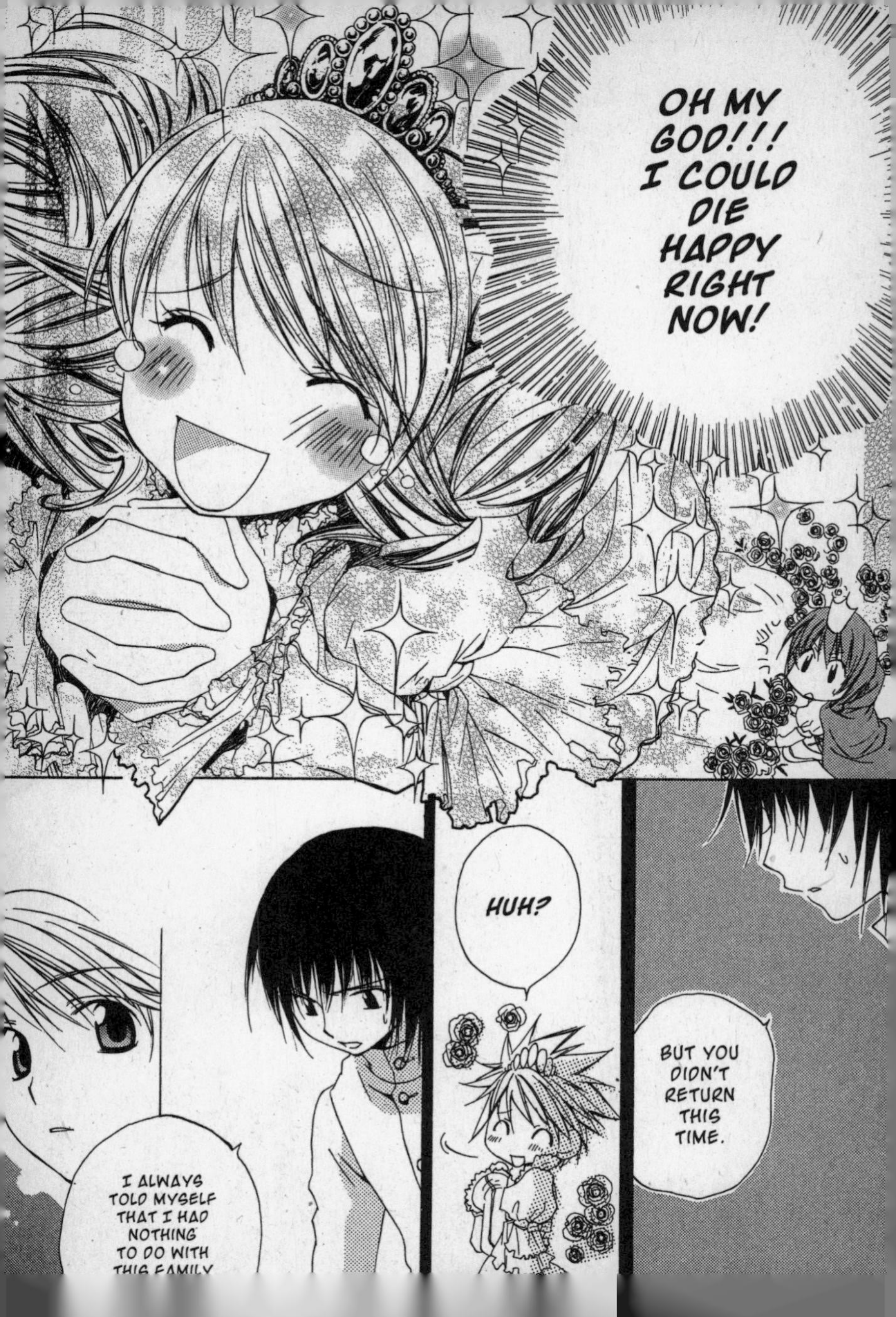
OH MY GOD!!! I COULD DIE HAPPY RIGHT NOW!
BUT YOU DIDN'T RETURN THIS TIME.
HUH?
I ALWAYS TOLD MYSELF THAT I HAD NOTHING TO DO WITH THIS FAMILY

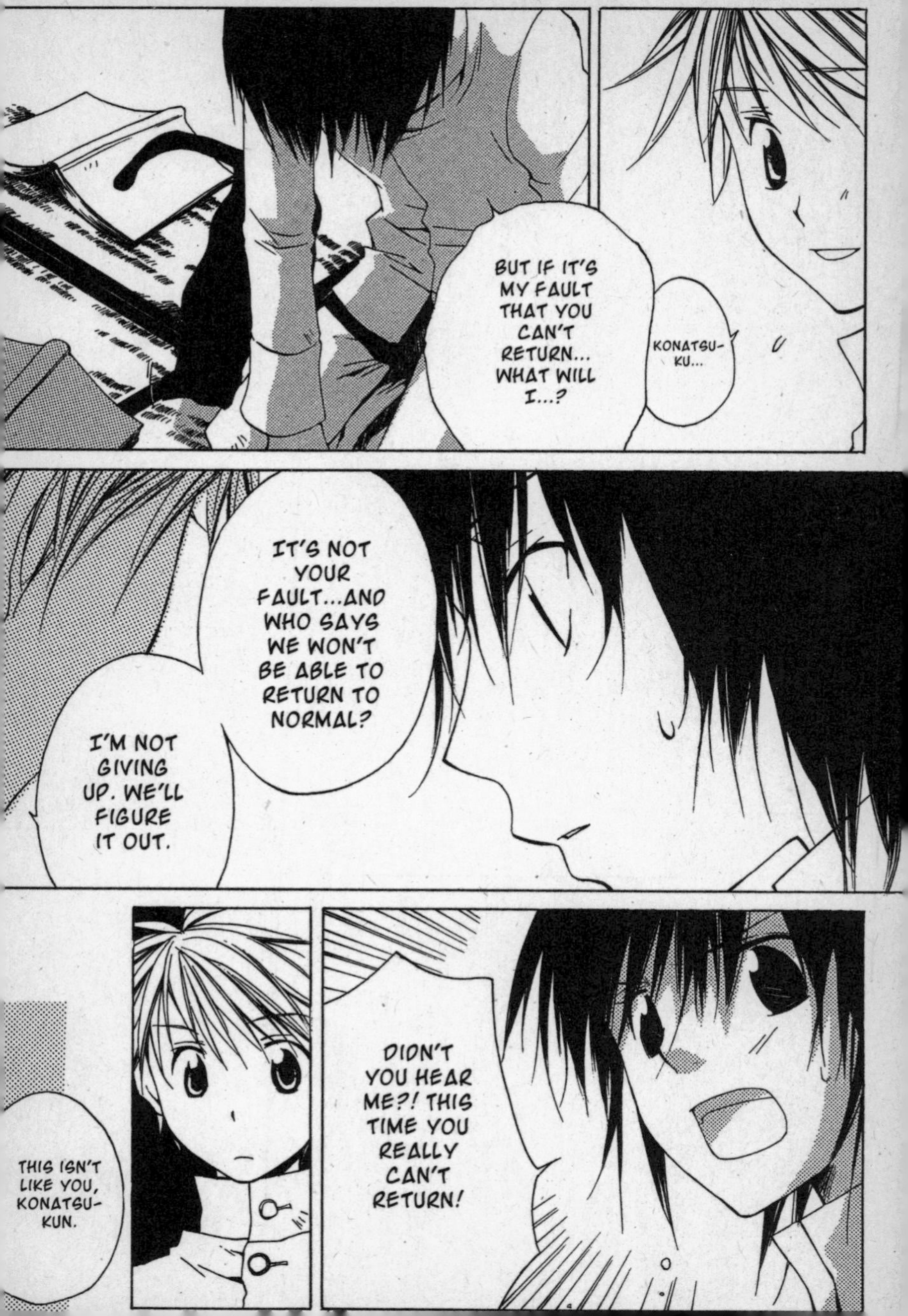
KONATSU-KU...
BUT IF IT'S MY FAULT THAT YOU CAN'T RETURN... WHAT WILL I...?
IT'S NOT YOUR FAULT...AND WHO SAYS WE WON'T BE ABLE TO RETURN TO NORMAL?
I'M NOT GIVING UP. WE'LL FIGURE IT OUT.
DIDN'T YOU HEAR ME?! THIS TIME YOU REALLY CAN'T RETURN!
THIS ISN'T LIKE YOU, KONATSU-KUN.

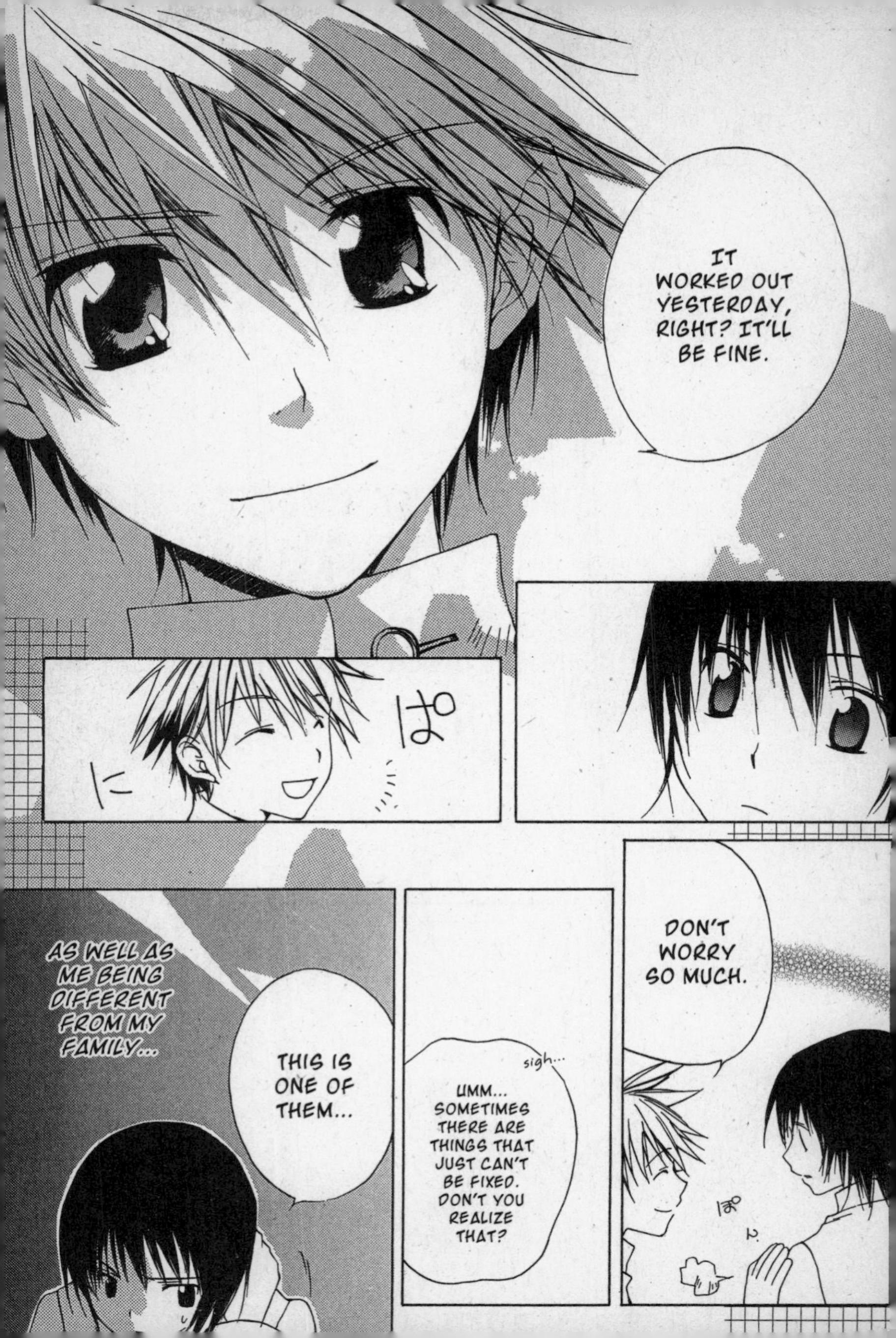
IT WORKED OUT YESTERDAY, RIGHT? IT'LL BE FINE.
ぱ
に
DON'T WORRY SO MUCH.
ぽ
ん
sigh...
UMM... SOMETIMES THERE ARE THINGS THAT JUST CAN'T BE FIXED. DON'T YOU REALIZE THAT?
THIS IS ONE OF THEM...
AS WELL AS ME BEING DIFFERENT FROM MY FAMILY...

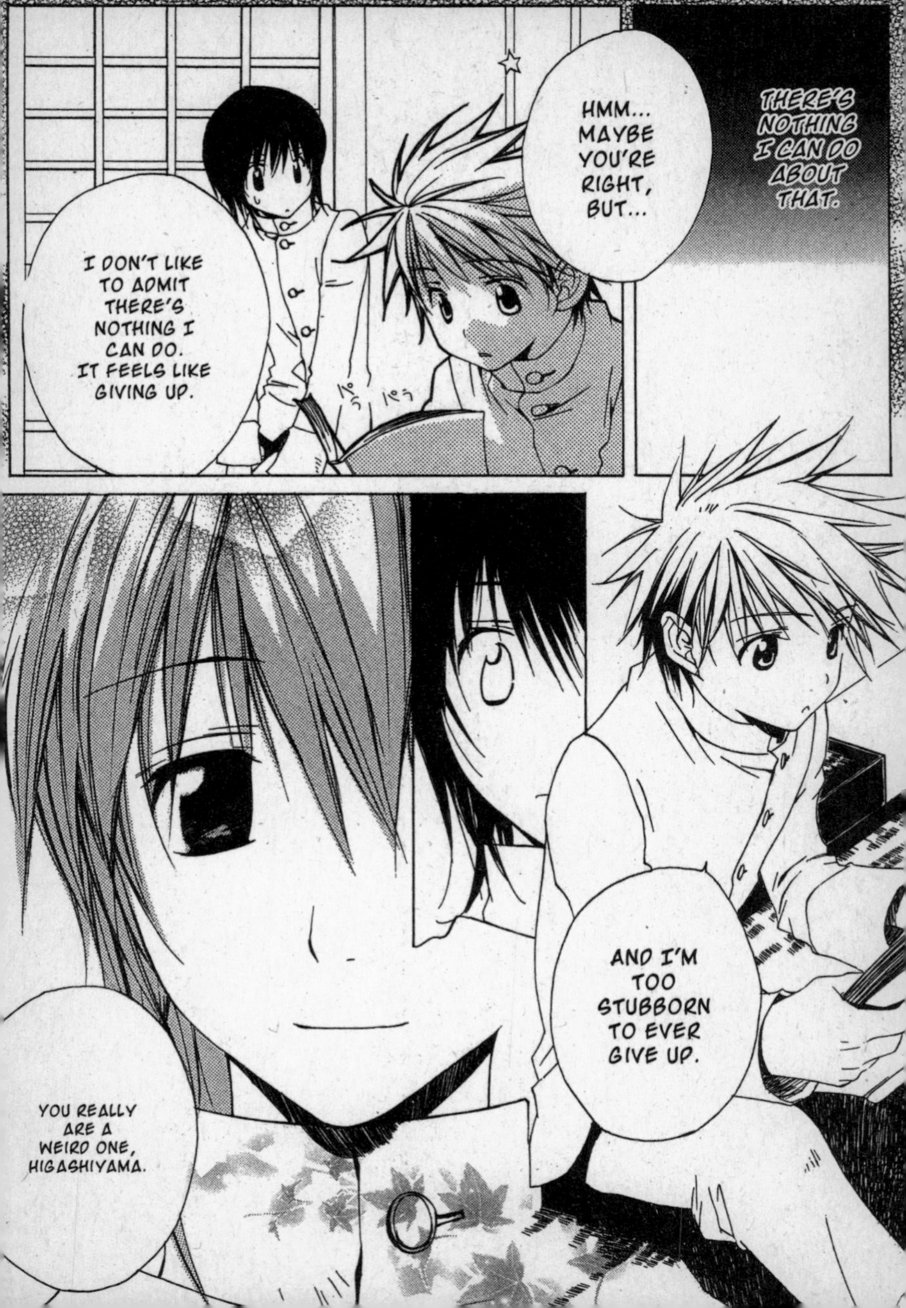
THERE'S NOTHING I CAN DO ABOUT THAT.
HMM... MAYBE YOU'RE RIGHT, BUT...
I DON'T LIKE TO ADMIT THERE'S NOTHING I CAN DO. IT FEELS LIKE GIVING UP.
パラ パラ
AND I'M TOO STUBBORN TO EVER GIVE UP.
YOU REALLY ARE A WEIRD ONE, HIGASHIYAMA.

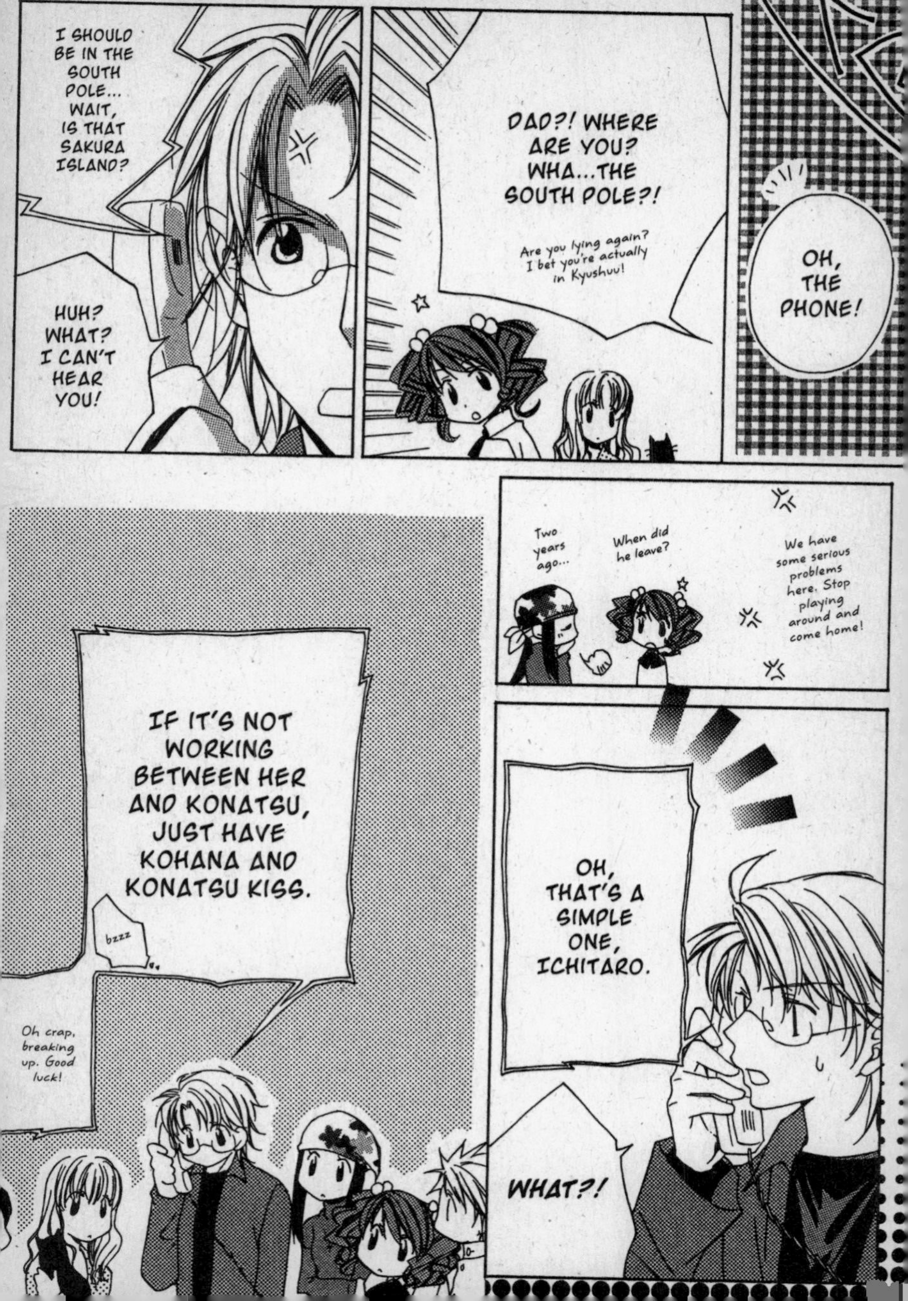
OH, THE PHONE!
DAD?! WHERE ARE YOU? WHA...THE SOUTH POLE?!
Are you lying again? I bet you're actually in Kyushuu!
I SHOULD BE IN THE SOUTH POLE... WAIT, IS THAT SAKURA ISLAND?
HUH? WHAT? I CAN'T HEAR YOU!
We have some serious problems here. Stop playing around and come home!
When did he leave?
Two years ago...
OH, THAT'S A SIMPLE ONE, ICHITARO.
WHAT?!
IF IT'S NOT WORKING BETWEEN HER AND KONATSU, JUST HAVE KOHANA AND KONATSU KISS.
bzzz
Oh crap, breaking up. Good luck!

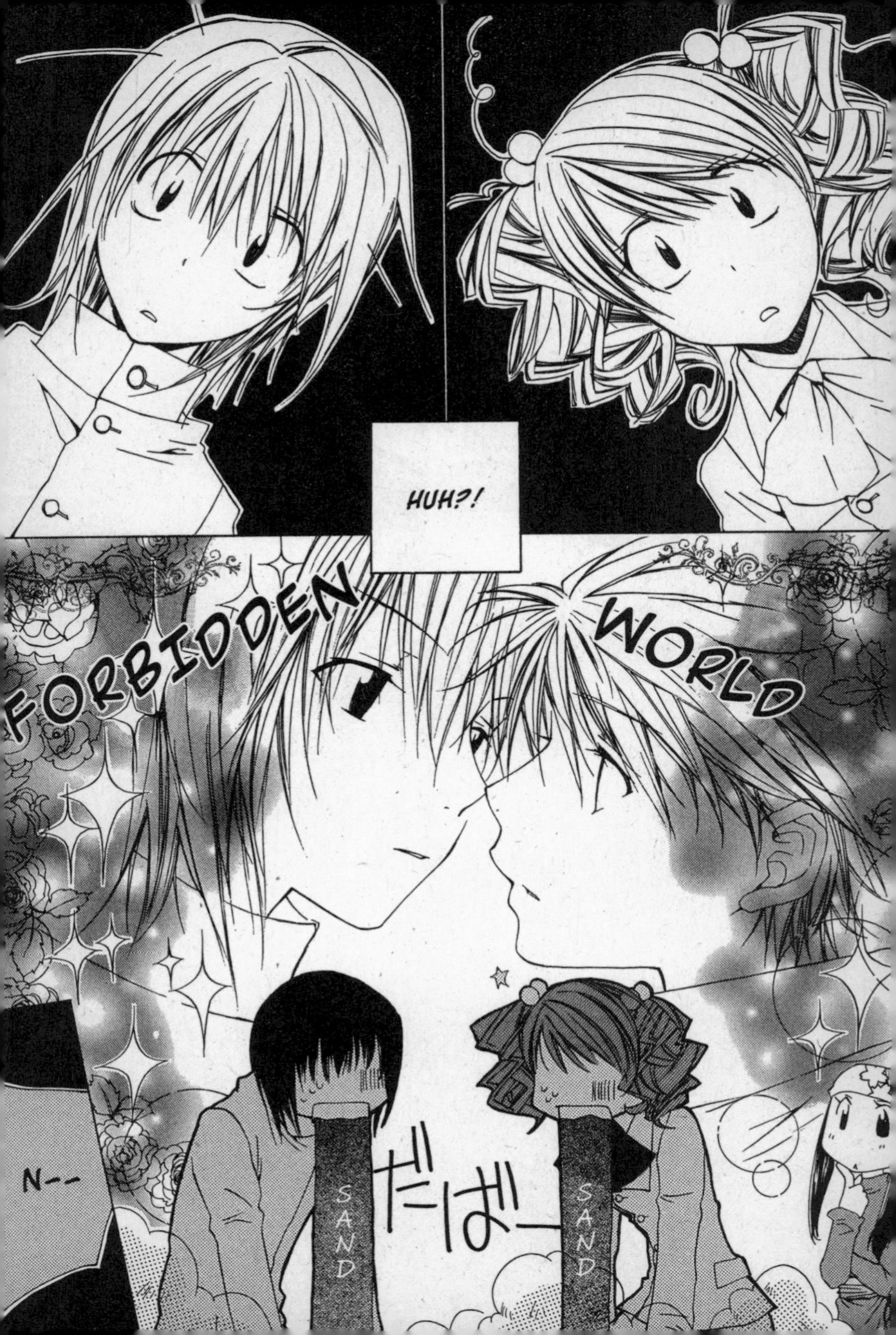
HUH?!
FORBIDDEN WORLD
SAND
だばー
SAND
N--

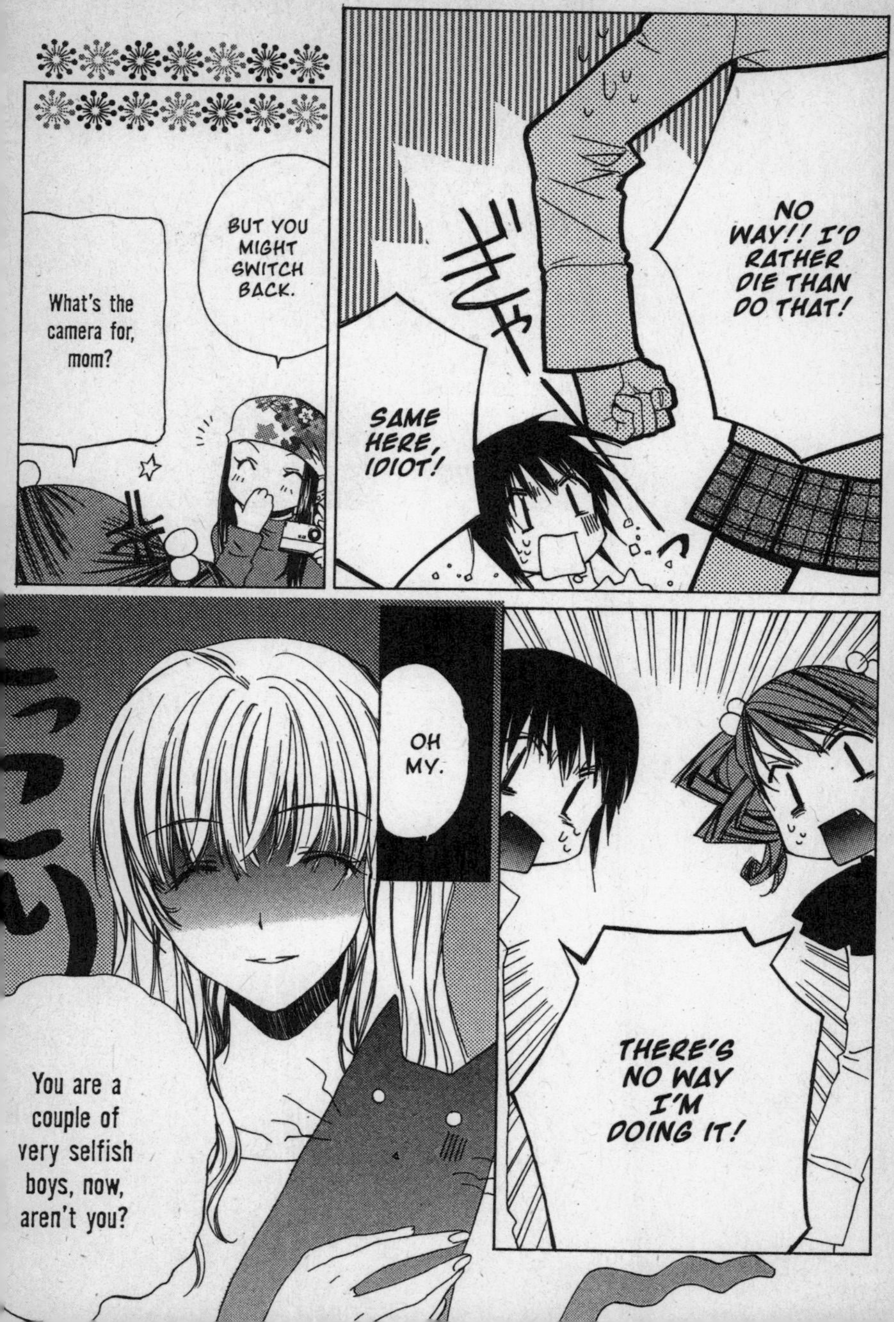
NO WAY!! I'D RATHER DIE THAN DO THAT!
SAME HERE, IDIOT!
BUT YOU MIGHT SWITCH BACK.
What's the camera for, mom?
THERE'S NO WAY I'M DOING IT!
OH MY.
You are a couple of very selfish boys, now, aren't you?

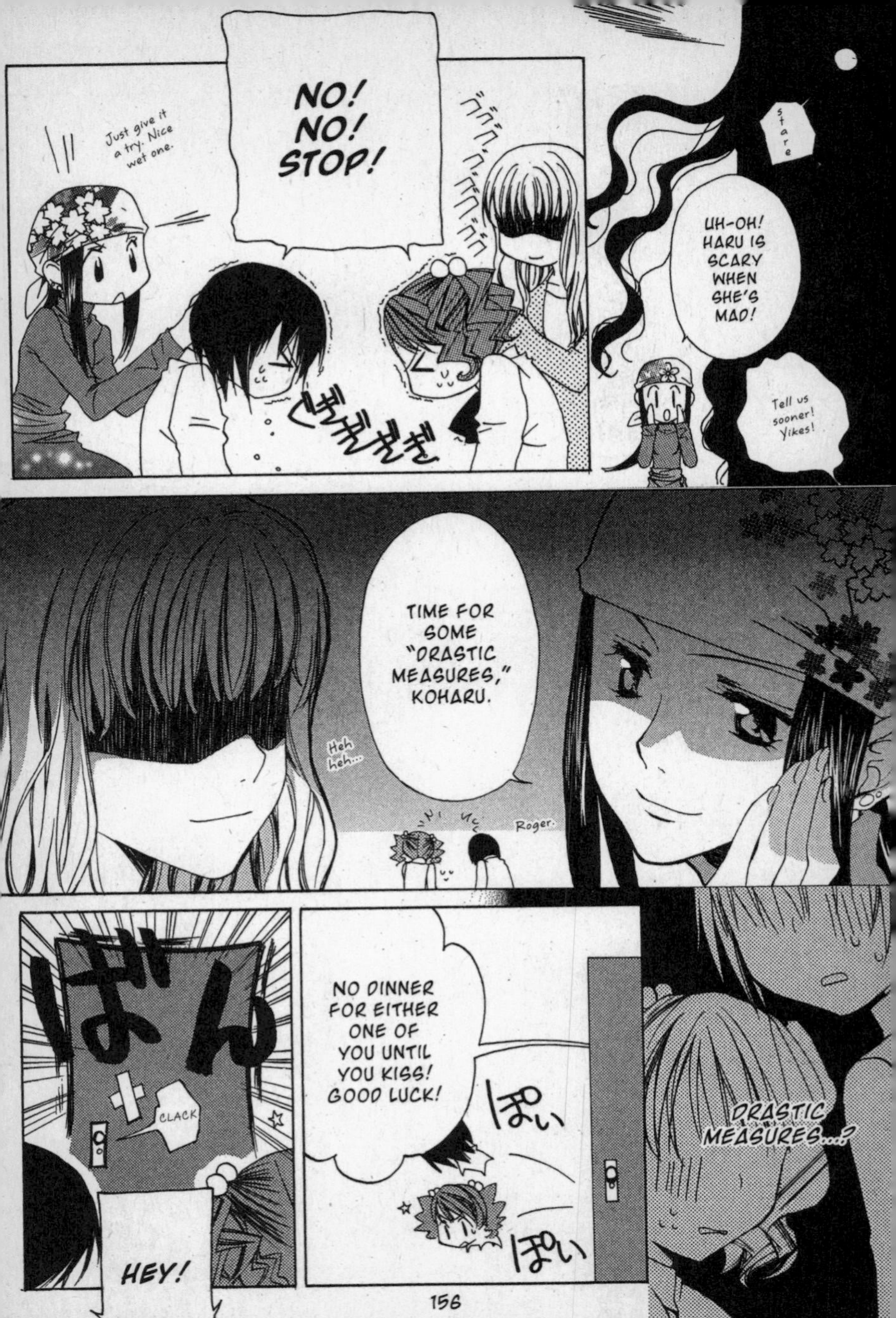

stare
UH-OH! HARU IS SCARY WHEN SHE'S MAD!
Tell us sooner! Yikes!
NO! NO! STOP!
Just give it a try. Nice wet one.
TIME FOR SOME "DRASTIC MEASURES," KOHARU.
Roger.
Heh heh...
DRASTIC MEASURES...?
NO DINNER FOR EITHER ONE OF YOU UNTIL YOU KISS! GOOD LUCK!
ぽい
ぽい
CLACK
HEY!

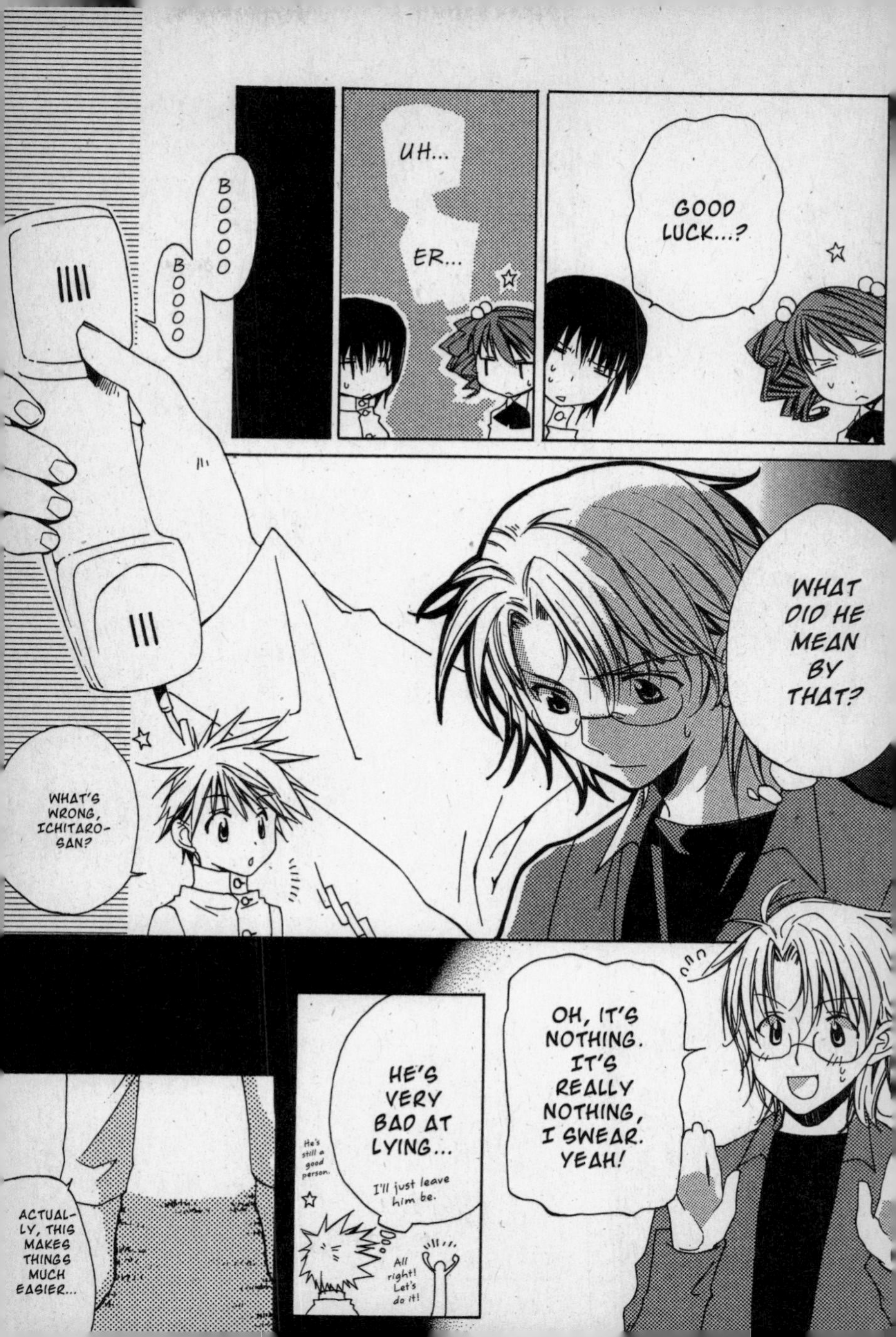
GOOD LUCK...?
UH...
ER...
BOOOO
BOOOO
WHAT DID HE MEAN BY THAT?
WHAT'S WRONG, ICHITARO-SAN?
OH, IT'S NOTHING. IT'S REALLY NOTHING, I SWEAR. YEAH!
HE'S VERY BAD AT LYING...
I'll just leave him be.
He's still a good person.
All right! Let's do it!
ACTUALLY, THIS MAKES THINGS MUCH EASIER...

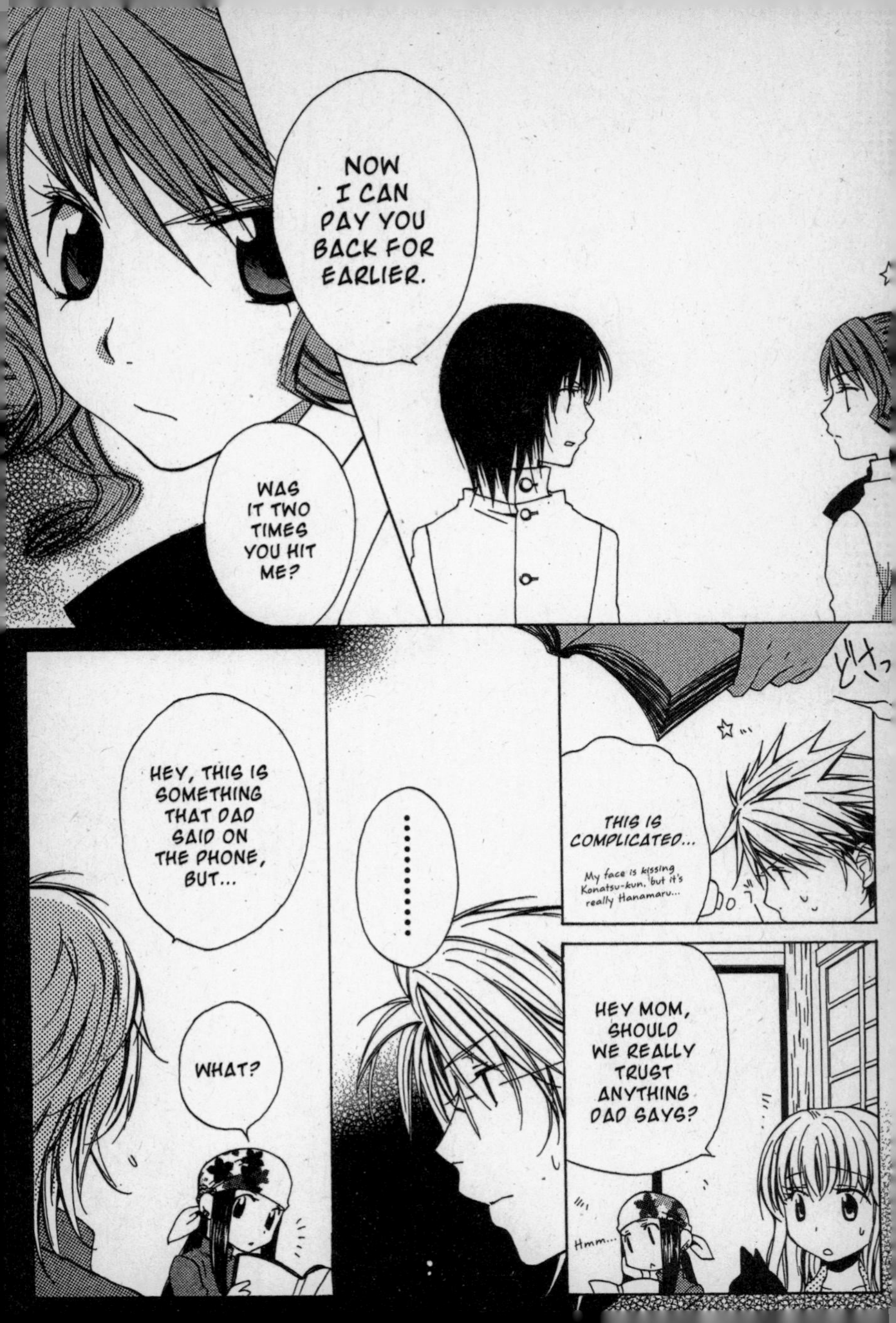
NOW I CAN PAY YOU BACK FOR EARLIER.
WAS IT TWO TIMES YOU HIT ME?
THIS IS COMPLICATED...
My face is kissing Konatsu-kun, but it's really Hanamaru...
HEY MOM, SHOULD WE REALLY TRUST ANYTHING DAD SAYS?
Hmm...
....
HEY, THIS IS SOMETHING THAT DAD SAID ON THE PHONE, BUT...
WHAT?

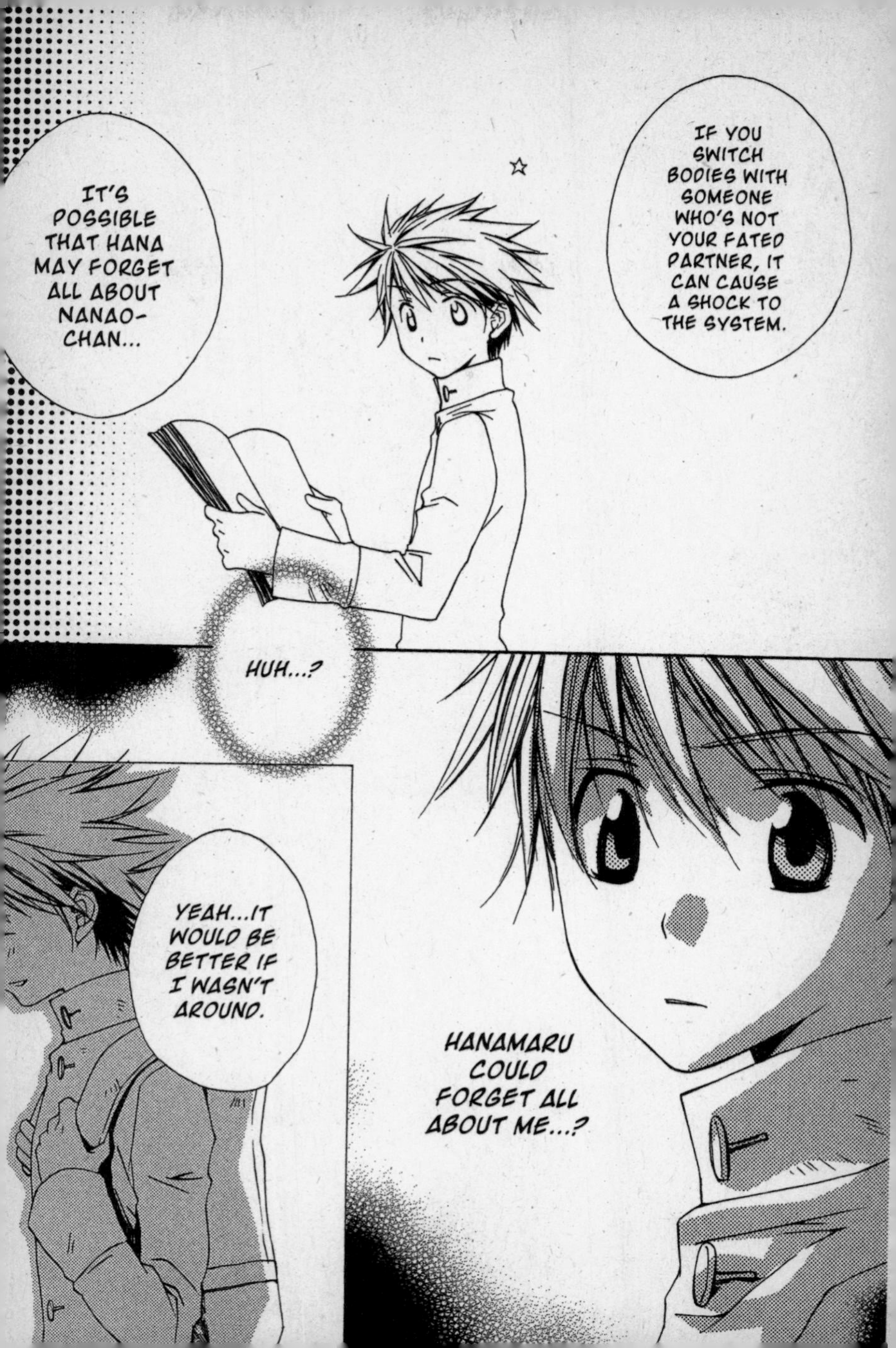
IF YOU SWITCH BODIES WITH SOMEONE WHO'S NOT YOUR FATED PARTNER, IT CAN CAUSE A SHOCK TO THE SYSTEM.
IT'S POSSIBLE THAT HANA MAY FORGET ALL ABOUT NANAO-CHAN...
HUH...?
HANAMARU COULD FORGET ALL ABOUT ME...?
YEAH...IT WOULD BE BETTER IF I WASN'T AROUND.

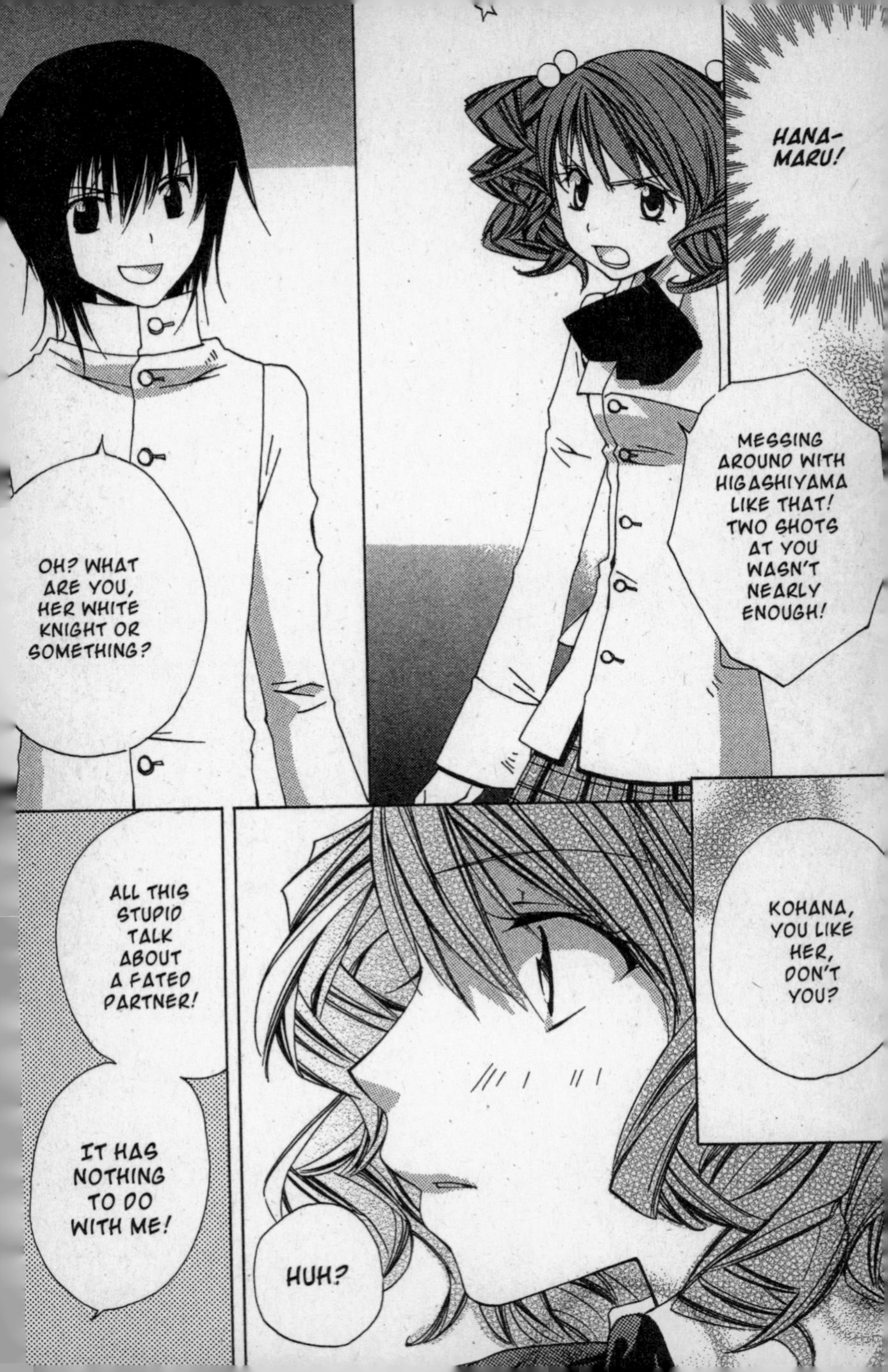
HANA-MARU!
MESSING AROUND WITH HIGASHIYAMA LIKE THAT! TWO SHOTS AT YOU WASN'T NEARLY ENOUGH!
OH? WHAT ARE YOU, HER WHITE KNIGHT OR SOMETHING?
KOHANA, YOU LIKE HER, DON'T YOU?
HUH?
ALL THIS STUPID TALK ABOUT A FATED PARTNER!
IT HAS NOTHING TO DO WITH ME!

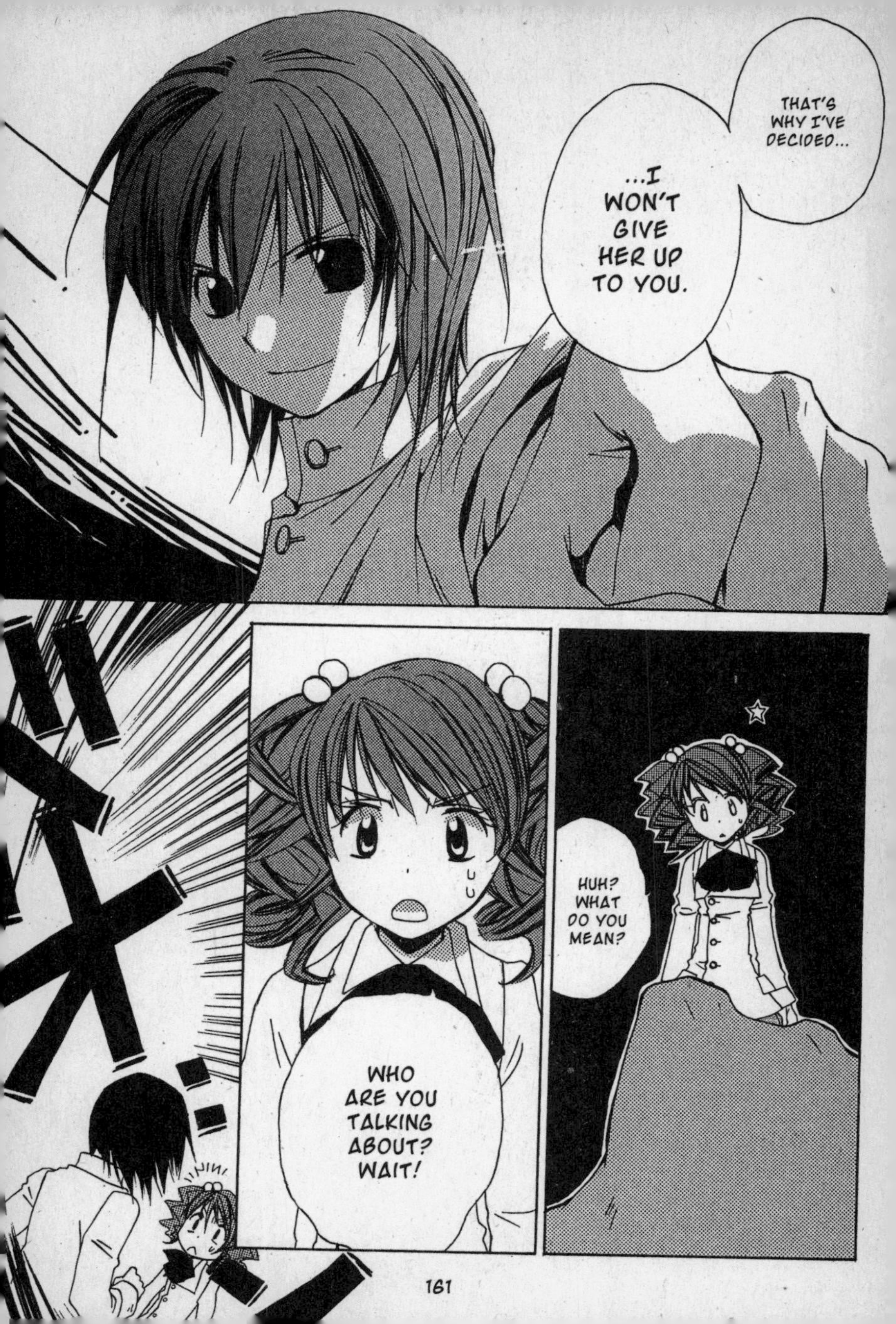
THAT'S WHY I'VE DECIDED...
...I WON'T GIVE HER UP TO YOU.
HUH? WHAT DO YOU MEAN?
WHO ARE YOU TALKING ABOUT? WAIT!

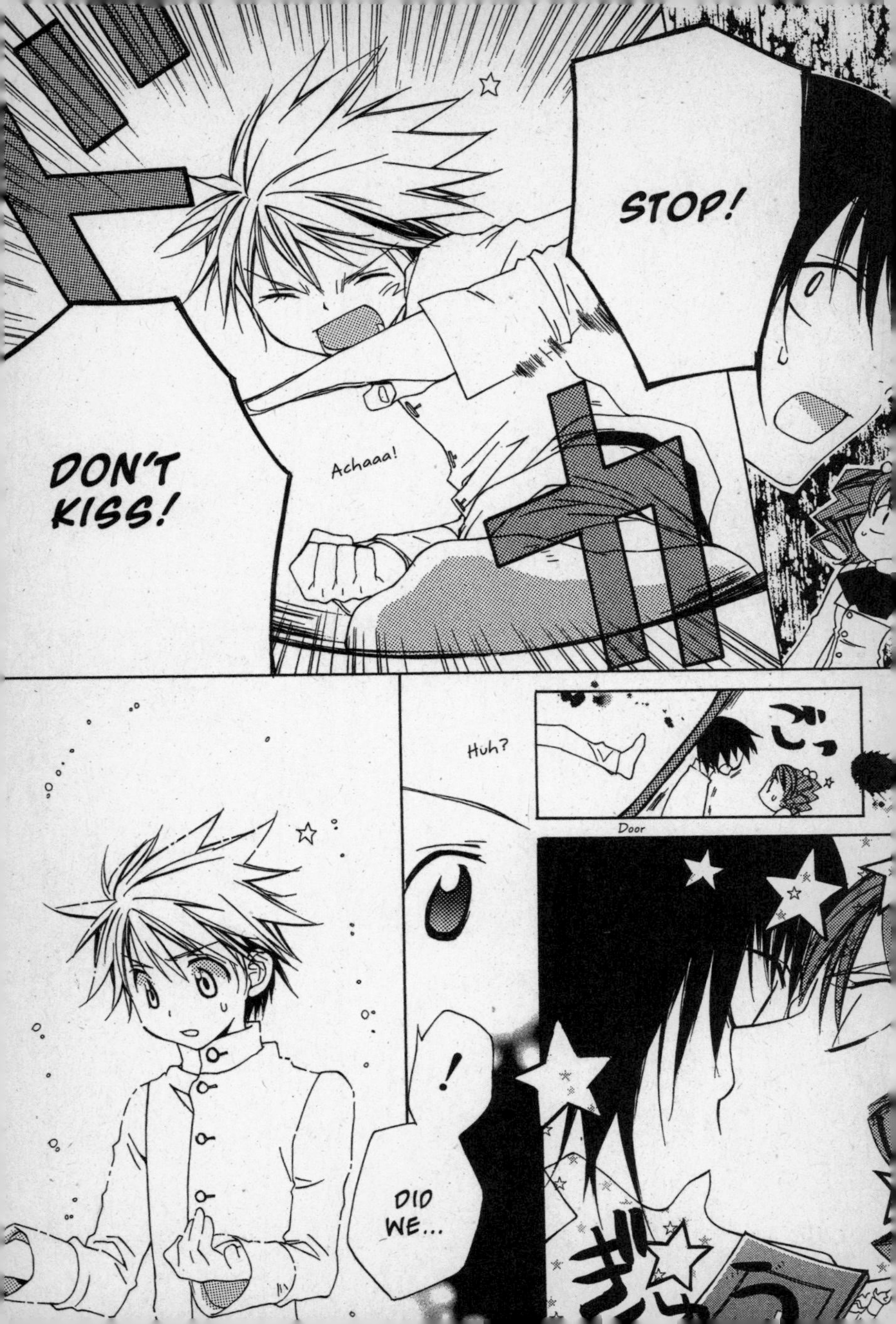
STOP!
Achaaa!
DON'T KISS!
Huh?
ごっ
Door
!
DID WE...

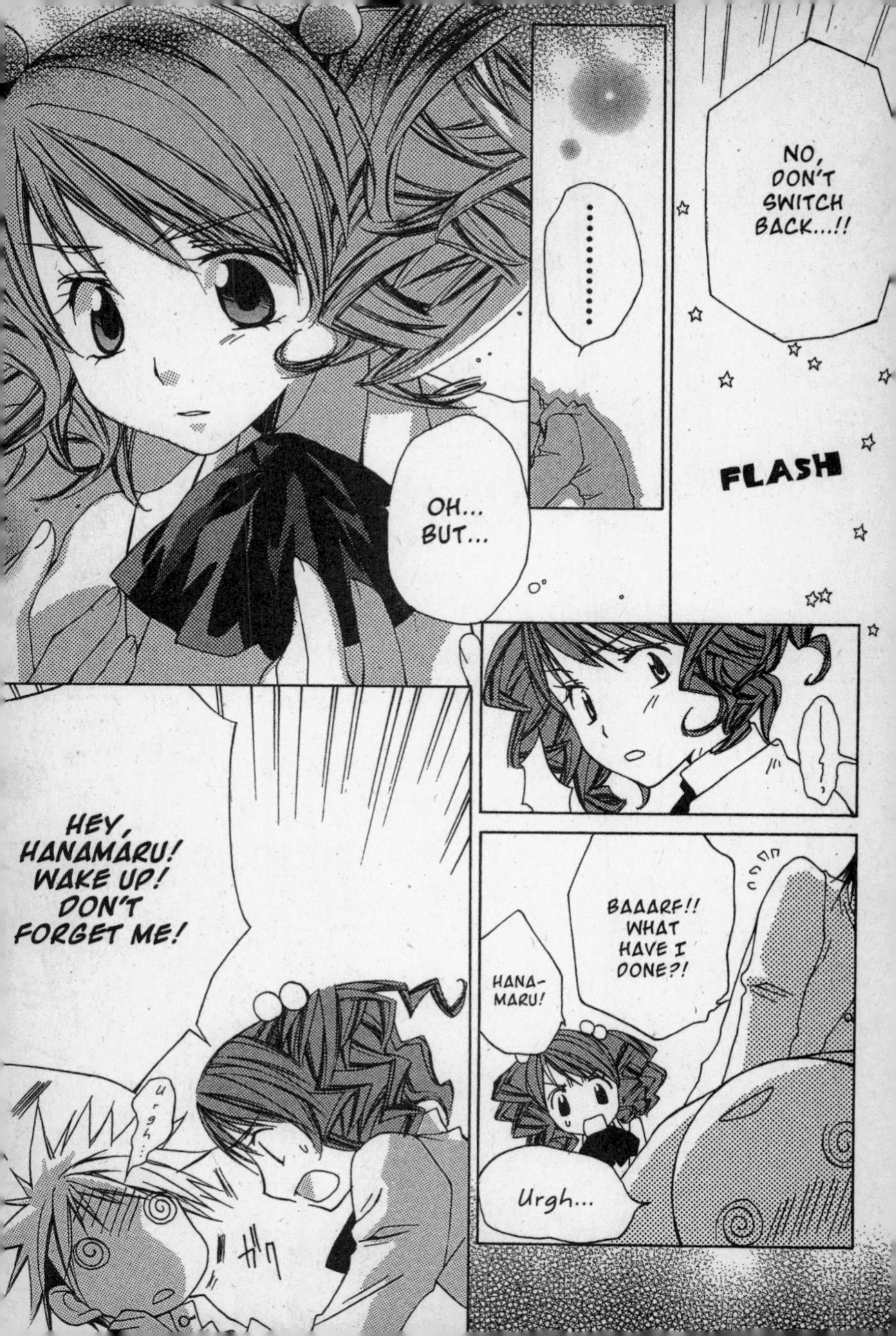
NO, DON'T SWITCH BACK...!!
FLASH
......
OH... BUT...
BAAARF!! WHAT HAVE I DONE?!
HANA-MARU!
Urgh...
HEY, HANAMARU! WAKE UP! DON'T FORGET ME!
Urgh...

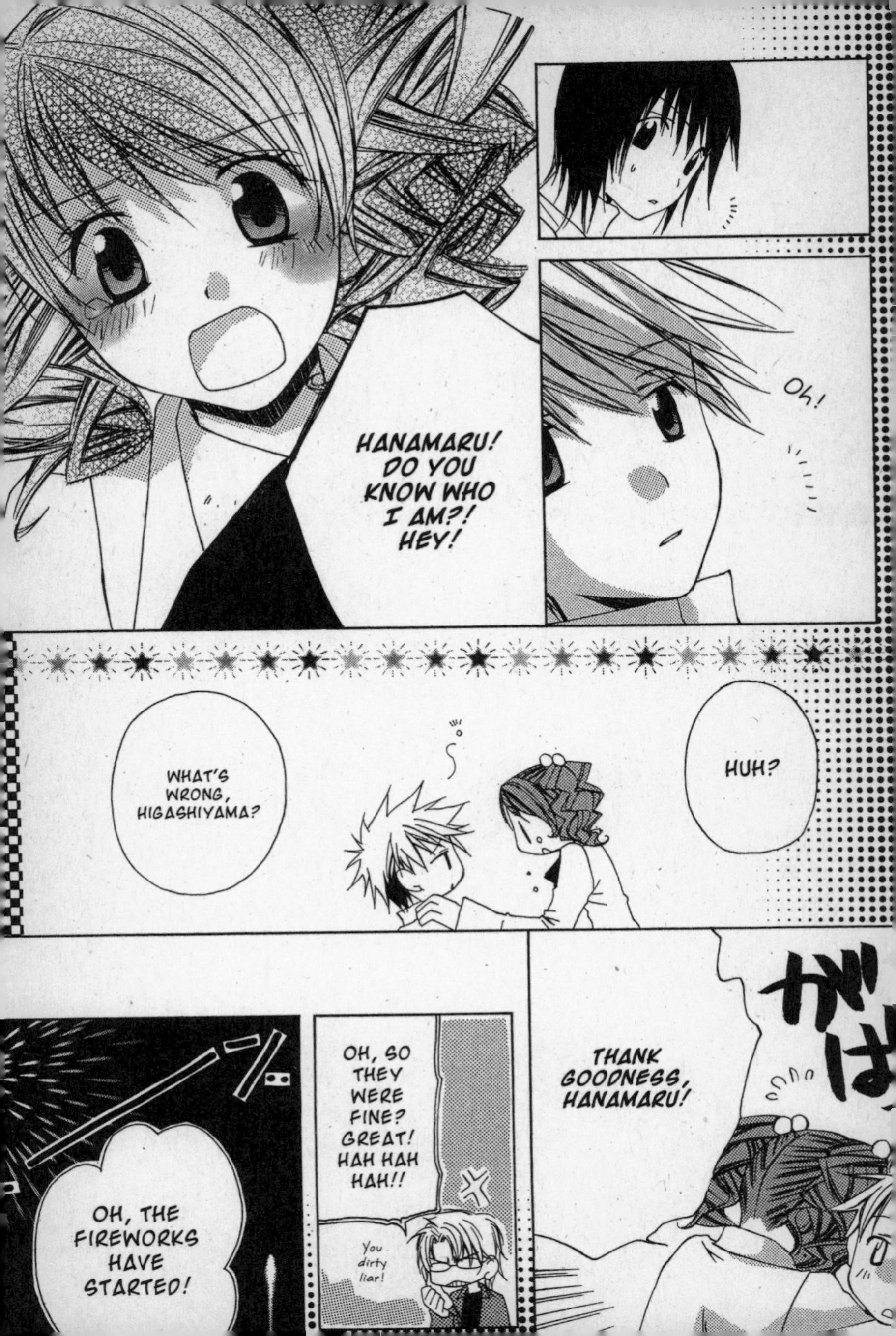
Oh!
HANAMARU! DO YOU KNOW WHO I AM?! HEY!
HUH?
WHAT'S WRONG, HIGASHIYAMA?
がは
THANK GOODNESS, HANAMARU!
OH, SO THEY WERE FINE? GREAT! HAH HAH HAH!!
You dirty liar!
OH, THE FIREWORKS HAVE STARTED!

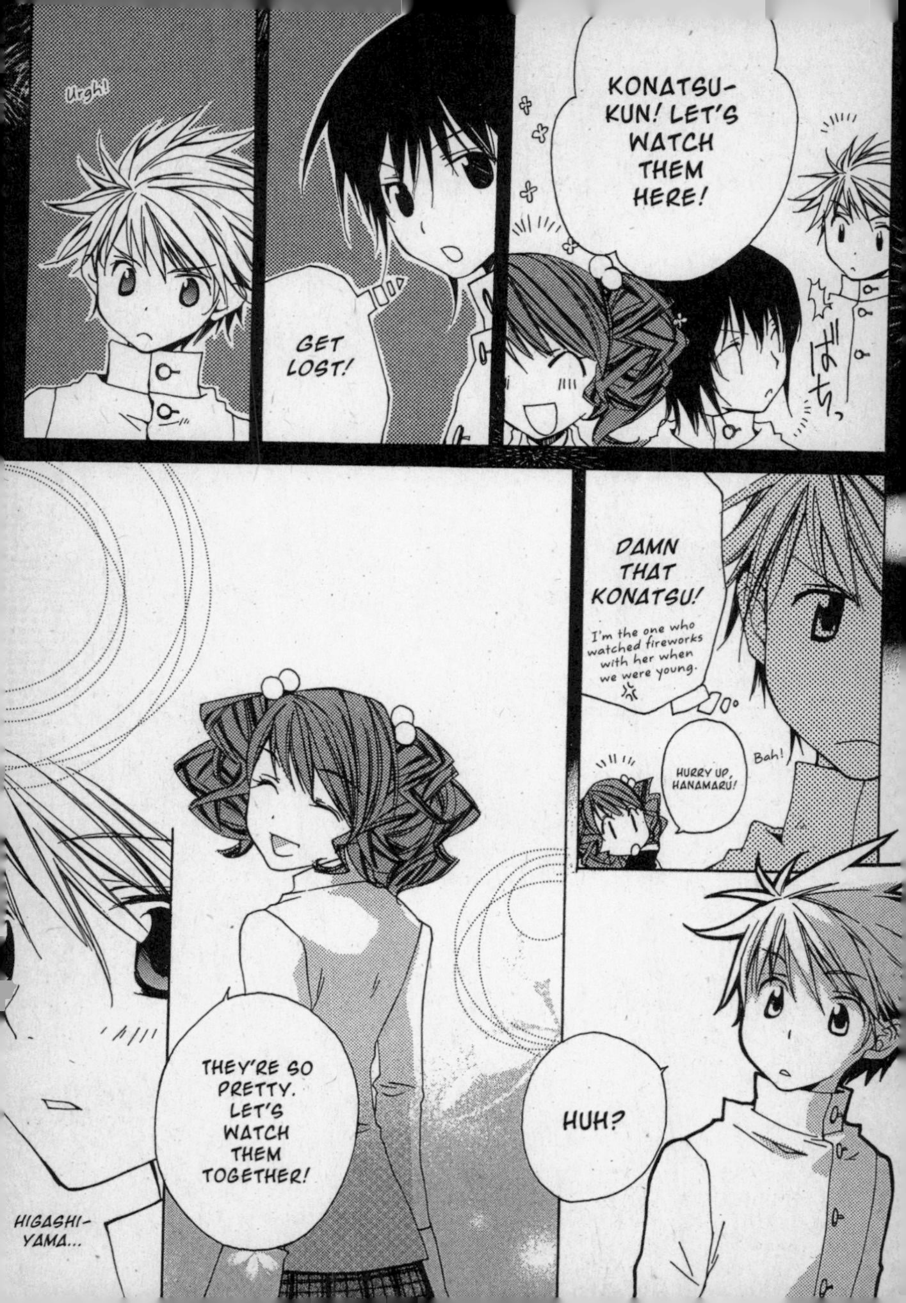
KONATSU-KUN! LET'S WATCH THEM HERE!
ぱち
GET LOST!
Urgh!
DAMN THAT KONATSU!
I'm the one who watched fireworks with her when we were young.
Bah!
HURRY UP, HANAMARU!
HUH?
THEY'RE SO PRETTY. LET'S WATCH THEM TOGETHER!
HIGASHI-YAMA...

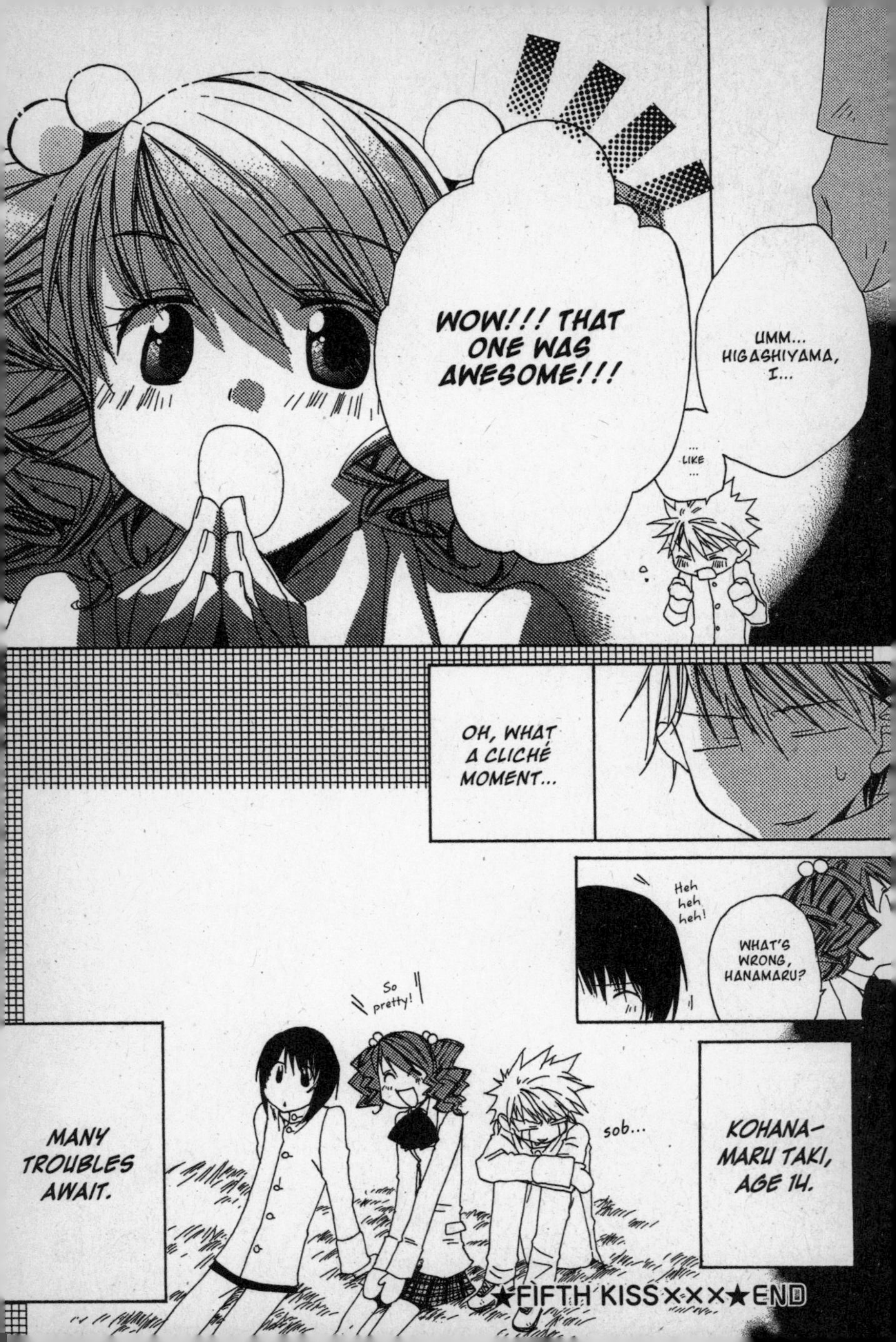
UMM... HIGASHIYAMA, I...
...LIKE...
WOW!!! THAT ONE WAS AWESOME!!!
OH, WHAT A CLICHÉ MOMENT...
Heh heh heh!
WHAT'S WRONG, HANAMARU?
KOHANA-MARU TAKI, AGE 14.
sob...
So pretty!
MANY TROUBLES AWAIT.
★FIFTH KISS×××★END

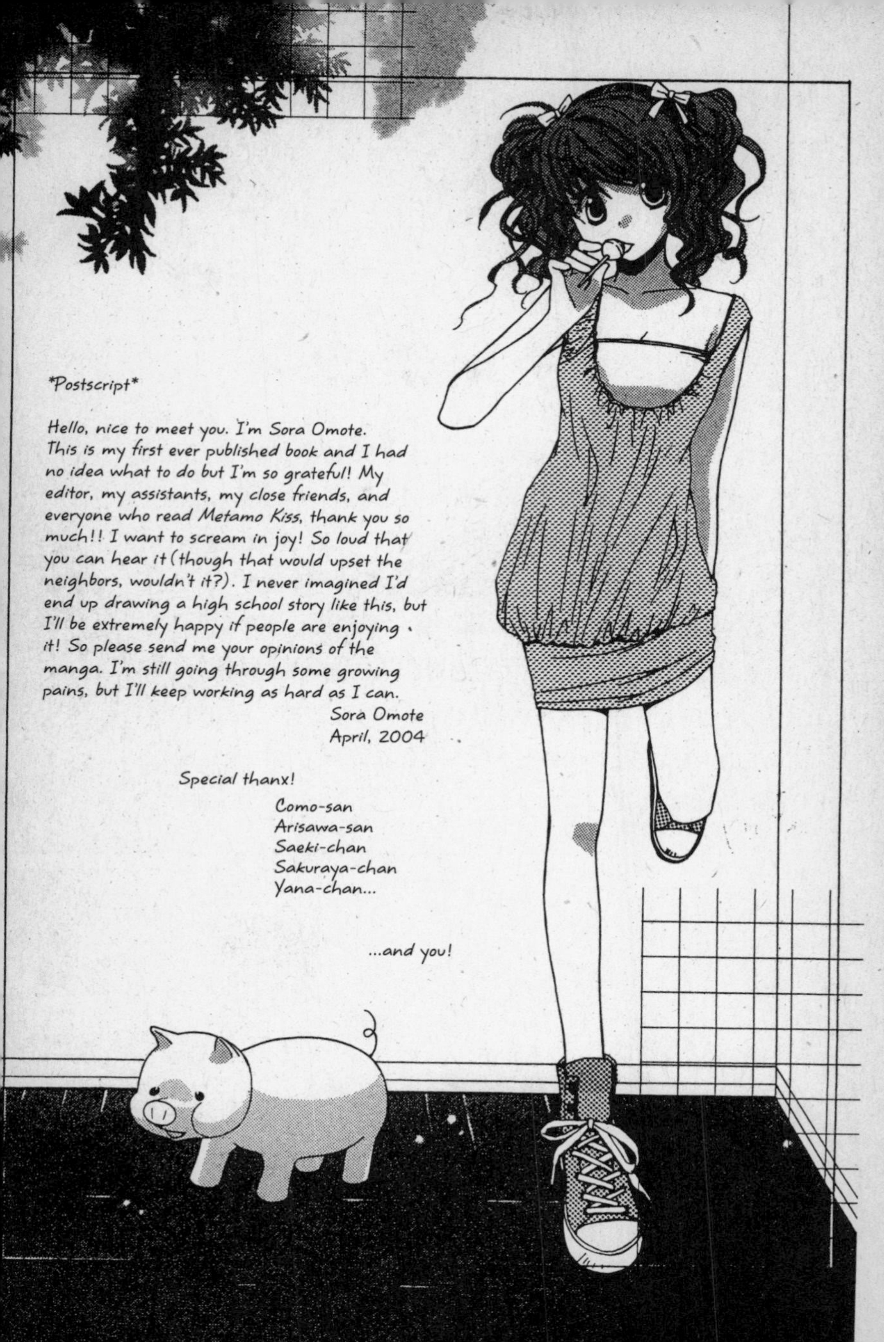

Postscript

Hello, nice to meet you. I'm Sora Omote. This is my first ever published book and I had no idea what to do but I'm so grateful! My editor, my assistants, my close friends, and everyone who read Metamo Kiss, thank you so much!! I want to scream in joy! So loud that you can hear it (though that would upset the neighbors, wouldn't it?). I never imagined I'd end up drawing a high school story like this, but I'll be extremely happy if people are enjoying it! So please send me your opinions of the manga. I'm still going through some growing pains, but I'll keep working as hard as I can.

Sora Omote
April, 2004

Special thanx!

Como-san
Arisawa-san
Saeki-chan
Sakuraya-chan
Yana-chan...

...and you!

Next Time in...

metamo KISS

Who would suspect that Hanamaru and Nanao could switch bodies? Who else but Madoka, the school's paranormal geek? This crazy stalker will do anything to uncover a newsworthy secret! As Hanamaru fends her off, Nanao trains for the big archery tournament...but what will happen when she and Hanamaru switch bodies on the day of the competition?!

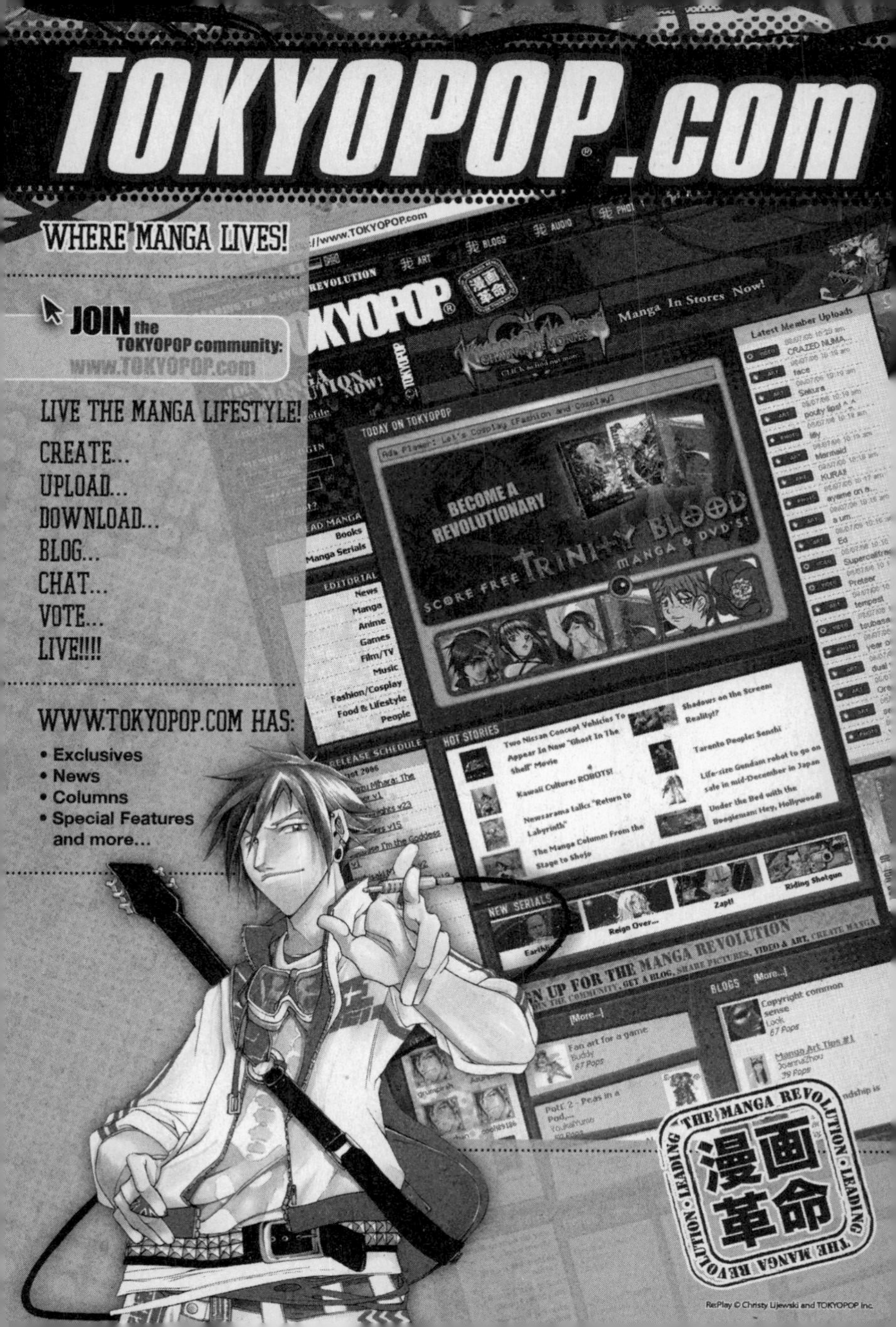
TOKYOPOP®.com
WHERE MANGA LIVES!
JOIN the TOKYOPOP community:
WWW.TOKYOPOP.com
LIVE THE MANGA LIFESTYLE!
CREATE...
UPLOAD...
DOWNLOAD...
BLOG...
CHAT...
VOTE...
LIVE!!!!
WWW.TOKYOPOP.COM HAS:
• Exclusives
• News
• Columns
• Special Features and more...
THE MANGA REVOLUTION • LEADING • THE MANGA REVOLUTION • LEADING
漫画革命
Re:Play © Christy Lijewski and TOKYOPOP Inc.

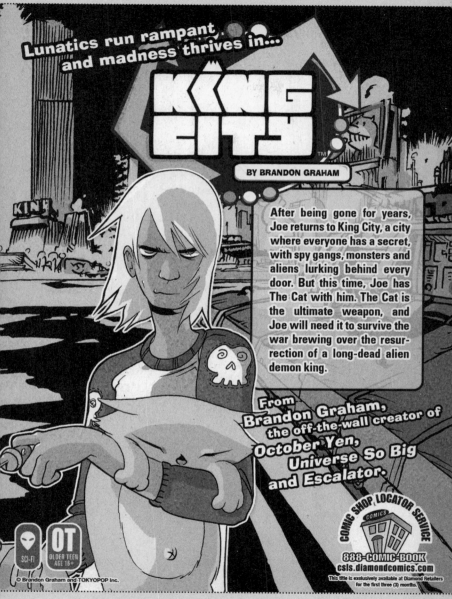

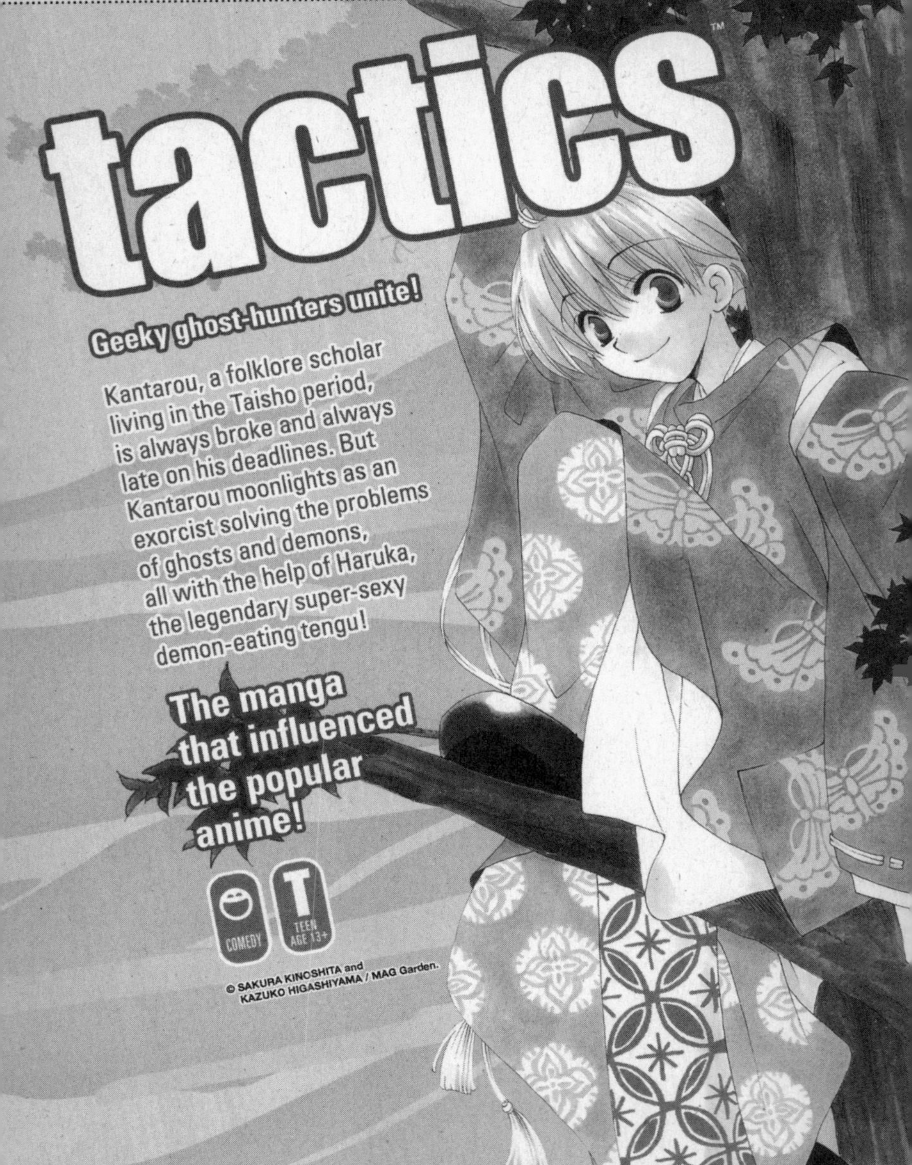
tactics™
Geeky ghost-hunters unite!
Kantarou, a folklore scholar
living in the Taisho period,
is always broke and always
late on his deadlines. But
Kantarou moonlights as an
exorcist solving the problems
of ghosts and demons,
all with the help of Haruka,
the legendary super-sexy
demon-eating tengu!
The manga
that influenced
the popular
anime!
COMEDY
T
TEEN
AGE 13+
© SAKURA KINOSHITA and
KAZUKO HIGASHIYAMA / MAG Garden.

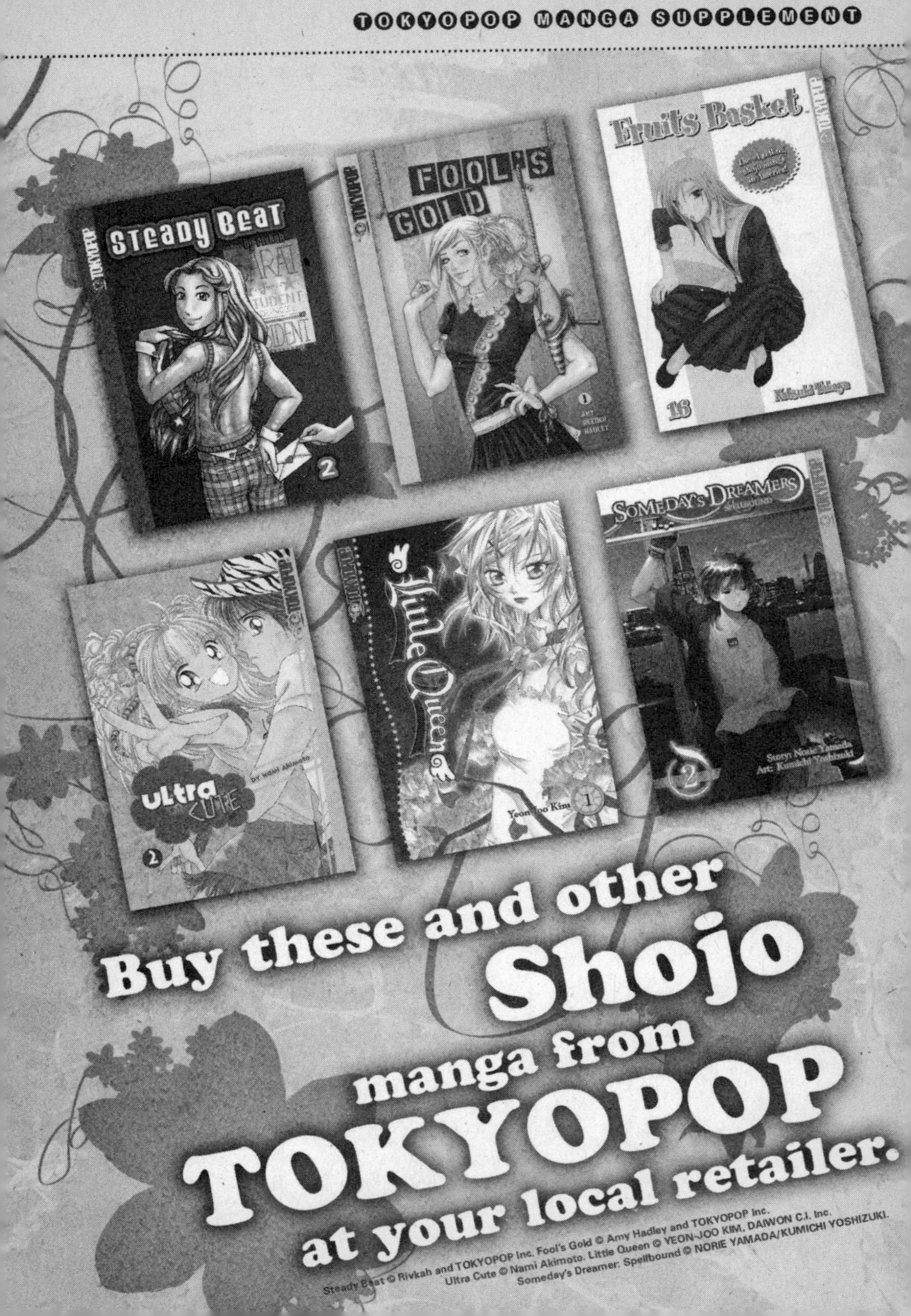
Steady Beat
2
Fool's Gold
1
Fruits Basket
16
ultra CUTE
2
Little Queen
Yeon-Joo Kim
1
Someday's Dreamers
Spellbound
2

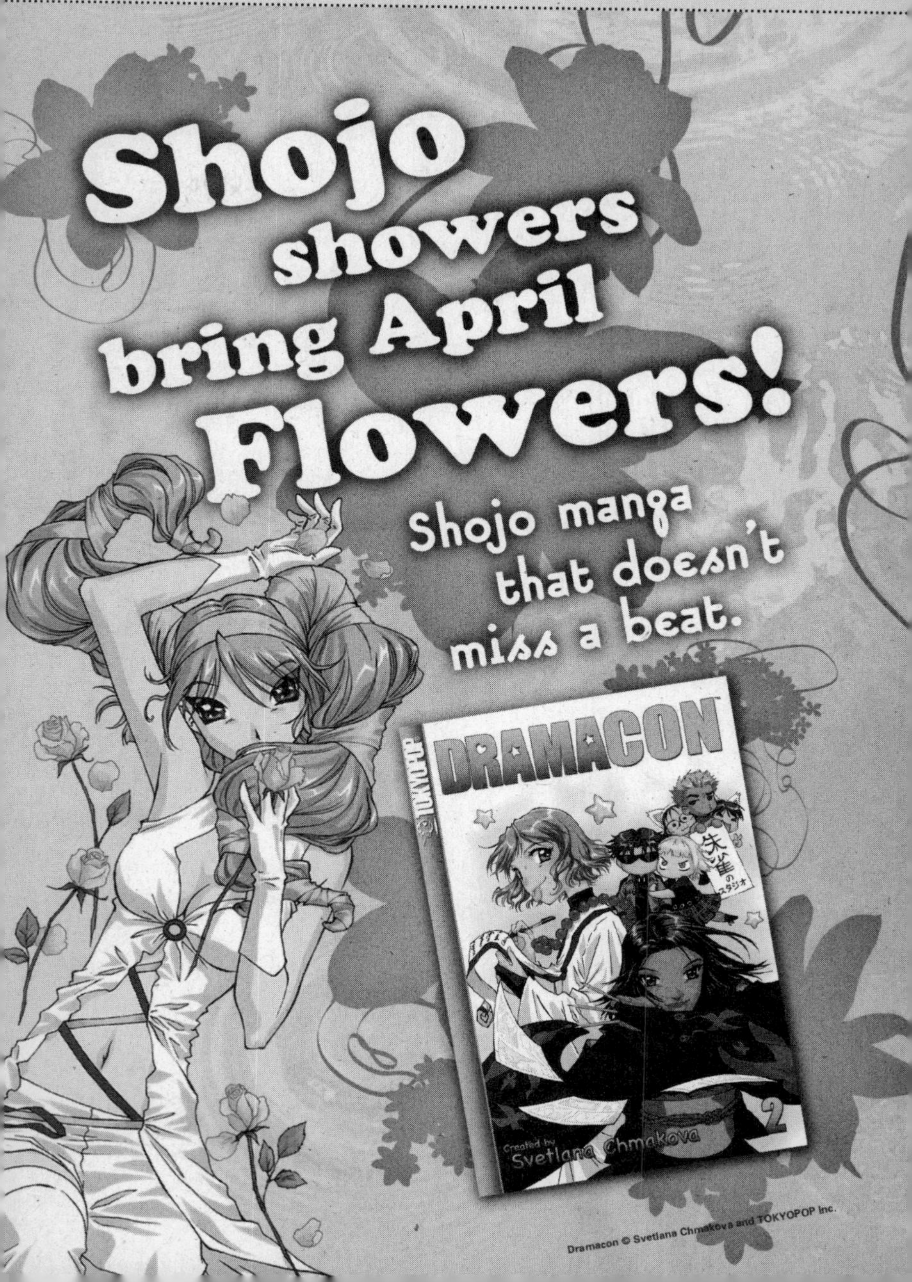
Shojo showers bring April Flowers!
Shojo manga that doesn't miss a beat.
DRAMACON
TOKYOPOP
Created by Svetlana Chmakova
2
Dramacon © Svetlana Chmakova and TOKYOPOP Inc.

STOP!

This is the back of the book.
You wouldn't want to spoil a great ending!

This book is printed "manga-style," in the authentic Japanese right-to-left format. Since none of the artwork has been flipped or altered, readers get to experience the story just as the creator intended. You've been asking for it, so TOKYOPOP® delivered: authentic, hot-off-the-press, and far more fun!

DIRECTIONS

If this is your first time reading manga-style, here's a quick guide to help you understand how it works.

It's easy... just start in the top right panel and follow the numbers. Have fun, and look for more 100% authentic manga from TOKYOPOP®!